# UKRAINE,
# THE MIDDLE EAST,
# AND THE WEST

The illustration displays *An Allegory of Science*, from Tadeusz Krusiński's *Histoire de la dernière révolution de Perse*, vol. I (The Hague: Gosse et Neulme, 1728). Krusiński was a Catholic priest and a Jesuit, who wrote about an Islamic country without prejudice, but rather with an insight and sympathy that was remarkable for his time, and his dedication of his book "To Science" fitted well into the period of the Enlightenment in which he lived. After his extensive travels in the Middle East, he taught in various places in what is today Ukraine, including at Lviv and at Kamianets in Podolia.

# UKRAINE,
## THE **MIDDLE EAST,**
## AND THE **WEST**

# THOMAS M. PRYMAK

MᴄGILL-QUEEN'S UNIVERSITY PRESS

Montreal & Kingston | London | Chicago

ISBN 978-0-2280-0577-3 (cloth)
ISBN 978-0-2280-0578-0 (paper)
ISBN 978-0-2280-0771-5 (ePDF)

Legal deposit second quarter 2021
Bibliothèque nationale du Québec

Printed in Canada on acid-free paper that is 100% ancient forest free
(100% post-consumer recycled), processed chlorine free

McGill-Queen's University Press gratefully acknowledges the financial contribution
of the Temerty Foundation and the Canadian Foundation for Ukrainian Studies
toward the publication of this volume. Publication of this volume was made
possible by the generous financial contribution of the НАУКОВЕ ТОВАРИСТВО
ІМ. ШЕВЧЕНКА В КАНАДІ / Shevchenko Scientific Society of Canada / Société
scientifique Ševčenko du Canada.

We acknowledge the support of the Canada Council for the Arts.
Nous remercions le Conseil des arts du Canada de son soutien.

LIBRARY AND ARCHIVES CANADA CATALOGUING IN PUBLICATION

Title: Ukraine, the Middle East, and the West / Thomas M. Prymak.
Names: Prymak, Thomas M. (Thomas Michael), 1948– author.
Description: Includes bibliographical references and index.
Identifiers: Canadiana (print) 20210101628 | Canadiana (ebook) 20210101652 |
     ISBN 9780228005773 (cloth) | ISBN 9780228005780 (paper) |
     ISBN 9780228007715 (ePDF)
Subjects: LCSH: Ukraine—Relations—Middle East. | LCSH: Middle East—
     Relations—Ukraine. | LCSH: Ukraine—Relations—Europe, Western. |
     LCSH: Europe, Western—Relations—Ukraine. | LCSH: International relations
     LCSH in literature.
Classification: LCC DK508.57.M53 P79 2021 | DDC 327.477056—dc23

Set in 11/14 Minion Pro
Book design and typesetting by Lara Minja, Lime Design

To my Iranian family and friends,
to my Ukrainian Canadian family,
and to all of my fellow Canadians
of Ukrainian, or partly Ukrainian,
ancestry, heritage, or affection

# CONTENTS

# Preface

IT WAS IN OCTOBER 1971, while Soviet premier Alexei Kosygin's Cold War visit to Canada was provoking furious protests, that I suddenly grasped the close ties between my ancestral Ukrainian homeland and the Lands of Islam – the *Dar al-Islam* (House or Abode of Islam). I was away in Europe, a young graduate student in history doing research for my master's thesis on the medieval Crusades to the Holy Land. I planned to visit several Roman Catholic monasteries in Austria and Belgium and had decided to take a side trip to Poland to meet some relatives (originally from eastern Galicia, in what is today western Ukraine) who had been separated from the rest of our family since 1913.

My Polish-Canadian uncle and I rented a car in Vienna, and, halfway to Poland, we stopped overnight in Prague, which was still rather dark and dismal after the shocking Soviet invasion of August 1968. In the parking lot of the Hotel International I spotted a sizable "Winnebago"-style van with a large sign: "From Alaska to Samarkand or Bust!"

I went up to the van and spoke with the owners, an elderly couple from Alaska. They had spent a year or so travelling in an enormous circle across western Europe, eastern Europe, and the Soviet Union to the legendary city of Samarkand in Uzbekistan, then crossed the mountains to Afghanistan, and over more, even higher mountains to Iran. From there, they motored across Turkey, and then through the Balkans back to central Europe and Prague to visit friends they had made along the way. They had taken warm clothing, camping gear, and extra gas tanks, and they had known about the new Soviet-built road across otherwise-impenetrable Afghanistan. They said the trip had not been too difficult. From that day forward, I dreamed of doing that same journey myself.

It was not to be – yet. My firm dedication to scholarship, and five decades of wars, revolutions, and related turmoil throughout most of those countries, have prevented such an ambitious undertaking. Nevertheless, that elderly couple had taught me something: East and West can sometimes come together in unexpected ways, especially when we open our eyes to new possibilities – encounters with strangers, and through study, books, film, and other media.

This book is a parallel journey of sorts, and consists of a mosaic of various elements, most rather colourful, and each revealing in its own way. My chapters deal with what I call "Oriental" and "Occidental" aspects of Ukrainian history and culture that have long fascinated me, but receive little attention in conventional treatments of the country.

During the Soviet period of Ukrainian history, which for most of the country lasted seventy years, from 1920 to 1989, contacts with the outside world were minimal, impeded by an almost-impenetrable "Iron Curtain" separating the Soviet sphere of influence from other parts of central and western Europe – and the rest of the world – and extremely thorough censorship, which tightly controlled contacts even among the "republics" of the sprawling Union of Soviet Socialist Republics (USSR, or Soviet Union). Although the USSR collapsed in 1991 and an independent and democratic Ukraine arose from its ashes, the isolation eased only gradually. Chronic political and economic problems made it difficult for Ukrainian academic, cultural, and scientific institutions to take up the new freedoms and establish productive relations with kindred institutions elsewhere. Moreover, it took a number of years for interested Ukrainians to learn foreign languages such as English, slowing efforts at exchanges and cooperation with colleagues and institutions abroad. This situation deeply affected my areas of scholarship, especially cultural and political history, but also related fields such as biography, art history, literary studies, folklore, even philology.

In a modest way, I seek to address certain lacunae in the scholarly literature with the chapters in the present volume. I crafted the essays on which I base some of these chapters over the course of many years, starting in the 1990s; a number of them have circulated in manuscript form among my close colleagues – a version of chapter 6 has appeared online and of chapter 8 in *Polish Review* (details in first note of those chapters). Most, however, are more recent, written especially for this book. I offer all of them today in the hope that they will augment the growing literature on Ukraine crystallizing on an ever more international scale and beginning to produce constructive dialogue with scholars in that country as well.

East and West are major themes in Ukrainian history, and, as the reader will soon discover, contacts were varied and often ancient, some dating back to pre-history, long before the nations that we see today formed out of the earlier Slavonic or Slavic peoples (Europe tends to use "Slavonic," and the United States, "Slavic"; we Canadians use both, and our professional journal is titled *Canadian Slavonic Papers*). Ancient and medieval times saw Slavonic contacts with both Iranian peoples to the east and Germanic peoples from the west. During the High Middle Ages pilgrims and adventurers of various sorts travelled to the Middle East and wrote about their journeys. Early modern times saw close and repeated contacts with both the Turkic world and with the expanding West. The periods of the Reformation and the Baroque experienced an increase in religious travellers to the Holy Land and adjacent countries, and the Enlightenment and modern times added scholars and scientists, émigrés and exiles.

Meanwhile, other notable figures tightened relations with western Europe and spread Western influences throughout the lands that are today known as Ukraine. By the eighteenth and nineteenth centuries, even some major western European intellectuals and writers took up their pens to describe "Ukrainians," calling them usually "Cossack," "Ruthenian," or "Little Russian," but also often simply "Russian." All these themes – Ukrainian contacts with the outside world, and outside influences on Ukraine – are "fragments" of a much larger story, and are touched on here. It is my sincere hope that these contacts, and these varied influences back and forth, will interest both readers concerned with Ukrainian history and culture and those interested in international history and cross-cultural contacts, and that they will find something of unexpected value in this unusual and quite original collection that I title *Ukraine, the Middle East, and the West*.

THOMAS M. PRYMAK, Toronto
January 2019

# Acknowledgments

IT IS MY PLEASURE to thank various people and institutions that helped me to gather the materials for this book and to write it. Over several years, some of my closest friends and colleagues read one or more of the chapters in this volume, or advised me about them. Foremost among these was Professor Paul Robert Magocsi of the Chair of Ukrainian Studies at the University of Toronto. My association with him and his chair has made possible much of the research here and enabled me to use the university's great John P. Robarts Library (one of North America's largest), which holds one of the best collections of *ucrainica* in the Western world. This also holds true for its substantial collection of materials on the Middle East, and its magnificent collection of French literature and history. At the Robarts Library, Ksenya Kiebuzinski and, before her, Mary Stevens were a great help to me. With Ksenya, in particular, I share a special interest in French-language materials on Ukraine. Halya Ostapchuk of the Saint Vladimir Institute Library in Toronto was also very helpful.

Parts of the manuscript were read by scholars at the University of Toronto, including the Ottoman Turkish specialists Professor Victor Ostapchuk and Ms Maryna Kravets. Professor Maria Subtelny of the Department of Near and Middle Eastern Civilizations, who many long years ago was my first instructor in the Persian language, advised me on Shevchenko's impressions of central Asia; the late Professor Bohdan Budurowycz of the Department of Slavic Languages and Literatures, who was also a noted Latinist, checked parts of the manuscript.

A distinguished but still-anonymous peer reviewer for the *International History Review* proposed ways for me to improve an earlier version of the chapter on early modern Tatar slave raiding in Ukraine. Other anonymous peer reviewers for McGill-Queen's University Press made extensive and constructive suggestions about the whole text. Years ago, the late Maria Zaputovych kindly typed part of the manuscript into a computer for me, and more recently, my son Cyrus Prymak helped me to negotiate other arcane mysteries of contemporary computers. I also thank the editors of the *Polish Review* for their permission to reprint the chapter on "Rembrandt's 'Polish Rider' in Its East European Context" and the Frick Collection in New York City for permission to reproduce the painting itself. The generous financial support of the James Termerty Family Foundation, the Shevchenko Scientific Society, Toronto Branch, and the Canadian Foundation for Ukrainian Studies is also gratefully acknowledged.

I should also like to thank my editor pro tem at McGill-Queen's, Richard Ratzlaff, for all his assistance with this difficult manuscript. Managing editor Kathleen Fraser put considerable effort into this volume. It has been many years in the works, and I am glad that they could help me so much further along to the final goal.

As well, I should like to express my gratitude to my close colleagues at the University of Toronto, Roman Senkus and the late Andrij Makuch, editors at the Canadian Institute of Ukrainian Studies Press, for many interesting conversations and tips about our field. Finally, I wish to thank my Iranian wife, Yassamine (or Jasmine) Kalhori-Prymak, the descendant of a distinguished Kurdish tribal leader from Gilan-e-garb in the Zagros Mountains of western Iran, not far from the magnificent rock carvings of Darius the Great at Bisitun. A native of Tehran, she helped me with many a translation question and was a constant inspiration to me to continue work on my subjects of interest, still unfamiliar to so many inhabitants of present-day Ukraine. Quite understandably, in recent years they have had other, rather more important concerns on their minds.

# Abbreviations

| | |
|---|---|
| AN URSR | Akademiia nauk Ukrainska radianska sotsialistychna respublika (Academy of Sciences of the Ukrainian Soviet Socialist Republic), Kyiv |
| CIUS | Canadian Institute of Ukrainian Studies, Edmonton and Toronto |
| MHSO | Multicultural History Society of Ontario, Toronto |
| NANU | Natsionalna akademiia nauk Ukrainy (National Academy of Sciences of Ukraine), Kyiv |
| NTSh | Naukove tovarystvo im. Shevchenka (Shevchenko Scientific Society) |
| PAU | Polska academia umiejętności (Polish Academy of Learning), Cracow |
| PIW | Państwowy Instytut wydawniczy (State Publishing Institute), Warsaw |
| PSB | *Polski słownik biograficzny* (Polish Biographical Dictionary) |
| PWN | Państwowe wydawnictwo naukowe (State Publishing House), Warsaw |
| RM | Russian Museum, St Petersburg |
| RSFSR | Rossiiskaia Sovetskaia Federativnaia Sotsialisticheskaia Respublika (Russian Federal Soviet Socialist Republic) |
| TG | Tretiakov Gallery, Moscow |
| UkSSR | Ukrainian Soviet Socialist Republic |
| USSR | Union of Soviet Socialist Republics |
| UVAN | Ukrainska vilna akademiia nauk (Ukrainian Academy of Sciences in the United States), New York |

FIGURE 1. *Ahatanhel Krymsky*. From A. Krymsky,
*Tvory v p'iaty tomakh*, vol. III (Kyiv: Naukova dumka, 1973),
frontispiece.

Ahatanhel Krymsky (1871–1942) was an outstanding Ukrainian Middle East scholar,
an "Orientalist." Krymsky (Figure 1), as his surname indicates, was of Crimean Tatar
background and sympathies, but also accepted a clearly Ukrainian national identity
and was dedicated to the national awakening. He wrote extensively on Islamic and
Middle Eastern culture in both Russian and Ukrainian and was an expert on the
various Steppe peoples of central Asia, especially those of Turkic linguistic affiliation.

FIGURE 2. *Lesya Ukrainka,*
early-twentieth-century illustration.

Krymsky's contemporary Lesya Ukrainka (Figure 2) – the pen name of Larysa
Kosach (1871–1913) – was a great poet. She spoke about ten languages and translated
numerous western European works into Ukrainian. She was outraged by the
historical enslavement of so many Ukrainians by the Turks and Tatars, but also
visited Egypt, wrote a cycle of poetry on Egyptian themes, and penned a play on
the love between the Prophet Mohammed and his young wife Aisha.

FIGURE 3. *Ruthenian Country Folk in Austrian Galicia Going to Church on Sunday,*
by Juliusz Kossak (1824–1899), illustration. From Władisław Zawadzki,
*Obrazy Rusi Czerwonéj* (Poznań, 1869), 1.

When the Austrians annexed Galicia in the 1790s, they knew a bit about the Poles in
its western parts, but little about its eastern inhabitants, with their different language
and form of Christianity. The Austrians revived the old Latin term "Ruthenian" to
designate the Eastern Rite residents and renamed their church "Greek Catholic"
to raise its stature and bring it on a par with the Poles' "Roman Catholic" church.
The Polish painter Juliusz Kossak (1824–1899) toured the province and depicted its
peoples in an album published in 1869. In Figure 3, devout country folk head to a
wooden Ruthenian church in the foothills of the Carpathians, with the rolling plains
of Podolia in the far distance. In 1906 a group of Ruthenians went as pilgrims to the
Holy Land led by Metropolitan Andrei Sheptytsky.

FIGURE 4. *The Church of Saint Sophia* (Kyiv), by Abraham van Westerveldt. From a sketch (1650s), reproduced from O.I. Rudenko and N.B. Petrenko, *Vichnyi iak narod: Storinky do biohrafii T.H. Shevchenka* (Kyiv: Lybid, 1998).

The great Metropolitan Cathedral of St Sophia in Kyiv (Figure 4), a UNESCO World Heritage Site, founded in 1011, as pictured in the 1650s by the Dutch painter Abraham van Westerfeldt (1620–1692); and the ruins of the Golden (Southern, or Great) Gate of Kyiv (Figure 5) depicted in 1870 by the Polish graphic artist Napoleon Orda (1807–1883). In the 1650s, the Poles and the Cossacks were still struggling for control of the city, and the drawing shows the Orthodox style of the church and Roman Catholic influences in the great crucifix in the square before it. Just as the Church of St Sophia symbolized the continuity of Ukrainian Christianity from medieval to modern times, so the ruins of the Golden Gate symbolized the destruction caused to Kyivan Rus' by thirteenth-century Mongol invaders from the east.

FIGURE 5. *The Ruins of the Golden Gates in Kyiv* (1870), by Napoleon Orda.
From a drawing from "Zoloti vorota," in Kyiv entsyklopediia online at
http://wek.Kyiv.ua/uk.

FIGURE 6. *Tatars Taking Ukrainians into Slavery*, undated engraving.
Courtesy of Andrew Gregorovich, *Forum: A Ukrainian Review*, no. 44
(spring 1980), 32, from the collection of Eugene Kurdydyk.

From about 1450 to about 1750, Tatar raiding parties (heirs of the Mongols)
systematically carried off hundreds of thousands of country folk, townsfolk, and
others into captivity, perhaps a million or more in total, although statistics are
sketchy. Many, especially the old, the weak, and children, did not make it even as
far as the Crimea. Those who survived were sold into slavery, many in the slave
markets of Istanbul and other cities of the Ottoman Empire. Christian raiders in the
Mediterranean, such as the Knights of St John in Malta, attacked Muslim shipping
and North African coastal cities to free Christian slaves and carried off many
Muslims into captivity, although the Tatar raids on the Ukrainian Steppes seem
to have been more intense, more regular, and more destructive.

FIGURE 7. *Liberation of the Slaves from Turkish Captivity*, by Opanas Slastion, drawing. From *Shevchenkivskyi slovnyk*, 2 vols. (Kiev: Instytut literatury im Shevchenka, 1976), I, plate between pp. 208 and 209.

Figure 7 portrays a scene from Taras Shevchenko's "Hamaliya," about the liberation of Ukrainian slaves in Turkey by the Cossack Hamaliya. The poem was inspired by a story by the neo-Cossack Mykhailo Chaikovsky / Michal Czajkowski (a.k.a. Sadyk Pasha) and by various reflective songs (*dumas*) and other sources.

In the nineteenth century, folklore about Tatar slave raiding and Turkish captivity was kept alive by itinerant blind minstrels, such as Dmytro Skoryk (Figure 8), who played their *kobzas* (multi-stringed instruments) and sang their mournful *dumas*, usually travelling with a young guide. Heading the list of *dumas* inscribed on Skoryk's portrait is the legendary *Plach nevolnykiv* (Lament of the Slaves).

Both drawings are by museum curator, artist, and illustrator Opanas Slastion (1855–1933), who also played the *kobza*.

FIGURE 8. *Kobzar Dmytro Skoryk*, by Opanas Slastion, drawing (before 1930).

FIGURE 9. *Imam Shamil*, nineteenth-century
magazine illustration.

Imam Shamil ruled Dagestan 1834–59 and became renowned for his forces' resistance
to Russian invaders. His mountaineer's dress seemingly was paralleled by the
Russian and Ukrainian Cossacks sent to oppose him, and the lines of cartridges
along his chest, and *kinjal* (long knife) hanging at his side, became standard Cossack
dress by the end of the nineteenth century.

FIGURE 10. *Honoré de Balzac,*
nineteenth-century drawing.

FIGURE 11. *Prosper Mérimée,*
nineteenth-century drawing.

Portraits of the writers as young men: Honoré de Balzac (Figure 10), rendered in
1901 by J. Allen St John (1875–1957), based on a drawing by Louis Boulanger, and
Prosper Mérimée (Figure 11). Balzac, a royalist and deeply conservative, lived in
Ukraine 1848–50, but it seems to have been for him an unrealistic dreamland about
which he knew little, apart from his brilliant and devoted wife, Ewelina Hańska,
née Rzewuska, and her magnificent château, Verkhivnia. The liberal Mérimée wrote
much more about Ukraine, but never visited it. While critical of Russian serfdom, he
was generally quite russophile. He was fascinated by the freedom-loving Ukrainian
Cossacks and by the Ukrainian writer Nikolai Gogol, and wrote a biography of the
Cossack hetman Bohdan Khmelnytsky.

FIGURE 12. *Sketch of Ilya Repin's Defiant Zaporozhians* (1878),
by Ilya Repin, pencil drawing.

*Zaporozhian Cossacks Writing a Satirical Letter to the Turkish Sultan* (1891) (see Plate 13) was Ilya Repin's (1844–1930) masterpiece. He worked on it from 1878 to 1891. Although he kept adding new elements, his original, 1878 conception of happy Cossacks grouped around a table, with the secretary of the army penning the letter, never changed. His inspiration came from an article by the Ukrainian historian Mykola Kostomarov. Though living near Moscow and later near St Petersburg, Repin always remembered Ukraine and returned to Cossack themes when in self-imposed exile in Finland, just outside St Petersburg.

FIGURE 13. *Victory Song of the Zaporozhians*, by Józef Brandt. Nineteenth-century magazine illustration from Volodymyr Nadiak, *Ukraina kozatska derzhava* (Kyiv: Emma, 2007), 301.

Polish artist Józef Brandt (1841–1915) loved to paint Cossacks, Tatars, horses, and cavalry scenes. He rendered action and movement superbly, but spent very little time on faces. By contrast, the Ukrainian master Ilya Repin was a magnificent portrait artist, but seldom depicted movement. Brandt's *Victory Song of the Zaporozhians* was exhibited in St Petersburg at the same time in 1891 as Repin's *Zaporozhian Cossacks* and attracted some attention. But Ukrainians, perhaps partly out of national pride, much preferred Repin's canvas. Nevertheless, Brandt's mounted Cossacks helped create the modern idea of Cossacks as wild but very skilled cavalrymen. In fact, they began as daring river boatmen (some even crossing the Black Sea to raid the Ottoman Empire), became famous as courageous infantrymen under Hetman Bohdan Khmelnytsky, and only much later developed renown as horsemen.

FIGURE 14. *Professor Mykhailo Hrushevsky and His Government as Repin's Defiant Zaporozhians,* by Józef Brandt. Magazine illustration from Volodymyr Nadiak, *Ukraina kozatska derzhava* (Kyiv: Emma, 2007), 301.

During the Ukrainian Revolution of 1917, the graphic artist P. Kotsky recalled "The Olden Days in Ukraine" in this caricature of Ivan Repin's iconic *Zaporozhian Cossacks* (see Figure 12; Plates 13, 14), which shows Professor Mykhailo Hrushevsky and his colleagues of the Ukrainian Central Rada (the autonomous Ukrainian government), in Kyiv. They were struggling against the centralizing tendencies of Kerensky's Russian Provisional Government in Petrograd. Hrushevsky is the white-bearded, Taras Bulba figure on the far right; Oleksander Lototsky, his minister for religious affairs, is either the secretary writing the Cossack letter to Sultan Kerensky, or the bespectacled Cossack pointing him out in the distance; the Cossack at the back holding his cap up high is probably the historian Dmytro Doroshenko; and Symon Petliura is the clean-shaven Cossack sitting opposite Professor Hrushevsky.

Steppes, forêts, deserts
VICTOR HUGO, "Mazeppa" (1829),[1]
describing Ukraine


Ukrainians are one of the most orientalized . . . of the western peoples.
MYKHAILO HRUSHEVSKY (1918)


"Ukraine, like [the god] Janus of [ancient] Rome, has two faces:
one turned towards the West, and a second turned towards the East."
But of this second, eastern face, we know practically nothing.
IVAN KRYPIAKEVYCH (1966)

# Ukrainian History in Context

## Writing History: People or Territory?

ABOUT A HUNDRED YEARS AGO, a new political entity appeared on the map of Europe. For most of the twentieth century, it was neither independent nor sovereign, but it existed. That entity was the Ukrainian Soviet Socialist Republic, which had its roots in the revolutions and wars of 1917–1921 in what had once been the southern European provinces of the Russian Empire and, to some degree as well, in territories a little to the west, in the Habsburgs' Austrian Empire, which had disappeared from the map in 1918. The Ukrainian SSR was a constituent or "union" republic of the USSR that had arisen as a compromise measure between the short-lived Ukrainian People's Republic, which had embodied the independentist national strivings of the Ukrainian people in 1917, and Moscow's enduring centralist tendencies, which increased in years following. In 1991, however, that compromise republic, the Ukrainian SSR, declared its independence from the Soviet Union and became an independent state called "Ukraine." These developments came as a surprise to many both in the West and in the former USSR itself, but had antecedents stretching far back into the history of eastern Europe and worthy of explanation. Historians in the "new" country reverted to the theories of predecessors largely ignored or repressed throughout most of that stormy century (when Communist dictatorships ruled about half of the world), but now, quite suddenly, very important.[1]

In the decades around 1900, in a number of ways, those pre-Revolution Ukrainian scholars had begun to define a new field of "Ukrainian history," or rather "the history of Ukraine," as they put it. Two principal streams emerged – "national" and "territorial." Mykhailo Hrushevsky (1866–1934) was writing the history of a people or a nation. He began with pre-history and the ancient Scythia of Herodotus and carried through the Sarmatians, Goths, Huns, Antes, early Slavs, and others to Kyivan "Rus'" (the Slavonic name); he continued it across the Middle Ages, when first Lithuania, and then Poland, ruled most of what is today Ukraine; and he then passed into modern times, when first Muscovy, and then the Russian and Austrian Empires, were ascendant. However, the great historian stressed the role, throughout all of this, of "the popular masses" in history, concentrating on those whom he considered ancestors of the modern Ukrainian people, and he emphasized their continuity through the many social and political changes on their lands through the centuries. For the nineteenth century, he focused on the national movement and largely ignored national and religious minorities. In general, his approach, which elevated the heretofore-ignored majority of "southern Russia" and stressed its continuity through many centuries and many political disruptions, is called the "national" or "ethnic" approach to Ukrainian history.[2]

A contemporary of his saw things quite differently – a Polish nobleman from Volhynia province in "right-bank Ukraine" (west of the Dnieper River), whose nascent local patriotism embraced "Ukraine" in another, territorial context. Wacław Lipiński/Viacheslav Lypynsky (Polish/Ukrainian spellings) (1882–1931) argued that all of the country's inhabitants, not just ethnic Ukrainians, and all social classes, and not just the "masses," had played a role, that the upper or ruling classes had contributed much, and that the focus should be on a definite territory rather than simply on one nationality or social group.[3]

During the Cold War, when almost all of Ukrainian ethnic territory was controlled by the Soviet Union and made up one of its "Union Republics," these two views were underplayed or banned in favour of the Soviet class-based view of history, which stressed Russian primacy and connections throughout. But Ukrainian émigré circles discussed them, and a new generation of historians debated them. The national approach was defended in particular by leading members of the Ukrainian Historical Association, centred in the United States and Canada, but with many European members. Its long-time president, Lubomyr Wynar (1932–2017), argued that the

Soviets had repressed most aspects of Ukrainian national history and that Hrushevsky's ideas and work had to be kept alive by Ukrainian historians living in "the Free World." Moreover, he clearly distinguished between "nationalistic" history, as represented by the Ukrainian "integral" nationalists of the 1930s and 1940s (who did not much like Hrushevsky's alleged pacifism, respect for democracy, socialism, and revolutionary bent), and "national" history, which preserved the general direction of that scholar's work, but played down his revolutionary credentials, and also added his ostensible "state-building" experience during the Ukrainian Revolution of 1917–21.[4]

Wynar's view was shared by most émigré Ukrainian historians of the late Cold War era, but not all. In particular, Omeljan Pritsak (1919–2006) of Harvard University resurrected Lypynsky's ideas and preached a non-ethnic, territorial approach that appealed to a handful of influential Ukrainian scholars in the West. Pritsak was initially not a Ukrainian historian per se, but an "Orientalist," who specialized in the Turkic peoples of central Asia and the Steppe (grassland plains), or Eurasian Steppe, which stretches from the Carpathian Mountains east to Manchuria, with Ukraine in the Pontic Steppe, and he knew something about Ottoman Turkish history. But he thought that those peoples and regions had helped shape Ukrainian history and belonged in the national narrative, which explained much of his affinity for non-ethnic, "territorial" Ukrainian history, although he also accepted Lypynsky's emphasis on the role of the national elites across the ages. For most of his career, Pritsak was very critical of Hrushevsky, despite helping to create and then holding (1975–89) the Mykhailo Hrushevsky Chair in Ukrainian History at Harvard University, even though that disappointed many younger, American-trained scholars who hoped to teach high-level Ukrainian history.[5]

Western debates about Ukrainian history took place mostly in little-known Ukrainian-language émigré journals, despite the appearance of two great, translated "narratives" or surveys, by Hrushevsky (published in 1940), and by Lypynsky's most notable follower, Dmytro Doroshenko (1939). But those pioneering surveys seemed very much out-of-date by the 1960s and 1970s, after all that had happened in the interim,[6] and new narratives were required.

The first came out in 1988: Orest Subtelny's *Ukraine: A History* clearly took Hrushevsky's national or "ethnic" approach, even sharpening that focus by stressing "statelessness" through the centuries and hence "modernization" mostly by the foreign rulers. Subtelny (1941–2016) seemed to believe that this reality sidestepped Ukrainian culture, which remained very traditional. (So Ukrainian national culture even today is sometimes disparaged by Russians and others as being largely "peasant based.") His book had a pessimistic tone: he apparently remarked that it was a real miracle that Ukraine had survived. For the general public, Subtelny was one of the first historians to survey the country's misfortunes and disasters – an approach forbidden in the USSR. Translated into Ukrainian and Russian, his book had an enormous effect on both the public and young historians, then beginning their work in newly independent Ukraine.[7]

In 1996 Paul Robert Magocsi's *History of Ukraine*, with many attractive maps, exposed the general public in the English-speaking world to the territorial approach. Magocsi (b. 1945) devoted substantial sections to Ukraine's national and religious minorities and, unlike Pritsak, carried their story beyond the early Turkic peoples of the Steppe and concentrated on Jews, Poles, Germans, and several other groups. Many of these minorities had considered themselves "Russian," but Magocsi's work gave them clear recognition and thus a conceptual framework and an incentive to re-orient themselves to the new Ukrainian reality.

Moreover, unlike Subtelny's book, which read well and had a clear narrative, Magocsi had a more neutral, encyclopaedic tone, and a more positive spirit; Ukrainian history was not a complete disaster, but more "normal" than was previously thought, with its own share of victories and progress, as well as difficulties; and he seemed quite impatient with the theme of "victimization." The very existence of the Ukrainian SSR seemed to him real progress – a quasi-national state that partially fulfilled the nineteenth-century national awakening and the nationalist activism of the early twentieth.[8]

Of course, many new ideas and debates have taken place since Subtelny and Magocsi's tomes appeared. For example, today, some historians, in particular Volodymyr Kravchenko, see the Ukrainian SSR not as a kind of quasi-national Ukrainian state but as a miniature USSR with its own national regions, its many enclaves with Pan- or "All-Union" status, its "Hero Cities" by Pan-Union designation, its Crimea (a "Pan-Union resort"), its Donbas ("the Union's Stokehold"), and so forth. Sebastopol, Kyiv, and Odessa were all such "Hero Cities." Of course, perceptive observers who knew the relevant languages could notice that Ukrainians were second in rank after Russians in the USSR, but Kravchenko detected echoes more of the old Russian Empire, with its triune nation of Great, Little, and "Belorussian" branches, than anything of a national Ukrainian character. Such an interpretation, which definitely raised national expectations with regard to history, clearly revealed how far Ukrainian national consciousness had advanced since Subtelny and Magocsi started writing their general histories.[9]

And so, Ukrainian national consciousness, especially based on ethnic distinctiveness, was a variable thing. But so too is the very concept of a Ukrainian national territory, which has changed greatly over time and has gradually shifted westward. So in the nineteenth century, Ukraine was still very much a vague concept that stretched eastward well into Kursk and Voronezh provinces of old "Russia" and southward into the Kuban, where the descendants of the Zaporozhian Cossacks were then settled. Thus the Ukrainian national poet, Taras Shevchenko (1814–1861), was invited by his friend the Cossack commander Otaman Yakiv Kukharenko to visit the Kuban, "our Cossack Ukraine." And major Ukrainian figures such as the historian Mykola Kostomarov and the painter Ivan Kramskoi were both born and raised in those intriguing but neglected provinces that today lie in Russia.[10]

## Borderlands or Former Colony?

Meanwhile, the provinces west of Kyiv province – Volhynia and Podolia – were not always considered part of "Ukraine." Certainly, this was mostly true for the Polish nobles who owned much of the land, as we can see in the writings of Honoré de Balzac, who toured the region in the mid-nineteenth century (see chapter 6, below).[11] And we do not even speak of Transcarpathia, Galicia, and Bukovina even further west – disputed "borderlands" claimed by various peoples. They all had the seeds of a Ukrainian national consciousness and a devoted intelligentsia that remained very small until late century. So from the nineteenth century to the end of the twentieth both the name and the national concept of Ukraine spread steadily westward until it included Galicia and those other western parts, but lost some of those eastern parts, and eventually solidified into today's "Ukraine."[12]

Indeed, in the Slavonic tongues "Ukraine" means "borderland," which sometimes serves as the organizing principle for books on Ukrainian history. Certainly, just as in the late Middle Ages what is today Ukraine constituted the eastern flank of "Christendom" facing the Lands of Islam (*Dar al-Islam*), so later it came to be the easternmost part of "Europe," facing the Crimean Khanate and the Ottoman Empire to its south, and various nomadic, non-Slavonic tribes to its east. As one recent historian has so eloquently put it, Ukraine has often been the very "Gates of Europe." But was it really always a borderland, or "frontier," as American historian William H. McNeill called it, or was it sometimes more "a colony?"[13]

In other words, was it ever a colonial entity to be used and exploited by its neighbours, and to be settled and absorbed, or was it something else? Many Ukrainian historians, beginning with Hrushevsky himself, saw the sixteenth-century Polish push into Ukraine as a colonial enterprise (as did some of the Poles themselves), and years later, during the Cold War, some anti-Communist Ukrainians in the West, especially émigrés, saw Soviet efforts in Ukraine in terms of colonialism and imperialism. After 1991, this view became very strong in Ukraine. So in 1994, when the Ukrainian art historian Yury Belichko considered the career of the distinguished painter Ilya Repin (1844–1930), who was born and began his long career in Ukraine, flourished in St Petersburg, but ended as an exile in Finland, he put it this way:

> [In Soviet times, Repin] was very seldom accounted among Ukrainian artists. This very fact testifies to that cultural process that began in Ukraine after the Pereiaslav Treaty of 1654 [by which the eastern part of the country became a vassal of Muscovy] and of which Repin is a concrete example. Ukraine produced geniuses, but because of its colonial status was not able to provide them with an appropriate field for their endeavors. They fell into the orbit of Russian culture, while at the same time reaching the level of [other] European achievements. Such persons in the best of circumstances retained [only] some distant memory of their homeland, and a feeling of obligation towards the spiritual betterment of their own people. Here Repin's case is amazingly similar to that of the notable Ukrainian, Nikolai Gogol [Mykola Hohol in Ukrainian]. And he stands together with other famous products of Ukraine such as [the artists] L. Borovykovsky, D. Levytsky, M. Gay (Ge), A. Kuindzhi, I. Kramskoi, and M. Yaroshenko.[14]

Throughout most of the Soviet period, such "colonial status" (Belichko's term) was thoroughly enforced, and such giants' Ukrainian connection was played down for the sake of Russian greatness. This was true not only of artists, but also of statesmen, scientists, musicians, historians, architects, and various literary figures, especially from earlier Ukrainian and Russian history, so that outsiders, even many scholars, were seldom aware of the very real differences between them and genuine Muscovite and Russian-origin figures.[15]

Moreover, within the nineteenth-century Russian Empire, state and society would brook no talk of Ukrainian separateness or independence, either in politics or in literature, although early in the century, it was still quietly discussed in positive terms by much of the nobility of eastern, or left-bank Ukraine (east of the Dnieper), most of it descended from the old Ukrainian Cossack officer class. Despite periods when Ukrainian traditions were more accepted, and Ukrainian literature was published (though as a local variant of Russian patriotism), in general, this older nobility and its heirs faced a solid wall of rejection by the Russians, or *Moskali*, as the Ukrainians called them. Myroslav Shkandrij, a Canadian specialist on the subject, explains:

> The unanimity of Russian conservatives, liberals, and socialists on the question of Ukraine's incorporation and assimilation stems in large part from the fact that the country has always been seen as an early and crucial test case of successful imperial expansion and assimilation. Any challenge to its success has carried enormous consequences for the Russian self-image and has been dealt with in uncompromising terms. The dissolution of the Russian–Ukrainian link has always threatened the imperial identity of Russia itself, the symbiosis of nation and empire that Russian intellectuals have so frequently extolled. These intellectuals have always been called upon to provide justifications for imperial growth and to defend an increasingly monolithic conception of Russian identity. The very idea of a Ukrainian identity, of course, threatened both.[16]

Such was the situation in the Russian Empire right up to 1917, when suddenly the whole thing fell apart. The formation of the USSR gave the so-called Union Republics a certain leeway within the formula "national in form and socialist in content," but over the next seventy years the Russian state's centralizing tendencies repeatedly reasserted themselves, and on the eve of dissolution it was a very tight-knit, frozen entity, with anything but the genuine federal system and democratic liberties that its constitution proclaimed. Indeed, some observers abroad would quite consciously refer to it as the "Soviet Empire," and even the question of Ukraine's colonial status was sometimes adumbrated by émigrés, though not much more widely than that.[17]

Ukraine's political independence after 1991 changed much of this, but the legacy of Soviet "colonialism" remains, although "post-colonial" historians generally ignore the country. In fact, they seem to group it with Ireland and, despite the two countries' common second-class status within vast imperial entities, set them aside, concentrating on Europe's former overseas empires.[18] Does this have something to do with the difference between those great maritime empires versus contiguous continental empires, or is there some kind of lingering ignorance, reverse racism, or, at least, moral inequivalence, at work here?

Indeed, many left-oriented, post-colonialist historians seem to know or care very little about either Ireland or Ukraine and often do not even distinguish between Ukraine and Russia, despite notable differences dating back to medieval times. And this is revealed even in the very names of the two countries. In this way, in the eighteenth century, eastward-oriented and Orthodox Muscovy officially accepted the new name *Rossiia* (based on the medieval Greek for Rus'), while the regions to its south and west, long associated with either Lithuania or Poland, and mostly Catholic, were referred to generally as *Ruthenia* (based on the medieval Latin for Rus'). Thus did the respective choices of names reveal the general orientations of what later became Russia and Ukraine.[19]

## Outline of This Book

This general question of east and west informs the title of this book in a different way, and I should like to expand on a few matters mentioned in the Preface. I am concerned here not so much with Ukraine's ostensible westward orientation (as opposed to Russia's eastward) as with eastern and western influences on Ukraine itself and, especially, Ukraine's forgotten influences and contacts with others west and east.

So part I, "A Complex History: Ukraine and the *Dar al-Islam*," and some elements of the other chapters treat the country's contacts with the Middle East, especially the Islamic Middle East. The first two of its three chapters deal with the many cultural luminaries who wrote about or visited the region – primarily in the early modern era (chapter 1) and in the nineteenth century (chapter 2). This includes iconic figures such as the Igumen [Abbot] Daniel, the first medieval pilgrim from Kyivan Rus' to leave an account of his visit to Palestine, and many centuries later, Ahatanhel Krymsky (of Crimean Tatar ancestry), the first modern, professional Ukrainian "Orientalist" scholar to do formal research in that part of the world.

Of course, not all these travellers were "ethnic" Ukrainians. For example, not only the Igumen Daniel, who lived long before the name "Ukrainian" was coined, and Ahatanhel Krymsky, claimed today by both Crimean Tatars and Ukrainians, but also certain Jews from what is today Ukraine, visited or lived in the Middle East for long periods. These include characters as diverse as Sarah, the beautiful but controversial wife of the charismatic seventeenth-century Jewish prophet Sabbatai Zevi; Sarah grew up in what is today Ukraine, but married Sabbatai Zevi in the Ottoman Empire. Then there was the twentieth-century religious figure Muhammad Asad, Pakistan's first ambassador to the United Nations, born to a Jewish family in Austrian Galicia, whence came his happy memories of his childhood summers among Ruthenian country folk.[20]

These notable figures indicate the great variety of Ukrainian contacts with the Middle East. The relevant chapters of this book, especially in part I, look at nineteenth-century or earlier travellers with – to us – somewhat fuzzy national identities, such as the collector of Arabic thoroughbreds "Emir Rzewuski"/"Emir Revusky" and the "neo-Cossack" Mykhailo Chaikovsky/Michał Czajkowski.

Chapter 3, also in part I, treats more specifically slave raiding by Tatars in Ukraine and its reflection in Ukrainian folklore. Such activity was a very big business, during its earlier periods surpassing even the much better-known transatlantic trade. Invaders raiding lands, seizing their people, and enslaving them shattered and scarred families and communities and tore people from their homelands into an uncertain and often-miserable existence, although slaves' fates varied greatly, depending on where they were taken. The Black Sea slave trade remained significant for about three centuries (1441–1783) and left its dark imprint, still barely explored, on the Ukrainian national psyche and narrative.[21]

The formation in 1648 of the Ukrainian Cossack "Hetmanate" within the Russian Empire, following the triumphant Cossack insurrection against the Roman Catholic, noble-dominated Polish–Lithuanian Commonwealth, transformed the geopolitical situation in eastern Europe. Because of these wars, the slave trade suddenly expanded. But during the later years of the Hetmanate, it went into a steady and irreversible decline. Two figures dominate the history of the Hetmanate: founder Bohdan Khmelmytsky (c. 1595–1657; hetman 1648–57) and its most highly cultured ruler, Ivan

Mazepa; hetman 1687–1708). Throughout this period Ukraine and its Cossacks attracted the attention of both western Europe and the Ottoman Empire – see, for instance, the French-language geography and map of the country by Guillaume le Vasseur Sieur de Beauplan (cited frequently cited in chapter 3 below) and the histories of the Ukrainian Cossacks by Pierre Chevalier, J.B. Scherer, and others. Khmelnytsky became known a bit in western Europe, but his apparently difficult name stifled interest, according to the French novelist Prosper Mérimée, who wrote a book about him in 1865 (see chapter 7 below).[22]

In contrast, Ivan Mazepa (1639–1709) – see Plates 2 and 3; the artist for Plate 2 also rendered (Plate 1) one of Mazepa's predecessors, Petro Doroshenko (1627–1698) – became at home an enduring symbol of Ukraine's western longings and fascinated many people in western Europe during his reign and ever since. In the Romantic era some European painters and writers made him a kind of exotic hero. Voltaire had noted his 1708 rebellion against Peter the Great's Russia and observed: "*L'Ukraine a toujours aspiré à être libre*" (Ukraine has always wanted to be free). Voltaire was widely read across all of Europe, including his story of Mazepa as a young man being tied naked to the back of his horse and set off to die in the steppe by a cuckolded husband, although he of course survived to allegedly recount the tale. The story eventually reached the young Polish poet Antoni Malczewski, whom Polish scholars suspect mentioned it to Lord Byron. Influenced by Voltaire's account, Byron wrote the narrative poem *Mazeppa* (1819) and in turn inspired other poets such as Józef Bohdan Zaleski, Aleksandr Pushkin, and Victor Hugo (in *Les Orientales*, 1829) to do the same. Soon artists such as Delacroix, Géricault, and Vernet, and musicians such as Liszt and Tchaikovsky took up the Mazepa theme. Together, all these writers and artists, for well over a century, made Mazepa the best-known Ukrainian figure in western Europe.[23]

The Mazepa legend within the Russian Empire, the Soviet Union, and Ukraine itself has affected how the man is today seen in the West. During the Great Northern War (begun 1700, pitting Denmark, Saxony, Poland, and Russia against Sweden and allies), at a crucial time in his country's history, Mazepa turned west and tried to orient his country in those directions. Mazepa, disillusioned with Russian rule, in 1708 allied with Charles XII of Sweden, who promised Ukraine independence, or at least a very wide-ranging autonomy. However, the Swedish forces were badly defeated at Poltava (1709) and Mazepa died soon afterwards. But he has inspired later

Ukrainian patriots and nationalists who have rejected the Russian connections. At the same time, he has remained a villain in Russian literature and historiography, and this basic disagreement over his character still shapes the writing of history in both countries.

Well into the twenty-first century, the Russian version of the "traitor" Mazepa, anathematized by the Russian Orthodox church, supposed enemy of the Ukrainian people, and disgraced by the glorious Russian victory over his Swedish allies at Poltava, dominated Russian writing on him, and remained present even in independent Ukraine. As late as 2011, the Ukrainian historian Yaroslav Dashkevych still had to deconstruct this caricature. He pointed out that all great modern national rebels, beginning with George Washington, have been accused of being "traitors" to the imperial power until their countries finally gained their independence. Dashkevych noted that priests' condemnations of religious "heretics" have never extended to political rebels otherwise loyal to the church, such as Mazepa. Priests used to re-proclaim this ban in the official liturgy of the church on certain days every year – proving, the writer noted, the church's scandalous subservience to the Muscovite state and its irreligious Tsar Peter. Only Russian clerics continue to denounce Mazepa.

Dashkevych next turns to Ukrainians' attitudes towards Mazepa. He concludes that Russia's ferocious repressions of the Ukrainian Cossacks and the Ukrainian people before and after the Battle of Poltava in 1709 (especially its massacre of the population of the Cossack capital at Baturyn), in contradiction to the Russian myth about Mazepa's unpopularity, clearly showed whose side that populace favoured. And finally, he notes that the "glorious" victory of Poltava became a central pillar of Russia's imperialist propaganda (and later its nationalist propaganda) in its opposition to Mazepa's vision of independence, even though two years later it was defeated by a Swedish/Ukrainian ally, the Ottoman Empire, during the Prut campaign of 1711. These wilful distortions are still dominant in Russia, and still influence much Western writing about its history.[24]

More generally, in Russia, the Cossacks are seen primarily as border folk, wild and unruly, useful only to serve the tsar at the outer limits of the empire. They were always peripheral to the Muscovite and the Russian state, where Moscow and the tsars dominated. By contrast, in Ukraine, the Cossacks are absolutely central to the national history. For many people, they simply defined Ukraine and Ukrainians, and in the national mythology they almost always stood for liberty and national as well as personal freedom. They almost always resisted serfdom, countered Turkish and Tatar attacks, and opposed the more baneful influences of Poland and Muscovy, although sometimes they also cooperated with those more powerful states. Indeed, for many Ukrainians, the well-educated and administratively adept Mazepa, who was also a poet and a patron of architecture and the arts, represented not only order and good government, but higher culture and civilization itself. Moreover, even that illustrious painter Ilya Repin (1844–1930) greatly esteemed his defiant Zaporozhian Cossacks. Repin's vast 1891 canvas, more than a decade in creation (the subject of chapter 9, below), portrays them writing their boisterous and scatological reply of 1676 to an ultimatum from the Ottoman sultan. Nevertheless he thought quite highly of them. Irrepressably cheerful, "[they were] the intelligentsia of their time," he observed to a literary friend in 1889, "most of them had an education." The contrast with old Muscovy, dark, backward, and autocratic, could not have been greater.[25]

In part II of this volume, "A People Finds Its Voice: Maksymovych and Shevchenko," we examine the initial phase of the nineteenth-century Ukrainian national awakening. We begin (chapter 4) with the historian, folklorist, literary scholar, and biologist Mykhailo Maksymovych (1804–1873). Although biology was Maksymovych's first calling, and the German philosopher F.W.J. Schelling's idealistic "nature philosophy" his main interest, he soon picked up the early Romantic fascination with folklore and language. Following the examples of the Brothers Grimm, the Serb Vuk Karadžić, and many others, he turned to the folksongs of his own people as a key to its national spirit. He wondered about how "Great Russians" (i.e., Russians) and "Little Russians" (Ukrainians) related to each other in this new context. He ended up creating the geographical label "Eastern Slavs" to replace "Russians," which then often covered the peoples today called Russians, Ukrainians, and Belarusans. Philologists and then linguists eventually borrowed it to distinguish these people's languages – descended from the languages/dialects of Kyivan Rus' and written in the Cyrillic alphabet – from those of the Western and South Slavs. Maksymovych's thought and career clearly reveals the influence of western European models on the Ukrainian national awakening. However, he did not completely divide "Ukrainian" from "Russian" identity, only set the ball rolling.[26]

Chapter 5 turns to the national poet, Taras Shevchenko (1814–1861), whom Maksymovych greatly admired. Although Shevchenko knew Russia well, he looked back to a time when his beloved homeland was inhabited by free Cossacks, beholden to no one, and he could also see the firm Muslim resistance in the Northern Caucasus to Russian imperial culture, and sympathized with it. In his great poem "Kavkaz" (The Caucasus, 1845) – first circulated in manuscript form to avoid censors and finally printed in Leipzig in 1859 – he revealed himself a local Ukrainian patriot, but also a fiery opponent of Russian imperialism in general. Scholars of his work would probably agree on his being revolutionary – but perhaps not on whether he favoured "national" or "social" revolution. His simultaneously "national" and "international" poem "Kavkaz," treated in this chapter, is a centrepiece of this book.[27]

Part III, "From Paris to Verkhivnia and the Sich: The French Connection," deals with the French writers Honoré de Balzac (1799–1850) and Prosper Mérimée (1803–1870). The former, as we saw above, had close personal relations with Ukraine, and he married a rich Polish aristocrat from the right bank (west of the Dnieper), where Poles held most of the land and Ukrainian peasants worked it. Balzac actually lived with her in Ukraine for much of the last two years of his life, but took sick while there and returned to Paris, where he died. Prosper Mérimée, however, never visited the country but knew its history and ethnic and national composition much better than did Balzac. He was especially fascinated by those soldiers of the steppes called "Cossacks," and he wrote a major French-language biography of their hetman Bohdan Khmelnytsky (c. 1595–1657). Yet neither Balzac nor Mérimée seems even to have heard of Taras Shevchenko, who was their contemporary and already famous.[28]

Part IV of the current volume – "Contested Canvases: Rembrandt's 'Polish Rider' and Repin's Satirical Cossacks" – consists of two chapters on art history. The first deals with Rembrandt's mysterious painting *The Polish Rider* (c. 1655), which today hangs in the Frick Collection in New York. The chapter explores the rider's identity and points to some intriguing

Ukrainian connections. The figure, originally thought "a Cossack Rider," most likely was of "Ruthenian" origin from the Grand Duchy of Lithuania. But "Ruthenian" and "Polish" had different meanings in that era, which forms the thrust of the chapter. I also mention the theory espoused by some modern-day Ukrainians that the model was Ivan Mazepa, who was in Holland roughly when the picture was painted.

Chapter 9 treats Ilya Repin's great 1891 painting of the Zaporozhian Cossacks responding to the Ottoman sultan. During his lifetime and since, Repin has been Russia's most beloved painter, and this was his masterpiece. Its influence was enormous, and it has provoked endless interpretations. This chapter zeroes in on the era's conflict between realism and the avant-guarde and on the famous nineteenth-century debate over the nature and meaning of Orientalist painting and "Oriental" studies, especially relating to Islam and the Middle East. It also addresses the historicity of the event depicted and the historical interaction of Islam and Christianity, starting with the sultan's letter to the Cossacks, precedents for which date back perhaps to the Prophet Mohammed himself.[29]

The book ends with three appendices. The first concerns the varying meanings of *Saqaliba* (Slavonic peoples) in the medieval Muslim world. The second looks at philology – words of eastern or "oriental" provenance in modern Ukrainian. It treats such basic loan-words and concepts as *Boh*, or *Bog* (God), in the various Slavonic languages, and *khata*, a small house or "peasant cottage," in Ukrainian and Belarusan, as well as rather obscure (to Westerners) artefacts such as the *kobza*, a stringed musical instrument widely used by blind and elderly nineteenth-century itinerant folk musicians, and then popularized by the fiery poetry of Shevchenko, who took inspiration from such folk artists. That poet's ideas about Islam and Muslims in general form the third appendix.[30]

## Reconnecting Ukraine with East and West

In brief, the book is indeed a mosaic treating Middle Eastern and western motifs in Ukrainian history and culture. For many years, Soviet policy be-littled or banned discussion of these outside influences and contacts with the wider world. All good things, it declared, came to Ukraine from Russia, not the West, and most certainly not from "the East." But I believe that this is simply untrue and that both the Middle East and the West have contributed much to Ukrainian culture, and it is not all – despite Russian propaganda – bad. In other words, I seek to neutralize the lingering negative effects of extreme Soviet censorship, which sought to isolate Ukraine in the present and cut it off from its external contacts in the past. In this way, the Soviets played down early Ukrainian contacts with the Islamic world, promoted negative stereotypes of the Crimean Khanate and the Ottoman Empire, almost censored the Khanate itself out of existence, and imposed negative labels on Ukrainian figures such as Mazepa, who defied Russian authority. The Soviets also concocted new labels to denigrate Polish, Austrian, and German influences in the country during the following centuries.[31]

This type of censorship was ferocious with regard to Mazepa, who was consistently labelled a selfish aristocrat and traitor to Russia. It did not matter to the Soviet censors that when Peter the Great left Ukraine to its fate during a foreign invasion, it was he who betrayed Mazepa, not the other way around. And as for Voltaire and his early positive attitudes towards Mazepa and Ukrainian independence, these were simply censored out of everything written in the USSR after 1930. At that time, Stalin achieved his ascendancy, crushed the national intelligentsias in the Union Republics, and then "liquidated" the national Communists and re-imposed tight Moscow control over the entire USSR. Voltaire was a progressive, and therefore could never have praised a figure such as Mazepa. It was Voltaire's later, pro-Russian writings, which, as we saw above, were commissioned and paid for by Tsarina Elizabeth, that were propagated widely in the Soviet Union, and especially in the Ukrainian SSR, where the French author's famous statement that "Ukraine has always wanted to be free" never once was mentioned or alluded to in the encyclopaedias or history texts.[32]

The case of Oriental studies is almost as clear. They began in the nineteenth century, their importance alluded to by Hrushevsky in 1917, during the Revolution, when he wrote that "Ukrainians are one of the most orientalized . . . of the western peoples,"[33] and finally, were precariously established in Ukraine in the 1920s when Ahatanhel Krymsky (1871–1942) pioneered Turkish, Persian, and Arabic studies in the Pan-Ukrainian Academy of Sciences. Krymsky had several promising students, who did some good work during the 1920s. But Stalin's rule and the end of the earlier Soviet policy of "ukrainianization" froze such developments. Krymsky was disgraced, the academy ferociously purged, the master's students and friends arrested or executed, and the few who managed to survive precariously, such as Vasyl Dubrovsky, a Turkic specialist, fled to the West during the Second World War. The lonely figure of A.P. Kovalivsky, who worked primarily in Kharkiv, not Kyiv, and wrote a valuable study of the Arab traveller Ibn Fadlan, was one of the very few prominent survivors. Ibn Fadlan visited the Volga, not Ukraine, perhaps a key to Dubrovsky's survival.[34]

Indeed, after 1930 such an impartial source on Ukrainian–Muscovite relations as the Orthodox Christian Arab Paul of Aleppo (1627–1669), a Syrian Church deacon, who described his voyage across both Muscovy and Hetman Bohdan Khmelnytsky's Cossack Ukraine, was for many years virtually ignored in Soviet Ukraine and in the USSR generally, which banned his works. In the 1950s a Ukrainian émigré encyclopaedia published in Latin America offered a rather lengthy article on Paul and explored his distinctions between a fearful, unfriendly, and oppressive Muscovy ("The cunning Muscovites oppressed us and reported everything about us: 'God save us and liberate us from them!'," he writes), and an open, pleasant, and educated Ukraine ("the Land of the Cossacks"). "Throughout the Cossack Land," he continues, "there was one thing that simply amazed us: almost everyone with very few exceptions, even some of the women and girls, could read and knew the Order of the Liturgical Services in Church and could sing the hymns. The priests [even] teach the orphans and do not allow them to wander in ignorance through the streets." No wonder Paul and his small company of clerics breathed a sigh of relief on re-entering golden-domed Kyiv after their unpleasant stay in Muscovy!

In the mid-1980s, Paul's work was edited, published, and commented on in Soviet Ukraine's neighbour, the People's Republic of Poland, where scholars could already breathe a bit more freely. But the relevant parts on "the Land of the Cossacks" appeared in full in Ukraine only in the early twenty-first century. As indicated by this stunning example, "Oriental studies," once so thoroughly censored, now flourish once again in Ukraine itself.[35]

Indeed, it was not only Eastern sources such as Paul of Aleppo, and western European writers such as Voltaire, but even the very founders of so-called scientific socialism, Karl Marx and Friedrich Engels ("Western" in both insights and prejudices), who were thoroughly censored throughout most of the Soviet period. So, for example, Marx's *Secret Diplomatic History of the Eighteenth Century*, published posthumously by his daughter in the 1890s, never appeared in full in the USSR until its very last days, when the censorship was collapsing. Marx depicted Imperial Russian foreign policy in a very negative light and maintained that it was simply an extension of the brutal, aggressive, and exploitative policies of old Muscovy, and its predecessor, the Mongol Horde. He attacked both Ivan the Terrible and Peter the Great and contrasted old Kyivan Rus' (of allegedly Norman, read "Occidental" lineage) to Imperial Russia (of Mongolian, read "Oriental" origins) and (with special regard to *Rus'* versus *Rossiia*) thought them more different from each other than "Franconia" in medieval Germany from "France" on the territory of what had been Gaul, than Saxony on the continent from Essex in Britain, or even than England in Europe from New England in North America. "The bloody mire of Mongolian slavery, not the rude glory of the Norman epoch," Marx concluded, "forms the cradle of Muscovy, and modern Russia is but a metamorphosis of Muscovy."[36] Such opinions were simply not allowed in Stalin's USSR, or even permitted in the long years after his death, when the unity of the multinational Soviet state was a prime concern of Russian officialdom, and the state prestige of Russia always paramount.

The contrast between Kyivan Rus' and Russia, however, was from Mykhailo Hrushevsky's time (1890s on) onward an axiom of Ukrainian history, and, of course, although he was not really a "Normanist" at all, Hrushevsky claimed Kyivan Rus' more or less for Ukraine alone. But also, Marx, who learned a fair amount of Russian late in life, applied himself to internal affairs in Russia, and in the late 1870s read some of the work of the nineteenth-century Ukrainian historian Mykola Kostomarov, and also of his contemporary, the Ukrainian émigré political philosopher Mykhailo Drahomanov. Marx noted Drahomanov's criticism of tsarist policy on Ukrainian literature and language, carefully read his description of Kyiv's 1840s oppositional Brotherhood of Saints Cyril and Methodius (patron saints of the Slavonic world), and was fascinated by the fiery, indeed revolutionary, poetry of Taras Shevchenko. More generally, he seemed to like republics of various sorts, including old Novgorod in northern Rus' (which he did think truly Slavonic) and a "Cossack Christian Republic" in Zaporozhia in central Ukraine, for both may have seemed to him somewhat "progressive," and both turned out to be Muscovy's victims.

Marx also noted Kostomarov's description of the revolt of the Russian Cossack Stenka Razin (1630–1671), and his account of the Ukrainian Cossack Hetman Ivan Vyhovsky (d. 1664), who wished to turn Cossack Ukraine away from Muscovy and back towards Poland. He probably misread some of Kostomarov's intentions (he too had to deal with the

Russian censors) and saw rather too much violence in Razin's revolt, and although he noted Vyhovsky's politics, he did not seem to see the long-term national significance of his political turn westwards, which Mazepa was to repeat, and again Ukraine more recently. But still, he clearly noted differences "in customs, character, ideas and ways of life" between "Little Russians" and Muscovites, and even strengthened Kostomarov's vocabulary from Ukrainian "dissatisfaction" with the Muscovites to "hatred." Of course, such opinions, or even topics, could not be openly discussed in the USSR, where censors tightly controlled everything to do with Ukrainian nationalism and independence, and even these brief notes on Ukrainian affairs could not be printed.[37]

Later Marxist literature stressed usually Marx and Engels's general view of the "non-historical and reactionary" nineteenth-century Slavonic peoples of eastern Europe, especially the Ruthenians or Ukrainians of Galicia, and the post-Stalin Soviets were all too happy to simply ignore anything that threatened their view of the world importance of Imperial Russia and the USSR. In the Soviet Union, Marx's *Secret Diplomatic History of the Eighteenth Century* was published in full only in 1989 as the Berlin wall came crashing down, and his notes on Kostomarov's *Vyhovsky* only in 1993, after Ukraine itself had achieved independence.[38]

It is these sorts of repressed contacts with the outside world, both east and west, though particularly the Middle East, that form the core of the present book. Never thoroughly discussed, and for decades completely censored, they did at times constitute a resonant dimension of Ukrainian history, art, literature, and legend. Their censorship impoverished Ukrainian culture in ways and deprived it of a normal and healthy cosmopolitanism. This book is a modest attempt to correct that historical error and enrich that culture with motifs that truly belong to it and are the heritage of every thinking and feeling person concerned with the culture of that oft-troubled but not entirely unique land.

# ONE

A Complex History:
Ukraine and the *Dar al-Islam*

CHAPTER ONE

# From Abbot Daniel to Count Potocki: Middle East Travel to 1800

EUROPE HAS ALWAYS HAD an interest in and fascination with the part of the world today called "the Middle East," the lands to its south and east, which have since the seventh century been the heartlands of the Realm or House of Islam (*Dar al-Islam*). Although such interest can be traced back to ancient Greece and Rome, which borrowed much from those lands – even their alphabets and measures of time – it grew considerably after Europe's conversion to Christianity, which also originated in the Middle East. Indeed, even after the Arab conquest of Palestine, Syria, Iraq, and North Africa in the seventh and eighth centuries, this curiosity continued, and pilgrims, merchants, soldiers, and sailors of various sorts travelled there until the European discovery of the Americas and the end of the Middle Ages. Since then, despite frequent wars and religious and other conflicts, such contacts have never been completely broken, and advances in travel, especially new ocean-going and much faster ships, increased such voyaging in modern times, especially in the nineteenth century.[1]

Most modern research and writing on these contacts concern western European pilgrims, Crusaders, travellers, and such, with very little written, at least in English, about the eastern Europeans, especially the Slavs. But Slavonic Europe too played a role in this "contact between civilizations," if one may use this much-disputed term. The present chapter surveys and investigates a major aspect of these eastern European contacts: the experiences, voyages, and writings of Ukrainian (or "Ruthenian," to use an old term, from the medieval Latin for Rus') and Polish pilgrims, travellers, adventurers, exiles, scholars, and artists, most of them from the vast but under-populated eastern borderlands of old Poland, especially the Ukrainian Steppe lands that in the nineteenth century came to be called in Polish "*Kresy*" (plural of edge).[2]

The reasons why these Kresy, and especially those Polish–Ukrainian borderlands, produced so many travellers, especially in the nineteenth century, are unclear, but they were the focal point of Ottoman Turkish and Crimean Tatar influence in that part of Europe, north and east of the Carpathian Mountains – the region that W.H. McNeill once called "Europe's Steppe Frontier" – and, especially during the post-Napoleon Romantic period, they saw numerous uprisings against Russian imperial rule. Certainly, some of those Ukrainian/Polish (or Polish and Ukrainian) adventurers and exiles looked to the Ottoman Empire and the Lands of Islam for help against that Russian dominion and, on occasion, found it. Nevertheless, simple interest in and fascination with "the Orient" motivated many travellers.[3]

## Abbot Daniel and Other Medieval Pilgrims

As occurred from western Europe, many medieval and early modern Polish and Ukrainian travellers visited the Middle East. The very first were unnamed pilgrims to Palestine from "the Land of Rus'." (The Slavonic *Rus'* becomes in medieval Greek sources *Rosia* [later "Russia"], and "Ruthenia," later Ukraine, in medieval Latin.) These pilgrims appear briefly about 1022 in the old *Life of Saint Theodosius* of Kyiv, about three decades after the formal conversion of Kyivan Rus' to eastern, or Byzantine (Greek) Christianity in 987.

The first pilgrim whose name we know was St Varlaam of the Kyiv Lavra (monastery), who went to the Holy Land about 1062. But the first who left a record of his journey was the Igumen (or Abbot) Daniel of Chernihiv, who went on pilgrimage to the Holy Land in the early twelfth century, c. 1104–8 – shortly after the formal break between the Latin and Greek churches in 1054 (called in the West the "Eastern Schism") and between the First Crusade (1096–99) and the Second Crusade (1147–50) to the Holy Land.

The Igumen Daniel visited Constantinople, Cyprus, and what is today Lebanon on his way to the Crusader states, which then controlled the Holy Land, and he left a detailed account – *Puteshestvie igumena Daniila* (Pilgrimage of Igumen Daniel) – about the Holy Land itself. He writes much about the religious shrines and places that he visited, but his work is notable for its lack of hostility towards his Latin Christian brethren. He seems to have been especially impressed by his hospitable reception by (the Crusader) King Baldwin of Jerusalem, who was trying to mend relations between eastern and western Christianity. The distinguished British Byzantinist Steven Runciman used Daniel's "very instructive" journal to support his theory that, even after the "Eastern Schism," relations between the Latin (Catholic) west and the Greek (Orthodox) east really soured only after the Fourth Crusade (1202–4) and the Latin conquest and sack of Constantinople in 1204: "He was made equally welcome at Greek and Latin monasteries. He was shown particular favour by King Baldwin I. At the ceremony of the Holy Fire [at the Holy Sepulchre – Christ's] he saw Greek and Latin clerics working in harmony, though he noted with interest that while the Greek lamps in the tomb were lit miraculously, the Latin lamps had to be lit from them."[4]

Modern Russian scholars stress King Baldwin's reception of Daniel, whom they see as a kind of semi-official representative of "the entire Russian land," not just of the Kyivan region or principality. They also often ignore his magnanimity towards the Latins, and emphasize his "patriotic" Russian sentiments. By contrast, historians of Ukrainian literature point out how Daniel's written Slavonic resembles modern Ukrainian, rather than Russian, and they interpret his "Land of Rus'" as primarily the central or original Rus' lands, predecessor of modern Ukraine. Moreover, they never refer to Kyivan Rus' as "Russia," implying a separate polity and even culture from that later state and empire. And so, both Ukrainian and Russian scholars claim Daniel, although he wrote in a Kyivan form of Slavonic.[5]

Among Ukrainian historians, for example, the assessment of Daniel's writings by Mykhailo Hrushevsky (1866–1934) is crucial. He mentions Daniel's work several times in the third volume of his great *History of Ukraine-Rus'*, which series has still not lost its scholarly value, and he devotes several pages to it in the second volume of his *Istoriia ukrainskoi literatury* (History of Ukrainian Literature). He notes that Daniel's journal is the only surviving pilgrim's account from early Kyivan Rus' literature and has proved extremely popular, surviving in numerous manuscripts, and was especially rich in descriptions of the Holy Places and apocryphal tales about Christ, the Virgin Mary, and other biblical topics. And so, he concludes, Daniel's writings were neither geographical nor historical, but primarily literary. This was clearest, he says, in Daniel's emotional description of his first sight of Jerusalem and in his stirring accounts of baptisms in the Jordan River, the ceremony of the Holy Fire in Jerusalem, and his meetings with King Baldwin.[6]

Nevertheless, Daniel's pilgrim journal, which, more recent historians agree, is very much a literary work,[7] influenced later writers on and travellers to the Middle East, and even artistic depictions of that region. For example, some medieval or late medieval East Slavic representations show the River Jordan flowing from two separate sources, the rivers Yor and Dan, based on an early medieval legend recorded by Daniel. As late as the sixteenth century, Daniel of Korsun (Danylo Korsunsky) described Palestine much as his namesake had, correcting and amending his source only slightly. Even writers such as Dobrynia Yadreikovych (later Archbishop Anthony of Novgorod and, for a time, bishop of Przemyśl/Peremyshl in Halych/Galicia), who seems to have been in Constantinople both before and after its sacking in 1204, penned much briefer accounts of Palestine, poorer in actual facts and much more schematic, although Anthony is still quite valuable on Constantinople itself.[8]

Moreover, one pilgrim, probably a Kyivan, wrote a very vivid account of the capture of the Byzantine capital, preserved in an older version of the Novgorod Chronicle. This piece suggests how those tragic events were viewed in Kyivan Rus' and is of use to historians of the Byzantine Empire. Indeed, one Soviet scholar concluded that it formed an invaluable source for those events, together with the Old French account by Geoffrey of Villehardouin and the Greek chronicle of Niketas Choniates.[9]

Among Roman Catholic Poles, pilgrimages to the Holy Land began about 1200, although the earliest pilgrims left no surviving memoirs. The late medieval Polish historian Jan Długosz (1415–1480) claimed that in 1147 the prince of Mazovia, Bolesław Kędzierzawy (the curly-haired), helped the German King Conrad III en route to the Second Crusade, although this may be much more legend than history. Długosz, who defended Polish rights on the Baltic against the claims of the Teutonic Order, also reported that in 1154 Henryk, prince of Sandomir, organized a pilgrimage or Crusade to the Holy Land, visited the Holy Sepulchre, and helped King Baldwin militarily, and there seems to be independent evidence for this. Indeed, shortly before that, plans had even been laid for the great preacher of the Second Crusade, Bernard of Clairvaux, to visit Poland and preach there.[10]

Thereafter, brief notices of other pilgrims appear in the sources, although throughout the Crusading period little is known about them, for in general Poles seem to have paid more attention to crusades against pagans in the Baltic area than those to the Holy Land. Later, however, one Mykola the Ruthenian of Cracow went east in 1330, and the pilgrim Jan Winko, in 1446 when he reached Jerusalem, seemingly converted to Islam. Winko remained in the Holy Land, but never completely broke off relations with Christians, in particular the Franciscans, who called him "the Turk."[11]

## Early Modern Travellers

By the sixteenth century, Ruthenian and Polish pilgrims to the Holy Land were much more plentiful, and many were writing about their travels. In 1512, the first description of Palestine by a Pole was published anonymously in Cracow. The names of many other pilgrims, however, are well known, such as Jan Łaski (1456–1531), bishop of Gniesno and primate of Poland, and Mikołai Krzysztof Radziwiłł (1549–1616), "the Little Orphan," one of the most powerful magnates of the Lithuanian part of the great Polish–Lithuanian Commonwealth, who began life as a Calvinist, but converted to Catholicism. While seriously ill, he pledged to the pope that, should he recover, he would travel to the Tomb of Christ. He fulfilled his pledge in 1582–83, visiting Cyprus, Syria, Palestine, and Egypt to see various places associated with Christ. In Egypt, he even acquired an interest in ancient mummies and took one home with him. Upon his return, he refused all high political appointments and wrote a detailed description of his travels that quickly came out in Polish, Latin, German, and East Slavonic. Fluidly written and filled with interesting materials on sacred and secular history and geography, it remained a valuable source for travellers till the mid-nineteenth century.[12]

A generation later, the Ruthenian pilgrim Meletii Smotrytsky (1578–1633) was born in Podolia (today in western Ukraine), studied under both the Orthodox and the Jesuits, as well as in various Protestant universities in Germany, and became one of the best-educated and most cosmopolitan eastern Christians of his time. Smotrytsky started as a fiery defender of Orthodoxy in the Commonwealth, but after years of study and reflection on the trials of his times, the murder in 1623 of Archbishop Josephat Kuntsevych (now a saint), the leader of the Ruthenian Uniate church (in communion with Rome, founded 1595–96, under the Union of Brest), and, finally, a soul-searching journey to Constantinople, Jerusalem, and other places in the East, he converted to that "Uniate" church. His meetings with Ecumenical Patriarch Cyril Lucaris, who was favourably disposed towards Calvinists, and with other Orthodox leaders and hierarchs in the East, made a deep impression on him, but not favourable to those in "schism" with Rome.

On his return to the Commonwealth, Smotrytsky penned an ostensible description of his journey, which urged communion with Rome. *An Apology for the Pilgrimage to the Eastern Lands* (1628) contained more about theology than geography, but did describe the places that he visited, and it remains a landmark of Ruthenian, or Middle Ukrainian, literature, and of the polemics surrounding the Church Union.[13] Like Smotrytsky, several other learned Ukrainian pilgrims made their way to the Holy Land during this era, and some left accounts, including Danylo Korsunsky, Varlaam Linytsky, and the Monk Serapion.[14]

Moreover, Belarusans (at the time also called "Ruthenians"), most of whom, like Ukrainians, lived in the Grand Duchy of Lithuania, and were culturally very close to them, had long been producing a similar literature, which was widely read in Ukraine as well as in Belarus'. Princess Efrosiniia of Polotsk (1104–1167), now a saint, visited the Holy Land while the Crusaders still held it. Ignatius Smolnianin went on pilgrimage in the late fourteenth century and left a detailed description of the Byzantine Empire's increasing vulnerability to the Ottoman Empire. A certain fifteenth-century Varsonofy from Belarus' travelled to the Holy Land twice and prepared the first description of Egypt by any author from the East Slavic lands.[15]

Two centuries later, the famous Belarusan poet Simeon Polotsky (1629–1680), who had studied at the Mohyla Academy in Kyiv but later took service with Tsar Alexis I of Muscovy, wrote several highly polemical works castigating Islam and the Islamic countries, including *Skazanie o Makhomete i ego bezzakonnoe zakone* (The Legend of Mohammed and His Lawless Law) and *O brane* (About Abuse), arguing that it was right for Christians to treat Muslims badly. He also translated into Slavonic those parts of the medieval Latin encyclopaedia of Vincent de Beauvais that treated of Islam. Simeon is famous for introducing the Baroque style, which he had picked up in the Commonwealth, particularly in Kyiv, into Muscovite literature, and the Baroque period especially was notorious for its religious intolerance and fiery religious polemics of all kinds.[16]

In vivid contrast, almost a century earlier the anonymous author "Michael the Lithuanian" wrote positively about the Muslim Tatars of the Crimea, apparently to embarrass his fellow countrymen into better behaviour. He certainly saw many positive traits in Muslim Tatar culture, despite the frequent Tatar raids on Lithuania (after 1569 part of the Polish–Lithuanian Commonwealth), and despite the repeated wars between the two states. Michael's tract, written in Latin in about 1550 and bearing the title *De moribus Tartarorum, Lithuanorum et Moschorum Fragmeti X* (Ten Fragments on the Manners of the Tatars, Lithuanians, and Muscovites), was printed in Basil in 1615 and became relatively well-known in western Europe.[17]

The 1453 fall of Constantinople to the Ottomans, the spread of Renaissance ideas from Italy, the discovery of the Americas, and the outbreak of the Protestant Reformation marked a new era in European history, but on the Ukrainian Steppe, besides pilgrimages and polemics, certain other patterns of contact with both "east" and "west" remained strong. The Black Sea slave trade began in ancient and medieval times, but took on new and more intensive forms during the early modern era. So from about 1450 to about 1750, that is, for a full three centuries and more, the Crimean Tatars (who, together with Muscovy, were the major successors to the Mongols in Steppe Europe) systematically raided the Ukrainian lands along the southeast border of the Grand Duchy of Lithuania (later the Polish–Lithuanian Commonwealth) and carried off many hundreds of thousands of captives (over the centuries most probably a million or more) to be used as domestic and agricultural labourers in the Crimea and sold into slavery in Istanbul, from where they were dispersed all over the Middle East and North Africa. This trade was very extensive and even gave rise to the very English word for an unfree person, bondsman, or "slave," derived from the late medieval Latin *sclavus*, recoined by Italian slave traders in the Crimea, who designated their captives thus from their ethnic name "Slav." In this way, the new word replaced the ancient name for an unfree bondsman or slave, which had been *servus* in ancient Rome.[18]

These captives acquired by the Tatars on the Steppe generally called themselves *Rus'ki* , but Latin and western European sources often labelled them "Ruthenians," sometimes confused with modern "Russians" by modern historians, who are unacquainted with the early modern history of Ukraine and Muscovy. The original Kyivan Rus' (founded late ninth century), or "Ruthenia," was largely in what is today Ukraine and neighbouring

lands, while the early "Muscovy," much further north, became the centre of modern Russia, and its neighbours called its inhabitants *Moskali*, or
Muscovites. So some historians label as Russian one of the most famous of
all these Ukrainian-origin slaves, the concubine Roxelana (= Ruthenian
woman), who became the wife of Suleiman the Magnificent (sultan 1520–
66), although she was certainly from Poland–Lithuania, in fact, probably
from what is today western Ukraine. Known in the harem as "Hürrem Sultan" (the Cheerful One), she soon became the most influential woman in
the Ottoman Empire, corresponding with the king of Poland and other
dignitaries, and building major mosques and other buildings in Istanbul,
Palestine, and elsewhere.[19]

Of course, the numerous harem women of Islamic Turkey were only one
aspect of this enormous slave trade. The sultan's administration was also
made up largely of European-origin slaves, most of whom at some point
had converted to Islam. Many of these were from the Balkans, but some
were from the Commonwealth, principally the Ukrainian provinces, and so
were many of the rowers on Turkish galleys, and many others. On average,
during the height of this trade, perhaps five thousand slaves per year passed
through the slave markets of the Crimea to Istanbul, and the total number
of European- and Commonwealth-origin slaves in the empire must have
numbered in the hundreds of thousands, perhaps even more.[20] Chapter 3
below explores the Black Sea slave trade in detail.

However, other people from the Commonwealth lived in or visited the Ottoman Empire in the seventeenth century. Ambassadors, diplomats, and
more distinguished hostages also passed this way. So the famous Cossack
leader Bohdan Khmelnytsky (d. 1657) was taken captive after a great battle
and spent two years in Tatar and Turkish captivity, where he learned much
about Islamic culture and the Turkish and Tatar languages. His modern
biographer, George Vernadsky, writes that the young man did not waste his
time: "[Khmelnytsky] mastered the Turkish language, which later proved
of exceptional value to him, for it enabled him to conduct personally his
negotiations with Turkish envoys, as well as the Crimean Khan. Beyond
this, he collected much information on the habits of the sultan's court and
administration, which, again, was to be of use later on. He also became
acquainted with the Greek clergy at Phanar, a suburb of Constantinople

where the Greek patriarch had kept his quarters since the conquest of the city by the Turks in 1453." All these connections, and his ecclesiastical contacts, proved invaluable when he later attempted to found an independent Cossack polity in central Ukraine after 1648.[21]

Moreover, the Polish king Jan III Sobieski (1629–1696), who thirty-five years after Khmelnytsky's successful insurrection lifted the Ottoman siege of Vienna in 1683, had earlier accompanied a Polish embassy to Istanbul, where, like the Cossack leader, he learned some Turkish, something of the Ottoman court, and even more about the Tatars. His modern biographer, Zbigniew Wójcik, notes that this experience widened Sobieski's linguistic and cultural world and was "the first step on the road to a future political career, his first very modest action in the international arena, [and] his first lesson in political life."[22]

Sobieski's court translator of Turkish documents, Franciszek Meniński (1620–1698, born François Mesgnien in Lorraine), spent much time in Istanbul, where he perfected his knowledge of Oriental languages and learned much about high Ottoman culture. He also went on a pilgrimage to Jerusalem, later producing in Latin an influential, multilingual explanatory dictionary of Turkish–Persian–Arabic, still useful on the history of those languages.[23]

The sixteenth and seventeenth centuries saw also a vigorous polemical literature in both Polish and Ukrainian attacking the Ottoman Empire, Islam, and Muslim society, but probably no more scornful than Muslim accounts of the *Kafir* (Unbelieving) north – *Dar al-Harb*, the Realm or House of War. These Christian tracts concentrated on the Ottoman Turks then threatening Christendom, and largely ignored Persia and other Muslim lands further east. Some writers even held up Islamic society as a virtuous model to contrast with Christian Europe. So the Polish Protestant poet Mikołaj Rej was a bit of a turkophile, and several Orthodox Ukrainian polemicists against the Catholic Church and the Church Union of 1695–96 praised Muslim society for its religious tolerance, something they did not see in Roman Catholic parts of Europe. Such polemics revealed the authors' contact with real life in the Muslim world, and, as we saw above, one such writer, Meletii Smotrytsky, later travelled in the Middle East, although it changed his mind in ways with which those other Orthodox polemicists most certainly could not agree.[24]

Eastern European contacts with the Islamic east extended well beyond the Ottoman Empire into Persia, the Land of "the Great Sophy," as its ruler was sometimes called in English travel literature. Certain travellers went as far as India, and recorded their journeys. The best example was a man from Tver, in northern Muscovy. In 1466, the merchant Afanasy Nikitin travelled through Iran to India, where he noted the religious practices, nakedness, and dark complexion of the people, and, in the absence of Christian churches, he preferred to worship with the monotheistic Muslims, in their mosques. He recorded a brief, but fascinating account of his adventures, considered a masterpiece.[25]

The renowned Italian traveller Pietro della Valle (1586-1652), who spent 1614–26 in the Middle East and south Asia took back to Europe from Iraq examples of ancient cuneiform writing on clay tablets, toured the ruins of Babylon, and reached the court of Shah Abbas the Great at Isfahan; he also sought a great anti-Ottoman alliance of Persia, the Ukrainian Cossacks, and western Europeans. In Persia, he befriended a Zaporozhian Cossack from central Ukraine, who had been sent to conclude such an alliance with Persia's Shia Muslims against the Sunni Turks.[26]

Two generations later, Russia's Peter the Great (reigned 1682–1725) invaded Persia in 1722 and sent a detachment of Ukrainian Cossacks along with his army. This event appeared in the extensive diary (1717–67) of the erudite Ukrainian military officer Yakiv Markovych (1696–1770), and later in the anonymous and fanciful *Istoriia Rusov* (History of the Ruthenians) (1827), which long circulated widely in manuscript form among the Orthodox gentry of left-bank (eastern) Ukraine before appearing in print in 1846.[27]

Difficulties of communication and distance had prevented Pietro della Valle's anti-Ottoman combination from succeeding, and by 1683 the Ottomans were at the gates of Vienna, threatening Habsburg hegemony in central Europe until Jan Sobieski arrived with a large relief force. About two-thirds of his Commonwealth army came from what is today Ukraine, including from the old Kyiv province Podolia, Red Ruthenia, and Volhynia, and a small unit of Ukrainian Cossacks accompanied the host. Meanwhile, other Ukrainian Cossacks in alliance with the Poles created a diversion in Ottoman Moldavia, helping to relieve Vienna. Sobieski himself put much faith in his Cossack supporters, although fewer arrived at Vienna than he had hoped.[28]

The Ottoman defeat at Vienna was epochal, ending a centuries-long encroachment on European territories. From 1683 to 1699, the Habsburgs and their allies pushed the enemy back, liberating Hungary and other lands.

In Ukraine, the Poles recovered the large province of Podolia, the Cossacks largely freed themselves, and the Tatars lost most of their offensive edge. Warsaw was filled with booty captured from the Ottoman camp at Vienna, Polish nobles sported Turkish attire, and Franz Kulchytsky, believed to be a former Zaporozhian Cossack, opened one of Europe's first coffee-houses, using coffee beans from the Ottoman camp awarded him for his services at the siege of Vienna – an early instance of the growing fashion for things Turkish ("la Turquerie"), which spread across Europe, reaching its climax in France and England in the mid-eighteenth century.[29]

## Three Eighteenth-Century Travellers

The eighteenth century saw three outstanding travellers to the Middle East from Poland and the Ukrainian lands. The Ukrainian Vasyl Hryhorovych-Barsky (1701–1747) from Kyiv spent twenty-five years journeying throughout the Ottoman Empire and especially the Levant. As a student of the Orthodox Mohyla Academy in Kyiv he acquired an interest in the Holy Places in the Islamic East, especially Orthodox monasteries, and after a visit to Italy he went to Constantinople and Mount Athos. On route, he learned Greek and composed a journal of his travels across Anatolia, Syria, Lebanon, Egypt, and the Holy Land, where he stayed in various monasteries and described the locals, their languages and customs, and the economies, history, and physical geography of the region. He took monastic vows in Antioch, but could never quite settle down. His journals included over one hundred and fifty drawings and pictures and vividly recounted his many adventures, as well as describing churches, shrines, and monasteries.

These journals represented a new form of literature in the eastern Slavonic world, and some modern scholars consider them the first real Slavonic autobiography. They became enormously popular after his death, circulated in manuscript, and went through six printed editions between 1778 and 1819; when a four-volume edition of his journals came out, it greatly impressed N.G. Chernyshevsky, the ideological leader of the Russian revolutionary intelligentsia, as Soviet historians once liked to note.[30] Moreover, his drawings of Egyptian monuments and other antiquities were so accurate that at least one Soviet historian claimed that they excelled those produced a century later in the great *Description de l'Egypte* commissioned by Napoleon.[31]

The scholarly Jesuit Tadeusz Krusiński (1675–1751), originally from Poland proper, taught for several years at Ostroh in Volhynia and died at

Kamianets-Podolsky, both in right-bank Ukraine, and is best known for his writings on Iran. In the early eighteenth century, within the Catholic church, various national communities seemed to focus their missionary work in specific regions of the world. Thus Spain was most concerned with the Americas (much of it part of their empire) and North Africa, France with Syria and the Levant, and it fell to Poland to treat with Iran.

Of course, Polish diplomats had long been active in Persia, but Krusiński was the most talented, cultured, and observant, and the best linguist, becoming court translator for the Safavid Shah Hossein. He was in Iran when the Gilzai Afghans under Mahmud Hotak toppled the long-standing Safavid dynasty and witnessed the sack and partial destruction of Isfahan: "The most famous [city] of the East . . . exceeds Constantinople in Bigness, Populousness and Magnificence of Buildings and Riches." Even today, the saying "*Isfahan, nisf-e jahan!*" (Isfahan is half of the world!) is universally known in Iran.

Krusiński described these events in a lively fashion and gathered information on the Afghan invaders, then largely unknown in Europe. He was the first modern European scholar to describe the Hindu Kush and prepared the first European history of Iran. He wrote a great deal in Latin on his experiences in Iran, most famously a history of the Afghan invasion – *Relatio de mutationibus Regni Persorum* (almost immediately translated into English as *A History of the Late Revolutions in Persia*[32]) – which appeared in several other European vernaculars and Ottoman Turkish. It became one of the first books printed in the Muslim world, where Islamic scholars were suspicious of this new technology from the *kafir* north. The book was referred to by John Malcolm in the next century, Percy Sykes a century after that, and all subsequent historians of Iran.[33]

Count Jan Potocki's (1761–1815) influential family held enormous estates in Podolia in western Ukraine. Throughout his life, he travelled widely in Europe, but also visited Turkey, Egypt, and North Africa, including Morocco in the Arab far "west" (*Maghreb*). He took part in at least one raid by the Knights of St John of Malta against Muslim shipping in the Mediterranean and in this way acquired a lively interest in the Middle East. He was also a politician, who took part in Poland's famous Four Year Sejm, or Parliament, which passed the Constitution of May Third (1791) intended to reform the Polish–Lithuanian Commonwealth, and he was a scientist and the first person to fly in a hot-air balloon above Warsaw.

During his varied travels, Potocki acquired an interest in the strange and the occult and in later life began writing on these subjects in French. These interests eventually led to his suicide at his château in Podolia. Aside from penning numerous works on Ukrainian archaeology and ancient history (some copies of which he sent to Thomas Jefferson and are today in the Library of Congress), he wrote travel books and horror stories with supernatural and grotesque motifs. His example spurred his kinsman Count Wacław Rzewuski/Viacheslav Revusky – nicknamed the "Emir" – to travel in the Levant, which subject we explore below in chapter 2.[34]

## CHAPTER TWO

# From the "Emir" to the Metropolitan: Middle East Travel (1800–1914)

THE FIRST STAGES OF UKRAINIAN TRAVEL to the Middle East were dominated by pilgrims visiting the Holy Land and other such places of interest. But by the eighteenth century adventurers of other sorts had followed those first pilgrims and the profle of Middle East travel changed. The next century saw scholars and political exiles as well as artists and writers of other kinds set out on such journeys, and the historical record becomes much richer.

## Four Orientialists and Three Writers (1800–70)

Like Count Jan Potocki, whom we met in chapter 1, his kinsman Count Wacław Rzewuski/Viacheslav Revusky (1784–1831) (Plate 4) belonged to one of the great families of right-bank Ukraine, but his father, like the Potockis, had (in 1792) joined the Confederation of Targowica against Polish king Stanisław Augustus Poniatowski and the 3 May Constitution, which alliance aided the Russian Tsarina Catherine II in the last partitions of Poland. The family thereby earned eternal ignominy among patriotic Poles. The younger Rzewuski seemed to feel this opprobrium and perhaps as a result travelled extensively abroad.

After the last partition of Poland in 1795, Rzewuski resided in Vienna, joining the Austrian army. But science and scholarship interested him more, and he worked closely with the Orientalist scholars J. Klaproth and Joseph von Hammer-Purgstall. Also in Vienna, he studied Arabic with a Maronite priest, Antun Ariba, and Turkish with a political émigré named Ramiz

Pasha. In 1812–13, he was back in Volhynia (in Russian-ruled Ukraine), where, with the influential Polish educator and tsarist administrator Tadeusz Czacki, he founded the famous Lyceum at Kremenets. At the Congress of Vienna in 1815, Rzewuski met Tsar Alexander I and his wife, Caroline of Wittenberg, and suggested that they finance his proposed expedition to Arabia to search for thoroughbred horses to replenish European stocks decimated in the Napoleonic Wars. The tsar agreed, and Rzewuski set out for Constantinople, Syria, and Arabia with a medical officer and a small troop of Ukrainian Cossacks.[1]

For about two years (1818–20) Rzewuski travelled widely across Anatolia and throughout the Arab lands. He dressed in Arabic garb, took up the local manners, and mixed easily with the Bedouin, who respected him and called him, fittingly, "Goldenbeard." He adopted the names Emir Taj al-Fahr (crown of glory [= Wacław]) and Abd-al Nishan (slave of the sign). The French philosopher Jean-Jacques Rousseau and his idealization of "the Noble Savage," unspoiled by urban civilization, may have inspired him.

"Goldenbeard" was looking constantly for the best horses for export to Europe and making abundant notes on the lands and peoples he met. Eventually, he settled in Aleppo. In Palmyra, he met the English adventurer Lady Esther Stanhope, like him an enthusiast for the Islamic world. All the while, he wrote about his discoveries and adventures for various Polish and western European newspapers and journals and told the Arabs about the power and might of the Russian tsar. Indeed, one modern Polish historian believes that he was a tsarist agent, working quietly against British and French influences in the region. Eventually, a great revolt against Ottoman rule caused him to leave Aleppo, and he returned to Constantinople and arranged to have his horses sent to Europe, where some went to the armies of the post-1815 Congress Kingdom of Poland (Russian Poland) and of Imperial Russia.[2]

On his return to Ukraine, Rzewuski maintained his interest in Arabic and Islamic culture. He studied Arabic manuscripts and amassed a great collection, continued to dress in Arabic clothing, and actually shocked the tsar when his activities and look were reported to him; the tsar ordered that he immediately shave his "Goldenbeard."[3]

Rzewuski wrote several notable manuscripts, articles, and reports that he published in von Hammer-Purgstall's multilingual journal (which he co-sponsored), *Mines de l'orient/Fundgruben des Orients* (= Eastern Treasures), Europe's first journal dedicated to the Middle East. He composed studies with titles such as *Arabic Melodies*, *Greek Melodies*, and *Reflections*

*on the Ruins of Palmyra.* Bucking his family traditions, he wrote a musical score for Niemcewicz's *Śpiewy historyczne* (Historical Songs), which
became enormously popular among patriotic Poles. But his magnum opus
was his manuscript narrative in French on his journey through the Middle
East, about his adventures there (vol. I), Arabic horses and horsemanship
(vol. II), and other, related matters (vol. III). The work featured Rzewuski's
own drawings and expert Arabic calligraphy. It was frequently consulted in
Cracow where it was stored, but remained unpublished until 2014.[4]

Rzewuski's interest in "the East" extended to Europe's Steppe frontier,
and he held court at his château at Savran in right-bank Ukraine, where
he cultivated Cossack traditions, studied Ukrainian folk music, especially
historical songs, collected Ukrainian musical instruments, and patronized
various poets and artists, including the Ukrainian poet and "Torban"
player Tymko Padura, who wrote Ukrainian lyrics and poetry using non-
Cyrillic Polish letters. Padura composed a *duma*, or epic reflective song,
in Rzewuski's honour, and his *Hej Sokoly* (Hey, Falcons!) remains one of
Poland's best-known Ukrainian folksongs and serves as the theme song of
the flying aces of today's Ukrainian Air Force.[5]

However, when the Poles revolted against Russian rule in 1830–31,
Rzewuski joined the insurrection with his Arabic thoroughbreds and
his private regiment of Cossacks. He disappeared in pitched battle with
the Russians, and his body was never found. Afterwards, wild rumours
circulated that he had escaped at the last minute and gone to Arabia, where
he fitted in quite well and lived to a ripe old age. Polish Romantic-era
writers composed poetry and stories in his memory, and the tale of "Emir"
Rzewuski, the Cossack Arab from the Ukrainian–Polish borderlands,
entered into Polish national legend.[6]

Today Rzewuski's colleague von Hammer-Purgstall is known primarily
for his ten-volume *Geschichte des osmanischen Reiches* (History of the
Ottoman Empire, published 1827–35), which, for the first time, synthesized
European scholarship with the information contained in the Ottoman
chronicles. But he was also one of the first major European translators
and historians of Persian literature, especially the fourteenth-century
poet Hafez. His translation of Hafez, in particular, had a profound effect
on Europe, inspiring Goethe's *West–östlicher Divan* (Poems of West and
East, 1819) – *divan/diwan* being Persian/Arabic for a collection of poems –
a leading Romantic work. It combined Enlightenment admiration for the
"wisdom of the East" with the Romantic quest for the exotic. Goethe's *Divan*,

together with Byron's Oriental poems, especially *The Giaour* (from Turkish for infidel = Arabic *kafir*, 1813), and in Poland various takes on Byron's *Mazeppa* (1819), became a key Romantic work, immediately imitated all over Europe. At least one Ukrainian scholar believes that it even influenced the new Ukrainian-language literature that emerged after 1900.[7]

Von Hammer's personal life too was influenced by "the Orient": he began each day praying *insha'allah* (If God wills it) and went to bed with a *masha'allah* (Whatever God wills). Moreover, despite being a pioneering historian of the Ottoman Empire, he preferred the poetic Persians to the "decadent" Turks and long dreamed of going to Iran. As a result, the conservative Austrian chancellor Prince Metternich blocked his advancement in the foreign service, probably fearing that it would harm Austrian–Ottoman relations. But that left von Hammer more time and energy for Ottoman history, to the eventual benefit of Turkish historians everywhere.[8]

Great writers too were drawn intensively to Eastern themes. Poland's national poet, Adam Mickiewicz (1798–1855), composed two major works devoted to "the Orient." *Sonety Krymskie* (Crimean Sonnets, 1826) was inspired by his brief stay on that peninsula and in its old capital of Bachisaray, and *Farys* (1828), by the exploits of Emir Taj al-Fahr, "Goldenbeard" (Count Rzewuski). Like parts of Goethe's *West–östlicher Divan*, *Farys* resembled a *qasideh*, a brief Persian or Arabic storied or purposeful poem, but becoming here a manifesto of extreme individualism and love for liberty, dwelling on the limitless desert and his subject's adventures. In contrast to Byron's pessimism, *Farys* pointed the way to victory over all obstacles.

In central and eastern Europe, *Farys* was read as a concealed call to national freedom and soon spawned Polish Romantic spin-offs, such as Juliusz Słowacki's (1809–1849) *Arab* (1832) and Karel Baliński's *Farys-wieszcz* (1844). Słowacki, like Rzewuski from right-bank Ukraine, also imitated Chateaubriand and Lamartine in his own *Podróż do Ziemi Swiętej z Neapolu* (A Journey [1836–39] to the Holy Land from Naples) and elsewhere evoked Byron's Greek adventures. *Podróż* refers constantly to Ukraine, the land of his boyhood and youth and, according to one modern Polish historian, associates the Arab desert with the Ukrainian Steppe and "identifies the Bedouin with the Free Cossack."[9] Many lesser Polish works touched on similar themes, often concealing national patriotism only lightly under Oriental language and motifs. Moreover, the fact that so many of the authors were, like Potocki, Rzewuski, Mickiewicz, and Słowacki, from the eastern borderlands (*Kresy*) has not yet been properly explored by political and literary historians.[10]

Mickiewicz's Ukrainian counterpart, the Ukrainian "national poet," Taras Shevchenko (1814–1861), never set foot outside the Russian Empire, but had some very clear feelings about the Muslim peoples, who struggled against their Russian overlords. He was very sympathetic to the Muslims of the northern Caucasus and their great leader, Imam Shamil, then fighting a ferocious rearguard action against the Imperial Russian army, which was seeking to pacify and subdue them. One of Shevchenko's good friends had been conscripted into the fight and died at the hands of the resistance, but the Ukrainian poet championed those Caucasians.

In memory of his friend, in 1845, he penned his powerful "Kavkaz" (The Caucasus), which raised the specter of Prometheus, bound to a rock, high in the Caucasus, with the imperial eagle tearing at his flesh. Although Cossack Ukraine's oppression by the Muscovites is a major theme, it also seems a general protest against oppression anywhere. Shevchenko never visited the Middle East, but he was convicted of insulting the tsar's family for his rebellious poetry, sentenced to serve as a common soldier in central Asia, and forbidden to write or paint (he was a painter and artist by profession). In central Asia, he was able to see the local Kazakhs and other peoples and surreptitiously both painted the locals and wrote some poetry, thereby living the liberation theme of the Romantic movement, which involved the Islamic world.[11] Chapter 5, below, explores Shevchenko's creation of "Kavkaz" in detail.

A great many travellers from other parts of Poland and Ukraine than the *Kresy* (Shevchenko's birthplace too) went to Eastern lands or the Middle East. One of the most notable was the Russian writer of Ukrainian origin Nikolai Gogol/Mykola Hohol (1809–1852), who visited Palestine in 1848 on his return to the Russian Empire from western Europe. He seems to have read Igumen Daniel as interpreted by the historian Nikolai Karamzin, and had even assured a lady friend that he would write a full description of his voyage and those lands – which he never did. In fact, his personal troubles soured his impressions of both Jerusalem and Palestine as a whole: it seemed not to flow with milk and honey, but be rather a very barren place indeed, to judge from his few general and very brief remarks in private letters. After his return to

Russia, his psychological problems only intensified, and he eventually starved himself to death, trying to atone for what he believed were his many sins.[12]

The "neo-Cossack" Mykhailo Chaikovsky/Michał Czajkowski (1804–1886) was known in his own time all over central and eastern Europe, both in the Balkans and north of the Carpathians, as (Mehmed) Sadyk Pasha. Although he wrote usually in Polish, his subjects were either Ukrainian ("Cossack") or Ottoman Turkish, for he spent most of his active life in the Ottoman Empire as an adventurer, political intriguer, soldier, and writer, working tirelessly for what he believed was his ancestral "Cossack" heritage.[13] A descendant of the Ukrainian Cossack hetman Ivan Briukovetsky, he was born into a somewhat-polonized family near Berdychiv in Kyiv province shortly before that region transferred from Polish to Russian rule. Just before the last partition of Poland, his father, Stanisław, had held a senior administrative post in the local government (including Podkomarz of the Zhytomyr district), but his family raised and educated him to value Cossack traditions and Ukrainian folk culture. Indeed, as his memoirs noted, he was named after the Archangel Michael, protector of the Zaporozhian Cossacks and patron saint of the city of Kyiv. He grew up a local patriot, loyal to the idea of a resurrected Poland and esteeming Cossack Ukraine.[14]

But Chaikovsky as a youth preferred adventure to study and, when sent to Warsaw, complained that it was "not Cossack." As well, as an Eastern Rite, or Greek Catholic, he disliked the Roman Catholic traditions of old Poland and blamed the Jesuits for turning the Poles and Ukrainians against each other in the seventeenth century. Moreover, he sympathized with the enserfed Ukrainian peasants, and, when the Polish insurrection of 1830 began and a Russian officer came to arrest him, his peasants defended their master and almost hanged the police official. Chaikovsky then freed his serfs and, together with his Cossacks, immediately joined the rebellion, serving under Karol Różycki.[15]

But the insurrection failed, and Chaikovsky went into exile in Paris. There he turned to literature, writing novelettes on Cossack themes and complaining again that his fellow Polish exiles, even those from Ukraine, were not "Cossack" enough. His numerous books, written in Polish but filled with ukrainianisms, dealt mostly with Ukrainian history, the most famous being his *Powieści kozackie* (Cossack Novels, 1837), translated into French as *Contes kosaks* (1857), although his two-volume tale, *Weryhora* (1838), about the legendary Ukrainian seer who predicted the Commonwealth's collapse and rebirth, also made a big impact. Throughout, the author extolled Cossack bravery, attacked Russian autocracy, criticized the old Polish landlords (*szlachta*) for oppressing the common Ukrainian people, put Jews and Jesuits on the same footing, and wrote that it would be better for modern Cossacks to make peace with the modern Poles and be under the distant lordship of the Ottoman sultan rather than the closer pressure of the Muscovite tsar.[16]

Meanwhile, in exile, Chaikovsky began to shift politically to the right. Eventually, he came under the influence of Prince Adam Czartoryski (1770–1861), who convinced him to transfer from the Greek to the Latin rite and in 1841 to go to Turkey to work against Russian influences in the Ottoman-ruled Balkans; he also attempted to firm up Ottoman resistance to Russia. The French foreign minister, François Guizot, and the Turkish ambassador in London, Reshid Pasha, supported this enterprise. In Istanbul, our Cossack quickly adapted to local conditions. The Ottomans were still friendly to Russia because of the revolt of Egypt under Mohammed Ali, but soon came their *tanzimat* (internal reform), when the sultans modernized administration, education, and the armed forces to better compete with the threatening European powers, especially Habsburg Austria and Imperial Russia. European technical experts were welcomed, and the affable Chaikovsky, with his military experience and literary talents, soon fitted right in. He dressed like a Turk, fez and all, sat cross-legged on a carpet, and shared his tea in small glasses with other European and Polish exiles who followed his example, usually taking him for a Turk at first glance.

Chaikovsky opened the Polish Agency, which worked to counteract Russian spies and agents in Turkey, who were using Panslavic sentiments to raise the Balkan Slavonic peoples against their Ottoman overlords. Following Prince Czartoryski's plans, Chaikovsky proposed a gradual move towards independence for Christian Balkan Slavs. Despite some brief success in Serbia and Bulgaria, the pro-Russian tendency prevailed in both countries.[17]

Chaikovsky also hoped to establish a Polish colony on the Asian side of the Bosphorus. Polish refugees, deserters from the Russian army, veterans of the insurrection of 1830, and Slavs redeemed by the Polish Agency from Turkish servitude filled the colony, named Adampol after the exiled Czartoryski, but known in Turkish as Polonezköy (Polish village). It flourished during the nineteenth century and still exists.[18]

Chaikovsky's importance grew immensely after the failure of the revolutions of 1848 in central Europe, especially in Hungary. Thousands of defeated insurgents sought political asylum in the Ottoman Empire. Chaikovsky and his numerous Ottoman contacts worked to protect them and settle them in Turkey, and, despite Russian and Austrian pressure, many became soldiers, administrators, doctors, and technicians. But Russian insistence on rebels' repatriation did not let up, and eventually affected even Chaikovsky. To escape deportation, he, like many others, converted to Islam, and he took the Muslim name Mehmed Sadyk Pasha, or Sadyk Pasha, for short (Plate 5).

About this time, in the early 1850s, he organized his regiment of Ottoman Cossacks. He travelled to Dobrudja, near the mouth of the Danube in Moldavia, to mediate a dispute between Russian Old Believer Cossacks and descendants of the Zaporozhian Cossacks, who had fled to Turkey in 1775 after Catherine the Great destroyed their headquarters at the Sich in central Ukraine. Sadyk convinced many of them to join a new body of Ottoman Cossacks to serve the sultan in the event of war with Russia. Polish and Hungarian refugees, Balkan Slavs, Jews, and other men joined the unit, which was given old Cossack flags and insignia issued or captured by Ottoman forces in the seventeenth and eighteenth centuries. The highlight, Sadyk later wrote in his memoirs, was a Zaporozhian standard that the sultan had presented to Phylyp Orlyk, successor in exile to Hetman Mazepa, when the Zaporozhians first entered Ottoman service – on one side, a red field with a silver Muslim half-crescent, and on the other, a white field with a golden cross of Orthodoxy.[19] Only the Ottoman *tanzimat* reform era (starting in 1839) made possible this amazing combination.

During the Crimean War (1853–56), the Ottoman Cossacks saw service in Romania and the Balkans, but never raided Ukraine – Chaikovsky's dream. In Ukraine, rumours spread about his activities, and there were some Cossack disorders in the countryside. The 1845 constitution of the Brotherhood of Saints Cyril and Methodius (patron saints of Slavdom) in Kyiv, a quasi-conspiracy broken by the tsar's police in 1847, supposedly echoed similar writings by émigré Poles in western Europe – possibly Chaikovsky's. Although accurate information about the Brotherhood emerged in Ukraine only much later, its example inspired the Ukrainian national movement.[20]

After the Crimean War, Sadyk Pasha's influence declined. The death in 1861 of Sultan Abdul Mejid (reigned since 1839), his patron, other personnel changes in the Ottoman government, reforms in Russia, and intrigues against him by fellow Polish exiles, especially General Zamoyski, who had replaced him at the Polish Agency, pushed him to reconcile with Moscow. He came to see some hope for Cossackdom in these changes, and Count Nikolai Ignatev, the Russian ambassador in Istanbul, eventually convinced him to return to Ukraine in 1872. Accepting an amnesty, he retired from Ottoman service, converted to Orthodoxy, and, with a young Greek wife, set off for Kyiv. He settled in the countryside and completed his detailed memoirs of his time in Ottoman service. Excoriated by many Poles, but welcomed with some puzzlement by others, he died in 1886.[21]

It is difficult to fit Chaikovsky into any nineteenth-century historical or national category. He had served both Poland and Turkey, but always claimed to be a loyal Cossack first. The mid-century Ukrainian national awakeners, who generally looked back fondly on their Cossack history, did not quite know what to make of him. For example, when Nikolai/Mykola Petrov wrote his pioneering history of Ukrainian literature, he omitted Chaikovsky and those authors who wrote in Polish. Mykola Dashkevych, in his influential, book-length review of Petrov's study, seemed puzzled by Chaikovsky. In him, the reviewer concluded: "Polish Cossackophilism reached its apotheosis, and simultaneously its extreme limit, and turned into an absurdity. Along with this, in the course of history and a very adventurous life, Chaikovsky found out in practice the difficulty of putting into action his dreams of the re-establishment of Poland and Ukrainian Cossackdom."[22] But Dashkevych wrote in the face of stringent censorship, which rejected any overt expression of Ukrainian or Polish nationalism and, especially, independence. In his life, Chaikovsky, far more than Krusiński, Potocki, or Rzewuski, helped bridge Ukrainian (Orthodox), Polish (Catholic), and Ottoman (Muslim) cultures.

Aleksander Chodźko (1804–1891), a Pole from the Lithuanian part of the *Kresy*, ventured east as far as the Persian province of Khorasan, which neighboured Afghanistan, and throughout the Persian Empire. Everywhere he went, he made copious notes on places, people, events, and languages and customs.

Chodźko was one of three brothers in a patriotic Polish family of gentry origin. He attended university at Vilnius (now capital of Lithuania), where he mixed with Adam Mickiewicz, Antoni Edward Odyniec, and other members of the patriotic secret Society of Philomaths. More widely read than the others, he explained to them the tenets of the rising Romantic movement and Byron's motives. He too began to write poetry with exotic and Oriental motifs, and Mickiewicz, a close friend and rival, thought him the best poet of this circle.[23]

However, the tsar's police soon discovered the Philomaths and sent them to prison or into exile. Chodźko spent about a year in captivity, but on his release in 1821 went to the Oriental Institute in St Petersburg to study Oriental languages. Under the Azerbaijani professor Mirza Jafar Topchybashi, he specialized in Persian and related languages and excelled; on his graduation, the imperial government sent him to Iran as consular translator and representative.

He began his work in Tabriz in Persian Azerbaijan, but later went to Tehran, and then to Rasht on the Caspian Sea, in Gilan province. He studied the local language, a tongue quite different from literary Persian, and later did the same in Iranian Kurdistan. He listened to local music and the historical songs of the Azeri, Gilaki, and Kurdish peoples and later wrote about them. Gilan, with its mountains and greenery, was probably his favourite part of Iran, and he has left us a detailed historical and geographical description. In 1835, he crossed Iran with the Englishman Henry Crestwicke Rawlinson (1810–1865), who copied the magnificent trilingual cuneiform inscription of Darius the Great at Bisitun and, after much study, deciphered it, revealing to European scholars (and eventually also Persian and Arab readers) the ancient languages of Persia and Mesopotamia.[24]

In Iran, Chodźko also made friends with the Polish exile Izydor Borowski (c. 1770–1838), who had served in the Polish Legions in Italy, with anti-Spanish rebels in South America, with British forces, and finally in the Persian military, fighting against the Uzbeks, the Turkomans, and others. After illustrious service in Persia, where he helped reform the military under Fath-Ali Shah (reigned 1797–1834) and his sons, Borowski died in 1838 at the siege of Herat, which aimed to recover it for the Kajars.[25]

After eleven years (1830–41) serving Russia in Iran, Aleksander Chodźko went to Paris, where he met up with Mickiewicz and other friends from Vilnius, who convinced him to leave the Russian foreign service and interested him in the mystical movement of Andrzej Towiański, who turned out to be a charlatan. Under Towiański's baneful influence, and with some confidence because of his loyal service, he wrote to Tsar Nicholas I, asking him to mend his authoritarian ways, to no effect. During the Crimean War

(1853–56), Chodźko joined the French civil service and wrote a handbook of Turkish for Allied soldiers; after the war, he applied for the professorship in Oriental languages at the Collège de France. It went to a Frenchman, but, in compensation, Chodźko was in 1857 given the Chair of Slavonic Literatures, which Mickiewicz had held.[26]

Chodźko's most fruitful period of Middle East studies was in Paris. He published a major work in English on Azeri folklore – *Specimens of the Popular Poetry of Persia as Found in the Adventures and Improvisations of Kurroglou the Bandit Minstrel* (London, 1842; 2nd ed., 1864) – which was translated into French (by George Sand) and German. He also published a grammar of Persian, that handbook of Turkish for soldiers, those studies of Gilaki and Kurdish (on the Suleimani dialect), and other books on Persian song and folklore. Also, he wrote on Persian theatre – the famous Tazias, the distinctive Shia religious plays similar to the miracle and passion plays of medieval western Europe.[27]

Chodźko's work on the Slavonic world followed a similar pattern to his Oriental studies. *Chants historiques de l'Ukraine* (1879) summarized the longer work on popular historical songs in the original Ukrainian by Volodymyr Antonovych and Mykhailo Drahomanov, adding material on relations with the Turkic world. He also published on old Slavonic legends (1859), on Poland's "southern provinces," on Bulgaria, and on Russia. As well, he compiled a *Grammaire paléoslave* (1869) and a great *Polish–English Dictionary* (1851), the first of its kind. Later he returned to his first love, Persian language and literature.[28]

Louis Léger, his successor at the Collège de France, considered Chodźko's studies of Persian culture more original and important than those on Slavonic Europe.[29] In both fields, however, Chodźko made a solid contribution and, despite the growing influence of "positivism" and "organic work," held on to his Romantic beliefs, including the idea that the essence of any nation or people lay in its language and folklore, especially its historical songs – a concept that moved many other Slavonic scholars of that time (see, for example, Mykhailo Maksymovych in chapter 4 below) and went right back to Herder and the Brothers Grimm. Indeed, that idea may relate to the facts that Chodźko hailed from those same Lithuanian or Ukrainian borderlands of Poland as Potocki, Rzewuski, and Chaikovsky and that he, like the latter two in particular, supported the subordinate Polish and emerging Ukrainian cultures and peoples, which were crystallizing new identities. In any event, European knowledge of the Middle East was a quite unexpected beneficiary of this quest, and Chodźko's detailed documentation of Persian, Kurdish, and Azeri languages and dialects, and songs, remains a treasure trove for Iranian ethnographers.

The life and career of another Polish Orientalist from Vilnius contrast starkly with those of Rzewuski, Chaikovsky, and Chodźko. Józef Sękowski/ Osip Senkovsky (1800–1858), who also studied at the university in Vilnius and went directly into philology, early on translated into Polish parts of Dante's *Divine Comedy* and other works. Studies under Polish historian Joachim Lelewel seem to have turned him to travel literature, where he quickly focused on Turkey and the Middle East. With financial backing from the local Polish Freemasons and the Russian patron of historical studies, Count Rumiantsev, he spent the years 1819–21 exploring Turkey, the Levant, Egypt, the Nile as far south as Nubia, and Ethiopia. He improved his Turkish and Arabic, visited historic sites and ruins such as those at Troy and Baalbek, and explored Egypt's magnificent antiquities.[30]

On his return to Vilnius, Sękowski was offered a new professorship in Oriental studies, but he accepted a similar position at St Petersburg, where he taught for most of his career. Publication of his two-volume compendium of Turkish and other Oriental sources for Polish and Ukrainian history was financed by J.U. Niemcewicz, the famous compiler of historical songs illustrating Polish history.[31] The work focused on the *Kresy* bordering on the Islamic world, especially Ukraine with its Cossacks and Tatars, and some materials in it critical of the old Polish–Lithuanian Commonwealth aroused strong criticism in Poland; a certain Pietraszewski, in an almanac called *Haliczanin* (The Galician) in the Austrian sector of divided Poland (partly in today's Ukraine), accused Sękowski of falsifying Turkish sources. Yet the French father of modern European Arabic studies, Silvestre de Sacy, praised similar work by Sękowski, and most modern scholars, including Olgerd Górka, a Polish specialist in Crimean history, concur.[32]

Sękowski later published some of his own critical remarks, especially on some of von Hammer-Purgstall's work, on Champollion's decipherment of hieroglyphics, and on Karamzin's history of Russia, which enjoyed wide popularity in that empire, especially in official circles; he also published studies of Egyptian papyri and other matters.

In mid-career, Sękowski became an Imperial Russian censor, while simultaneously writing as Baron Brambeus, quickly becoming known for his biting wit and sarcasm. He renounced his hereditary Polish title and became known as a "careerist" renegade, whose fierce denunciations of Romantic nationalism and revolution completely alienated him from most patriotic Poles, despite being sometimes praised for his lax censorship. By the time he retired, he had alienated even Russian society with his sharp criticisms of the so-called national school of writers such as Nikolai Gogol and Vassarion Belinsky (the former an idol of the Ukrainian national movement, the latter, of Russian revolutionaries), and with his own, openly satirical history of Russia. Indeed, given his great learning and talent for satirical pedantry, it was often difficult for his innocent Russian readers to distinguish the valuable from the absurd in his writings.

Thus Sękowski explained to his astonished public that Nestor's chronicles of Kyivan Rus' had originally been written in Polish, that Hebrew differs from Chinese only in intonation, and that the ancient Persians spoke Belorussian (Belarusan) and their cuneiform inscriptions can be read only in that tongue! The deeply earnest left oppositionist N.G. Chernyshevsky was taken in by these jests and penned a ferocious rebuttal, although one reviewer of Sękowski's two-volume collection of Oriental sources for Polish history had earlier seen that much of his "criticism" of old Poland was no more than "a clever joke." In the end, the famous Russian émigré Alexander Herzen pointedly called him "the Mephistopheles of Nicholas I's [reactionary] era." Today, he is known better as an influential Russian journalist and literary critic than as the pioneering Polish Orientalist that he once was.[33]

Even more than Chaikovsky and Chodźko, Sękowski was clearly a child of the Romantic age. But if Byron's struggles for personal freedom and national liberation influenced the first two, Sękowski clearly became a defender of Imperial Russia and, like Chateaubriand, de Maistre, and certain others, an enemy of revolution, though without their conviction or religious feelings.

## Scholars, Writers and Artists, and a Pilgrim (1870–1914)

By the 1870s and 1880s, the Romantic sensibility was disappearing in most of Europe, and in Poland, Ukraine, and eastern Europe, most members of a new generation were pursuing national objectives in a much less revolutionary way. This was the era in Poland of "organic work" for the national culture and independence, and in Russia, including Ukraine, of so-called small-deeds liberalism, which favoured practical work on behalf of democratic and national ideals. Advances in transportation and communication were facilitating tourism of a more modern type, while old-fashioned adventurers and exiles became less common. Religious pilgrimages too were made easier and became more frequent, especially to the Middle East. During the period before 1914, Polish and Ukrainian travellers to the Middle East included scholars and artists, as well as tourists and pilgrims. The people we look at in this section seem characteristic of these years: the scholars Aleksander Jabłonowski and Ahatanhel Krymsky, the artists or writers Stanisław Chlebowski, Jan Matejko, Józef Brandt, Ilya Repin, Lesya Ukrainka, Ivan Trush, Mykola Yaroshenko, and Danylo Mordovets, and the pilgrim Metropolitan Count Andrei Sheptytsky.

Aleksander Jabłonowski (1829–1913) was a Polish historian of the Slavonic national awakenings. When studying the Balkan South Slavs, he noticed strong Turkish influences on their cultures. He participated in the Polish uprising of 1863–64 and was jailed for a while, but afterwards worked for a rich Polish family in Kyiv and became more and more interested in Ukrainian history. He made two great trips through the Middle East, in 1869–70 and in 1886.

On the first journey, Jabłonowski and his brother, a doctor working in Turkey, traversed Anatolia to Kurdistan, Syria, and Iraq; then went on to Lebanon, Palestine, and Egypt. Like Chodźko in Iran, he took copious notes and kept a journal. He described historical monuments, especially at Babylon and Karbela in Iraq, Palmyra in Syria, and Heliopolis, near Baalbek in Lebanon. He also recorded the geography, climate, languages, and customs, especially for the Kurds and Arabs. Although he is known today primarily for his works on eastern European history, his studies of the Middle East, first published in Polish journals, were collected after his death and reprinted in his volume VI of his *Pisma* (Collected Works). In his autobiography he detailed his travels through Kurdistan and elsewhere.[34]

Ahatanhel Krymsky (1871–1942) (Figure 1) was the region's first and only modern and professional "Orientalist" scholar during this last period before 1914. Though from a thoroughly russified family, he was of Crimean Tatar background and grew up among the Ukrainian people, and he consciously chose to serve both peoples. At the Halahan College in Kyiv he imbibed the egalitarian spirit of the Ukrainian national movement. Teacher Pavlo Zhytetsky introduced him to the federalist and socially radical ideas of the Ukrainian émigré scholar Mykhailo Drahomanov, and the young Krymsky quickly adopted them. Already interested in "the East," he studied next at the Lazarevsky Institute of Oriental Languages in Moscow and was soon sending Ukrainian-language articles and translations to Austrian Galicia, which allowed publication in that language. He collaborated closely with the radical western Ukrainian writer Ivan Franko, with whom he shared many political and social ideas.[35]

After graduating, Krymsky received a stipend to perfect his knowledge of languages in the Middle East and in western Europe. He fell in love with Lebanon and its people, so spent both years there, improving his classical Arabic, gathering materials on the "modern" Arabic literatures, and composing Ukrainian poetry in an Oriental style, which became *Palmove hillia* (Palm Leaves), published much later, compared in style by one American scholar to Goethe's *West–östlicher Divan*.[36]

On returning to Russia, Krymsky continued at the Lazarevsky Institute and at Moscow University while exploring Ukrainian studies and general history. He grew close to the notable Russian/Ukrainian geologist Vladimir Vernadsky, who, like him, admired Drahomanov. After further studies, he obtained a position at the Lazarevsky Institute, where he remained for twenty years, forging his reputation as one of Russia's leading Oriental and Islamic scholars.

Krymsky published mostly in Russian, though still sending Ukrainian-language articles to Galicia for publication. He was a prolific scholar, as well as a poet and a prose writer. His many lectures in Arabic, Persian, and Turkish literature and history were gathered into collections and published for his students, who lacked such preparatory materials. Krymsky also wrote on Islamic subjects for the *Entsiklopedicheskii slovar Brokgaus i Efron* (The Encyclopaedic Dictionary of Brockhouse and Efron) and the *Granat*. Leo Tolstoy remarked that he himself "read the Koran according to Krymsky."[37]

Krymsky's pamphlet in both Russian (1899) and Ukrainian (1904) – *The Muslim World and Its Future* – called for the modernization of Islamic culture and institutions, especially those within the Russian Empire. These ideas also inspired his close relationship with Ismail Bey Gasprinsky (or Gaspirali), the so-called national awakener of the Crimean Tatars and leader of the Jadidist (modernist) movement among Muslims in the Russian Empire, which urged education for the Islamic peoples, still wed predominantly to older, religious ideas about culture and society. Krymsky, who considered himself one with these peoples, was quite critical of such "religious fanaticism" (his term), although he studied and greatly admired the religious poetry produced by the Sufis and other Persian poets. Parallel to these activities, he supported the growth of literature and spread of higher education among Ukrainians, even writing a text on Ukrainian grammar, and he seems to have seen both of these causes as "anti-imperialist" or at least "anti-colonial."[38]

During the Russian Revolution, Krymsky moved from Moscow to Kyiv, where, after the collapse of the imperial order and censorship and the declaration of Ukrainian independence in 1918, he helped found a Pan-Ukrainian Academy of Sciences, to promote research and its publication in the Ukrainian language, and became the academy's permanent secretary. During the 1920s, that institution flourished and Krymsky published many works in Ukrainian, elaborating on several of his earlier Russian-language studies of Iranian and Turkish history and literature, especially a general history of the Ottoman Empire up to the death of Suleiman the Magnificent. At a time when the scholarly study of Ukraine, heavily censored under the tsars, was proliferating, Krymsky argued for Eastern studies: of Iran, to illuminate the influence of the early Iranian tribes, such as the Scythians, Alans, and others on the Steppe; of Turkey, to explain the significance of the Khazars, Polovtsi, and Pechenegs, as well as the Tatars, Ottomans, and modern Turks; and of the Arab world, to place all these peoples within the Islamic context. Arabic studies also opened up new sources for Ukrainian history – for example, as we saw above in the Introduction, the travel journal of Paul of Aleppo described at first hand and in a sympathetic way the great Cossack revolt led by Bohdan Khmelnytsky (1648–54) against Polish rule.[39]

The 1930s saw Stalin's physical destruction of the Ukrainian Academy, the exile or execution of most of its leading members, and the complete russification of whatever was left. Krymsky himself was forced out of Kyiv and had to retire to the countryside. In retirement, he reworked his earlier manuscripts and materials, which were published by Soviet printing houses decades later, after Stalin's death. They included a new history of Arabic literature and a book on the Persian poet Nizami and his contemporaries, which came out under the auspices of the Azerbaijan Academy of Sciences. The Ukrainian Academy, which also recovered somewhat during this cultural "thaw," published Krymsky's *Tvory* (Collected Works) in five volumes, including his literary efforts with Eastern motifs and his scholarly studies of the Islamic world.[40] His multi-volume "History of the Khazars," the first such work ever written, is said to have remained unpublished in the Academy archives. Krymsky himself did not escape Stalin's purges. He was arrested in 1941, was deported to central Asia, and died in a prison camp in Kazakhstan in 1942.[41]

Of the eight artists and writers we consider in this subsection, Stanislaw Chlebowski was undoubtedly the most closely bound to the Middle East and spent the longest time there, being known much better outside Poland and Ukraine than inside. Stanisław Chłebowski (1835–1884) was born to a Polish family in Podolia in right-bank (western) Ukraine. He studied painting in Odessa and St Petersburg and in Paris, where he worked briefly under the outstanding "Orientalist" painter Jean-Léon Gérôme. But in 1864, the Ottoman sultan, Abdul Aziz, invited him to Istanbul to be his court painter. There he had to please the sultan with works that his employer commissioned and often supervised, but even so he completed memorable pieces on historical themes, and also on street life in the Ottoman capital and elsewhere – perhaps most notably *Mehmed the Conqueror Entering Constantinople in 1453* (1873) and *The Sultan Beyazet as a Captive of Tamerlane* (1878). He also rendered battle scenes touching on Polish–Ottoman relations, such as *The Battle of Mohacz* (took place 1526) and *The Battle of Varna* (of 1444). Chlebowski eventually tired of painting only for the sultan and returned to Europe, and finally Poland, where he died, not quite fifty. He never did return to his native Podolia in western Steppe Ukraine.[42]

Unlike Chlebowski's, Jan Matejko's stay in Turkey in 1872 was extremely brief. Jan Matejko (1838–1893) was a native of Cracow, which he loved, and never left for any length of time. Nevertheless, under the influence of a story Chlebowski told him, he painted two watercolours, both on the theme of the Bosphorus. One of them depicted a sultan's concubine, a young woman from historical Poland, which included Ukraine, being thrown into the water to drown, a victim of her own indiscretions and harem intrigue. Matejko was a patron of and felt affection for the "Ruthenians" of eastern Galicia. He painted a fanciful picture of the Cossack leader Bohdan Khmelnytsky and his ally the Tatar Khan before the Gates of Lwów/ Lviv in 1648, and another of Jan III Sobieski at Vienna, relieving the city of the great Ottoman siege in 1683.[43]

Józef Brandt (1841–1915) was fascinated by Eastern themes. His specialties were battle scenes and depictions of horses and cavalry charges, especially those involving Cossacks and Tatars. Many of his canvases portrayed Zaporozhian Cossacks, whom many Europeans considered every bit as exotic as Persians or Arabs and who on occasion also took on Oriental characteristics themselves. For example, *A Mounted Arab Carrying a Child* and *Testing a Horse*, the latter portraying a man in a turban and Oriental dress, both merged his interests in horsemanship and Eastern themes. The same was true of his *Return from the Battle of Vienna* (1869), where the victors were carrying back to Poland Oriental loot, including camels, captured at Vienna, and *Fight for the Turkish Standard* (1905) (Plate 6), which depicted in a very realistic way a closely fought equestrian battle between gentry of the Polish–Lithuanian Commonwealth and Turks. Mounted Zaporozhian Cossacks were also a favourite topic of his. All these works reveal his close attention to the details of Eastern weaponry and dress.[44]

A major canvas by the Ukrainian-born and much-admired painter Ilya Repin (1844–1930) – *Zaporozhian Cossacks Writing a Satirical Letter to the Turkish Sultan* (1878–91) – successfully combined authentic Ukrainian faces and elements with an Oriental theme (see chapter 9, below). It became the best-known Ukrainian painting of all time, a favourite of both Tsar Alexander III and Soviet leader Joseph Stalin. His Ukrainian contemporaries proudly thought that Repin's technique far surpassed that of Józef Brandt, and that his Cossacks were much more authentic. Certainly, he paid just as much attention to the details of Oriental weaponry and dress, and the faces of his Cossacks were less stylized and more realistic, taken from real-life descendants of the Cossacks themselves. In every respect, Repin's superiority as a portrait artist showed in this great canvas, although he never captured movement in the way that Brandt did. Repin visited the Holy Land only very briefly in 1898, but his friend and close collaborator the historian Dmytro Yavornytsky (1855–1940), whom the artist painted into his iconic picture as the scribe writing that mocking letter to the sultan, actually toured Greece, Turkey, and Egypt, where he met up with the great poet Lesya Ukrainka.[45]

Lesya Ukrainka (1871–1913) was the pen name of Larysa Kosach, born the niece of political philosopher Mykhailo Drahomanov, who helped shape her education; she grew up in a cultured, activist family and knew something of about ten languages (see Figure 2). Ukrainka went to Egypt in 1909, seeking a warm climate and relief from the tuberculosis that would soon kill her. But while there, she quickly furthered her serious interest in the local antiquities and in ancient Egyptian inscriptions, and her stays there informed her cycle of poetry *Vesna v Yehypti* (Spring in Egypt, 1910), of which the most famous poem, "Hamsin," evokes the hot wind and sandstorm blowing in from the desert. These poems supplemented her earlier writing on Middle Eastern themes, both biblical and Islamic.[46]

Moreover, through letters to her first cousin, Ariadna Drahomanova, and her husband, the Galician Ukrainian impressionist painter Ivan Trush (1869–1941), Ukrainka aroused the interest of that artist in the Middle East and inspired him to visit Egypt and Palestine. In 1912, he spent two full months there executing numerous pictures of Egypt's antiquities and people, especially night scenes; the Sphinx by moonlight fascinated him. Trush never forgot that sojourn and returned to the subject later. His personal catalogue of paintings lists over fifty on Middle Eastern themes, little studied to the present.[47]

Similarly, the Ukrainian painter from Poltava, Mykola Yaroshenko (1846–1898), like Lesya Ukrainka mortally ill with tuberculosis, visited Italy, Syria, Palestine, and Egypt. His paintings from his journeys have also attracted little attention. He was a marvellous portrait artist, and a striking painter of genre scenes and mountain landscapes. (He lived the last years of his life near Kislovodsk in the Caucasus, where he died.) His portraits of young university students, especially *Kursistka* (The Female Student), are quite striking, and those of prominent figures, such as the painters I.N. Kramskoi (from Sloboda Ukraine) and Mykola Gay, or Ge (from Poltava), and the writer Vladimir Korolenko (from Volhynia) are also very good. For the Russian public, however, his depictions of the Muslim-majority High Caucasus, with its exotic flavour, were probably his closest association with "the Orient."[48]

Danylo Mordovets/Daniil Mordovtsev (1830–1905), the descendant of a Zaporozhian Cossack, grew up in the Saratov region of Russia, but remained a Ukrainian Cossack patriot. He knew many prominent Ukrainians, such as the poet Shevchenko and the historian Kostomarov, and he wrote many stories and novels in both Ukrainian and Russian on Cossack themes and also addressed Tatar slave-taking. In the 1880s, he travelled throughout the Middle East as well as western Europe; his writings include "A Trip to the Pyramids," "A Trip to Jerusalem," "Across Italy," "Across Spain," and "A Guest of Tamerlane."[49]

Metropolitan Andrei Sheptytsky (1865–1944) was the head (1901–44) of the Ruthenian Greek Catholic church in Austrian Galicia, which region fell to Poland after the First World War and a briefer Ukrainian–Polish conflict. He was the scion of an aristocratic Ruthenian-origin Polish family long connected with the Greek Catholic church. Consequently, when the Ukrainian national movement arose in the late nineteenth century, he accepted his role as a national leader, the shepherd of his Galician Ukrainian flock, who tried to bridge Catholicism and Orthodoxy. Having gone to Palestine privately the previous year, in 1906 he organized a great pilgrimage of some five hundred Galician Ukrainians and sixty-six Poles to the Holy Land (see Figure 3). Afterwards, with the twelfth-century pilgrim Igumen Daniel of Chernihiv (see chapter 1, above) in mind, the prelate commissioned two of the clergymen to write about the pilgrimage: "How the Ruthenians Walked in the Footsteps of Daniel." The learned and saintly Sheptytsky, mediator between East and West, is indeed a fitting figure with which to end our survey. A few years later saw the start of the First World War, which blocked access to the Middle East to all but essential personnel. The ensuing four years of conflict ended the Ottoman Empire and transformed the Middle East, to say nothing of what it did to Russia and Ukraine.[50]

## Conclusion

By way of conclusion, Ukraine and Poland, especially the *Kresy* (eastern borderlands), long inhabited by both peoples, contributed to travel in the Islamic Middle East in just as many ways as western Europe. We saw in chapter 1 that, just like the western Europeans, the medieval travellers from eastern Europe were pilgrims and Crusaders, and the early modern era saw more pilgrims, such as Mikołai Radziwiłł, but also captives of war, diplomats, and missionaries. If during the earliest period, notices by or about them were somewhat sketchy, during the eighteenth century some accounts became quite detailed, as with Hryhorovych-Barsky and Krusiński, and remain of use to historians, geographers, and anthropologists. Of course, the Romantic period saw much more travel to the Middle East, and the *Kresy* made its special contribution, with adventurers and rebels such as Rzewuski, Chaikovsky, and Chodźko, and even Mickiewicz and Słowacki, spending much time and effort in the region or writing about it.

The political activities of rebels such as Chaikovsky and Mickiewicz put paid to the notion that these visitors were imperialist agents of one sort or another. Rather just the opposite; like the Ukrainian poet Shevchenko, they were clearly anti-imperialists, who were willing to give their all, including even their lives, for the liberty of their homelands and to check the empire that ruled them. And this actually happened to Mickiewicz, who died in Istanbul. Moreover, in the decades before 1914, the great age of positivism and nationalism, the Ukrainian *Kresy* in particular continued to contribute to the phenomenon with scholars such as Jabłonowski and Krymsky, writers such as Lesya Ukrainka and Dmytro Yavornytsky, and artists such as Repin, Trush, Yaroshenko, and Chlebowski, living in or visiting Egypt or Turkey. These figures too, especially Krymsky, who identified closely with both Ukrainians and the Crimean Tatars, were clearly rebels, who opposed the imperial international order of their time, which, they believed, severely oppressed their homelands. Though little-known in either the contemporary West or today's Middle East, their contribution to the history, politics, and culture of the region was real and deserves to be acknowledged.

## CHAPTER THREE

# Tatar Slave Raiding and Turkish Captivity in Ukrainian History and Legend

THE THREE-HUNDRED-PLUS-YEAR HISTORY of the Crimean Khanate (1441–1783), which extended northward from the Black Sea to include much of the Ukrainian, or "Pontic" Steppe, has generally been ignored by Western historians. No recent general history exists in any western European language, and Crimean Tatar slave raiding into Ukrainian, Polish, and Russian lands, though frequently noted in the sources, has attracted little attention.[1] Indeed, even in the Soviet Union after the 1930s, discussion of the khanate's place in eastern European history was strictly forbidden, and the Tatars were assigned a solely negative role in Russian and Ukrainian history: they were ostensibly aggressive and destructive nomads attacking a peaceful Slavonic agricultural population or, to use an older vocabulary, wild Muslim steppe folk threatening Christian civilization. This combination of Western silence and pre-Soviet and Soviet stereotype has long obscured certain aspects of eastern European and Ottoman Turkish history and requires serious correction.[2]

This chapter seeks to address these issues in several ways. It presents evidence about Tatar raids on Ukrainian lands and outlines their great impact on the Ukrainian psyche and culture. It also challenges the stereotypes about the Crimean Khanate in Ukrainian, Polish, and Russian scholarship and presents a more nuanced and refined picture of its place in Ukrainian history and of Ukrainian captives' fate in the khanate and in the Ottoman Empire. I examine early modern documents, histories, travelogues, and such, and also older Ukrainian folklore collected and codified in the nineteenth century, to explore Tatar slave raiding and Turkish captivity. I also look at why Western historians have neglected these phenomena and whether Ukrainian folk tradition is accurate.[3]

During the last twenty years or so scholars have examined the history of slavery in the Middle East and Europe – for its tentacles spread wide – and this literature too occasionally mentions our subject.[4] With regard to Ukraine in particular, the echo of Edward Said and Bernard Lewis's debate about the "Orientalist" bias in scholarship gradually began to influence the work of Ukrainian historians, whose Soviet-era predecessors were almost completely cut off from Western developments. The resulting critique, as we see below, questioned the traditional stark juxtaposition of forest versus steppe, agriculturalist versus nomad, civilization versus barbarism, and Christian versus Muslim.[5]

## Geopolitical Context

Slave raiding in the region antedated the Crimean Khanate and the conflict between Christendom and the Lands of Islam. Eastern Europe, especially the Ukrainian Steppe lands (ancient Scythia and Sarmatia), had been sources of slaves for the Mediterranean basin for ages. Ancient Rome and Byzantium used people from this area, whom they considered "barbarians," in their galleys. Early medieval Moorish rulers of Islamic Spain and other Muslim countries highly valued their slaves from Kyivan Rus' and neighbouring countries, called *Saqaliba* in Arabic (from "Slavs"/"Slavonians"), who included eunuchs, castrated in Christian southern France, as Islam forbade the barbarous practice. Ibn Butlan (d. 1063) and later Muslim writers generally praised the bravery and other warlike characteristics of the Slavs and recommended use of the males as military slaves.[6] Females slaves too were long in great demand. "All my troubles," complained the Persian poet Nasir-i Khusraw, "come from the [Volga] Bulgars; they constantly bring mistresses from Bulgar to tempt a man; they are as beautiful as the moon; their lips and teeth should not be so beautiful, because the passion for their lips and little teeth is so great that it makes a man bite his own lips."[7]

Establishment of Italian trading colonies in the Crimea after the Fourth Crusade (1202–04) allowed direct commerce between the Ukrainian steppelands and Italy. Fourteenth- and fifteenth-century records of the Italian slave trade reveal large numbers of Slavic, Circassian, and other bondsmen from the Black Sea area. During this period Genoese in the

Crimean city of Kaffa (Caffa in Italian orthography) made this place a major centre of the European and Middle East slave trade, and the ethnic term "Slav" (*Sclavus*) entered Latin to mean "slave" (replacing the ancient *servus*), a usage that spread to most western European languages, including English.

Thus the Tatars under the Giray clan who laid claim to the Mongol inheritance of the Golden Horde and established themselves in the Crimea in the early fifteenth century, and the Ottoman Turks who conquered Kaffa and the other Genoese colonies in the Crimea in 1475, only continued and augmented the Black Sea slave trade, and Christian merchants from Italy gave us the modern English term "slave."[8]

Indeed, under founder Haji Giray (d. 1466), the independent Crimean Khanate was friendly to the Christian Polish–Lithuanian Commonwealth, which, after the decline of Kyivan Rus' and the Mongols' retreat, ruled most of the Ukrainian-populated areas north and west of the Black Sea. It was only under Haji's successor, Mengli Giray (who ruled intermittently between 1466 and 1478 and then 1479–1515), that the Crimean Tatars recognized the overlordship of the Ottoman sultan (1478), allied with Orthodox Muscovy, and carried out their great sack of Kyiv (1482), launching their long conflict with the Ukrainians of the settled agricultural lands. Liturgical vessels plundered from Kyiv's cathedral of St Sophia, founded in 1011 (Figure 4), near where stood the Golden Gate of Kyiv (Figure 5), were later handed over to Ivan III of Muscovy, and, it seems, a great many captives ended up on the slave markets of the Crimean peninsula.[9]

Russian historians traditionally downplayed Muscovite instigation of this great raid on a Christian city, but they did emphasize that thereafter Tatar slave raiding of Ukrainian-populated territories became an almost annual event. When the Tatars were not doing that in alliance with Muscovy, they were raiding Muscovy in alliance with Poland–Lithuania or on their own. That general pattern of alliances and raiding would last some three hundred years, almost until the destruction of the Crimean Khanate in 1783. In general, these alliances involved practical politics and had very little to do with religion or any generalized Christian–Muslim enmity, even though, as William H. McNeill pointed out many years ago, a steppe "no-man's land" came to separate these two worlds throughout our period.

## Estimating the Losses

Moreover, in the Ukrainian folk and historical tradition the juxtaposition of the two worlds was clear. The Cossack–Tatar conflict occupied a prominent place in that rich heritage, which explicitly described the Tatar raids and evoked the "Lament of the Poor Slaves in Turkish Captivity," to name a classic example. The historical songs and epic *"dumas"* (*dumy*) sung by wandering blind musicians – bandura and kobza players – are major motifs of nineteenth-century Ukrainian national culture.[10]

These songs were deeply moving. Thus when in the 1880s the Ukrainian-born Russian painter Ilya Repin heard the "Lament of the Poor Slaves in Turkish Captivity" played by such musicians, he "cried more than a single tear," and he later incorporated this supposed Christian–Muslim conflict into his great painting of the *Zaporozhian Cossacks Writing a Satirical Letter to the Turkish Sultan*. This enormously popular painting (see chapter 9, below) continues to influence Ukrainian and Russian, that is, "East Slavic," sensibilities to the present day.[11] Indeed, Christian–Muslim conflict and the ostensible horrors of Tatar captivity seemed to know no limits in the folk tradition and entered Polish as well as Ukrainian folklore. So, according to one such folktale recorded in Poland rather recently, captured Christians were kept in cages and fed with milk and nuts. When they were so fat that they could not walk, they were roasted and eaten by the savage Tatars.[12]

For many years, certain pioneering historians (considered rather sophisticated in their own time) seem to have exaggerated the scale of Tatar raiding almost as much as did simple peasants. Thus the distinguished pioneer of modern Polish historiography, Adam Naruszewicz (1733–1796), is said to have stated that Poland–Lithuania lost to Tatar raids in total "anywhere from ten to twenty million inhabitants" (*kilkanaście miljonów mieszkańców*). Similarly, a recent Ukrainian historian wrote that "in separate years [Ukrainian demographic losses to the Tatars] . . . reached several hundreds of thousands of people. In general, it was a shame for a Tatar to bring back less than ten people."[13]

Both the Ukrainian and Polish folk traditions and eastern European historians of this issue have seldom been questioned by modern historians. Indeed, early modern European chroniclers and nineteenth- and twentieth-century historians (Ludwik Kubala, Tadeusz Korzon, and others), impressed by the ostensible power and ferocity of the successor Horde of Crimean Tatars, usually estimated its strength at some 100,000–200,000 warriors. But in the 1930s, one Polish revisionist historian, Olgierd Górka, challenged such figures. He studied the census figures compiled by the Russian conquerors of the Crimean state and in a tightly argued and highly critical essay concluded that in the sixteenth and seventeenth centuries not more than 250,000 people inhabited the Crimean peninsula. Of these, he believed, only some 180,000–200,000 were actually Tatars, while the remainder were of many other nationalities: Italians, Greeks, Armenians, Karaites, Jews, Turks, and even some Frenchmen. Most of these outsiders lived in Kaffa and the other "larger" cities under direct Ottoman rule. As well, Muslim sources – chroniclers such as Sa'deddin and Rashid Efendi, and correspondence between the sultan in Istanbul and the khan in Bakhchesaray – uniformly speak of very small forces, sometimes as few as 10,000 warriors. Consequently, Górka concluded that even at the height of its power, the Crimean army had at most 20,000–22,000 warriors.[14] Of course, these estimates reconfigured the Tatar raids and the Black Sea slave trade. For if the number of Tatar marauders was so modest, how could so many Ukrainians and other Slavs been taken as *yasir* (from Arabic *asir/* Tatar *yesir*: prisoners-of-war/slaves)?

Górka's revisionist thesis was published in the late 1930s, so the outbreak of war dented its impact. After the war, all of eastern Europe was under Communist rule, and Crimean Tatars, falsely, for the most part, accused of collaboration with the Germans, had been deported to central Asia. Thus there was simply no incentive for Russian, Ukrainian, or even Polish historians to seriously consider Górka's ideas. During that era, his thesis was generally ignored or rejected.

Indeed, even late in the Communist era, the popular Polish historical synthesizer Leszek Podhorodecki thoroughly rejected Górka's thesis, arguing that he had ignored the great emigration of Tatars from the Crimea to Turkey before 1778 and had omitted the vassal Nogay and Bujak Tatars from his figures. Podhorodecki estimated the population of the khanate before its decline at 300,000–350,000 and its armed forces at 40,000–50,000.[15] Other students of Crimean history, knowledgeable in Oriental languages but unaware of, or at least less aware of, Górka's arguments, cite without comment primary sources estimating the Crimean forces as high as 80,000–100,000 warriors.[16]

Other historians too thought in terms quite different from Górka's. Many who studied the devastation inflicted by the Tatars based their accounts on Polish and Ukrainian sources familiar with local conditions rather than on chroniclers' descriptions of the Tatar armies. Thus the Ukrainian historian Mykhailo Hrushevsky, while agnostic about the size of Mengli Giray's armies, notes that their early-sixteenth-century depredations destroyed almost all of Steppe Ukraine south of the forest line (only cities and fortresses maintained by the state seemed to have retained any population).[17] Similarly, in 1964, the Polish historian Maurycy Horn, who examined the local archives of heavily populated Red Rus' (the Ruthenian province), found that from 1605 to 1633 in this region, far from the Crimean Khanate, at least twenty-six major raids destroyed about half of the towns and villages and reduced the population by 120,000–150,000. In 1618, the worst year, 57 per cent of the villages were destroyed.[18] Thus, if Horn is correct, the Tatar armies, whatever their size, significantly devastated the Ukrainian countryside and reduced the population.

From Horn's figures, fairly well documented down to the village level, it seems that Tatar raids took on average 4,210–5,350 people each year from Red Rus'. If we project – a dicey game – these figures over the two hundred and fifty years of intense Tatar activity, they amount to loss of between 1,051,500 and 1,337,500 people. To this we must add losses in all the other Ukrainian provinces – less heavily populated but more exposed to Tatar attacks – and also a further fifty years of less intense slave raiding. Horn himself was reluctant to estimate total losses beyond his period and region, but other scholars have been less reluctant.

The Polish scholar Bohdan Baranowski wrote prior to the publication of Horn's study and relied entirely on European historians contemporary to events. He guessed that "over the course of the centuries the number of persons taken away as *yasir* from the territory of the old Polish–Lithuanian Commonwealth was about a million or perhaps more."[19] In so far as his estimate dealt with all Ukraine and adjacent areas in ethnic Poland, rather than just Red Rus', his guess seems fairly conservative.

More recently, the Ukrainian historian Yaroslav Dashkevych, who could use Horn's archive–based figures, estimated that "not less than between two and two and a half million people were taken captive and killed" by the Tatars during their two hundred and fifty most active years.[20] This figure seems quite high, but breaks down to 10,000 per year and includes both captives and persons killed by the Tatars. Moreover, the Turkish historian Halil Inalcik and the American historian Alan Fisher, who apparently both consulted the same Ottoman archives, agree that in 1578 – the only year for which records have thus far been analysed – *at least* 17,500 slaves were sold in the Kaffa slave market, the principal emporium selling Ukrainian and other Slavonic captives to Turkey.[21]

This figure accords well with our knowledge of the role of the slave trade in the finances of the Ottoman state, which was taking in 100,000 gold ducats per year from the trade – four gold ducats per sale, thus 25,000 transactions annually.[22] Clearly the Black Sea slave trade was a large-scale enterprise, and recent Ukrainian-language surveys of early modern Ukrainian and Crimean Tatar history at least mention it.[23] However, examination of surviving Tatar and Ottoman documents has only just begun, and until this task is completed, no firm total numbers about the *yasir* from the Slavonic lands north of the Black Sea can be given. Moreover, the firm data that we do have are not always uniform, and complications of other kinds sometimes arise. For example, the reports on which Horn relied so heavily may have exaggerated demographic losses for taxation or other purposes, and often did not distinguish between abductions and escapees. Thus the ghost of sceptics such as Olgierd Górka still lurks.[24]

## Tatar Logistics

In contrast to the little-studied archives, literary sources (European and Turkish travellers' accounts, historians, and polemicists) and ethnographic sources (Ukrainian, and to a much lesser extent Polish and Russian historical songs) give a detailed and vivid picture of Tatar raids and Turkish captivity, and testify to their importance in the general history of the Ukrainian Steppe. According to such sources, the Tatars developed their raiding style into a military/commercial art. Summarizing the work of various Polish historians, Leszek Podhorodecki has identified three types of raiding expeditions: large, mid-sized, and small.

The first kind of raid – a *sefer* – engaged the entire military might of the Horde. These raids were led either by the khan himself or a high-ranking member of his clan, either the *kalga sultan* (second in the line of succession) or the *nurredin* (third). They sought plunder and captives but also had military and political objectives. For example, these ventures could put military or political pressure on an opponent, draw his forces from another theatre of operation, affect territorial arrangements, or simply cripple or destroy his defences. Very often such operations were coordinated with foreign allies or followed an "invitation" from the Ottoman sultan. They caused enormous devastation by fire and sword and killed or abducted thousands of people. Podhorodecki estimated an average of about five thousand prisoners from each such expedition.[25]

A mid-sized expedition (*chapul*, hence the Ukrainian *chambuly*) involved a few thousand Tatars led by some aristocrat, a *bey* or a *mirza*. These were principally for plunder, but also applied military and economic pressure and extracted "gifts" for the Tatars. If continuing over a long period, they could even rearrange territorial holdings. Of course, such attacks were much less destructive, but, well organized, a single one could take as many as three thousand *yasir*.[26]

A small raid – *besh bash* (five heads) – was the most frequent type and needed only a few hundred or, at most, a few thousand attackers. Such ventures were often undertaken without the knowledge of the khan or even against his wishes and could even injure his political interests. Many involved Nogay or Bujak Tatars – unruly border elements and somewhat superficial Muslims, only formally subservient to the Crimean khan. Sometimes Turkish slave dealers loaned poor Tatars horses and equipment in exchange for expected *yasir*. In the seventeenth century, Hasan the Lame of Ochakiv, a well-known slave trader, financed many such expeditions. One of these raids could expect to kidnap up to two hundred and fifty people.[27]

The Tatar armies were made up of mounted archers, and always travelled light and fast. Mobility and surprise were their advantages, but a determined enemy, even small groups of Cossacks or other soldiers equipped with firearms, could easily deflect them or force them to retreat empty-handed. The Tatars almost always avoided strong points and fortresses, and the agricultural Slavs could usually retreat to such places.[28]

Crimean Tatars followed many "paths" (really general directions, avoiding river crossings) to the populated regions of northern Ukraine and neighbouring lands, but used especially three on the right bank of the Dnieper and one on the left. The "Black Path" (*Chornyi Shliakh*) led through Cherkasy, Korsun, Kyiv, and then swung sharply west to Lviv; the Kuchman path ran from Ochakiv on the Black Sea through Bar and then to Lviv in Red Rus'; the Volos, or Pokuttia, path followed the Dniester River to Lviv. The left bank of the Dnieper offered only the Muravian Path (*Muravskyi Shliakh*). These four main routes covered the enormous area from the confines of ethnic Poland to the southern borders of Muscovy, and the Tatars, travelling swiftly by day or night, often took Ukrainian villagers by surprise.[29]

Once they had arrived in the area to be ravaged, the Tatars established a main base (*kosh*) from which they fanned out over the countryside looting and pillaging where there was no resistance, and bypassing any defended locations. Having captured as much plunder and as many captives as possible, the Tatars bound or chained their prisoners and, herding them like cattle, retreated by forced marches as quickly as possible. The Habsburg diplomat Sigismund von Herberstein and other sources seem to imply that the very young, the old, the infirm, and anyone who might delay the retreat were dispatched immediately, and without mercy.[30]

## Becoming a Slave:
## From Village to Kaffa and then Istanbul . . .

This painful process made an indelible impression on the remaining settlers (see Figure 6). As we saw above, a considerable body of folklore grew up, especially a vast body of Ukrainian historical songs and laments. Of the initial capture of prisoners by the Tatars, we read lines such as these:

> Ukraine lamented that there was nowhere to survive.
> The Horde trampled the children and left none alive.
> They trampled the little ones; the big ones they took,
> They tied them in fetters . . . to the khan for a look.[31]

Other verses describe other stages on the long road to Turkish slavery.

Once the Tatar raiders had returned to the khanate, they divided the loot – including the captives – among themselves. Firstly, those Tatars who had incurred losses during the expedition were recompensed. For example, if a Tatar had lost a horse or some armour, he was compensated the equivalent in booty: valuable objects, livestock, or *yasir*. A detailed register of all booty and captives was prepared, and the khan or other leader of the expedition received a portion. Occasionally the leader would resign some of his portion to his warriors.[32] The French engineer Beauplan, who seems to have interviewed more than one eyewitness, paints a sorrowful picture of this division of the spoils:

> That day [and same] night they bring together all their booty, which consists in slaves and cattle, and divide it among themselves. It is a sight [that] would grieve the most stony heart to see a husband parted

from his wife, and the mother from her daughter, without hopes of ever seeing one another, being fallen into miserable slavery, under *Mahometan* infidels, who use them inhumanely. Their brutish nature causing them to commit a thousand enormities, as ravishing of maids, forcing of women in the sight of their parents and husbands, and circumcising their children in their presence to devote them to *Mahomet*. In short, it would move the most insensible to compassion to hear the cries and lamentations of those wretched *Russians* [Ruthenians or Ukrainians]; for those people sing and roar when they cry. These poor creatures are dispersed several ways, some for *Constantinople*, some for *Crim Tartary* and some for *Anatolia*, etc.[33]

The ethnographic evidence supports Beauplan's testimony, for folksongs on this very theme have been preserved and analysed. Here are a few typical lines:

Oh you Turkish land, Busurman faith,
You, the Christian bane!
You have separated father from mother,
Sister from brother,
And husband from wife again![34]

Contemporaneous Muslim sources such as the Turkish traveller Evliya Chelebi, who was very sympathetic to the Ukrainian captives, confirms this picture. At one point he even quoted an ostensible Muslim proverb: "Whosoever sells a man, cuts down a tree, or breaks a dam, is cursed by God in this world and in the next."[35]

After this division of the spoils, the captives were driven on to the great Crimean port at Kaffa (Kefe in Turkish) or to one of the other Turkish Black Sea ports: Bilhorod (Białogród in Polish, Akkerman in Turkish), Ochakiv (Özü in Turkish), or Kilia. Russians captured on the borders of Muscovy were taken to Azov (Azak in Turkish) and from there by sea to Kaffa. On at least one occasion, and probably many more, captives from Ochakiv were also taken by sea to Kaffa,[36] which remained the greatest slave emporium on the Black Sea throughout the period.

It was usually at this point that negotiations for ransoming of the nobler or wealthier captives were begun. Armenians and Karaite Jews, communities of whom lived both in Poland–Lithuania and in the Crimea, generally served as intermediaries.[37] Prisoners from the gentry (*szlachta*) were, of course, highly prized for their redemptive value, and, because they were so valuable alive, were much better treated than the common folk. Sometimes, however, negotiations for noble prisoners broke down, and a captive gentleman would be badly treated, perhaps even tortured, and then sold for use as a common galley slave.[38] Nevertheless, almost all prisoners aspired to the treatment meted out to the gentry. Marcin Broniewski writes: "The condition of captives is very miserable among the Tartars, for they are grievously oppressed by them with hunger and nakednesse, and the Husbandmen with stripes, so that they rather desire to dye than to live. Many of them moved with the present calamitie, and follie, tell the Tartars that they are Gentlemen, and have wealthy and rich parents and friends. They promise of their owne accord a great and almost inestimable ransome."[39]

Indeed, sometimes common Cossacks were redeemed by their families. In one widely quoted historical song, a young Cossack captive tells the grey pigeon to take greetings to his Christian homeland:

Remind them of my Cossack fate
Let my father and mother know my troubles
Let them sacrifice their wealth
To free my Cossack head from wretched slavery![40]

The great majority of prisoners, however, were not redeemed, but were sold into Turkish slavery.

Today Kaffa (Teodosiia) is a small city on the south-east coast of the Crimea. Its main architectural monuments are the remaining city walls and turrets of the Genoese fortress, a thirteenth-century church, and a seventeenth-century mosque. But in its heyday under the Ottomans it was a major Black Sea port. Sultan Selim the Grim spent part of his minority there, as did his son, later Suleiman the Magnificent (Suleiman the Lawgiver, in Turkish tradition). At that time, Suleiman probably first became acquainted with a Slavonic language, most likely Ukrainian itself. Considering the number of slaves that passed through it, Kaffa must have possessed a very large slave market with many traders. Turks and Tatars certainly engaged in the trade, but whether the non-Muslim minorities also participated is more uncertain.[41]

In Kaffa, the slaves were sorted according to sex, age, and skills, and sold individually to local buyers, or again in large numbers for further shipment to Istanbul or even Persia. Another sixteenth-century eyewitness, Michael the Lithuanian, pseudonym of a "Ruthenian" (Ukrainian or Belarusan) nobleman, generally very positive about the Tatars, condemned the slave trade. He describes the degradation of his compatriots from the Kingdom of Poland, their imprisonment in dark places, and their rotten food, not fit even for dogs:

> It is necessary to say what they do with such people. Namely, when the time for trading comes, they lead these unfortunates in groups into the square of the marketplace, which has many people in it. They are bound around their necks in groups of ten like cranes flying in single file, and they sell them by tens at auction with the auctioneer loudly shouting to raise the price that these are new slaves, simple, not cunning, only just arrived from the king's people and not from the Muscovites. This is because the Muscovite people are cunning and deceitful and are very lowly valued on the slave market. And so this type of merchandise is evaluated with great care in Tavria [Crimea] and is bought by foreign merchants for a high price in order to sell it even more highly to distant and wild peoples such as the Saracens, the Persians, the Hindus, the Arabs, the Syrians, and the Assyrians.

Michael remarks that Kaffa's was the most notable slave market on the peninsula because of its convenient location and insatiability – "not a city but a great vampire which drinks our blood."[42]

Some of the captives sold in Kaffa were bought by locals and remained in the Crimea. Most, however, went on to Istanbul. The voyage from Kaffa to Istanbul took ten days by sea, with sometimes a stopover at Sinop on the north shore of Asia Minor. Once in Istanbul, the slaves were examined by the sultan's officials, and the best and brightest men and the most beautiful women were selected for his household and his harem. The remainder were sold on the open market by one of the many slave dealers in the city, who were organized into a special guild. The Turkish traveller Evliya Chelebi says that in his day they numbered about two thousand; but other sources reveal that of these only thirty-nine had a government licence, the rest being watchmen, guards, and helpers of various sorts. Still, the trade was brisk; the salary of one major market official, the *Esirhane emini*, required the sale of some two thousand slaves annually.[43]

## The Price of Slaves

In both Kaffa and Istanbul, the sale of each slave was taxed, according to the captive's origin rather than his or her ability. The Ottoman state derived substantial income from sales of slaves from Poland–Lithuania, even in times of peace. In 1527, for example, the grand vizier of Suleiman the Magnificent told Hieronomus Laszky, the Transylvanian ambassador: "Although we are not at war with Poland (because we have concluded a peace agreement to last three years), we have still collected over 50,000 ducats from her, not directly but through the Tatars, because those captives which the Tatars seize from the Polish lands are sold to Turkey, and our customs agents made money on it. For the last two years our agents in Kilia and in Kaffa have given us an income of 30,000 ducats more than usual."[44] So plentiful were slaves from Poland–Lithuania and Muscovy that the seventeenth-century Croatian traveller Juraj Križanić, who visited Greece and Istanbul, thought them spread throughout the entire east, including Greece, Syria, Palestine, Egypt, and Anatolia. When new captives arrived, he reported, the older ones would ask them: "Are there still any people left in Rus'?"[45]

Although there has been no systematic study of the price of slaves, prices varied according to place of origin, sex, age, physical condition, abilities, and supply. Individual differences were particularly great for females, and throughout the Ottoman period, it seems, whites were more costly than blacks.[46] At Akkerman in the mid-sixteenth century the average price of a typical Polish or Ukrainian captive was 2,250 aspers, or akçe in Turkish (about forty to fifty gold pieces), although the figure could double for an especially talented or handsome individual. This was slightly lower than the cost of a good horse. Of course, the prices paid at Istanbul and Edirne, the largest slave emporia in the heartland, were slightly higher and rose steadily over the next century.[47]

We do have a vivid description of the pricing system in Istanbul. It is of rather late date (the early 1700s) but seems to correspond with what we know of earlier times, especially about the high value put on Circassians. The author was Demetrius Cantemir, a long-time resident of the city, who eventually became prince of Moldavia, an unsuccessful rebel, and then an exile in the Russian Empire. Cantemir writes:

But of what esteem the *Chercassians* are with the *Turks*, may be guessed from the Price which the Sellers put upon their Captives. They value them in the first place, because their Virgins are more beautiful than all others, better proportion'd in their Bodies, capable of Instruction and of great modesty, and their young Men, as they think, more sharp in their Wit, and capable of making the best Artificers. The next in their esteem are the *Polanders*, then the *Abaze* [a Caucasian people], then the *Russians* for the hardness of their Bodies and their enduring of Labour, which considerations often send them to row in the Grand Sinior's Gallies, then the *Cossaks*, then the *Georgians*, and last of all the *Mengrelians* [another Caucasian people].

Cantemir continues:

The *Germans*, *Venetians*, and *Hungarians* (whom they are wont to call by the name of *Ifrank*) are by them thought incapable of all drudgery, by reason of the softness of their bodies, and the Women of giving pleasure proper to their Sex from the hardness of theirs. So that were Slaves produc'd in the Market out of all these Nations of the same age, strength, or beauty, a *Chercassian*, Man or Woman, would be sold for 1000 Imperial Crowns, a *Polander* for 600, *Abaza* for 500, a *Russ* or *Cozac* for 400, a *Georgian* for 300, a *Mengrelian* for 250, a *German* or *Ifrank* for still less.[48]

This price range given by Cantemir seems wide, and most slaves apparently fell somewhere in the middle. Moreover, we do not know, for example, even whether by "Polander" Cantemir meant any subject of the Polish–Lithuanian Commonwealth, or just ethnic Poles. Similarly, did "Russ" mean any East Slav at all or (much less likely) primarily Muscovites, who were only just then beginning to refer to their country as "the Russian Empire"? Such difficulties notwithstanding, the prices quoted here do give a general sense of the relative value of captives from various European nations. Presumably, the figures for African slaves, who were rarer in Turkey than in Egypt and whom Cantemir does not even seem to consider, would have been somewhat lower.[49]

# Where the Slaves Went

As Cantemir indicated, so also in earlier times, many of the Slavic captives sold at the market in Kaffa or in Istanbul, especially strong young men with no special skills or professional training, went directly into the sultan's navy, where they served as galley slaves. Joseph Pitts heard about this practice from as far away as Egypt, and Juraj Križanić, who was strongly slavophilic, wrote that in the Turkish galleys that he observed almost all of the slaves were "Russians" (i.e., East Slavs: Ukrainians, Belarusans, and Russians). The demand for such personnel was constant and very great, and at times the sultan would ask the khan directly for help in supplying his special needs. Thus in 1646 Sultan Ibrahim "invited" Khan Islam Giray III to raid Muscovy and the Commonwealth to supply him with slaves for a number of new galleys that he had ordered built to relieve the Venetian siege of his army in Crete.[50]

Ukrainian captives filled a large part of this need during this period. The archival records of the Knights of St John of Malta show that, on the fifteen Turkish galleys they captured at about this time, they liberated 2,483 Christian galley slaves (see Figure 7), of whom a full 1,230, or almost half, were of Ukrainian origin or nationality. The Italians came a distant second, with 271, and the Poles third, with 202. Captives from almost every other nation of central, southern, and eastern Europe were to be found.[51] The very Ukrainian and Russian words for punitive exile – katorha or katorga (widely used in nineteenth-century Russia) – derive ultimately from the Turkish word for galley, kadirga, adopted from Byzantine Greek.[52]

Some of the most touching Ukrainian historical songs about Ottoman captivity deal with the galley slaves. The most famous by far is the duma (reflective song) "The Flight of Samuel Kishka from Turkish Slavery." Samuel Kishka (d. 1602) was apparently a Ukrainian nobleman and Cossack leader who was captured by the Turks and spent some time (supposedly twenty-five years) in captivity. He eventually made his way to freedom, and around him there grew a legend about his slave uprising. This legend, it seems, is based on a real incident (1620s) in which the Podolian nobleman Marek Jakimowski/Marko Yakimovsky, from Bar in central Ukraine, led a successful rebellion of Ukrainian, Polish, and Russian galley slaves, took over their ship, and sailed it to freedom in Sicily, and then Rome. From Rome, he and his companions made their way overland back to the Commonwealth (see Plate 7). The duma and the historical incident suggest that escape from the galleys did take place, and certainly marked the Ukrainian historical memory.[53]

Other Tatar captives in the Crimea met different fates, some of them apparently quite tragic. For example, if we can believe Michael the Lithuanian, "there were strong ones, who, if they were not castrated, had their ears cut off or their nostrils torn, or were branded with a hot iron on their cheeks or lips."[54] Although it is hard to understand why a slave-owner would deliberately mutilate and thus devalue his bondsman, and indeed such action was expressly forbidden by Islamic law, it is possible that some run-away slaves may have been branded. Moreover, we do know that before the empire's decline there were a certain number of white eunuchs guarding the harems and serving in the households of the sultan and of rich and influential Turks, where they were in great demand. (For example, white eunuchs were in charge of training the pages in the sultan's household.) But of who performed this terrible operation and where, we know much less. There is no information about eunuchs preserved in the Ukrainian folk tradition.[55]

Nevertheless, there is no doubt that some eunuchs originated in Slavonic Europe. Michael the Lithuanian writes: "All of the servants, eunuchs, scribes, and various craftsmen of these tyrants, and the better warriors, the Janissaries, whom they teach the art of war from childhood and from whom in the end they select their leaders and notables, come from our Christian blood."[56] Indeed, if a slave had some education or a special talent, his lot was almost certain to be better than that of his uneducated, or less talented compatriots. If they converted to Islam, such slaves could, and often did, rise to high positions in the sultan or khan's household. Of slaves from Poland–Lithuania, in the sixteenth century the governor of Yemen, Hasan Pasha, was evidently of Ukrainian origin, the Pole Jan Kierdej (son of the *starosta* or castellan of Terebovla/Trembowla in Red Rus') became a Turkish diplomat, and Joachim Strasz/Ibrahim Bey became principal translator at the court of Suleiman the Magnificent; in the seventeenth century Wojciech Bobowski/Ali Bey became a noted Ottoman scholar; and in the eighteenth century, Yusuf, the pasha of Bender, was of Ukrainian or Polish origin. Not surprisingly, several Poles, or Ukrainians, attained high positions in the khan's household in Bakhchesarai. One of them, Jan (Ibrahim) Bielecki, became the central figure in a famous poem by the Polish Romantic writer of the Ukrainian school, Juliusz Słowacki.[57]

Artists and musicians were especially highly prized by both Turks and Tatars. For example, the favourite singer of Khan Islam Giray III was a

"Polish" slave, as was much of the khan's chorus. When, on conclusion of a Polish–Tatar peace treaty in 1654, the choristers were given the chance to return home, none of them did.[58]

## Freeing of Slaves

The fact that slavery in the Ottoman Empire was not always a life-long sentence probably made it a bit more tolerable for Turkish bondsmen. In fact, in both the Crimea and Turkey proper the example of the Prophet, Islamic law, and popular practice encouraged both kindness to slaves and frequently their manumission. The Koran itself encouraged pious Muslims to free their slaves. There were several categories of manumission: unconditional (*melva*), made while the owner was still alive; conditional (*tedbir*); contractual (*mukataba*), usually on payment of some kind by the slave; *umm-i veled*, for a female slave who bore her master a recognized child; and even court-ordered, resulting from an owner's misbehaviour. Indeed, by the nineteenth century it became customary to emancipate slaves after only seven or nine years of service. (This seems to have been a distant echo of the ancient biblical injunction to free one's slave on the seventh year, although, unlike that injunction, it applied to a slave regardless of his or her origin, not just to a fellow "Hebrew," as stated in Deuteronomy, 15:1–3, 12–14.)[59] All this, together with the general lack of a colour bar in Islam, meant that Ukrainian and other Slavonic captives in Turkish service integrated quickly into Ottoman society, which helps explain why so few chose to return to their European homeland if they were eventually freed.

Such slaves who integrated into Ottoman society, converted to Islam, and "turned Turk," as it was said, proved very problematic for the Ukrainian folk tradition and are almost always denigrated. Thus, in the *duma* about Samuel Kishka, the overseer of the galley slaves was the "renegade" Liakh Buturlak, who asks Kishka to:

> Trample the Christian faith underfoot,
> Break the cross with your hands.
> If you will trample the Christian faith underfoot,
> You will be like a brother
> To our young Pasha![60]

It is highly doubtful, however, whether such outright hostility of the converts to Islam was more common than lingering affection for the land and faith of their youth. The contemporary historian of Ottoman Turkey Suraiya Faroghi gives several examples of rich and prominent Turks, especially women, probably former Christian slaves, who out of simple charity openly sympathized with mistreated captives and even admonished their masters to treat them better.[61] Thus it is clear that the Ukrainian folk tradition more probably reflects the attitudes of those who remained in the Christian homeland than the attitudes of those who survived the initial rigours of captivity and lived to be fully absorbed into Ottoman society.

Of course, not all the slaves sold in the market in Kaffa went on to Istanbul and other parts of the Ottoman Empire. The Tatars retained many and used them in domestic work or as farm hands. For these slaves, as for many in Istanbul, often life improved dramatically after purchase, for many domestic servants were treated as family members, and work in the fields was no worse and perhaps sometimes much better than being exploited serfs on the estates of the Polish or Ukrainian gentry and aristocracy. Moreover, according to Herberstein, no great admirer of the Tatars, agricultural slaves in the Crimea, as in Turkey, were generally freed after six years of servitude, but not allowed to return to their homeland.[62]

Once again, many of them seemingly did not even want to. For example, the Ukrainian chronicle of Velychko (early eighteenth century) tells the story of how the Zaporozhian Cossack leader Ivan Sirko (d. 1680) freed a large number of Ukrainian slaves and gave them the choice to come with him or return to the Crimea. When a large portion (three thousand, or almost half) chose the Crimea, saying they had property and work and could live better there than in Ukraine, where they had nothing at all, he had them all slain, after which he turned to the corpses and said: "Forgive us, brothers, but it is better that you face the judgement of the Lord God here instead of strengthening the Muslims in the Crimea to the detriment of our young Christian men and to your own eternal damnation."[63] The story, like so many folktales, may be somewhat apocryphal, but it does make the point that Tatar captivity did not always last and could have compensations over time.

## Women Slaves

Of all the people taken into Tatar and Turkish captivity, it was perhaps the women who had the best chance of a decent life. Almost all of them ended up as domestic servants or concubines of their Muslim masters and were treated as an integral part of the household. Attractive young women were especially sought after by the Tatars, who apparently called them "white *yasir*" (*bila cheliad* in Ukrainian) – not because of their white skin (which, indeed, could sometimes be of a lighter shade than that of the average Tatar or Turk), but rather because of the white scarves that young Ukrainian women used to cover their hair.[64] So valuable were attractive Ukrainian girls that Michael the Lithuanian exclaimed that in the slave market they were "worth nearly their weight in gold" and treated with care because of it.[65]

Such women were widely sought after because Islamic law allowed a Muslim man not only up to four wives at the same time, but also the use, as concubines, of any slave women he could own and support. If such a woman bore her master a child and he recognized this, the child was considered free, and the master – though not Ottoman sultans – sometimes freed and married the mother as well. As we saw above, even if he did not marry her, the woman acquired the privileged status of "mother of child" (*umm walad*). She could not be sold, and became free on her master's death. Thus slave parentage on the mother's side bore little stigma in Islamic societies, and the children of such liaisons often rose high in Muslim society.[66]

The most famous of such Ukrainian female slaves is undoubtedly Roxelana (Plate 8), the favourite, and subsequently the legal wife, of Suleiman the Magnificent, perhaps the greatest of all Ottoman sultans. Roxelana/ Hürrem (the cheerful one) was born seemingly in or near Rohatyn in Red Rus' (or "Red Ruthenia," today in western Ukraine), probably the daughter of a Ukrainian Orthodox priest. She was captured by the Tatars on one of their raids and sold into Turkish slavery. She entered Suleiman's harem about 1520, when he became sultan, and was soon influencing affairs of state. The execution of Suleiman's good friend the Grand Vizier Ibrahim (1536) and of his own favourite elder son, Mustafa (1553), are both ascribed to her, probably because they both kept her own sons from the throne. She seems to have influenced Suleiman's foreign policy towards friendship with Poland–Lithuania, and her correspondence with the king of Poland and with the wife of Shah Tahmasp of Persia has been preserved. Roxelana became a pious Muslim, although for her, as for Suleiman, fanaticism of any kind seems to have been alien. Never forgetting her origins, she had a mosque built near the female slave market in Istanbul. One of her sons, Selim, eventually succeeded his father as ruler.[67]

There were, of course, many other Ukrainian women who entered the harems of the Ottoman sultans. Besides Suleiman, Osman II (reigned 1618–22), Ibrahim (reigned 1640–48), and Mustafa II (reigned 1695–1703) all had either Ukrainian or Russian consorts, and the mothers of both Mehmed IV (reigned 1648–87) and Osman III (reigned 1754–57) were both Ukrainian. The last was known especially for her virtue, wisdom, modesty, and piety.[68] However, none of these women ever attained the power, prestige, and European renown of Roxelana.

The careers of female slaves such as Roxelana touched the Ukrainian folk tradition. One of the best-known *dumy* about Turkish captivity deals with a female Ukrainian slave named Marusia, a priest's daughter from Bohuslav in Kyiv province, who "turned Turk." She told some Cossack captives (in bondage for some thirty years) that it was Eastertide back home. They cursed her for this tantalizing news, but when their Turkish master went out, she kept his keys and freed the captives. In parting with the Cossacks, however, she bade them not ask her parents to ransom her, for she has "turned Turk and become a Muslim": "Because of the Turkish luxury I need, / And because of that miserable thing called greed."[69] This is again the viewpoint of the Christian homeland, but it does reveal awareness of the predicament and opportunities of many of the young female slaves.

## A Constant Struggle

Of course, a large body of historical literature and folklore concerns Ukrainians' efforts to protect themselves from Ottoman capture. Cossack–Tatar struggles constitute an entire genre. All of this folklore inspired a late-sixteenth-century Cossack offensive, which attacked Ottoman Black Sea ports, disturbed Ottoman shipping, devastated the countryside, and freed many slaves. This effort reached a high point about 1616, when the Ukrainian Cossack Hetman Petro Sahaidachny (d. 1622) captured Kaffa itself and freed a host of slaves.[70] Thereafter, the rise of an independent Cossack polity under Hetman Bohdan Khmelnytsky (1595–1657), the extension of Russian power southward into Ukrainian territories, and finally, the Russian annexation of the Crimea (1783) pretty much put an end to the Black Sea slave trade.

However, during the three centuries and more that it existed, it con-stituted a very big business, and Tatar slave raids played a large role in the history of the Ukrainian Steppe. Tatar armies and raiding parties of all siz-es continually harassed the population and caused enormous damage and loss of life. Over these centuries huge numbers of people – quite possibly a million or more – were carried away as *yasir* to be sold on the slave markets of Kaffa, Bilhorod, Ochakiv, Edirne, and Istanbul. Similarly, the raiding process and the transport of the captives to market caused incalculable human misery. War in early modern Europe was hellish, including in the Ukrainian lands. The Tatar raids were an extension – very widespread – of this mayhem, and led sometimes to Cossack liberating raids on the Crimea and Ottoman Turkey, even into the suburbs of Istanbul itself.

## Conclusion

The wars between the Ukrainians and the Tatars are well reflected in the Ukrainian folk tradition. Tatar raids are described in detail, as are the trials that the captives endured. But the folk tradition also depicted Turkish captivity, and in a uniformly negative light. While this tradition seems to have been fairly accurate about the raids, it is clearly less well informed as to the conditions of captivity and sought only a negative picture of the Islamic world. Recent historical studies show that there could be mitigating factors in captivity. The race-based "plantation-style" slavery so common in the Americas was largely absent in Turkey, the Crimea, and the Ottoman Balkans, where most Slavonic captives ended up.

Certainly, some aspects of Turkish captivity were very bad indeed. The galley slaves probably had it the worst – the Ukrainian folk tradition got that right. But Muslim slaves rowing Christian galleys probably suffered equally, and one should be careful about making moral generalizations on this basis alone. Moreover, other kinds of Turkish captivity could be much less onerous. Although the raiding process and transportation to market were undoubtedly traumatic, indeed, horrifying, for the poor captives, if they could make it safe and secure to a pious Muslim household, their prospects improved, and manumission, though not return to the Slavonic homeland, became a real possibility. In Ottoman Turkey often enough, household slaves were treated as members of the family and sometimes liberated after only a few years' service. This was also true in the Crimea.

Some women, and the children that they bore to Muslim masters, probably had it best. These women included even wives and mothers of the sultans themselves, like Roxelana. The prevalence of manumission, and Islam's legal colour-blindness, led to quick integration into and absorption by Ottoman and Tatar society and hence contributions to the general Turkish and Tatar gene pool. The discrimination so colourfully described above by Demetrius Cantemir was evidently completely forgotten after the second generation.

Thus most modern Turks and Tatars are unaware of their own or compatriots' possible Ukrainian and Slavonic ancestors, partly because lineage is always traced through the paternal line; but it is remembered in Ukrainian folk legend and in Ukrainian history. Roxelana, in particular, is well-known throughout modern Ukraine and in Turkey itself. Consequently, Western historians of Europe and the Middle East, traditionally un- or ill-informed about Ukrainian history, and even the Ukrainian name, should take some account of these facts in their descriptions of early modern Ukrainian history, while Ukrainian scholars, and Russian, Polish, and eastern European scholars generally, should discard old Soviet and pre-Soviet stereotypes about the Tatars, and refrain from drawing a picture that is completely dark. We may modestly conclude by saying that in those days captivity was at times the only alternative to death, and while the Tatars, like many other warriors of this period, sometimes did some terrible things to their captives, at the very least, they did not eat them, as folk legend claimed.

A People Finds Its Voice:
Maksymovych and Shevchenko

## CHAPTER FOUR

# Maksymovych and
# the National Awakening

These historic words of Iziaslav of Kyiv to Yury of Suzdal during the famous
[twelfth-century] struggle for the sovereignty of Kyiv, quoted by Maksymovych
to [his Russian friend] Pogodin as a summary of his polemic against him can serve
as an epigram of the great historical feat [of Maksymovych and] Ukrainian
historiography [1820–1920]: "We bow down before you! You are our brother!
But go back to your own Suzdal!"
MYKHAILO HRUSHEVSKY, "'Malorossiiskie pesni'" (1927)

MYKHAILO OLEKSANDROVYCH MAKSYMOVYCH (1804–1873) was a gifted
scientist and scholar at the start of the nineteenth-century Ukrainian
national awakening. He made solid contributions to botany and zoology, to
philology, including the history of the Ukrainian and Russian languages and
their contemporary development, and to folklore, literary studies, popular
education, history, and archaeology. He was a contemporary and friend of
both the Russian national poet, Aleksandr S. Pushkin, and the Ukrainian
national poet, Taras Shevchenko (see Plates 9 and 10); he was mentor to the
Ukrainian writer Panteleimon Kulish and the Ukrainian historian Mykola
Kostomarov and, like his close friend the humorous novelist Nikolai Gogol/
Mykola Hohol, advanced both Ukrainian and Russian national cultures.
At Maksymovych's death in 1873, the Ukrainian political figure Mykhailo
Drahomanov, paraphrasing Pushkin on Lomonosov, characterized
him as being "for Kyivan Rus' an entire learned, historical-philological

institution and together with this a living national personality."¹ Some
hundred and twenty years later, the Kyiv University historian Volodymyr
Zamlynsky acknowledged his predecessor as "the patriarch of Ukrainian
scholarship" (*patriarch ukrainskoi nauky*).² But exactly who was Mykhailo
Maksymovych, where did he stand in the history of Ukrainian–Russian
national relations, and what was his role in the modern history of Ukraine?³

Mykhailo Maksymovych was born on 3 (15) September 1804 on the
small homestead (*khutir*) held by his mother's family, the Tymkivskys,
in Poltava province in left-bank (eastern) Ukraine, into a family of old
Ukrainian Cossack officer lineage. Most members of the province's
landowning gentry had similar ancestry, and many cultivated a local
patriotism that esteemed the old Ukrainian hetmanate, or autonomous
Cossack state. The Tymkivskys were quite well educated, and early on
Mykhailo's maternal uncles schooled him at home. He later studied at
a nearby convent. From 1812 to 1819, he attended the Novhorod–Siversk
Gymnasium, or High School, whose founder and director was his relative
Ilia Fedorovych Tymkivsky. It is generally believed that the famous,
anonymous political tract on Ukrainian national autonomy, the *Istoriia
Rusov* (History of the Ruthenians, 1827), which circulated in manuscript
widely in this region at the time, was somehow linked to this town. By
the time Mykhailo graduated, he had imbibed much of the local or estate
patriotism of "Little Russia," and he seems to have taken this sensibility
with him to Moscow University.⁴

Maksymovych stayed for a while in Moscow with his uncle Roman
Tymkivsky, and after the latter's death he studied philology, then botany and
medicine, at the university. One of his biology professors, Mikhail Pavlov,
introduced him to Schelling's idealistic, spirit-oriented "Nature Philosophy,"
which was to influence several of his important early works. He took his
first degree in biology in 1823, his master's in 1827, and a doctorate in 1832.
The Polish Romantic poet Adam Mickiewicz was present at his defence
of his 1827 master's thesis, "O systemakh rastitelnogo tsarstva" (On the
Systems of the Flowering Kingdom), in which, as he later noted, "botanical
knowledge was filled out with the teachings of Nature Philosophy."⁵ His
first book, *Glavnye osnovaniia zoologii ili nauka o zhivotnykh* (The Principal
Foundations of Zoology or the Science of Animals), was published in 1824,
and *Osnovannia botaniki* (The Foundations of Botany) quickly followed.
During this period, Maksymovych's work in the physical sciences was so
pioneering that he had to invent a number of new scientific terms in the

Russian language, some of which passed into common parlance and are still used today. These endeavours brought him to the attention of the Russian literary figure Prince V.F. Odoevsky, who noted his work in the journal *Syn otechestva* (Son of the Fatherland), invited him to his home, and introduced him to Moscow literary circles.[6]

After receiving his doctorate in 1832, the young scholar was named professor of biology at Moscow University and director of its botanical garden. In the 1820s he had published in the newspaper *Moskovskii telegraf* (Moscow Telegraph), but by the 1830s he was drawing close to his fellow Moscow professor the literary critic N.I. Nadezhdin, whose journal, *Teleskop* (Telescope), printed many of his first notable philosophical statements.[7] Another close friend whom he met late in this period was the Ukrainian folklorist and historian Osyp Bodiansky, with whom he shared interests in Ukrainian antiquities.

Many Russian intellectuals were beginning to challenge their colleagues' unthinking imitation of western European models in literature and politics and began to explore the native Slavonic and Russian elements in their culture. *Narodnost* ("nationality") was in the air, and Maksymovych imbibed its general principles. He was not a Muscovite, however, but a native of "Little Russia" (central Ukraine), and he was to express the principle of nationality in his work not only in general "Russian" but also in specifically Ukrainian forms. Three publications reveal his thought processes of this time: his speech "On Russian Education," delivered on 12 January 1832 at the University of Moscow, his "Letter on Philosophy" (*Teleskop*, 1833), and his *Kniga Nauma o velikom Bozh'em mire* (Book of Naum about God's Great World, 1833).

In the first of these, Maksymovych argued that Russian education must balance western European with native Russian elements and that service to Russia was also a service to humanity in general; in the second, reflecting Schelling's Nature Philosophy, he declared that true philosophy was based on love and that all branches of organized, systematic knowledge that strove to recognize the internal meaning and unity of things, but most especially history, were philosophy; in the third, he put these two principles to work in a popular exposition of nature, the solar system, and the universe, in congenial religious garb for ordinary laypeople. He wrote this last *Book of Naum* in Russian but used very simple language, and intellectual historian Aleksandr Pypin believed he intended it primarily for the common folk of his native Little Russia.[8]

## *Malorossiiskie pesni* (Little Russian Folksongs, 1827)

During the late 1820s, when Maksymovych was most active in botany, zoology, and the other physical sciences, he was still attracted to literature and the humanities. Thus in 1827, when defending his master's thesis in botany, he published a non-science collection: *Malorossiiskie pesni* (Little Russian Folksongs). He researched this book in his spare time and during a summer gathered songs in Ukraine and read the Slavonic grammar of Josef Dobrovský and Vuk Karadžić's collection of Serbian folksongs. The stirring opening lines of Maksymovych's Introduction were a manifesto of the new national spirit:

> The time has arrived to recognize the real value of nationality (*narodnost*); the desire has arisen to create a truly Russian poetry! . . . In this regard, the monuments in which nationality is most fully expressed deserve our attention. Such are the essence of songs revealing spirit and feelings, and tales which show the fantasy of the people . . . "Stories are sweet, but songs are truth itself" says the proverb . . . In particular, this can be said of Slavonic songs, which we see are characterized by their grace. This grace can be a clear proof that poetry is the natural quality of the human spirit and that true poetry is its own creation.

But why Little Russian folksongs in particular? Maksymovych continues: "Thinking along these lines, I turned my attention to this subject in Little Russia and for the first time I am publishing a selection of the songs of this country, proposing that they will be interesting and in many respects useful for our [Russian] literature (*slovestnost*). I am completely convinced that they have an indubitable value and occupy one of the first places among the songs of the Slavonic peoples."

Cossack traditions were particularly strong in his homeland. "Arising like a comet," Maksymovych tells us, "Little Russia has long made its neighbours tremble." Its history was stormy; its people made up of Slavs, other Europeans, and Asiatics, who loathed slavery and thirsted for independence and the heroic. The stormy life of the Ukrainian steppe raiders, the simple life of the pastoralists, and the settled life of agriculturalists, he maintained, are all embedded in their national character and are reflected in their songs, which are preserved especially well by the women. Ukrainian songs, he observed, like the Ukrainian language, are intermediate between Polish and Russian songs. While Russian songs are deep, despondent, and submissive, Ukrainian songs are natural, passionate, almost like "conversations with the wind." In "Russia," it is the men who sing; but in Little Russia, it is the women (see Figure 3).[9]

Maksymovych's collection contained 127 songs, including historical songs and "*dumy*" (a term [*duma* sing.] the author coined for reflective epic songs), songs about everyday life, and ritual songs. He printed the volume in his proposed new etymological orthography for Ukrainian. It was not the first modern work on Ukrainian ethnography, history, or language – Kalynovsky's descriptions of Ukrainian wedding customs had been published in 1764, Bantysh-Kamensky's history of Little Russia in 1822, and Pavlovsky's grammar in 1818 – or even the first assemblage of Ukrainian folksongs – that was Prince Tsertelev's (1819). Yet Maksymovych's was by far the most extensive collection yet and the first to contain ordinary non-historical songs, to analyse and classify the material, and to go beyond mere antiquarianism or simple historical interest and invoke the new principle of nationality, which was now coming to the fore.[10]

Indeed, Maksymovych's little book was to raise new questions about Little Russia and its relation to Russia as a whole. His ideas were still ambiguous. He used the terms *Russkii* (Russian) and *Malorossiiskii* (Little Russian) and distinguished them as we do, Russian from Ukrainian. But he also applied *Russkii* as a generic term for both Russian and Little Russian, where we today say "Eastern Slavs." Nowhere in his Introduction does he apply the then-common term *Velikorusskii* (Great Russian) to northerners or *Ukraintsi* (Ukrainians) to southerners. Thus the youthful Maksymovych (he was only twenty-three) raised the question of nationality in Russia, and more specifically in Little Russia. His little book of folksongs was merely the first step in a decades-long process.

It had a profound effect on Maksymovych's contemporaries and on the development of national relations in Russia and what was to become modern Ukraine. The reviews were generally good. For example, in *Syn otechestva* (Son of the Fatherland) Orest Somov, who was Ukrainian-born, praised Maksymovych's knowledge of Little Russia and called this poetic, sunny, southern country "a Russian Italy."[11] Pushkin read the songs with interest; he soon met Maksymovych at the home of Count Uvarov, who complimented the botanist for his gift with words, to which Pushkin said: "We have known Maksymovych for some time and consider him [not only a scientist but also] a literary man (*literatorom*). He has given us the Little Russian songs."[12] In

Pushkin's poetic hymn to Russian glory, *Poltava* (1829), the folksongs clearly inspired the figure of the Ukrainian woman, Mariia Kochubei, "one of the first living Russian female personalities" in Russian literature.[13]

Maksymovych's songs electrified "Ukrainians." In November 1833, Gogol, thinking of writing a history of Ukraine, wrote to Maksymovych: "Ah my joy, my life, the songs! How I love you! What are these soulless chronicles that I am ploughing through compared to these sonorous living chronicles!"[14] Meanwhile, in far-away Austrian Galicia, where the local Ukrainian intelligentsia was just rising from its slumber, the "Ruthenian Triad" – Markiian Shashkevych, Ivan Vahylevych, and Yakiv Holovatsky – read Maksymovych's collection with enthusiasm – Holovatsky even copied it out by hand – and, following his example, published a collection of Galician songs in the Ukrainian vernacular of that region, which was to be a lasting and profound example.[15] Also, the songs stirred younger inhabitants of the region. The young Kostomarov later testified that he got hold of them in the late 1830s: "I was struck and then carried away by the sincere beauty of Little Russian popular poetry. I had never suspected that such elegance, such depth and fresh feelings could be found in the creations of the common people who were so close to me and about whom I unfortunately knew nothing."[16] Given such positive reactions, Maksymovych released *Ukrainskie narodnye pesni* (Ukrainian Folksongs, 1834) and *Sbornik ukrainskikh pesen* (A Collection of Ukrainian Songs, part 1, 1849). His use of the term "Ukrainian" may relate to the publication in 1832 of the Russian translation of Beauplan's famous map *Description d'Ukraine* (1639), which used "*Ukraina*" and "*ukrainets*" quite frequently, unlike Beauplan himself, who usually spoke only of "*Cosaques*."[17] At any rate, Maksymovych's turn to things Ukrainian and his eventually liberal use of the term "Ukrainian" were to resonate profoundly.

## St Vladimir University (1834–47)

Despite his great success in Moscow in biology and literature, Maksymovych was not happy there. The severe northern climate was hard on his delicate health, intensive work with microscopes was bothering his eyes, and academic politics and the jealousy of some of his colleagues were a challenge. His mother had long advised him to return home, he longed to do so, and shortly after her death the government announced its plans to create a new Russian university in Kyiv, so Maksymovych showed interest in the project. His "Russian" patriotism had earned him the confidence of Minister of Education Count Uvarov, who was formulating his ideology of "Orthodoxy, Autocracy, and Nationality," and Maksymovych would have liked to have been named professor of biology at the new institution, but in May 1834, after a certain amount of hesitation, he accepted positions there as professor of Russian literature and dean of the Faculty of Philosophy and, in October, "rector," or president. The new university, founded in 1834, was named after Grand Prince Vladimir/Volodymyr of Kyiv (c. 958–1015), a founder of Kyivan Rus'.[18]

Tsar Nicholas I, Count Uvarov, and Russian governing circles in general were planning a new and thoroughly "Russian" institution, to replace Polish institutions in Ukraine and other parts of the Russian/Polish borderlands that had bred Polish patriotism prior to the Polish insurrection of 1830–31. It was meant to solidify the new, supposedly "Russian" character of Kyiv and strengthen Russian claims to this city, which had for several hundred years been subject to the grand dukes of Lithuania and then the kings of Poland. His local roots and ostensible Russian patriotism made Maksymovych the perfect instrument of this policy.

He titled his public lecture at the university of 2 October 1837, which he delivered in the presence of Count Uvarov and other dignitaries, "On the Participation and Significance of Kyiv in the General Life of Russia." He proposed three phases of Russian history: religion (i.e., Orthodoxy), national independence, and autocracy, corresponding to Uvarov's policy of "official nationality." He saw Prince Vladimir (reigned 980–1015) as the enlightener of "Russia," Ivan III (reigned 1462–1505) as "gatherer" of the Fatherland, and Peter the Great (reigned 1682–1725) as its "transformer," but through it all, including the Lithuanian and Polish periods, Kyiv, with its old churches, its Orthodox Cossacks, and its famous theological academy (founded 1632), retained its place as the most ancient and holy repository of Orthodox Rus', hence the naming after the great enlightener himself, Prince Vladimir. Count Uvarov was so impressed that he rushed to the podium to shake the lecturer's hand on his very last word. Maksymovych's interpretation seemed to fully coincide with official policy on Russian nationalism and Russia's claim to Kyiv, but it hinted at major, unresolved differences.[19]

Government pressure to conform to official policy on the national question was one thing, but all was not well at the University of Kyiv. From its very founding in 1834, it had run into difficulties: there were many Poles with suspect loyalties on faculty, the student body was mostly Polish, and the government kept a close watch on both professors and students. The new rector had developed far-reaching scholarly plans for the university – including an encyclopaedia of what he called "Southern Rus'," a dictionary of the Ukrainian language, a scholarly journal, and further editions of Ukrainian songs – but few of these were realized. Maksymovych invited Gogol to come and teach, but this too did not work out.

The atmosphere of suspicion and the constant denunciations of university members took their toll. Maksymovych's delicate constitution and frayed nerves simply could not take it. By the end of 1835, he resigned his rectorship. He continued to teach and to care for the welfare of the university, but at thirty-one he was already partly retired to his country home at Mykhailova Hora (Michael's Mountain), south of Kyiv and overlooking the Dnipro River.[20]

However, the university's troubles continued. In the mid-1830s, a wide conspiracy among the Poles led by one Szymon Konarski was discovered and many students were implicated. In May 1837, the tsar himself arrived in Kyiv and threatened both faculty and students with severe reprisals for any disloyalty. This was the prevailing atmosphere when Maksymovych lectured before Uvarov and the others in October.

It did not help. All of his efforts to protect the university and its faculty and students from the imperial authorities were in vain. In 1839, the tsar closed the university down for several months and ordered many arrests. (Some students were actually sentenced to be executed, later commuted to long terms in prison.) Maksymovych's health only worsened. He had trouble lecturing, and his hands, legs, and eyes bothered him. In 1841, he retreated for two years to the countryside, and by 1845, at forty-one, he resigned from his professorship and fully retired.[21]

However, Maksymovych's career at the university had solid results. The institution survived and steadily grew, and several of his scholarly projects were carried out in the following years. At one level, he developed a close working friendship with the rector of the Kyiv Theological Academy, the famous preacher Inokentii Borisov, who shared with him an interest in Kyivan churches and antiquities. (Maksymovych was later to write much on these subjects.) So close were the two men that as early as 1840 Maksymovych confided to Borisov in writing his concerns about the oppression of the enserfed Ukrainian peasantry. This appearantly dangerous letter has not survived, but Borisov's reply, written in Latin to avoid police scrutiny, plainly remarked on Maksymovych's pained tears in this regard.[22]

Throughout his period as professor of Russian literature (*slovestnost*), Maksymovych deepened his knowledge of "Russian" (East Slavic) literatures and languages, and wrote extensively on these topics. Thus in 1837 there appeared his first major work on the famous *Slovo o polku Igoreve* (Lay of Igor's Campaign, late twelfth century), which defended the authenticity and antiquity of this questioned product of Kyivan Rus', compared it to the popular verse of Cossack Ukraine and northern Rus', and affirmed its "national" significance. Specialists usually note that he always stressed this work's "southern," or Ukrainian, language and linguistic connections, which he believed a product of southern, not northern Rus', and that he was convinced that, in both spirit and content, it closely resembled the surviving popular poetry of Cossack and nineteenth-century Ukraine; in other words, he saw an almost-genetic connection between the heroic epic of Kyivan Rus' and popular Ukrainian folklore of his own time.[23]

Even more important was Maksymovych's *Istoriia drevnei russkoi slovestnosti* (History of Old Russian Literature; Kyiv, 1839), which explored both the oral and the written "word" (*slovo*) in its various manifestations. He rejected the aesthetic method of classical criticism and used a historical-cultural approach that aimed to reveal the spirit and life of the people. He turned first to the national speech of Russia and placed it within its Slavonic context. Contradicting the Czech philologist Josef Dobrovský, he argued that "Russian" was not a South Slavic language but rather formed a separate "eastern" group of languages with two branches (*razriady*), "South Russian" and "North Russian," and that the former contained two dialects (*vidoizmenenia*), Ukrainian, or Little Russian, and Red Russian, or Galician. The North Russian branch he divided into two languages: "Great Russian," with four dialects (*narechie*), of which Muscovite was the youngest but most developed and "Belarusan" or "Lithuanian–Russian" intermediate between it and South Russian, but much closer to the former. Dobrovský, who usually focused on the written language, had completely overlooked this diversity of the "Russian" or "Eastern Slavic" languages. (Maksymovych used both terms interchangeably.) By contrast, Maksymovych's work concentrated on the vernacular, decentralized the question, and put language studies in closer touch with the life of the people. The argument that, to use today's terminology, Ukrainian, Russian, and Belarusan were part of a completely independent "Eastern Slavic" group of languages, which emerged before Rus' became a polity, was new and quite bold. Indeed, Maksymovych's researches facilitated the definitive emergence of the new term "Eastern Slavic."[24]

At the university quite aside from his work as a scholar, our professor had a profound influence on the younger Ukrainian intellectuals gathering in Kyiv. His very attractive personality certainly played a role. "The secret of Maksymovych's attraction as a professor, writer, and scholar," wrote such a younger contemporary, "was hidden in the personal traits of his character. He was not only a very gifted person, but also of high moral quality, sympathetic, considerate, and sincere, with a poetic note to his speech and in his relations with people."[25]

He met all three of the famous literary trio who stood at the very centre of the Ukrainian national awakening: the enserfed peasant boy turned fiery and melancholic poet and painter, Taras Shevchenko, the idiosyncratic and testy but very original writer Panteleimon Kulish, and the high-strung but prolific historian Mykola Kòstomarov – all of whom had been influenced by Maksymovych's *Malorossiiskie pesni*. Kulish was in the late 1830s his admiring student and in 1840 his co-author in his path-breaking almanac of *ucrainica* titled *Kievlianin* (The Kyivan); from 1843 on, Shevchenko became a close acquaintance and then friend who shared his interests in Ukrainian history and songs and who, with his full support, worked for a while for the Kyiv Archaeographic Commission, of which Maksymovych was a founder and guiding spirit; and Maksymovych also helped to bring Kostomarov to Kyiv, found employment for him, and, when Kostomarov was named professor of Russian history, avidly discussed Ukrainian history with him in the privacy of his own home. The four men shared many ideals, relating to the Ukrainian national awakening and the general Slavic renaissance. Together they planned to publish a journal in the various living Slavonic languages.[26]

It was not to last. In 1847, an informer reported to the police seditious conversations held by the young men. A suspicious ukrainophile and slavophile society, the Brotherhood of Saints Cyril and Methodius (patron saints of Slavdom), was discovered, compromising papers came to light, and all three young protégés, members of the group, were arrested, imprisoned, and sent off into punitive exile. The police reported:

From the papers of Kulish and [his colleague Vasyl] Bilozersky, several new names of people in the Slavic society have come to light: a bureaucrat from the office of the Kyiv Military Governor, Rigelman, the zealous partisan of Slavonic successes, the teacher from the Podolian Gymnasium, Chuikevych, Maksymovych, Bodiansky, and others. Although the main ideas of the love of Slavdom and, especially,

Little Russia, flow through their letters, it is still difficult to determine whether all of the named people took part in undesirable political activities or just shared in the scholarly work of these Slavophiles.[27]

The sickly Maksymovych was left more or less in peace, as two years before he had already retired to Mykhailova Hora.

## Mykhailova Hora and Moscow (1847–60)

The following years were very difficult for our former professor. His health was still not good; he was isolated in the countryside without books or friends and lived in great poverty. Nevertheless, he worked whenever he felt strong enough and turned more and more towards history and philology. He wrote a brief history of Kyiv (*Ocherk Kyiva*) and worked with the Kyiv Archaeographic Commission. His *Nachatki russkoi filologii* (Principles of Russian Philology, 1848) was very well received; the Russian lexicographer Vladimir Dal praised it, and it influenced the development of Russian philology. In 1849, Maksymovych felt strong enough to go to Moscow to find work and consorted with his old friend Gogol and with Sergei Aksakov, an early figure among the conservative Moscow slavophiles, who had not yet turned against the Ukrainian awakening. Maksymovych discovered in the papers of his friend Mikhail Pogodin the long-lost 1622 poem of Kasiian Sakovych in honour of Petro Konashevych Sahaidachny, hetman of the Zaporozhian army. In June 1850, he returned to Ukraine in the company of Gogol.[28]

His misfortunes, however, continued. In 1851, his father died, in 1852 Gogol did too, and the next year he lost to marriage his beloved sister, who had long cared for him. Finally, at forty-nine, he married a neighbour's daughter. Mariia Vasylivna turned out to be his saviour. She was a cheerful, warm, sensitive, and charming woman who played the piano well and knew a great many Ukrainian songs. She quickly became the light of his life and bore him both a son and a daughter. This marriage helped transform Ukrainian culture.[29]

In 1856, the slavophile Moscow journal *Russkaia beseda* (Russian Conversation) published the first part of Maksymovych's *Dni i mesiatsy ukrainskogo selianina* (Days and Months of the Ukrainian Villager). This wide-ranging work summed up his many years of observing "Ukrainian" peasants, more particularly those of the Kyiv and Poltava regions, especially near Mykhailova Hora. It laid out the folk customs of the Ukrainian village according to the calendar year.[30] The published parts of the work earned very positive responses, and the following year Maksymovych (with his new wife) went to Moscow to edit *Russkaia beseda*. He also released the first number of the almanac *Ukrainets* (The Ukrainian) – note the auspicious title – a continuation of his earlier almanac, *Kievlianin*. It included works on Ukrainian history and a Ukrainian translation of the Psalms and of the twelfth-century *Slovo o polku Igoreve* (The Lay of Igor's Campaign).[31]

In Moscow, Maksymovych reunited with many old friends, both Russian slavophiles such as Sergei Aksakov, and Ukrainian scholars interested in Slavdom and the national awakening, such as Osyp Bodiansky. (Maksymovych's long-time and absorbing correspondence with the latter has been preserved.[32]) Shevchenko returned from exile and with a friend went to visit Maksymovych and his wife. On 18 March 1858, Shevchenko, quite taken with Mariia Vasylivna, confided in his diary:

> We found him busy at work over *Russkaia beseda*. His wife was not at home. She was at church and fasting. But soon she appeared and the gloomy cloister of the scholar began to lighten up. What a beautiful sweet thing she is! And what is most charming about her is that she represents the pure and innocent feminine type of my country-man. She played several songs on the piano for us in such a pure and unaffected way that more than one great artist could hardly match. Where did that old antiquarian dig up such sweet pure goodness?[33]

On 25 March Maksymovych held a dinner in honour of Shevchenko, which included his old friends Pogodin and Shevyrev, and recited a verse he had composed in honour of the poet. He praised Shevchenko as a true poet of his people, who had returned unbroken by his hard experiences and would soon "sing new songs of human freedom."[34]

The poet and the scholar did not meet again until June 1859, at Mykhailova Hora. They were together for over a week, and Shevchenko painted memorable portraits of both his hosts. Mariia Vasylivna was also supposed to try to find a wife with similar qualities to her own for the poet, but fate intervened. Within a year and a half Shevchenko was dead, and Maksymovych pronounced a farewell verse at his funeral at Kaniv, almost across the Dnipro from Mykhailova Hora.[35]

## Turning to History (1860–73)

In the early 1860s, Maksymovych lived quietly in the countryside, corresponding with friends and colleagues and contributing to various Ukrainian publications. He collaborated in 1861 with Bilozersky, Kostomarov, Kulish, and the others on the journal *Osnova* (Foundation), in which he placed his famous "Letters on Bohdan Khmelnytsky." He had long wanted to see a real scholarly journal of Ukrainian studies, and this was the first. In 1864, after its failure, and while Moscow, with its circular partially banning the use in print of the Ukrainian language, began to turn firmly against the Ukrainian movement, he still managed to put out another number of *Ukrainets* – an almanac – but it did keep the idea of a journal alive.

In these various publications and others, our scholar defended the Ukrainian character of Gogol's stories from an attack by Kulish, who had accused him of not really being in touch with the Ukrainian folk, penned several articles on Kyiv and other Ukrainian localities, and wrote more on *Slovo o polku Igoreve*, which he had now translated into both modern Ukrainian and modern Russian verse. He also prepared a new, revised edition of his popular work on biology, *The Book of Naum about God's Great World*. (The twelfth edition of what can be called only a nineteenth-century scientific "bestseller" appeared only much later, after his death.)[36] But more and more, he was drawn to history.

Isolated at Mykhailova Hora, he could not do intensive archival research, but still managed to write a great deal and also published analyses of the works of other historians. Indeed, his favourite genre became the friendly public "letter" to his scholarly subject, with some personal memories of their experiences together and then a careful critique of their work. He used this technique with his old Moscow friend the Russian historian Mikhail Pogodin and the Polish writer Michał Grabowski, as well as the Ukrainians Kulish and Kostomarov. As he himself noted, his motto was: "*Amicus Aristoteles amicus Plato, sed magis amica veritas* (I am a friend of Aristotle, and a friend of Plato, but much more a friend of truth)." As this suggests, careful and courteous analysis rather than bold narrative formed the basis of Maksymovych's historical method here.[37]

Of course, Maksymovych tackled many of the most pressing questions of Ukrainian or Russian history. Thus he was critical of the Normanist theory of the origins of Rus' – that the Normans (Norsemen), a people whose relatives later ruled Normandy, England, and Sicily, created Kyivan

Rus'. Maksymovych criticized the theory's supporters August Ludwig von Schlözer, Nikolai Karamzin, and his own friend Pogodin and stressed the native Slavonic origins of this polity.[38] Having long rejected a unitary origin of the languages and peoples of Kyivan Rus', he was appalled when Pogodin, leaning on new arguments that evidence for the Ukrainian language was missing from surviving literary sources, theorized that it was the "Great Russians" who had originally populated this state, only to be driven north by the Tatars and replaced by the "Little Russians" immigrating later from the Carpathians. Maksymovych offered a three-pronged rebuttal: southern Rus' had always been populated by the Ukrainians and their direct ancestors, whose roots could be traced back to the Poliany, or pre-Christian tribes in the Ukrainian forests and steppes; the literary heritage of Kyivan Rus' had, unfortunately, been preserved only in the North (Muscovy) by monastic scholars who systematically edited out its South Russian elements; and the later Tatar devastation was never complete. Further, it was ancestors of the modern Ukrainians who had pushed west across the Carpathians, not vise versa.[39]

Similarly, Maksymovych criticized Michał Grabowski for stressing the Polish claim to Kyiv and to Ukraine. Grabowski contended that Ukraine had been colonized anew by the Poles after the Mongol/Tatar invasion, and that Polish influences on Ukraine were on the whole beneficial. Maksymovych retorted that it was the Lithuanians, not the Poles, who had liberated Ukraine from the Tatars, and who ruled it for two and a half centuries, and that the Poles governed the country directly for less than a century – between the Union of Lublin of 1569 and the Khmelnytsky revolt of 1648 – not enough time to repopulate and change an entire country, but sufficient to force the unpopular Church Union with Rome on the unwilling Orthodox Ukrainians and thus bring on the great revolt of 1648.[40]

Our many-sided scholar also wrote on other contentious historical subjects. Thus he was the first to explore the career of Hetman Petro Sahaidachny (hetman 1616–22), who in alliance with the Poles had attacked Muscovy, renewed the suppressed Ukrainian Orthodox hierarchy, and captured the great Turkish slave emporium in Kaffa. He also wrote on Bohdan Khmelnytsky, correcting his former protégé Kostomarov on many minor points and criticizing his innovative but somewhat uncritical use of Ukrainian folksongs and Polish chronicles as sources. He acknowledged his friend's artistry and beautiful exposition, as well as his unrivalled knowledge of the subject, but advised him to rework his monograph. The writer took the criticism to heart and did exactly that.[41]

Maksymovych was the first to write seriously on the Haidamak rebellions against Poland (1734, 1750, 1768), especially on the Koliivshchyna, or "Rebellion of the Pikes," of 1768, in which the common Cossacks – the so-called Haidamaks – massacred many Polish nobles, Catholic priests, and Jewish "estate bosses" or stewards. Polish legends depicted the Cossacks as simple thieves and brigands, but Maksymovych saw in them a natural reaction against Polish oppression, especially the "forced" Church Union. Even though he stressed religious and not social factors, his work on the 1768 uprising was so unsettling to the socially conservative authorities that it was banned by the Russian censor and published only after the author's death.[42]

In general, Maksymovych was very critical of the dominant Ukrainian histories of his time, the anonymously written *Istoriia Rusov* (History of the Ruthenians), Bantysh-Kamensky's *Istoriia Maloi Rossii* (History of Little Russia), and Markevych's *Istoriia Malorossii* (History of Little Russia). He thought the strongly autonomist and patriotic *Istoriia Rusov* inspiring, but too fanciful, and the strongly loyalist history of Bantysh-Kamensky better documented but too dry, indeed, even dead. In his opinion, Markevych too relied too much on the fanciful *Istoriia Rusov*. Even though Maksymovych had helped popularize Ukrainian historical songs, and knew they inspired the work of Kostomarov and others, he did not think them particularly accurate as historical sources.

Therefore he sought out as many new sources as he possibly could (given his delicate health) and published many of them. Perhaps his rediscovery of Sakovych's poem eulogizing Sahaidachny was his greatest new find, but he also did much critical work on the chronicle of Hrabianka and the new Cossack chronicles and other sources discovered in his time, and, as well, did some archaeological work on ancient arrowheads, and on Kyiv and its architecture, which had implications for Ukrainian history as a whole.[43] His attention to detail and to the particular make his works heavy reading but sustains their scholarly value.

The Ukrainian intelligentsia in Kyiv celebrated the golden jubilee of Maksymovych's literary and scholarly career in 1871, and the next year his friend and companion of his last years, the bibliographer and book collector Stepan Ponomarev, published a short biography of him. He was at long last elected a corresponding member of the Imperial Academy of Sciences in St Petersburg, and the Ukrainian scholars Volodymyr Antonovych and Oleksander Kotliarevsky were preparing the large, three-volume edition of his *Sobranie sochinenii* (Collected Works) cited so many times in this chapter.

Also in 1872, an institution that Maksymovych had long dreamed of, the Historical Society of Nestor the Chronicler, was finally founded in Kyiv, and he was immediately elected an honorary member. Moreover, the Kyivans, much to his delight, were arranging a great archaeological and historical congress for 1874. In the midst of all this activity, the elderly scholar, who was still living at Mykhailova Hora, quietly passed away. He was buried at his beloved country home and mourned by three generations of Ukrainians for whom he had been an esteemed mentor, courteous colleague, and faithful friend.

## The Impact of His Legacy

Where does Maksymovych stand in the development of the Ukrainian language and the history of Ukrainian literature? His *Malorossiiskie pesni* of 1827 was a landmark in both. It turned attention to the Ukrainian vernacular shortly after the Napoleonic Wars, when the literary elite was still somewhat enamoured of the French language and western European models. The innovative etymological orthography he crafted to print it was, as he himself argued, a way of presenting the Ukrainian vernacular without fully breaking with the Ukrainian past and its Church Slavonic–influenced book language. Furthermore, as he also argued, because it looked so similar to the written Russian language of the North – the language of Pushkin – Russians too could read it, provided a glossary was added.[44]

Nevertheless, it was a step backward from Pavlovsky's phonetic orthography of 1818; many of his Ukrainian contemporaries thought that it did not capture spoken Ukrainian. When he persisted in using it, he was criticized. Petro Hulak-Artemovsky wrote to him in French some time later, "Please allow me, kind sir, to say to you in all sincerity, which arises out of a deep respect for you, that this orthography, in my opinion, does not appeal to the taste of our countrymen, or to the spirit of the language itself. The Russians will read it as Russian, and the Ukrainians will have difficulties making out what it says."[45] In the end, it was rejected in favour of a more phonetically accurate system devised in the 1850s by Panteleimon Kulish – the basis of modern written Ukrainian.[46]

Maksymovych's literary views befell a similar fate. Although he staunchly defended the independence of the Ukrainian language, and almost worshipped the fiery and melancholic Shevchenko, his views on its development were very modest. For him, as for a great many people of that time, it was the language of the common people and seemed to him appropriate only for writings about them – primarily *belles lettres* and poetry – but not for scholarship or other such pursuits. He did not, it seems, expect Ukrainian literature in Russia to develop into a full field of literature.

Many in the younger generation could not understand why Ukrainian could not move from poetry and song to literary, scholarly, and eventually scientific prose. Indeed, the talented Kulish was soon translating into Ukrainian not only the Psalms, as Maksymovych had already done, but pretty much the whole Bible, as well as Goethe, Byron, and Shakespeare. Moreover, Maksymovych advised the Galicians, who were trying to stave off polonization of their tongue, but were free to choose their written language, to write everything in the Ukrainian vernacular and use the achievements of the Ukrainians in the Russian Empire. Consequently, there was a certain amount of equivocation in Maksymovych's views on literature.[47]

## Maksymovych at the Crossroads

Mykhailo Maksymovych, with his gentle and humane character and his Schellingesque love for man and nature, was in many ways a "universal man" of the classic Renaissance kind. He contributed prodigiously to both the physical sciences and the humanities, to botany, zoology, folklore, philosophy, education, language, literature, and history. Moreover, he was a poet, who saw a basic unity and purpose to all systematic and organized knowledge, and who considered all of life and science to be infused with meaning and direction. Thus, although he was certainly not a "great" poet, he was "a poet of scientific thought" and "a poet of scholarship," who was somewhat lyrical about everything that he wrote and everybody that he met.[48]

Maksymovych's universal interests and curiosity had a bearing on how he approached both the physical sciences and the humanities, and, indeed, even politics. He gleaned his idealistic philosophy from Schelling and applied it to his popular works on botany and zoology; and he learned his scientific rigour in the physical sciences but also applied it to his works in literature, folklore, and history. He was a true Romantic in his interest in the past, religion, and the common folk, but, given his mild, accommodating nature, was very timid about questioning the autocracy and public order of Imperial Russia, about which he had many private doubts; it was left to a younger generation already moving from Romanticism to Positivism to completely sweep away the last vestiges of classicism and "enlightenment hierarchy," if that is how, most generously, the tsarist system could be described.

Maksymovych stood at the crossroads. In his youth, European manners and morals, classical models, and the French and German languages had held unchallenged sway over elite Russian minds and feelings. In "Little Russia," the socially conservative estate or local patriotism – and political autonomism – of the kind promoted by the *Istoriia Rusov* were very popular. But it was Maksymovych and his generation who pioneered the concept of "nationality" in the Russian realm. In doing so, Maksymovych drew attention to the fact that "Russian" nationality existed in more than one form, and he raised new questions about the relations between Southern Rus' and Northern Rus', which during his time were becoming modern "Ukraine" and "Russia." These questions concerned their Slavonic and national characters, their languages, histories, and literatures. By raising the status of Southern Rus' and putting it on an equal footing with the North, he unknowingly helped launch the eventual separation of the two and the emergence of modern Ukrainian and Russian national identities.

But Maksymovych took only the first step. He did not accept the concept of mutually exclusive Ukrainian and Russian national identities that was to emerge later in his own century, or, even more clearly, early in the next century. For him there still existed a deep family kinship among the various parts of St Vladimir's Rus'. As late as his 1871 jubilee, he explained it thus:

> As a native of Southern Kyivan Rus', under the land and sky of my forefathers, to the present day I primarily have belonged to her and I will belong to her, primarily dedicating to her my intellectual activity. But together with this, growing to maturity in Moscow, I also loved and studied Muscovite Rus' as the sister of our Kyivan Rus', and as the second half of that one and the same *Holy Rus' of Saint Vladimir*, feeling and recognizing that in their ways of life and their understandings, one without the other is insufficient and one-sided.[49]

Deeply conservative in his instincts and interests, Maksymovych looked backward to the heritage bequeathed him by his Ukrainian forefathers. He was a true gatherer of a pre-national heritage. But in doing this, he aroused newer "national" feelings among members of the younger generation. Through his editions of Ukrainian folksongs, he stirred their interest in their native language and past; through his studies of *Slovo o polku Igoreve* he stressed the continuity of this Ukrainian past and deepened their Ukrainian feeling; and through his polemics with the Muscovite Pogodin and the Pole Grabowski, he started a way of historical thinking that was to culminate in Kostomarov's innovative claim about the existence of "Two Russian Nationalities" and Hrushevsky's about the independence of the Ukrainian historical process from the Russian within the context not of "Russia," but of the "Eastern Slavic" peoples, a term first coined and defined by Maksymovych himself.

Maksymovych's words quoted above indicate that he possessed a number of simultaneously held identities, some of which eventually became contradictory; that is, he identified widely with "Russia" as a whole, more narrowly with "Southern Rus'," and even more narrowly with "Ukraine," or the Kyivan region together with the entire area east of the River Dnieper; and he did this in a way that was typical of the nineteenth century. At the same time, as his correspondence with the Galicians showed, the area to the west of the Dnieper, stretching as far as Galicia (similarly a part of St Vladimir's Rus'), was also of a very special "national" interest to him, even though it was seldom marked as "Ukraine" in maps of his day and official Russia then had no political ambitions with regard to it.[50]

However, as well, Maksymovych was in some ways different from both his immediate predecessors – the gentry autonomists, who admired the *Istoriia Rusov* and held certain very real grivances against Moscow – and his successors, whom he had already taught to think along "national" lines. These differences were etched out in his positive though relegated attitudes towards Russia, the result of his intense intellectual formation in Moscow, and also in his innovative concept of ancient Kyiv's significance, both unusual for his time. Both his older contemporaries from the former hetmanate, those avid readers of the *Istoriia Rusov*, and the next generation, as represented by Shevchenko, Kostomarov, and Kulish, were centred more on Cossack Ukraine than on Kyivan Rus', and Moscow was completely absent from the education of the latter three. And this was to have enormous consequences with regard to Ukrainian national independence.

As the literary historian Serhii Yefremov aptly stated in the 1920s, although Maksymovych may have been very conservative and moderate in his ambitions for Ukrainian literature in "Russian Ukraine," and thus also for the future development of Ukraine as a full-fledged modern nation with a language and a literature of its own, his advice to the Galicians to develop their literature as much as possible in their native language – basically what was happening in the rest of what he called "Southern Rus'" – returned to haunt both his memory and his spiritual children in

"Russian Ukraine." After all, it was he who initiated the process by which the terms "Russians" and "Little Russians" started to give way to "Eastern Slavs" and "Ukrainians," and which ended two generations later in the deconstruction of the Russia into which he had been born and the extension of the term "Ukraine" to a vastly larger area, even west to Austrian Galicia and beyond. That is, Yefremov believed that Maksymovych started a process that eventually went much farther than he had intended.[51]

Moreover, as his ultimate heir, the influential Ukrainian historian Mykhailo Hrushevsky, pointed out to his countrymen some ten years after the great Ukrainian revolution of 1917,[52] there were two conscious principles inspiring Maksymovych's work that resonated through Ukraine's future. Firstly, unlike some earlier works, such as the popular but gentry-oriented *Istoriia Rusov*, his own varied writings stressed "the people" as the subject and the goal of Ukrainian scholarship. This was clear not only in his work on Ukrainian folklore and history, but even in his popularizations of the natural sciences, especially his *Book of Naum about God's Great World*. Secondly, he emphasized the continuity of Ukrainian culture throughout the centuries, extending even back to Kyivan Rus'. He traced this continuity in his studies of Ukrainian language, folk poetry, and history. The people and its millennium-old heritage, so argued Hrushevsky, as well as the names "Eastern Slavs" and "Ukrainians," as pointed out in this chapter, were the lasting legacy of the gentle hermit of Mykhailova Hora, whose deep personal and political conservatism did not prevent him from becoming a close friend of the fiery rebel Shevchenko and, in politics, a revolutionary force in the modern history of his native land.

## CHAPTER FIVE

# Shamil, Shevchenko, and the *Chef-d'oeuvre*, "The Caucasus": A Poem as Seen from Afar

AMONG UKRAINIAN LITERARY HISTORIANS AND SPECIALISTS, there is absolutely no doubt that the 1845 poem "The Caucasus" (Kavkaz) holds a central place in the so-called political, philosophical, or ideological writings of the country's national poet, Taras Shevchenko (1814–1861) (Plate 11), and in the history of Ukraine. Despite its brevity, it touches directly and unequivocally on a great many themes and motifs, with enormous psychological and emotional power. Moreover, its unique combination of plain language, simple exposition, and complex structure renders it an artistic masterpiece (*shedevr/chef-d'oeuvre/chédeuvre*) unsurpassed in his "political" verses.

Writing in the 1880s, a young Galician-Ukrainian scholar, the left-leaning Ivan Franko, called it "one of Shevchenko's best works," and sixty years later a Shevchenko scholar, the right-leaning Leonid Biletsky, a political refugee who had fled Stalin's Red Army and settled in Winnipeg, declared it "a political poem with the most deep personal and philosophical tones."[1] The western Ukrainian writer Bohdan Lepky commented: "Explosive and immediate in its power, 'The Caucasus' has no equal [in Ukrainian litera-ture]. This poem overturns, crushes, burns, strikes with irony, freezes with truth, and blinds with sparkling comparisons, until, with its memory of a sincere friend, it ends in quiet accord. An entirely extraordinary thing."[2] One of the most recent interpreters of Shevchenko, George Grabowicz, who has pioneered the concept of "myth" in Ukrainian literature, has labelled it "prophetic," "manichean," "millennial," and ultimately "one great philippic against structure in its various guises, from false religion, to false enlightenment, to finally, above all, the boundless imperial lust to aggrandize."[3]

But whence came this outraged attack on falsehood, lust, and Russian "imperialism," the last its main target? And what occasioned it? Despite its "mythic" or "millennial" qualities, the answers are both personal and political.

## Yakiv de Balmen

In July 1845 the poet's good friend Yakiv Petrovych de Balmen died, aged thirty-two. Shevchenko, already a celebrity in his homeland because of his first book of poetry, *Kobzar* (The Blind Minstrel, or The Kobza Player, 1840) (see Figure 8), had met de Balmen in 1843 during the poet's first tour of Ukraine and near the end of his art studies in St Petersburg. They met at a party or ball at the Volkhovsky residence in Poltava province in left-bank (eastern) Ukraine, where most of the local gentry and aristocracy were descended from Cossack officers and were well disposed to Cossack Ukraine and to the old "hetmanate," or autonomous state, founded by Hetman Bohdan Khmelnytysky in 1648, which had maintained its own army and administration despite Russian suzerainty. On the west or right bank of the Dnieper, a partly resurgent Polish state had crushed the western flank of that same Cossack Ukraine, which by the 1840s was only a poignant memory, revived by Shevchenko's fiery and melancholic verses.

Although de Balmen was of French and Scottish ancestry, and claimed an old French title (count), he and his circle were Ukrainian local patriots who treasured Cossack traditions. He and Shevchenko met up several more times, including at the de Balmen estate near the Volkhovskys'. The two young men joined an informal fraternity of local sons of the gentry, and both signed a humorous letter to the historian Mykola Markevych dated 22 January 1844. (In 1918 the Ukrainian Peoples Republic under Mykhailo Hrushevsky declared independence and dated it 22 January.) The poet signed that letter to Markevych "Hetman Shevchenko," and de Balmen signed "Military Captain (*yesaul*) Yakiv Dybailo." Shevchenko then continued on his journey across Ukraine, and de Balmen, together with a friend, transcribed a collection of Shevchenko's verse into Latin letters using Polish orthography and illustrated the manuscript with his own drawings.[4]

In 1845, Shevchenko returned to Poltava and his friend's estate. He learned from de Balmen's brother that his friend had been killed, fighting in the tsar's army against Caucasus mountaineers vigorously resisting Russian encroachments. Deeply disturbed by the tragic death, and struck by the irony of a Ukrainian patriot dying in the service of a rapacious empire oppressing Ukrainians and neighbouring Muslim peoples, Shevchenko penned "Kavkaz."[5]

Less than a year later, the poet finally saw de Balmen's manuscript and illustrations. By hand, he restored a few lines that the imperial censor had struck out and added the stirring first two lines of "Kavkaz":

Za horamy hory, khmaroiu povyti,
Zasiiani horem, krovoiu polyti.
(Mountain upon mountain,
Covered with cloud,
Seeded with woe, blood
All the way down.)[6]

In 1847, after the arrest of Mykola Kostomarov and the other members of the secret, democratically inclined Brotherhood of Saints Cyril and Methodius (Slavonic patron saints), with whom Shevchenko had close relations, authorities confiscated the de Balmen manuscript. After the 1917 Revolution it was transferred to Kyiv, and today it is preserved in the library of the Institute of Literature of the Ukrainian National Academy of Sciences.[7]

## War in the Caucasus

So the personal element certainly inspired that fiery poem. But so too did the political and military events that sparked it. If this story about Russian imperial expansion seems current and very new, it is also past and very old and spans four-and-a-half centuries. In the sixteenth century, Muscovy's Tsar Ivan the Terrible annexed the Muslim Tatar khanates of Kazan and Astrakhan; in the seventeenth, Tsar Alexis gained supremacy over the eastern parts of the Ukrainian hetmanate; and in the early eighteenth, Tsar Peter the Great began to dismantle that hetmanate and expanded Russian rule in the Baltic. In the late eighteenth century, Tsarina Catherine the Great participated in the three partitions of the once great Polish–Lithuanian Commonwealth, pushed the borders of her empire further west, and most immediately, in the 1780s, completed annexation of the Crimean Khanate, which faced the Black Sea.

With the extinction of that khanate, Ukrainian Cossacks, formerly quite independently minded, but now very much in Russian service, were resettled first along the Black Sea, and then along the Kuban River, and Russian-speaking Don Cossacks were settled along the Terek River north of the Caucasus Mountains. The "Caucasus Wall," in the foothills north of the main Caucasus range, seemed to block further Russian expansion southward.

Cossack settlement along the Kuban and Terek rivers led to creation of the Kuban–Terek Line as the empire's southern boundary. None the less expansion followed, including colonization by military and private landlords, but the rough terrain and the fierce resistance of Circassian, Avar, Chechen, and other warriors led to a long and difficult struggle, the so-called Caucasian War, which lasted through three-quarters of the nineteenth century.[8]

Western interpretations of Ukrainian and Russian history savour the image of the mounted Cossack, wild and terrifying, sweeping all before him. But this image is largely erroneous, and by about 1800 irrelevant, as technical innovation, advances in gunnery and artillery, and military discipline and tactics had rendered him largely obsolete. In fact, even in the Kuban and the North Caucasus, he was not always the most effective soldier. "The mounted natives," reads one striking military report, "are very superior in many ways to both our regular cavalry and the Cossacks."

> They are all but born on horseback and being used to riding from their earliest years, become extremely expert in this art and accustomed to covering great distances without fatigue. Having an abundance of horses not pampered in stables, they choose those only which are noted for their swiftness, strength, and activity . . . The mountaineers' weapons are their personal property, handed down from generation to generation. They value them highly, carefully preserve them, and keep them in excellent order . . . All domestic work is performed by the women, while the men who are sufficiently well-off do hardly any work at all. Their only occupation is raiding.

The report continues:

> The Cossack on the other hand, is an agriculturalist as well as a soldier. Being very often withdrawn from his military occupations by field work at home, he cannot use either horse or arms with the same

skill as the mountaineer; nor being for the most part of the time near his own house, is it possible for him to become acquainted with topographical details over a wide area . . . The Cossack . . . being on the defensive, spends most of the time vainly awaiting the enemy . . . Work and danger are almost his only lot – an insufficient compensation.[9]

Given these factors, the Kuban–Terek Line might well have become the empire's permanent southern border.

However, fate intervened. In 1801, the dying King George XII of the Kingdom of Georgia, south of the main Caucasus range, willed his realm to Alexander I of Russia, a fellow Orthodox Christian. In 1797, Georgia's Persian overlords had launched a particularly destructive invasion. Russia had already gone to war with Persia on occasion, the first time being in 1722, when Peter the Great invaded its northern Caspian provinces accompanied by a unit of Ukrainian Cossacks.[10] Now Alexander I annexed Georgia, aided by the Christian Ossetians, whose land formed a narrow bridge to Georgia, otherwise surrounded by hostile or unfriendly Muslim tribesmen and polities. Consequently, when the Russians began to expand southward, they arrived to conquer Caucasia (i.e., the whole region) from the centre and inside. It was those now-isolated northern tribesmen who exhibited the fiercest resistance to Russian rule.[11]

Over some seventy years, a series of competent and determined Russian generals ruthlessly crushed that resistance. A.P. Yermolov (1777–1861) set the tone for future commanders, Ivan F. Paskevych (1782–1856) was a Ukrainian nobleman with an aristocratic bearing from Poltava province, and Prince Aleksander I Bariatynsky (1814–1879) finally broke the resistance, able after the Crimean War ended in 1856 to transfer the bulk of Russia's now-numerous battle-hardened troops to the North Caucasus. Yermolov's term 1816–27 as viceroy of the Caucasus, military governor of the "line," and governor of Georgia established the basic strategy and tactics of Russian expansion.[12]

A veteran of the Napoleonic Wars and exposed to French influences, Yermolov held some progressive views that were critical of the autocracy. But in the Caucasus his principal tactic was to beat or scare the tribesmen to death. He steadily expanded Russian rule outward, conquered the East Lowlands, the so-called Shamkalate, made constant raids into the mountains, and built a great fortress in the north, which he boldly named Grozny (The Threatening), now capital of Chechnya. He once was reported to have said: "I desire that the terror of my name should guard our frontiers more potently than chains or fortresses, [and] that my word should be for the natives a law more inevitable than death. Condescension in the eyes of Asiatics is a sign of weakness, and out of pure humanity I am inexorably severe."[13]

Yermolov was also in these years ambassador to Persia, but with no time for diplomatic niceties. "My grim visage," he explained, "always expressed pretty clearly what I felt, and when I spoke of war conveyed the impression of a man ready to set his teeth into their throats. Unluckily for them, I noticed how little they liked this, and consequently, whenever more reasonable arguments were wanting, I relied on my wild beast's muzzle, gigantic and terrifying figure, and extensive throat; for they were convinced that anyone who could shout so vociferously must have good and weighty reasons."[14] Such ferocity was reciprocal. In 1829 the Russian envoy to Tehran, A.S. Griboedov, was ruthlessly murdered by Persians in the streets of their capital, his body left to rot amid a heap of corpses. Russia was hated for its expansion in the north, and the ambassador had sought apparently to protect escaped Armenian slaves.[15]

Yermolov was followed in the Caucasus by the more refined Paskevych, who, however, carried on most of his policies. He took the city of Kars in the western Caucasus and sent a Russian army to Armenia and Russian troops to Kurdistan in the south.

## Imam Shamil

Still, little progress was made in the north, where a Muslim revival move-ment led to an "Imamate," or religious state, in Dagestan, governed by a Sufi order, aiming to end tribal conflicts, blood feuds, and other impediments to the resistance. It also promoted simplicity, personal modesty, and disdain for worldly riches, banned pork and wine, and enforced a puritanical life on the mountaineers. It replaced *adat* (customary) law with Sharia, or Islamic law, and a series of leaders called imams preached *jihad* or *ghazavat* (Holy War) against the Russians. The last, and most illustrious and successful, of these, taking power in 1834, was Imam Shamil (1797–1871) (see Figure 9), whose followers were generally called *murids*.[16]

Although his forces were outnumbered and outgunned, Shamil's dar-ing tactics, personal bravery, dramatic escapes, and great charisma brought him many successes during almost three decades of struggle against the Russians. Being an ethnic Avar of Dagestan (Turkish for "Land of the Mountains"), and bearing one of the Arabic names of Allah, Shamil, meaning "universal" or "all-embracing," he was able to temporarily unite the mountain tribes, including even the ferocious Chechens, notorious for their blood feuds. But he was opposed by Muslim potentates of the eastern coast of the Black Sea, with more easy-going interpretations of Islam; as well, the Circassians of the north-west, most of them Muslim only in name, considered imam rule inappropriate for their more "feudal" social structure, which made allowances for different social and economic strata. But Shamil, like his predecessors, enjoyed considerable success in the high mountains and forests, where urban civilization had not yet extended its reach.

During the 1840s, Shamil performed his most spectacular feats, which became legendary in Caucasian, Russian, and even contemporary European history. The Russian army suffered some three thousand casualties at the siege of Akhungo, and in 1845 Shamil deteated Count Vorontsov in the Darango Expedition, destroying an entire Russian army of several thouasand men, including Shevchenko's friend de Balmen.[17] The most recent edition of Shevchenko's works (12 vols., 2003) is the only one ever in Ukraine to mention Shamil, discuss in some detail de Balmen's death, and quote an eyewitness:

> While [de Balmen] was on active service in the army, he was named deputy commander of the fifth corps of General O.M. Liders. During the Dargin expedition, when after the destruction of Shamil's residence, the army retreated to its old positions, Liders' corps, which followed the advance guard and was cut off from the main column, fell into a trap. The gorge was closed off. To re-establish contact with the High Command and with the goal of scouting out the situation that was developing, General O.M. Liders ordered his adjutant de Balmen out, and he was killed in a clash with the mountaineers in the district of the Shuan Heights.[18]

During the Crimean War (1853–56), Shamil remained active, even raiding Christian Georgia. During the conflict the French and British governments and most especially the Polish exiles and refugees in Ottoman Turkey tried to contact and support him, but never reached him. War's end brought the full force of Russia's enormous armies down on him, and they eventually captured him. By that time, he was already a legend across Russia and all of Europe. The Russians treated him honourably; he was received by Tsar Alexander II, and he was allowed, with his wives and suite, to live in Kaluga, a small town near Moscow.[19]

After several years in Kaluga, Shamil, old and unwell, asked to go on pilgrimage to Mecca. He gave his *parole d'honneur* to no longer oppose the tsar, became a Russian subject, and received the go-ahead. To prepare for his trip south he was given permission to move to the milder climate of Kyiv, where he stayed for two years.[20] Legend has it that inquisitive crowds gathered around his Kyiv home, and admiring radical students of the university and others (*raznochintsi*) threw notebooks with hand-written copies of "Kavkaz" at his carriage as it passed through the streets.[21]

From Kyiv, he went to Odessa and then on to Istanbul, where the court painter Stanisław Chlebowski, of Polish background from Podolia in right-bank (eastern) Ukraine, painted a famous portrait of him.[22] Shamil made it to Mecca, and died in Medina in 1871. His legend lived on; one of his sons served in the Russian military and another in the Ottoman, but in the 1920s a grandson returned to the Caucasus and again fought the Russians. Today a memorial plaque and a bust of Shamil grace Kyiv, and during the Russian–Ukrainian war, which began in 2014, his old house in Kyiv apparently became a gathering place for anti-Russian protesters, Ukrainian and Caucasian.[23]

## The Origins of "The Caucasus"

Shevchenko had heard something of the Caucasian War years before he wrote "The Caucasus" (Kavkaz). While he was studying in St Petersburg, it was a huge story, much in the newspapers – Russia's principal military engagement after it suppressed the Polish Uprising of 1830–31.[24] In the early 1840s, Shevchenko met Yakiv H. Kukharenko (1800–1862), lieutenant-colonel of the Kuban Cossack Army, defending the empire's southern flank against Circassian incursions in the Kuban and the western foothills of the Caucasus. Kukharenko was an amateur historian, ethnographer, and writer, already in contact with the historian Mykola Kostomarov and the Kharkiv circle of Ukrainian Romantic writers, who were also very interested in Cossack history, especially in the Zaporozhian ancestors of the Kuban Cossacks.[25]

Shevchenko became friends with Kukharenko immediately. One of his first letters to the colonel, dated early 1843, discusses ethnographic matters and a manuscript of Kukharenko's.[26] Many years later, before Shevchenko was returning home from central Asian exile, the now major-general wrote him on 8 August 1857: "Free yourself, dear friend, and come to our Cossack Ukraine!" But for some reason the poet decided on a more northern route instead. [27]

Their surviving correspondence never mentions Shamil, but in the early 1840s Kukharenko may well have told his new friend about the Caucasian resistance.[28] In October 1845, the poet's good friend O.S. Afanasiev-Chuzh-bynsky returned from the Caucasus and Transcaucasia, and Shevchenko questioned him closely about his impressions, as his interlocutor recorded in his memories of the poet. Thus Shevchenko must already have known something of Shamil, or his struggle, before he completed "Kavkaz" on 18 November 1845.[29]

If Shevchenko's poem offers few details of the Caucasian War, it is strong on its main drift and the merciless behaviour of both parties. But it places no hint of blame on those mountaineers, or on their unnamed leader. All of the poet's outrage is directed against rapacious Imperial Russia and its tsar, whom he held responsible for the terrible injustice inflicted on the freedom-loving mountaineers and his unfortunate friend.

"In its fundamentals," wrote the "Soviet" Ukrainian literary historian Mykola Zerov in the relatively liberal 1920s, "[the poem] is a romantic synthesis of nature and culture." His masterly summary of "Zavkaz" stresses Shevchenko's use of Prometheus, who pitied mankind and stole fire from the Gods for its use, but whom Zeus then tied to a rock high in the Caucasus with an eagle forever tearing at his flesh:

> The kindly, soft-spoken, warm-hearted but wild [*dykuny*] Caucasians are symbolized in the person of the Titan Prometheus, who was once tortured on these "blue mountains" "nestled in the clouds." Russian imperialism with its strong state organization, with its entire system of religious and political ideas, which sanctioned its attacks on those knights of the Caucasus Mountains, is symbolized by the eagle, which tears at his breast. Moral corruption and political hypocrisy enter the Caucasus together with the Russian Army. The most naked pillage is excused by Christian dogma. Sarcastic barbs like "From the Moldavian to the Finn . . ." follow one another in the poem with elevated pathos: ("For whom were you crucified, Christ, oh Son of God?"), and the poem ends with breaks in the tempo and a gentle, highly intimate lyricism ("and you, my dear and only friend have been driven to this").[30]

The intensity of Shevchenko's attack (one of several over the years) on the pseudo-benevolence of the all-powerful tsar,[31] and on the pseudo-Christian hypocrisy of the Russian imperial ideology, seems even more ferocious and timely while those Russians were attempting to destroy a Muslim culture and people, itself in the midst of its own religious revival.[32]

Nevertheless, after some time chained to those rocks with those eagles tearing at his flesh, Prometheus was eventually freed by Hercules. So even in this tortured symbolism, all was not yet lost. The central part of the poem was not given to weeping and despair, unlike the biblical epigram from Jeremiah at the start, but was rather a ringing call to arms:

> I vam slava, syni hory,
> Kryhoiu okruti.
> I vam, lytsari velyki,
> Bohom ne zabuti!
> Boritesia - poborete,
> Vam Boh pomahaie!
> Za vas pravda, za vas slava
> I volia sviataia!

In my humble translation, which hardly does justice to the piece, these lines read:

> And glory, mountains blue, to you,
> In blocks of frost encased!
> And glory, freedom's knights to you,
> Whom God will not erase!
> Keep fighting – you are sure to win!
> God aids you in your fight!
> Your fame and freedom grow not thin
> And on your side is right![33]

Such was the power of these ringing words in the vernacular Ukrainian that in the 1920s historian and political leader Mykhailo Hrushevsky made from them the motto and title of his émigré journal *Boritesia poborete!* (Fight and you will win!). The 1960s Ukrainian dissident poet Vasyl Symonenko likewise made them the motto of his stirring poem *Kurdskomu bratovi* (To a Kurdish Brother) at a time when the Kurds were under siege from occupying powers in mountainous Kurdistan. These words constituted the most important part of the first poem by Shevchenko ever translated into

English, in 1868 in the *Alaska Herald*, and were quietly omitted from the first collection of Shevchenko's poetry published in 1939 in the Chechen autonomous region of the USSR, although other of his revolutionary verses, such as his *Son* (The Dream) did appear.[34]

## Shevchenko, Shamil, and Echoes of the Caucasian War

Russian and Soviet accounts of Caucasian history could not ignore Shamil and his anti-Russian struggles but played them down, anxious to avoid furthering ethnic or national tensions. From the explosive, decentralizing conflicts of the Revolutions of 1917–21, through the time of partially re-asserted central control and more guarded sympathies and "liberation struggles" of the 1920s, Soviet accounts passed to an officially sanctioned "Great Friendship of Peoples" under Russian leadership of Stalin's time and later, playing down or denying anti-Russian efforts.[35] And the Russian/ Soviet authors of such accounts, and their Western counterparts, were duly impressed by the great empire's power, prestige, and culture and its dominant language and literature. Russian authors often noted the major Russian figures who wrote about the Caucasus and at times even acknowledged the continuing sufferings and oppression of its peoples. So mention of Pushkin, Lermontov, and Tolstoy seemed to be *de rigueur*.

But, despite their affection for the mountaineers, none of these icons, not even the sympathetic Tolstoy, went so far as Shevchenko. In his prose, Pushkin acknowledged Russian devastation, but not in his poetry, which exalted even the ogre Yermolov; while Lermontov lauded "the fearsome new Rome, which decorates the north with a new Augustus." And Tolstoy, of course, though a severe critic of the Russian state and its official religion, who painted a very positive picture of Shamil's lieutenant, Hadji Murat, never sanctioned the violence of those Muslim fighters in Chechnya, Dagestan, and Circassia, although he knew them much better than did either Pushkin or Lermontov, but tried only to understand and depict the ferocious conflict. None of those Russian writers displayed the outraged anger and fiery invective of the Ukrainian Shevchenko and so clearly took the rebel side. Zerov explains the difference as one between the pampered aristocrats and nobles, Pushkin and the others, and Shevchenko, the son of a serf, born into serfdom, who saw violence and oppression all around him and cried out in protest.[36]

Shevchenko's most recent biographer, Ivan Dziuba, who during Soviet days wrote the influential *samizdat* tract *Internationalism or Russification*, which argued for preserving Ukrainian culture in a tolerant socialist society, reiterated this point many times in writing on Shevchenko, postulating the poet's "internationalist" sympathies and position in this regard. In 2016 he noted that in 1930, just before Stalin's ascendancy, the Georgian writer Constantine Gamsakhurdia openly praised Shevchenko's spirited opposition to "the barbaric expansion of the Romanovs" and "greeted as brothers" the North Caucasus rebels.[37] Certainly, Shevchenko had a very profound effect on Akaki Tsereteli (1840–1915), the young Georgian student at St Petersburg University, whom he met in the spring of 1860 at one of his old friends Mykola Kostomarov's famous Thursday-evening parties. The three men discussed religious history, and Shevchenko suggested that Georgians and Ukrainians had a great deal in common. Tsereteli remembered that meeting and, when he became one of his country's great poets, acknowledged that he had learned much about national patriotism from the Ukrainian poet.[38]

But such international, or cosmopolitan ties between the southern nations are little known outside of Ukraine, Georgia, and even Russia. Western and non-Russian accounts of the Caucasian Wars, which followed the reports of Russian or Soviet historians, like those of Baddeley, Shauket Mufti, and others, do not even mention Shevchenko. They only paraphrase or mention Pushkin and Lermontov, and Mufti credits especially Tolstoy, who wrote so movingly about Hadji Murat, Shamil's lieutenant.[39] Whether they did this out of respect for Russian culture – and/or because they knew some Russian, but not Ukrainian language or culture, is unclear.[40]

Certainly, during the Cold War both Soviet Ukrainians (when allowed to) and Ukrainians living in western Europe, the United States, and especially Canada did their best to make Shevchenko better known, especially in English. But few of Shevchenko's major works, maybe just "Kavkaz," can be read usefully in translation without extensive annotation, which affects the reader's response. Such annotations were never done, despite several renderings into English, some of them quite good.[41]

Indeed, even in Soviet Ukrainian editions of Shevchenko's works, scholarly annotation was usually very weak and never mentioned Shamil by name, probably because of censorship. Even Yu.O. Ivankin's very detailed, book-length Soviet commentary to Shevchenko's poetry collection *Kobzar* (The Blind Minstrel, or The Kobza Player, 1840) referred to Shamil only once, in passing.[42] Until recently, only Leonid Biletsky's profusely annotated émigré, and fiercely anti-Russian Ukrainian-language edition spoke of Shamil.[43]

But if Shevchenko was the universalist and internationalist that biographer Ivan Dziuba made him out to be, then why did the West ignore him, unlike Pushkin and the others? Perhaps Ukrainian affairs have never mattered much here? But at least during the Cold War, human rights mattered, and today still do. Indeed, was Shevchenko so narrowly anti-Russian, only a Ukrainian patriot, that his angry verses repelled foreigners? At any rate, from the 1950s to the 2000s, both Westerners with democratic sympathies and Caucasian patriots generally ignored "Kavkaz." For example, a recent, strongly anti-Russian and pro-Chechen encyclopaedia of the Russian–Chechen conflict covers Pushkin, but ignores Shevchenko. Is it that this is because Ukrainian is little-known abroad, unlike Russian?[44]

## Critical Assessments of Shevchenko and "The Caucasus"

Opinion on the Ukrainian poet's nationalism versus his internationalism has always been divided, even among the people who knew him best. The Ukrainian novelist Panteleimon Kulish at one time thought him an excellent citizen, the poet of his people, and at another "a drunken muse," representing the worst of that people. The moderate St Petersburg Ukrainian historian Mykola Kostomarov considered him in no way radically anti-Russian – not "a Ukrainian separatist." In the substantially Polish Austrian Empire, another moderate, the Galician–Ukrainian writer Omelian Partytsky (1840–1895), championing "Kavkaz," wrote that Shevchenko directed all of his anger at Russia, ignoring his fierce criticism of the Poles, especially in *Haidamaky* (The Haidamak Rebels). Both he and Kostomarov seemingly strove to make the fiery poet acceptable to their own rulers, admitting his criticism only of their foreign rivals.

In the next generation, the Ukrainian socialist, federalist, and political thinker Mykhailo Drahomanov, who long lived abroad, was far more radical. He clearly saw this peculiar split between those two critics and concluded that Shevchenko had excoriated both Russian and Polish oppressors; he was a radical in his own way, but not necessarily "progressive." Drahomanov saw Shevchenko's rage as more like that of some biblical prophet than that of a man with a clear political program. So, it seems, Drahomanov was more critical of Shevchenko than his predecessors, as would be of most of his successors.[45] Yet he maintained high regard for the poet, and later, in exile in western Europe, popularized his endeavours in French, which reached Karl Marx, who, in his copy of Drahomanov's brochure *La littérature oukrainienne proscrite par le gouvernement russe* (1878), underlined the telling transnational phrase "from the Moldavians to the Finns, in every tongue, there is silence."[46]

About a decade or so later, Galician-Ukrainian radical Ivan Franko, in *Temne tsarstvo* (The Dark Empire), his detailed study of the political poems *Son* (The Dream) and "Kavkaz," pointed out that Shevchenko's political thought evolved. The poet started with a narrow Romantic elevation of Ukraine's Cossack past and criticized mostly its historical enemies – Turks, Tatars, Poles. But even in his *Haidamaky*, Franko noted, the poet thanked God that those violent days were passed, and he seemed to look forward to more friendly relations between Ukrainians and Poles. By the time he wrote "Kavkaz," concludes Franko, Shevchenko had become more "universalist," condemning "the Dark Empire," "from the Moldavians to the Finns," and sympathized openly with the Caucasian fighters. Franko's central thesis, that Shevchenko passed from localism to internationalism, proved valuable, and he even considered writing a doctoral dissertation on the subject at the University of Vienna. He never did that. But he did reprint this essay as a booklet for Shevchenko's centenary in 1914.[47]

In our times, George Grabowicz (born 1943) dismissed all specifics and historical circumstances and examples of Shevhencko's works and postulated that everything in them is primarily about good and evil, light and darkness – not local or national, but manichean and "mythic." His arguments quickly found a welcome public among Ukrainian literary critics, first in the West, and then later in independent Ukraine, who were used to thinking in either-or terms: émigrés idealized the national prophet, who raged against Russian domination; Soviets saw the prophet of social revolution, who raged against landlords and nobles and their oppression of the common people.[48]

Of course, the reality is that he was all of these things and more. Yes, he raged against the Muscovites and the Ukrainian nobles, but found some of his best friends and patrons among them, especially in Poltava province. Indeed, the stern and reactionary Nicholas I and his family freed him from serfdom, which reality must have troubled him when he turned so sharply against the tsar. Indeed, the resulting "cognitive dissonance" seems to have intensified his hatred of the injustices of the imperial system.

His life was full of such contradictions and psychological turmoil. For instance, not only did Yakiv de Balmen serve, if perhaps reluctantly, in the tsar's armies, but so too did the Cossack General Kukharenko. And what about the historian Kostomarov, who believed all states intrinsically evil, but bent over backwards to make things Ukrainian, including Shevchenko, acceptable to Moscow? And then there was the Poltavan Paskevych who crushed the Polish Uprising and fought in the Caucasus, decorated by the tsar and lionized in his Ukrainian homeland; and Kulish, who eagerly served the Russian administration in occupied Poland, but continued to contribute to Ukrainian literature, soon to be completely banned. [49]

Shevchenko's portrait of the anguished patriot de Balmen points to the more complicated nature of real life and a world far removed from dualism and myth. It is in this unlikely combination of fire mixed with melancholy, of hope mixed with dashed hopes, of compromise combined with endurance, and ultimately in noble ideals brought down to earth by bitter realities that Shevchenko's true genius lies. It is a genius that, despite the old claims of patriotic Soviet Ukrainian writers, is still not widely acknowledged today, although, Kulish and Drahomanov aside, it has never been seriously questioned in the fiery poet's homeland, and most probably never will be.

PART

# THREE

From Paris to Verkhivnia and the Sich:
The French Connection

## CHAPTER SIX

# All about Ève:
# The Realist Balzac's Ukrainian Dreamland

## *La comédie humaine*

HONORÉ DE BALZAC (1799–1850) is famous for his massive, multi-volume series of realistic novels and stories, collected as *La comédie humaine* (The Human Comedy). What is less known about him: he dreamed for many years of moving eastward to the Slavonic world and eventually spent almost two years on an estate in Ukraine about a hundred kilometres from Kyiv, on the west, or right bank of the Dnieper River, near the town of Berdychiv. The story of how this happened constitutes the real "novel of his life," as more than one of his biographers have put it.[1]

Balzac was of very modest origins. His grandfather had been a peasant from the south, his father a minor bureaucrat in revolutionary and Napoleonic France, and he himself added the "de" to his surname to make it sound more aristocratic. A spendthrift and poor businessman – he failed in mass-market publishing, Sardinian silver mines, and Ukrainian lumber – he ran up enormous debts and had to work day and night, literally in a monk's robe, and with endless cups of coffee, to pay off these debts. But he was an acute observer of the emerging bourgeois world around him and described its inhabitants in great detail in his penetrating stories and novels. He described the internal side of things, but also their causes, social and otherwise. He appeared to be driven by some unseen and unrelenting hand to describe in almost-encyclopaedic fashion the manners and morals of the entire, bustling society in which he lived. Many of his characters were consumed by passions and manias, be it greed, desire for honour, even love.

Balzac titled this great project in imitation of Dante's *Divine Comedy*, often considered the masterwork of medieval European literature. Like Dante, he divided his life's work into three parts: in his case, studies of manners, philosophical studies, and analytical studies, of which only the first part neared completion before he died. Balzac pioneered the use of the all-knowing, neutral narrator to tell his stories and created over two thousand characters in them. He described many of them in great depth, bringing them up recurrently, and did the same for his settings. This too was a completely new technique and has been imitated many times since. The American writer Elbert Hubbard once said that it was Balzac who discovered that not merely the heroic and the romantic, but every human life, is interesting, that life itself is a struggle, and that most battles are bloodless, and romance a dream, although all are very real. Moreover, Hubbard continued, he broke all the established rules of writing: he preferred prose to poetry, walked over French grammar, invented phrases, coined words, and used the language of ordinary people to "defile the well of classic French." The public loved it, but the critics did not, and it took him many years before he was eventually accepted as one of France's greatest writers.[2]

Politically, Balzac was a Legitimist, who supported the restoration of the absolutist Bourbon dynasty of France. He saw such a change as the only cure for the pettiness, untrammelled ambition, and "curse of money" thriving under the uninspiring King Louis Philippe (d'Orléans) (reigned 1830–48). And so, his criticism of French bourgeois society was sweeping, doubtless pushed to extremes by his own pecuniary difficulties. Yet this ultra-reactionary rightist was also idolized by the political left. His friend Victor Hugo considered him a genius and a revolutionary, and both Marx and Engels devoured his novels, the latter observing:

> Balzac gives us a most remarkable realist history of French society, describing it in the form of a chronicle, almost year by year from 1816 to 1848. He shows how bourgeois society, growing ever stronger, put ever more pressure on the society of the nobles, which after 1815 restructured itself, and in so far as it was possible, showed itself as a model of old French ideals. He reveals how the last remains of this model society steadily perished under pressure from the vulgar

money-grubber . . . Around this central picture, Balzac wound the whole history of French society in which I even recognize more in its economic detail . . . than in the books of all the specialists of that time taken together, including historians, economists, and statisticians.[3]

This resounding praise would return after 1917 to haunt Soviet authorities, seeking to contort Marxist "dialectics" to explain how such a perceptive observer of society as Balzac could be so blindly "reactionary."

But we are getting ahead of ourselves. By character, Balzac was anything but the refined and elegant aristocrat. His carriage was awkward, his manner coarse. He was short, with square shoulders and a deep chest. But he held his head high and had the poise of a man born to command. No scholar's stoop nor the genius's abiding melancholy for him, says Hubbard. His smile was broad and infectious, and he was always ready for fun: "He has never grown up; he is just a child," his mother complained when he was already past forty. Other women would say the same.

## Letters from *"L'Étrangère"*

Perhaps it was this youthful enthusiasm that so endeared him to women, for they were among his most avid readers and passionate admirers. Indeed, many of his stories and characters spoke directly to girls and women and their complex and often-frustrating situation. He seemed to have an understanding of mature women that other male writers of his time lacked. Although he was never close to his mother, many other women, from his sister to his older companion, Mme de Berny – "La Dilecta," as he called her – had taught him much about how women felt and thought, and they urged him to set it all down in writing, which he soon did.

The response was a steady stream of letters from female readers all over Europe. In 1832, he noticed one stamped at Odessa, in the Russian Empire, carefully written on quality paper and clearly from a very cultivated person. The letter praised his previous writings, but expressed disappointment with his latest book, which supposedly was much less sympathetic to women. The message was unsigned.

Balzac spoke of it to several friends. Then a second letter came, then a third, although none of these have survived. Finally, another, dated 7 November 1832, arrived. Vincent Cronin translates it:

Monsieur,

It would hardly be surprising should I, a foreigner, use expressions that seem to you rather un-French, but write to you I must, to tell you with all possible enthusiasm how deeply your books have affected me.

Your soul, Monsieur, is centuries-old; your philosophy seems to be based on age-long study, and yet I am told that you are still young. I should like to know you, yet I do not think I need to: a soul-instinct gives me a presentiment of you; I imagine you in my own way, and if I happen to see you I should say, "There he is!"

As I read your books my heart bounded; you raise woman to her rightful dignity and show her love as a heavenly virtue, a divine emanation; I admire the attractive sensibility of soul which allowed you to discover these things . . . I should like to write to you sometimes, to send you my thoughts and reflections . . . I have strength, energy, and courage only for what seems to me to join with my dominant feeling: Love! . . . I knew how to love and still do . . .

Again, the letter was anonymous, signed only *"L'Étrangère"* (the [female] foreigner).[4]

But it advised Balzac to put a note to its writer in the royalist French newspaper *La Quotidienne* (The Daily), the only French paper allowed into the Russian Empire. He was to sign it simply: "A. l'E – h.b." Balzac replied immediately and soon received further letters. Eventually, a trusted courier carried messages back and forth, although Balzac's correspondent remained anonymous. "I should be lost if anyone knew that I write to you and receive letters from you," she confided to him, vowing eternal anonymity.[5]

## Neuchâtel (1833) and Later

Before too long, however, another letter from L'Étrangère reported that she and her husband –for indeed she was married, with a young daughter – would soon be visiting western Europe and she might meet Balzac in Neuchâtel in Switzerland, but very discreetly. In September 1833, the two finally met. His unnamed admirer turned out to be beautiful, slightly over thirty, from eastern Europe, still young and vivacious, intelligent, very well read in European literature, thoughtful, sensitive, elegant, and aristocratic of manner. Ewelina Hańska, née Rzewuska, came from one of the great families of the old Polish–Lithuanian Commonwealth, related to Polish royalty, with large estates in Ukraine, by then part of the Russian Empire.

What a contrast to Balzac, the awkward and ambitious writer who only pretended to be an aristocrat! He was short, overweight, and not very good looking at all. But he still had something magnetic about him (Figure 10). "A happy wild-boar," was how one friend described him, and his ever good humour and infectious enthusiasm for life (he was only thirty-four) soon swept the young lady from Ukraine completely away. They vowed eternal love and met again the next December in Geneva, where they became lovers.[6]

But Ewelina's husband, Wacław Hański, was a problem. A Polish nobleman, he was about twenty years older than his wife and in bad health, but not expected to die soon. Balzac was introduced to him and was soon playing the role of a family friend. In fact, the two men got along quite well, agreeing on politics and having a mutual interest in the economics of agriculture, for Hański, it transpired, was one of the richest men in Ukraine and owned a vast estate in the province of Kyiv with thousands of hectares of good agricultural land and many thousands of serfs to work them. He and Ewelina – "Ève" to Balzac – lived in a great, neoclassical château called "Verkhivnia," with an enormous colonnaded portico, dozens of elegant rooms, a large library of thousands of volumes, furniture from around the world, rich Persian carpets, and hundreds of household serfs to look after them. The house had even its own hospital with a resident doctor. Ève and her daughter, Anna, were heirs to all this.

Balzac was quite swept away by his good fortune. Love! Beauty! Aristocracy! Enormous wealth! And Hański actually invited him to visit the family in Ukraine, sending him a large engraved print of his great home! Ève, however, held back. The situation was complicated and dangerous, and she knew it. After her return to Verkhivnia she continued to correspond with Balzac, and some of her letters were quite passionate. The separated lovers had to wait.[7]

Meanwhile, Hański lived on, despite his poor health. At one point, he intercepted some of Balzac's letters to his wife and was outraged. But the resourceful French writer, who was in the habit of writing to Ève almost every day, dreamed up an excuse, and the cuckolded husband, ever trusting, actually believed it or, at least, pretended to. This went on for several years, Balzac thinking more and more of his beautiful love in far-off Ukraine. This did not prevent him from having affairs with other women, and, indeed, word reached Ève about these, but again he talked his way out of the difficulty, and her suspicions were quieted. He never was to completely give up on his dreamy vision of Ukraine as a quiet oasis in the desert of life's troubles that he now dearly wished to visit.

## Who Were the Hańskis?

But what was Ukraine really like then, and who were the Hańskis? The answers to both questions are complicated. In the 1830s and 1840s, the name "Ukraine" was not used for the western parts of today's Ukraine, then under the Austrians, or even for other western provinces like Podolia and Volhynia. But it did cover the Kyiv region and lands further east, extending well into what are today parts of southern Russia, specifically the provinces of Kursk and Voronezh (Ukrainians and Russians then called the more eastern parts of these spacious territories "Sloboda [= free, non-serf] Ukraine." At that time, it was all ruled by the stern Tsar Nicholas I, with his infamous Third Department of political police. On the east, or left bank of the Dnieper River, which ran through the middle of the country, most of the nobility was descended from the old Cossack officer class, and part of the peasantry was still free, being designated as "state peasants." But on the western, or right bank, where the Hańskis lived, the nobility was almost all Polish, and the peasants were Ukrainian serfs, with far fewer state peasants around and a harder life for the common people. The towns had a very large Jewish population and very few Ukrainian residents. Thus, in this part of Ukraine, Russia ruled, Poles held the land, and Ukrainians worked it.[8]

Coming from one of the most distinguished families of old Poland, which had governed this part of Ukraine, Ewelina and her siblings might have had feelings for Poland, which had risen against the Russian occupiers in 1830–31; many refugees from that abortive effort lived in France. In fact, the three greatest landholding families of Ukraine – Branickis, Potockis, and Rzewuskis – sustained the Confederation of Targowica (a town in central Ukraine), which opposed the reforming king, Stanisław Augustus Poniatowski (reigned 1764–95) and the progressive constitution of 3 May 1791, which attempted to re-organize the Polish–Lithuanian Commonwealth and save it from its voracious neighbours. The Confederates brought on Russian intervention and Poland's partition.

Ewelina's father loyally served as a senator in the capital, St Petersburg; sister Caroline charmed both the Polish poet Adam Mickiewicz and the

Russian poet Aleksandr Pushkin before marrying a Russian general and spying for the Russians, and brother Adam served in the Russian military, helping put down the Polish Rising of 1830, and ending as commander of the Kyiv garrison. He died in 1888 at Verkhivnia, having purchased it from the Hańskis. After 1860, he engaged the artist Napoleon Orda as a music teacher, and Orda engraved the famous picture of that great house.[9] Brother Henryk, to whom Ewelina was closest, wrote tales of old Poland, including "The Zaporozhian," but became an apologist for Russian autocracy, declaring Poland dead. Ewelina seems to have had similar attitudes, though perhaps showing some interest in the Romantic writers of the Ukrainian School of Polish Literature, such as Antoni Malczewski and "the nightingale," Józef Bohdan Zaleski.[10]

There was one family member not indifferent to the Polish national cause, and also passionate about the Middle East, and deeply knowledgeable: Ewelina's uncle Count Wacław Rzewuski/Viacheslav Revusky (1784–1831), whom we met above in chapter 2. Aware of his family's anti-Polish stance, he went his own way, travelled extensively in the Middle East, dressed as an Arab "emir," bred Arabian horses, and even wrote a book on that subject. He had a château at Savran, also in right-bank Ukraine. He was a friend, sponsor, and prolific collaborator of the Austrian Orientalist Joseph von Hammer-Purgstall. Rzewuski patronized the poet Tymko Padura, who wrote in the Ukrainian vernacular about a time when Poles and Cossacks had fought together against common enemies like the Ottomans and the Muscovites. The "Emir," as he was called, joined the Polish Rising of 1830 but disappeared without trace in battle. It was rumoured that he had escaped to Arabia and lived on among the Muslims. Poets and authors such as Mickiewicz, Słowacki, and Wincenty Pol magnified his legend.[11]

The family of Ewelina's husband, Wacław Hański, was less exalted than the Rzewuskis but very rich. Hański himself was soft-spoken and sober and a great collector of books and artefacts. He once boasted that none of the furniture at Verkhivnia came from Russia; it was all imported. But he was no intellectual, and Ewelina could not share her intellectual adventures with him. Moreover, his bouts of depression were quite hard on her. He loved her, it was said, but was not in love with her and busied himself with his estates.

Hański had much prestige as marshal of the nobility of Kyiv province, but in that role carried out instructions from St Petersburg and from Military Governor D.G. Bibikov to disenfranchise the minor nobles, thus greatly speeding up russification. The 340,000 Polish nobles whom he helped to disenfranchise were reduced to peasants, were subjected to heavy taxation, lost access to higher education, and were often forced into the Russian military for twenty-five years of service.

Hański was known for his severity with his Ukrainian serfs. Ewelina's cousin Stanisław Rzewuski testified that years later these serfs recalled his brutal behaviour, at a time when noblemen could insult, beat, or even kill a serf virtually scot-free. More conscientious Polish noblemen like the writers Seweryn Goszczyński and Józef Kraszewski never ceased to denounce the savagery of some of their compatriots. The historian Daniel Beauvois speculates that perhaps Ewelina's romantic and idealized letters to Balzac reflected some kind of subconscious desire to escape from her cruel world.[12]

## St Petersburg Tryst (1843)

In 1842, a letter arrived for Balzac informing him that Hański had died. The debt-ridden novelist, now approaching the height of his fame, was ecstatic! He wrote to Ève anticipating their living together, but she had heard of his womanizing in France and "set him free." Her family, who had never liked or accepted the plebeian and vulgar Frenchman, contested the will to keep the estate from him. The court in Kyiv agreed, and the widow now had to go to St Petersburg to appeal the verdict. But Balzac continued to write passionate letters to her, and by the middle of the next year his tone had changed, and she invited him to join her and Anna in the Russian capital.

Balzac immediately went to the Russian embassy in Paris to apply for a visa. There the young diplomat Victor Balabin already seemed to know something of him. Within the embassy plans were immediately laid to make use of this popular, monarchist writer to counteract the scathing criticism of Russia in the new book *La Russie en 1839* (Russia in 1839) by the Marquis de Custine, whose father had been executed during the French Revolution and should, the Russians assumed, have looked favourably on their monarchy. Balabin disapproved of Balzac's appearance and manners but still recommended using him to counter de Custine's book.[13]

By the summer of 1843, Balzac was in St Petersburg with Ève. They had not seen each other in many years, and pursuit by creditors and terrible overwork had visibly aged him. But she was just as attractive to him as ever, and they got on well together. Largely at his urging, they planned marriage sometime in the future. The Russian government, however, stood in the way. Even if Ève won her lawsuit, she would not be allowed to marry a foreigner, as this would give him certain rights to the inheritance. Balzac had offered to become a Russian subject and go to the tsar to ask permission for their marriage, but the tsar would not see him, despite his fame and potential to do much for the Russian image abroad. Nevertheless, the couple spent two glorious months together in the Russian capital. They strolled the streets together, saw the sights, and made love. In the autumn, he returned to Paris, still hoping to one day marry Ève and see Verkhivnia.

Events then moved rapidly: news arrived that Ève was pregnant. Balzac was ecstatic and was sure it was a boy, whom he immediately named Victor. But she lost the child and won her lawsuit, so her daughter, Anna, could receive inheritance rights. Anna meanwhile had agreed to marry Count Jerzy Mniszech, owner of a large estate in Podolia, near Austrian Galicia. They travelled west for the ceremony and wed in Dresden. Balzac was a witness. By this time as well, Ève had begun sending Balzac money to pay off his ever-recurring debts, although she could never quite keep up with his free-spending habits.

## Verkhivnia, at Last (1847)

Nevertheless, by 1847 Ève's old objections to Balzac's visiting Ukraine had all dried up, and she finally invited him to Verkhivnia. He replied that for him Ukraine, with its wide steppes, peasants, and Jews, with its conjunction of "civilization and barbarism," as he put it, was the one place where he could discover "completely new people and things." In September, he travelled by train and then coach across the continent – uneventfully till western Galicia, which had been turned upside down by a great peasant uprising the previous year. The local Polish aristocracy had rebelled against the Austrian emperor, but the clever Austrians used the emperor's benevolent reputation among the peasants to turn them against their landlords. The result was a massacre, the last great "*jacquerie*" (violent peasant rebellion) seen in Europe west of Russia. By the time Balzac passed through, the rebellion was over and the peasants were now starving. Balzac blamed it all on the noble Polish rebels, whom he thought inspired by unrealistic Polish émigrés in France. "Let men die, but long live principles!" he exclaimed sarcastically. His prescription: replace Austrian rule with Russian autocracy and social order![14]

Crossing the border into the Russian Empire, Balzac felt he was indeed leaving Europe. He was greatly impressed by the wide spaces, endless fields

of wheat, empty lands and roads dotted with the great houses of Polish aristocrats, almost all in the neoclassical style: "those rare and splendid dwellings,"
he wrote, "surrounded by parks, with their copper roofs shimmering in the
distance." Finally, he reached Berdychiv, which he considered the beginning
of "Ukraine," where he was surrounded by a crowd of Jews, who, he later
claimed, suspiciously eyed his golden watch. "It was the desert," he later wrote
in his unfinished *Lettre sur Kiew*, "the kingdom of wheat, the Prairies of Fenn-
imore Cooper, and their silence. The sight filled me with dismay, and I fell into
a deep sleep. At half-past five, I was awoken [and] . . . saw a Louvre or a Greek
temple, gilded by the setting sun, overlooking a valley." It was Verkhivnia.[15]

Balzac spent four and a half months at Verkhivnia with Ève, Anna, and
Jerzy ("Georges" to Balzac). They all got on very well, and Balzac was happy. He had finally found his refuge from his relentless creditors, his oasis
in the desert. He even managed to do some writing, starting his *Lettre sur
Kiew* and composing a few other pieces. But at the same time, he seemed
oblivious to the injustice surrounding him. He took a very mixed view of
the peasants and serfs he saw and met, thinking them potential insurgents,
like the Polish peasants of western Galicia. Peasants, in Balzac's view, especially in France, were generally sly, greedy, idle, promiscuous, and not very
bright; but in "Russia," at least, so he thought, they were well controlled by
the tsar. In Ukraine, he believed them happy, secure under the benevolent
emperor. Unlike in France, they actually sang on their way to work! They
were like children, and serfdom was actually good for them. "In this paradise," he noted, "there are actually seventy-seven different ways of baking
bread from the abundant wheat!"[16]

Of course, Balzac, the great realist writer, was completely unaware of the
geographical, historical, and ethnographical peculiarities of the land he was
visiting: he had no accurate idea of where Ukraine actually began or ended
(simply following Polish traditions) or of the linguistic and cultural differences between Ukrainians and Russians (he thought Hański a "Ukrainian"
count). For him, Ève was his "north star," and Kyiv "the northern Rome."
Little did he know that Russians considered Ukraine their own South, their
"Russian Italy." Moreover, only a few months earlier the tsar's police had
imprisoned or exiled the brilliant national awakeners Taras Shevchenko, Mykola Kostomarov, and Panteleimon Kulish, leaders of the patriotic
Brotherhood of Saints Cyril and Methodius, which wanted to abolish serfdom and the Russian tsardom and replace them with a free federation of
independent Slavic states, centring on Ukraine.[17]

When Balzac went to visit Kyiv, he met some of the tsarist officials who had dealt with the Cyril-Methodians. The historian I.I. Funduklei, the civil governor of Kyiv, gave a large banquet in his honour, which local notables, both Russian and Polish, attended. A cultured man, Funduklei had earlier tried to warn Kostomarov of his impending arrest. Had he succeeded, the sentences would probably have been much lighter. Mikhail Yuzefovich, a school official of Ukrainian background, had turned against the Cyril-Methodians and pursued nationally conscious Ukrainians throughout his decades in government service. Three of Balzac's letters to him have been preserved. And there was also Bibikov, the military governor, to whom Balzac eventually had to apply for permission to stay in Ukraine. Bibikov had forwarded the reports on the Brethren to St Petersburg, where they were read by Crown Prince Alexander. There is no evidence that Balzac knew about any of this.[18]

## Paris–Verkhivnia–Paris (1848–50)

In January 1848, Balzac "very sadly" left his Ukrainian dreamland for France and his literary obligations and creditors. The next month, early in Europe's year of revolution, Louis Philippe was overthrown, and a new French republic declared. Balzac predicted its quick demise, but he was upset with these events and the complications for his work. He fled back to Ukraine just as soon as he could obtain a visa. The tsar, by now very suspicious of Frenchmen, granted it, but noted in the margins of the request: "Yes, yes, but under strict surveillance." On 20 September 1848, the besieged writer again departed for Ukraine.[19]

This time he traveled a bit more slowly, and after crossing the border into the Russian Empire, stopped at Vyshnevets, the great castle/palace complex that was the pride of the Mniszech estate in Podolia. The castle had been built in the seventeenth century and renovated several times by the famous Vyshnevetsky family, which had included Dmytro Ivanovych Vyshnevetsky, who became the legendary Cossack hetman Baida (d. 1653), and Poland's King Michael I Wiśniowecki (reigned 1669–73) – "the Ruthenian king," as some have called him. At this time, Balzac dreamed up the idea of using Ukrainian lumber from the Mniszech estates to export to France, which was desperate for railway ties. But, as usual for Balzac, this project never took off. The writer continued eastward and by 2 October had arrived at Verkhivnia.

Balzac settled in quite well, expecting to write a great deal, trapped, as it were, by the snow and ice of the long Ukrainian winter. He was, of course, well-liked by Anna and Georges, but also by the household servants, who found him "wise" and "considerate." He missed his Parisian cuisine, but soon grew to like the local tea blends and the food products made from millet, buckwheat, oats, barley, and even tree-bark. (Ukrainians traditionally made excellent sherbet from poplar sap; and *kasha*, or buckwheat porridge, has long been a staple.) Balzac was treated as the "old man of the family," surrounded by respect and affection. "The domestic who serves me here was recently married," he wrote his sister in France, "and he and his wife came to pay their respects to their masters. The woman and man actually lie down flat on their stomachs, touch the floor three times with their heads, and kiss your feet." The Frenchman's conclusion: they really knew how to do things right in "Russia"![20]

Although word eventually came that he would be permitted to wed Ève, Balzac's health took a sharp turn for the worse that winter. It had been bad for years, constantly aggravated by late hours, overwork, and too much coffee. His heart was ailing, and now he caught a terrible cold. It seemed that life was finally beginning to drain from him, he who had always been so strong. By springtime, Ève, seeing the writing on the wall, finally had mercy on him and agreed to marry. On 14 March 1850, they wed at a small ceremony in the Church of St Barbara in Berdychiv. Both of them fell sick on the way back to Verkhivnia.

She quickly recovered. But he did not. He blamed the Ukrainian winter for his illness, which the local physicians could not cure, and decided to return to Paris, to a house he had bought and furnished with his wife's Ukrainian money, but the trip to France only aggravated his condition, and everyone soon knew that he was dying. He passed away in Paris on 15 August 1850, in his debt-ridden house, filled with expensive art and artefacts from all over Europe, and the large print of Verkhivnia, given to him so many years before by Hański, still hung prominently on the wall. Balzac had never ceased to dream of that paradise on earth he called "Ukraine," but of which he really knew, or chose to know, so little.

At his graveside, Balzac's friend Victor Hugo pronounced a funeral oration, which stressed the nation's unity in mourning at his passing. But Marxist literary historians, both then and now, have seen the French writer's life as filled with what they call "contradictions." Political of course: a reactionary and supporter of absolute monarchy whose writings battered down the falsehoods and exposed the injustices of bourgeois French society, and so fulfilled a "progressive" function. As a result, through much of Soviet history, Balzac was frequently translated into Russian, printed and reprinted, and widely read by Russians and Ukrainians. During periods of political thaw, Ukrainian translations also appeared, also consumed widely.[21]

However, the non-Marxist historian may take this point about "contradictions" beyond economics and politics, and see the great irony of the foremost founder of "realist" European literature, who was totally "unrealistic" in his personal life. He remained to the end an unthinking child in his finances, a hare-brained businessman always concocting disastrous new schemes, a sociologist who could not see the forest for the trees, a lover who strove always for the unreachable, the forbidden, and the distant, and last of all, a dreamer, who saw paradise where it was not. He was, in fact, no realist in life, but rather a hopeless romantic, and the tragedy of his biography was fully revealed by his late marriage and early death, just returned from a dreamland that bore no relation whatsoever to reality. The terrible revolutions and wars that consumed that dreamland in the century following his death proved it beyond any possible doubt.

As to Ukrainian attitudes towards the French writer, these remain divided. Although Ukrainian historians tend to admit his towering role in European literature, they obviously dislike some of his attitudes towards their homeland and his ignorance of its history. For example, the left-leaning émigré in France Ilko Borshchak, put off by Balzac's "miserly" notes on Ukraine, in contrast to Hugo and Mérimée's more sympathetic and substantial contributions, only grudgingly admitted his greatness.[22] And D.S. Nalyvaiko, though still constrained by Soviet censors on the very threshold of the Gorbachev reforms, compared him to Homer, Dante, Shakespeare, Tolstoy, and Gorky, and called for a complete Ukrainian-language edition of his works, which was never done. Nalyvaiko argued that what Tolstoy was for Lenin, Balzac was for Marx.[23] Most troubling for Ukrainians seems to be not just Balzac's ignorance of Ukrainian culture and history, but his extreme views on class and empire, although, of course, they could not openly say that until 1991.

Verkhivnia today is a school of agronomy in an independent and democratic Ukraine, where the great-grandchildren of serfs study in the halls and parlours where Honoré de Balzac and Ewelina Hańska once walked and sat, discussed literature, and sipped birch juice. It is said that in 1917 the last private owner of the estate, still a Rzewuski, seeing the storm of revolutionary destruction all around him, and before fleeing west, beseeched the local peasants not to burn it to the ground. Those simple Ukrainian peasants, so it seems, were far more "civilized" than Balzac ever thought.

## CHAPTER SEVEN

# La Guzla, Gogol, and the Cossacks: Prosper Mérimée Looks East

## A Passion for Far-off Places and Unusual Subjects

PROSPER MÉRIMÉE (1803–1870) was a distinguished French writer and novelist who was widely read throughout the nineteenth and twentieth centuries. All over the world he featured on the curriculum for students of French, so virtually all of them at some time read his short novels, which – brief, direct, with exciting plots, exotic settings, and strong characters – readily appealed to young people. His classical style but Romantic content made for easy but interesting reading.

In politics, this innovative writer was an inveterate liberal. During the restoration of the monarchy that followed Napoleon's 1815 defeat, he was a critic of the absolutist Bourbons; after 1830, when a constitutional monarchy was proclaimed, and his fellow liberals came to power, especially the ministers François Guizot and Adolphe Thiers, he held various government posts; after the Revolution of 1848, which eventually led to the re-establishment of the liberal "Empire," he was close to the court of the Emperor Napoleon III, by whom he was appointed senator.

During most of his life, Mérimée combined public service with literature, where he repeatedly revealed his devotion to the historical heritage of France and his interest in far-off places and unusual subjects. Mérimée, it is said, was both "a liberal" and "a conservationist," and, known for his dryness and *froideur*, he had what one particularly perceptive critic called "a cold passion" for the events of life. These very visible contradictions, together with his vacillating between Romantic and post-Romantic, defined much of his literary career.[1]

Nietzsche characterized him as a refined artist, much taken with the past, who actually despised "the spongy" liberalism (*schwammingen Gefühle*) of his own time. That is, he was unimpressed by small beauties and little charms, which he was ready to sacrifice to a strong will, and so remained a pure rather than a great soul, while being "pessimist enough to be able to play along with the comedy [of life] without being sickened by it."[2]

Nietzsche, of course, was an extremist and very jaded. But such debates about Mérimée were so frequent that one contemporary declared that he never belonged to any literary school at all – neither a Romantic nor a classicist, neither a naturalist nor an idealist, always measured, never exaggerating. He always sought only elegance and perfection of the word. And the English expression "Brevity is the soul of wit" suited him perfectly – although he did not write much, what he wrote was always interesting, significant, even jarring.[3]

Attracted to exotic locales and foreign countries, this "hyper-Frenchman," as Guy Dumur called him, "who embodied all of the qualities and faults of his race," eventually learned some Russian, and introduced and interpreted Russian literature for the French.[4] And late in life he wrote two important studies of the Ukrainian Cossacks, especially their great leader, or hetman, Bohdan Khmelnytsky (d. 1657), who had ended Polish rule in Ukraine and established a de facto independent Ukrainian state.[5]

When Mérimée took up Khmelnytsky as a subject, the name "Ukraine" had been long gone from maps, and the Ukrainian Cossacks almost completely forgotten in western Europe. As a lad, Mérimée had been shocked to see "Russian" Cossacks occupying Paris at the end of the Napoleonic Wars. Shortly afterwards, Lord Byron and Victor Hugo wrote their famous poems on the Cossack leader Ivan Mazepa (1639–1709; hetman 1687–1708), but little accurate information about Ukraine was available to the general public. Older French writers like the seventeenth-century engineer/cartographer Guillaume le Vasseur Sieur de Beauplan, working in the Polish–Lithuanian Commonwealth, and the eighteenth-century historian of the Ukrainian Cossacks, the Alsatian Jean-Benôit Scherer, were by then little read, as indeed was even Napoleon's expert on the Cossacks, Charles-Louis Lesur. Thus Mérimée helped spread the word about Ukraine wherever French was known.[6]

Modern Ukrainians and Russians are proud that such an eminent French author paid such serious attention to their homelands, and Soviet experts considered Mérimée a bourgeois but relatively "progressive" writer, who, as they put it, took up literary arms against "feudalism" and religion. His novellas were assiduously collected, and a Russian-language edition of his collected works came out in six volumes in the 1930s, and again in the 1960s, and his two major works on the Ukrainian Cossacks appeared in Ukrainian in the 1990s. But who exactly was this French writer with a peculiar name, so honoured by the Soviets, and what did he actually write about Ukraine?[7]

## A Three-Phase Career

Prosper Mérimée (Figure 11) was the son of the artist/civil servant Léonor Mérimée and a relatively well-educated mother, Anne Moreau, a grand-daughter of the prolific writer Mme Jeanne-Marie Leprince de Beaumont, author of *Beauty and the Beast*. His parents were supporters of Napoleon, "Voltaireans" of a sort, indifferent to religion, and gave him an unusual, non-Christian first name (which embarrassed him throughout his life), and almost certainly did not even have him baptized. He attended the Lycée Napoléon in Paris (later the Collège Henri IV). That school maintained the rationalist traditions of the French Enlightenment, and Napoleon was still greatly admired there. In consequence, Prosper remained either indiffer-ent or hostile to organized religion throughout his career; but he early on acquired a nagging interest in superstition and magic. This peculiar combi-nation lasted his whole life and popped up again and again in his writings, including those about eastern Europe.

Literary historians and biographers generally see three phases in Mérimée's writings – roughly 1820–30, 1830–50, and 1850–70. First, in the 1820s, under the Bourbon Restoration (1815–30), he dabbled in drama, liter-ary "mystifications" or fakes, folk poetry, and prose, especially storytelling with anecdote, plot and personality central. When he was seventeen, in 1820, he translated the Scot James Macpherson's *Ossian* (1760), about the legendary past, progenitor of modern literary hoaxes. In 1825 Mérimée's *Théâtre de Clara Gazul* (1825) appeared, supposedly the rediscovered plays of a female Spanish writer, but actually by Mérimée himself. Even though Mérimée dressed up in Spanish women's garb and posed for the frontis-piece, only a few friends recognized him.[8] In 1827, he published *La Guzla, ou choix de poésies illyriques, recuellies dans la Dalmatie, la Bosnie, la Cro-atie, et l'Herzégowine*, ostensibly a collection of "Illyrian" or Serbian and Croatian folksongs.

Other early works include the stories in *La Jaquerie* [sic] (1828), on a medieval peasant revolt; *Tamango* (1829), about a Black slave in the United States; his tragic Corsican short story *Mateo Falcone* (1829); and *L'enlève-ment de la redoute* (1829), about the French siege of the Shevardino redoubt, near Borodino, Russia, in September 1812.

His first great historical novel, *Chronique du règne de Charles IX* (1829), was a "cloak and dagger" tale about France's late-sixteenth-century Wars of Religion and the St Bartholomew's Day Massacre of 1572, a volume disparaging religion. But the social implications of these revolutionary stories were unmistakable, and Soviet authors often noted them.[9]

In his second phase, during the constitutional monarchy of Louis Philippe (1830–48), Mérimée's attraction to the shocking anecdote and strong personality came to the fore, and he proved himself a master of the new short novel or novella, best exemplified in *Colomba* (1840), set in untamed Corsica, and *Carmen* (1845), the story of a wild gypsy girl set in Spain, and the inspiration for Bizet's fiery opera. He was appointed France's inspector general of historical monuments and began writing reports on his frequent travels to preserve those treasures, many badly damaged or destroyed during the Revolution. Both the great Cathedral of Notre Dame in Paris and the walled town of Carcassonne in the south owe much to him for their preservation. It is an irony of history that this sceptical Voltairean actually helped to preserve France's religious heritage.[10] And his growing interest in Russian writers led to his fascination with the writings of Nikolai Gogol, who visited Paris in 1836–37 – Mérimée even translated Gogol's new, and eventually iconic play *Inspector General* – perfect for France's official of the same title.

Third and finally, under Louis-Napoléon (president 1848–52 and emperor Napoleon III 1852–70), Mérimée turned more and more to the study of history. He began with a treatise in two parts on classical Rome and the pre-history of Julius Caesar's political career, which earned him election to the Academy of Inscriptions. But he soon tired of the project and turned to the Slavonic world, which had suddenly become very important during the Napoleonic Wars. History, not literature, became pre-eminent.

## An Evolving Historical Sensibility

Indeed, the nineteenth century saw the birth of a new idea about history and its relationship to science and knowledge in general. Science had already swept away so many of the old religious-based ideas about personality and society, and psychology and sociology were emerging. Although "facts" had always been respected by the best of historians, fact turned into organized knowledge about humankind and its communities was now put on a much firmer basis. Mérimée himself shared this new respect for facts and saw in it a deeper, truer reflection of society than could be afforded by fiction. Seemingly, he was a pioneer of that approach – "the noble dream" of historical objectivity. In 1856, he expressed these sentiments in certain of his essays and letters, which biographer A.W. Raitt summarizes:

> "In my eyes history is something sacred" [Mérimée wrote]; factual truth is sacrosanct, and the cardinal sin is to tamper with it, whether in the name of morality or in subservience to some abstract theory. The historian's prime aim should be the "discovery of truth"; vain embellishments and preconceived ideas must be forsworn. The overriding duty of a historian is to be "detached and fair"; his function is not to prove a thesis but to 'collect numerous facts and subject them to impartial criticism."
> . . . [Mérimée continues,] "I wrote so many novels in years gone by that now I only like history . . . For my part, I know of no more interesting problem than the complete dissection of a historical character."[11]

And indeed, even though today we see his biases vis-à-vis religion and his juxtapositions of "civilization" and "savagery," "civility" and "barbarism," this noble dream remained his method as he wrote later in his career about Ukraine, Russia, and Slavonic Europe as a whole.

Soviet historians and writers, both Russian and Ukrainian, pleased with his attention to their little-known countries, exaggerated Mérimée's importance in French literature and played down his misgivings about their cultures, especially his juxtaposing of "civilization" and "barbarism." So a major Soviet literary encyclopaedia published in the 1930s under general editor A.V. Lunacharsky, the most prominent of all Communist cultural officials, accorded Mérimée five pages, complete with four handsome illustrations. The article evaluated Mérimée according to Soviet Marxist theory, but said very little about his Russian/Ukrainian period. It started with the writer's early writing, during the absolutist Bourbon restoration:

> [After the success of *La Guzla*,] Mérimée gave himself over to [more] serious work. In 1828, his historical drama/chronicle *La Jacquerie* [*sic*] came out. It was a remarkable attempt to depict the positive

traits of the uprising of medieval peasants, sharply reflecting [not only medieval times, but also] the shifts which were happening in the social life of France during the epoch of the feudal-Catholic reaction in the twenties of the nineteenth century, when arose the rebellious inclinations of the petty bourgeois elements and their intelligentsia. Among the shorter novels of 1829, together with the negrophile novel *Tamango*, it is necessary to mention *L'enlèvement de la redoute*, a sparkling page in the Napoleonic Wars, and *Mateo Falcone*, devoted to the heroization of that spiritual simplicity and feeling of honour which Mérimée considered characteristic of the Corsican peasantry ... The anti-feudal and anti-clerical positions of the class group, whose ideologist Mérimée was, stood in the traditions of the Great French Revolution and the Empire, but to a much greater degree came out of the pre-revolution free thinking of Voltaire and the materialistically inclined salons of the eighteenth century ... Mérimée actively opposed the influence of aristocratic romanticism then developing its literary mystifications ... He avoided lyricism, [rather giving himself over to] the laconic, and even a dryness of exposition with a complete lack of the declamations typical for the purple patches [*krasnorechiia*] of the romantics.[12]

These stiff Marxist prescriptions, alluding to Mérimée's disgust with the conservative Romantic postulates of the religious writer Chateaubriand, had some basis in fact, and re-appeared in a second Soviet literary encyclopaedia of the 1960s. They were generally followed in all Soviet works.[13]

Mérimée was a contemporary of Hugo and Balzac and knew them both well. He was a friend of the French writer Stendhal (1783–1842), twenty years his elder, who had been in Russia during the Napoleonic Wars and may have sparked his initial interest in eastern Europe, as in his *L'enlèvement de la redoute* (1829), about Shevardino, a major engagement of the French, Poles, and Russians on the eve of the great Battle of Borodino. Both Hugo and Balzac wrote about Ukraine, Balzac even spending much of the last two years of his life there (see chapter 6, above), but Mérimée studied the country more closely and in the 1850s and 1860s wrote much more about it, especially about serfdom, history, and literature in the Russian Empire, which soon brought the Ukrainian Cossacks and the Ukrainian people to his attention.

## Far-off Places: *La Guzla* and Shevardino

Mérimée began his career with two great literary hoaxes: *Théâtre de Clara Gazul* (1825) and *La Guzla, ou choix de poésies illyriques* (1827). The latter, filled with folk ballads about bandits and brigands, vampires and the evil eye, was a Balkan take-off on Macpherson's *Ossian* (which Merimée had translated when he was seventeen). *Ossian* had enthralled the European public and turned its attention to far-away times and places, especially the misty Middle Ages, which were just then beginning to replace Greece and Rome as popular subjects for writers.

Mérimée knew practically no Serbo-Croatian, or, for that matter, any other Slavonic language, but scraped together much of his material from a published collection of modern Greek folksongs and used a few Slavic words and phrases to great effect in his supposed translation, which appeared under a Balkan-sounding pseudonym, Hyacinthe Maglanovich. A *guzla*, the public was informed, was a one-stringed musical instrument used by Balkan bards. Later, more perceptive critics would add that Guzla was also an anagram of Gazul![14]

As it turned out, the public loved these ostensibly "Illyrian" songs, and the verses fooled not only the French, but even the Russian poet Pushkin and the Polish poets Adam Mickiewicz and Aleksander Chodźko, who all translated parts into their respective languages. Pushkin titled his "Songs of the Western Slavs." The German writer Goethe saw through the sham, but only because Mérimée had sent him a signed copy.[15]

Distant places figured as well in other early works we met above: *Tamango* (1829), *Mateo Falcone* (1829), and *L'enlèvement de la redoute* (1829), about Shevardino.

## The Inspector (General): Mérimée and Gogol (1830s–1840s)

Two decades later, Mérimée's contacts with the Slavonic world deepened when his cousin Henri Mérimée, a seeming personal and literary rival, visited Russia, and wrote *Une année en Russie* (1847) At that time, Mérimée also came to know S.A. Sobolevsky and other Russian visitors to Paris.[16] Another decade later, he also met Ivan Turgenev, a Russian writer sympathetic to Ukrainians, who helped him to understand the ukrainianisms scattered through the works of Nikolai Gogol, which had captured his interest as early as the 1830s. Sobolevsky, in particular, knew both Mickiewicz and

Pushkin, and called Mérimée's attention to the latter. As a result, the French writer was soon busy learning Russian and after a time began reading Russian literature in the original. He quickly grew to love Pushkin, who shared his terse, straightforward, almost classic style, and love of strange stories, and considered him the foremost creator of modern Russian literature and one of the greatest of European poets, whose countrymen – previously hesitating between the traditional written Slavonic and the spoken language – would thereafter write only in their living, spoken tongue.[17]

But from the very start, Mérimée's writings on Russia revealed a critical outlook on its autocracy and its serfdom, which made most of its people semi-slaves. In an early review of Baron von Haxthausen's account of travels in that empire, Mérimée condemned the system and predicted a great explosion, a peasant uprising, or "*jacquerie*," that could destroy civilization in that part of the world.[18]

Such uprisings had long intrigued Mérimée, who seemed fascinated with violence and was always trying to fathom the basic passions and inner character of life, especially in foreign locales and specifically documented examples. His historical studies of Castile's Don Pedro the Cruel (1848) and Russia's Peter the Great (articles, 1864–68) particularly reflect these interests. On Peter, the French Mérimée specialist Paul Léon quotes a typically diffident, even flippant, letter that the author once wrote to a friend: "I am immersed in the history of Peter the Great and will give the public a part of it. He was an abominable man surrounded by abominable riff-raff. The whole thing amuses me enormously."[19]

In treating of these hotly contested personalities and events, Mérimée's habitual coolness might be said to have frozen – he had not lived through France's Terror of the early 1790s nor did he have a chance to experience the Russian "Red Terror" and Civil War. Like many rather naïve Western intellectuals in the twentieth century, he came to see Peter and his reforms somewhat positively, just as later on some Western intellectuals saw some benefits to Stalinism.

In the 1830s Mérimée also wrote on Gogol, who brought his attention once again to the Cossacks, on Mazepa, whom he thought the last Ukrainian ruler to act on behalf of independence, and on Marko Vovchok (1833–1907), born Mariya Vilinskaya, who, in such works as *Narodni opovidannia* (Folk Stories, 1857), described the extreme hardships of peasant life. The French writer did not quite know what to make of Gogol, whom he compared to Balzac in his focus on the tragic and the ugly in life, and was appalled by the peasants' terrible living conditions as described by Vovchok, assumed they would cause the peasants to rise up and "disembowel their lords" (*éventrer leurs seigneurs*), and in the end would be "taken as socialist preaching in France." Still, he was determined to translate her story *Kozachka* (The Cossack Girl), which he never published.[20]

Mérimée was fascinated by Gogol's stories of the Zaporozhian Cossacks in his *Taras Bulba* (1835) and, despite his imperfect knowledge of Russian and ignorance of Ukrainian, translated both Gogol and Vovchok into French, with the help both of Turgenev and of his renderings of Vovchok into Russian. Mérimée wrote to Turgenev that he intended his translation of Vovchok to be read to his friend the Empress Eugénie herself, whom he had known as a child in Spain and continued to be friendly with during the reign of Napoleon III.[21]

He was not the only Frenchman puzzled by Gogol. For example, Paul Léon quotes Turgenev's letter to his French lover, Pauline Viardot, after Gogol's unexpected early death in 1852: "It will be difficult for you to appreciate the enormity of this loss. One must be a Russian to feel it. The most penetrating spirits among foreigners, a Mérimée, for example, have only seen an English type of humourist in Gogol. His historical importance has escaped them."[22] Turgenev, of course, like most of his contemporaries, despite acknowledging Gogol's uniqueness, saw Ukrainians as merely a special southern variety of Russians.

While in Paris in the winter of 1836–37, Gogol revealed quite different opinions from Turgenev about the Ukrainian nationality. A legend long existed that Gogol met Mérimée during his stay in Paris. This legend originated, as the Mérimée specialist Henri Mongault points out, in the salon of one Mme Aleksandra Smirnova (née Rosset), a great beauty, who was born and grew up in Ukraine and met Gogol that same year in Paris. They became quite close and soon spent a great deal of time together in Rome. She had earlier charmed both Pushkin and Lermontov and often entertained Russian writers at her home in St Petersburg. (Prince Viazemsky even called her "*Notre Dame de littérature russe*.") After her death, her memoirs, edited and published by her daughter Olga, discussed Gogol at length.

Mongault, however, claims that Olga added much erroneous material, including the 1836 or 1837 Paris meeting with Mérimée. He notes that the two men differed in character and political opinions so probably moved in different circles in Paris. In Paris, Mérimée frequented liberal, Bonapartist circles, and Gogol probably the more conservative, religious ones of mystics like Mme Svetchine, or even Adam Mickiewicz and the liberal Catholic priest Hugues-Félicité de Lamennais. Scholars such as Thierry Ozwald believe that Gogol was quite a loner in Paris and lived quietly.[23]

Other sources, however, report that Gogol did socialize in Paris, but with a small circle of intimate Ukrainian friends, and among Polish rather than Russian émigrés, who kept apart because of the Polish insurrection of 1830–31. He met even with the Polish émigré poets Mickiewicz and Józef Bohdan Zaleski, with whom he got along famously, and discussed the controversial theories of another Polish émigré, Franciszek Duchiński, who believed that Russians, unlike both Ukrainians and Poles, were not really Slavs, but linguistically Slavonized descendants of the Finnish or what he called the "Turanian" peoples. Zaleski later noted that Gogol was delighted by these ideas of Duchiński's. Zaleski, a major poet of the so-called Ukrainian School of Polish Literature, was born and raised in Ukraine and considered himself a fellow Ukrainian (spólukraincem) of Gogol's. Gogol may have changed his opinions on Duchiński's theories later in life, but these conversations in Paris, as well as the differences emphasized by Mongault, tend to suggest that he and Mérimée probably never met, and that, if they had, they would not have been able to become friends.[24]

But Mérimée did develop a lively interest in Gogol and eventually translated some of his stories into French, despite their many unfamiliar ukrainianisms. He became the first French translator of Revizor (The Inspector General, 1836/42), previously rendered into literal French by some Russian émigrés in Paris and corrected only by a native French speaker who knew no Russian.

Mérimée's position as "inspector general" of historical monuments probably piqued his interest in Revizor. But Mongault points out that in 1845 the literary critic Charles-Augustin Sainte Beuve reviewed Taras Bulba and others of Gogol's works favourably in the renowned Revue des deux mondes, in the issue in which Mérimée's Carmen first appeared, so he almost certainly read it. Sainte Beuve singled out Gogol's story of the Zaporozhian Cossack leader Taras Bulba, who killed his own son for collaborating with the Poles for the sake of a beautiful Polish woman. Sainte Beuve repeatedly compared Gogol's style and interests to Mérimée's. Mongault quotes Sainte Beuve:

> When he briskly takes command, and gives his first absolute orders, the speech of the newly elected Kochevyi [Field Hetman, or Cossack Commander-in-Chief, Taras Bulba] reminds me of that spicy turn of

realism that Monsieur Mérimée could have written . . . I have heard it said by some spiritually inclined Russians that there is in Gogol something of Monsieur Mérimée. These kinds of comparisons are always hazardous, and do not do anything good in the long run. What is certain though is that Monsieur Gogol is less concerned with idealizing than with observing; that he does not withdraw from the rude and the nude side of things; and that he has no hesitations in doing this. He is most concerned with human nature and in his time must have read a lot of Shakespeare.

Mongault implies that it was this review that really sparked Mérimée's interests in Gogol, similar in style and absorbed in people on the fringe of civilized life – in this case, the reputedly "wild" soldiers of the Steppe, the Cossacks.[25]

French scholars have also compared Gogol's *Taras Bulba* and Mérimée's *Mateo Falcone*, as Sainte Beuve did above – especially the endings, where a father kills a traitorous son – and wondered about possible borrowings. Mongault, following the renowned French Slavist Louis Léger, says publication dates – 1829 for *Mateo Falcone* and 1835 for *Taras Bulba* – rule out Mérimée, and he also dismissed Gogol's borrowing it, since – here he agrees again with Léger – Gogol was not particularly interested in French literature. Mongault adds that fathers killing sons is common in all "primitive" literatures, and the two authors most probably came up with the same idea independently.[26]

Early on, Mérimée greatly admired Gogol. In an 1851 essay he compared him to Rabelais and to current English humourists. He understood that Gogol was enriching the Russian language with his southern speech and compared it to the influence of le Midi – the south of France – on French. He even compared Ukraine's role within Russia to the Midi within France, although he thought that Gogol's Ukrainian patriotism was unique – he had a kind of prejudice against "the rest of the Empire." "For me," he sagaciously wrote, "I find him to be impartial enough and rather general in his criticisms, but [at the same time] too severe for those [Russians], who are the subject of his observations."[27]

As for other Slavonic writers, Mérimée seemed to know nothing of the Ukrainian poet Taras Shevchenko and his *Kobzar* (The Blind Minstrel, or The Kobza Player, 1840) and was left cold by the Russian authors Lermontov and Dostoevsky. He acknowledged the last's *Crime and Punishment*, but thought him too much an imitator of Victor Hugo. Mérimée (the Frenchman!) actually considered this a slight to Russian culture, and suggested that Dostoevsky would have been better off imitating Pushkin. Moreover, given his aversion to Romantic melodrama, he had no sympathy for Poland and its literature, even Mickiewicz, whom Gogol greatly admired, but whose religiosity and enthusiasm would have repelled the French author. In fact, the numerous Polish émigrés in Paris, most of them Romantic nationalists, also held no interest for him. Yet his fascination with Ukrainian Cossacks only increased.[28]

## Mérimée on Ukrainian Cossack History (1850s–1860s)

These interests soon bore fruit. In 1852, the year after his article on Gogol, Mérimée published the play *Les débuts d'un aventurier*, about False Dmitri, who, with the help of Poles and Ukrainian Cossacks, overthrew Tsar Boris Godunov in 1605 and claimed Muscovy for himself. In this drama, and in his more carefully composed *Épisode de l'histoire de Russie : Les faux Démétrius* (1852), he postulated that the man was no Muscovite at all, but probably a student of the learned schools in Kyiv, then under Polish rule, who tired of his studies and joined the Zaporozhian Cossacks in southern Ukraine, where he learned about the arts of war. This hypothesis contradicted all Russian, Polish, and Ukrainian historians of that time, but brought much new attention to Ukrainian history and to its Cossacks. Mérimée painted Dmitri as intelligent and generous, too mild and lacking in ruthlessness to hold onto the Russian throne (he was murdered in 1606). Mérimée scholar A.W. Raitt considered *Épisode* the French writer's most original and successful study of Russian history.[29]

Mérimée wrote extensively and well on Russian and Ukrainian history. One essay (1854) outlined the Ukrainian Cossacks' history from their fifteenth-century origins to the death of Hetman Ivan Mazepa in 1709. A book-length essay of 1865 covered the successful Cossack revolt against the Polish–Lithuanian Commonwealth in 1648, led by the greatest Ukrainian Cossack leader, Hetman Bohdan Khmelnytsky.

The first work, *Les Cosaques de l'Ukraine et leurs derniers Atamans* (1854), outlined the origin of the Cossacks on the Dnieper River defending the exposed peasants of that rich land against Tatar raiding parties and increasingly demanding landlords, many from Poland. Relying on the most recent discoveries in philology (one of his special interests), he traced "Cossack" back to its root in the Turkic languages as a "freebooter" or independent soldier, who owed allegiance to no ruler. He stated that the Zaporozhian Cossacks of central Ukraine were the oldest of all the Cossack Hosts, lived without women at their headquarters, or *Sich*, on the Dnieper River, and provided a model for the Cossacks of the Don River, who were mostly refugees from Russia, not Poland or Lithuania. Both Hosts, he correctly stated, originated as boatmen, were transformed into infantrymen, and only much later acquired their reputation as cavalrymen, in which guise they entered Paris after Napoleon's final defeat.

Mérimée's study next outlined Bohdan Khmelnytsky's Cossack insurrection of 1648 against the Poles, the turmoil and chaos that followed his death in 1657, and Hetman Ivan Mazepa's revolt against Peter the Great in 1708. Mérimée thought Khmelnytsky, who was so little known in western Europe, had sought only to liberalize Polish rule but, by turning to the Muscovites for help and agreeing to the Treaty of Pereiaslav, which recognized the tsar's overlordship, brought to his people a much heavier burden, and he himself soon regretted his actions. Mérimée concluded that the suppression of Mazepa's revolt ended Cossack dreams of independence and even of a clearly defined, independent Cossack stratum within the Russian Empire.

For this study, Mérimée used Russian, but also French sources, the latter including Voltaire on Mazepa (whom he corrected on the spelling of Mazepa's name and on the youthful Cossack's famous but apocryphal naked horseback ride); the cartographer Beauplan (who wrote on the eve of the Khmelnytsky revolt); and the Swedish historian J.A. Nordberg (who had penned a detailed history of Charles XII of Sweden, with whom Mazepa allied himself against Peter the Great). This survey of Ukrainian Cossack history was fluidly written, relatively well researched, and quite informative for the general European public, who knew nothing of Cossackdom. It dovetailed with Napoleon III's foreign policy and was published during the Crimean War (1853–56) in the official journal *Le moniteur universel*, so was relatively brief.[30]

As a result, it was Mérimée's second study of Ukrainian Cossacks – *Bohdan Khmelnytsky* (1865) – that became his main contribution to popularizing Ukrainian history in the West. In the 1860s, he came across the Ukrainian historian Mykola Kostomarov's superb two-volume biography of Khmelnytsky and was simply carried away by it. He loved Kostomarov's use of local colour, his exciting narrative, and, most originally, his use of folklore and folksong as historical sources and to enliven chronicles and documents. (Mérimée had done something a bit similar in his Corsican tales, *Colomba* and *Mateo Falcone*.) About Kostomarov's study of Don Cossack rebel Stenka Razin, who rose against Muscovy in 1670–71, Mérimée wrote:

> Monsieur Nicolas Kostomarof, author of some very well regarded historical and archaeological works, has written the life of this wild hero [*de ce héros sauvage*]. He has endeavoured to collect not only all the printed documents and manuscripts from the archives and libraries of Russia, but also local traditions and folksongs which often can reveal better than official reports the passions of the masses ... He believes that the historian, without losing his character of [fair] judgment, can and must make use of drama and poetry. The reflections and dress of these ornaments do not negate truth; to the contrary they succeed when they are chosen with taste and discernment, in the same way that a portrait done with a close attention to detail adds to the image of the principal figure.[31]

This captured Kostomarov's general approach to writing history. On the one hand, Kostomarov later became more critical of oral sources grounded in folklore and revised some of his findings accordingly. On the other hand, he always found "popular poetry" a useful guide to the spirit of the people. By the time Mérimée discovered him, Kostomarov had become a very popular "historian-artist," the most popular in the Russian Empire, who, because of strict censorship, partly hid his Ukrainian sympathies, especially vis-à-vis Ukrainian independence, beneath a thin façade of pan-Russian patriotism. For example, at a time when the new term "Ukrainians" was still not widely used, he typically spoke of the "North Russian" and "South Russian" "nationalities" (singular: *narodnost*). Mérimée, who sometimes saw through this façade (possibly with Turgenev's aid), and who loved folk poetry, resolved to write at least an extended French paraphrase of Kostomarov's life of Khmelnytsky, despite his serious difficulties with its many Ukrainianisms.[32]

The work proceeded very slowly, and at times Mérimée despaired of it, writing to a friend, "I am still not finished with this animal of a Chmielnicki."[33] But in the end, although he was already aged and ill, Mérimée's *Bohdan Khmelnytsky*, following Kostomarov, painted Ukrainian history and the Ukrainian Cossacks in the brightest and most garish of colours, fully reflecting the excitement and the seemingly unrestrained violence of

those times. It outlined the heavy oppression of the peasants in the old Polish–Lithuanian Commonwealth, and summarized Khmelnytsky's possible
impressions when he visited Warsaw to take his personal grievances to the
king: all around him, he saw chaos and disorder, the nobles' arrogance, the
ineffective government, private armies all over the land living off pillage,
and not least "the brutalized peasants, who were ready to follow anyone
who would carry fire and sword to [the castles of] their masters."[34]

And when the Ukrainian insurrection came in 1648, Mérimée described
the Poles impaling the Cossacks, and the Cossacks flaying the Poles. Still,
he criticized some of Kostomarov's sources and disagreed with some of
his positions – for example, that Cossacks had burned alive some fifteen
thousand Jews at the capture of the town of Bar, as was related in the
sources, and that Khmelnytsky, after his first great victories in Ukraine, had
decided not to enter and destroy Poland proper out of lingering patriotism
for the old Commonwealth. Instead, Mérimée proposed that Khmelnytsky
actually needed Poland in the dangerous political scene in central and
eastern Europe – he was just being practical. Mérimée saw him as a brilliant
military leader and tactician who skilfully united his people while playing
off his enemies, one against the other. Moreover, Khmelnytsky was "the
elected leader of a small nation surrounded by powerful neighbours [who]
devoted his whole life to the struggle for independence." He continues:

> Nations like to find in their chosen leader the qualities and even the
> defects of their national character. Bohdan Khmelnytsky was, as it
> were, the perfect type of the Cossack. He was brave, cunning, and
> enterprising; he had an instinctive understanding of war. His intem-
> perance, his real or assumed brutality, was no more creditable to him
> among the Russians [sic] than Henri IV's love-affairs were shocking
> to the French. Few rulers have been more absolute; none observed
> more carefully the laws and customs of his country. Within the con-
> fines of the Zaporozhian Army, he seemed to be only the humble
> executor of the decisions of its assembly. All his power consisted in
> persuasion based on his unalterable attachment to its interests.[35]

Mérimée concluded by saying that Khmelnytsky did not aim to create a
new nation, at least in the modern sense, but rather sought to raise the
Cossacks to an aristocratic class similar to that which already existed in
Poland. In his exciting narrative, Mérimée, ever conscious of the need for

local colour, introduced new Ukrainian words into the French language, many of them in Russian guise from Kostomarov.[36]

Mérimée's colourful book was a moderate success and, amazingly, is still in print today. Some authors, such as A. Zhukovsky (Arkady Joukovsky), a Ukrainian émigré living in France, and Thierry Ozwald, a Frenchman, argue cogently that it was no paraphrase at all but rather an original work of interpretation, which clearly used a much wider range of sources than was once previously thought. Zhukovsky in particular speculates that Mérimée saw Khmelnytsky as "a kind of Father of the Cossack nation," who, as Mérimée wrote to a friend, "seems to have invented the [modern] war among nationalities."[37]

Mérimée, however, completely misread Kostomarov's basic purpose, which was not sensationalist. The latter did colourfully describe the violence of various Cossack revolts against the Polish and Muscovite governments, but not out of any love for or fear of revolt, or fascination with violence, but rather simply to debase these uprisings, so as to pacify the censors, who hated revolts of all kinds. So Kostomarov, in that earlier book on Stenka Razin, detailed the "savagery" of the Russian Cossack revolt against Moscow (again repeated by Mérimée in his own narrative of those same events) for that reason, and he may have done the same for Bohdan Khmelnytsky and his peasant followers' ostensible "barbarism." Otherwise, the French writer did greatly admire Khmelnytsky for his try at independence and clearly distinguished between the professional fighting men – the actual Cossacks – and the peasants. But generally, Mérimée, and perhaps others like even Karl Marx himself, who, as discussed in the Introduction to this volume, also relied on Kostomarov for eastern European and Russian history, took this depiction of extreme violence to be Kostomarov's real interpretation and passed it on to the general European reading public, which was thereafter greatly influenced by it.[38]

## Mérimée's Ukrainian Legacy

Of course in the century that followed, Soviet historians and writers, both Russian and Ukrainian, pleased with the attention Mérimée brought to their little-known countries, and promoting a Marxism of their own type, tended to play down his criticisms, especially of the peasants' "barbarism," or justify it as a natural reaction to the nobles' harsh oppression. For Ukrainians, hamstrung by Soviet censorship, which touched on both democratic and national strivings, Mérimée was a very rare nineteenth-century Western writer who paid serious attention to their culture.

Thus during the occasional cultural thaws they released a few studies of this Frenchman, which ignored or minimized his criticisms and disregarded his fascination with egregious violence. So Dmytro Nalyvaiko, writing in 1970, basically ignored the Frenchman's negative impressions of Gogol and stated that his historical narrative about Khmelnytsky and others closely reflected later Soviet prescriptions about social divisions within the Cossack polity and the Ukrainian struggle "against the yoke of the Polish aristocrats."[39]

It was only after 1991 that these same Ukrainian intellectuals could talk about Mérimée more freely, and they finally prepared Ukrainian translations of his historical works dealing with their country. In the first Ukrainian-language printing of *Bohdan Khmelnytsky*, which appeared in the journal *Zhovten* (October) in 1987, the translator gave three reasons for doing so: Mérimée had expanded the general history of the Slavonic peoples (Ukrainians, Poles, and Russians), had called Zaporozhia "a democratic republic" in Ukraine, and had, by the breadth of his interests, revealed himself to be "a citizen of the world." The translation was geared to fill a "blank spot" in Ukrainian history, which purpose also fitted in with the new spirit of the times.[40]

Of course, these Ukrainian publishers and writers continued to ignore Mérimée's contrast of "civilization" and "barbarism" (e.g., Ukraine). Again reflecting Kostomarov, Mérimée saw some Cossacks aiming at a higher, more civilized status in society, but it was the general violence and chaos of the Cossack revolt that caught everyone's attention, including Mérimée's. And that is still striking today when one reads his work on Khmelnytsky.

Nevertheless, Mérimée really helped publicize Ukraine's history, despite his harsh judgments of its history, his anti-religious biases, his stress on violence, and his reliance on Russian-language sources. For example, although he followed his contemporaries in calling these Cossacks, or their peasant followers, "Russians," and ignored Kostomarov's distinctions between North and South Russians, he did write about "Ukraine," not "Little Russia," as so many others did. This was a clear national interpretation of Ukrainian history, hitherto banned by the tsar's censors. Moreover, he also referred to Ukraine as "a country" rather than simply a region – another important advance.[41]

Finally, he also could see a difference between the *sauvage* Don Cossack leader Stenka Razin, who behaved atrociously and ended badly, and the more cultured Zaporozhian leader Khmelnytsky, who, despite the ravages of his peasant followers, was a man of some wealth and education, enjoyed substantial success, and died peacefully in his bed surrounded by respectful attendants. And Mérimée seemed to acknowledge that these rebellious inhabitants of Ukraine formed, or rather tried to form, "a Cossack nation" with its own native nobility and ruler. In other words, Mérimée had a notion of that imaginary Ukrainian past captured by Gogol in his *Taras Bulba* (1835), but no inkling – knowing nothing of Shevchenko's *Kobzar* (1840) – of what that work looked towards: a future Ukraine with its own new literature in its own independent language. Indeed, so taken was Mérimée with the Ukrainian past, with Ukrainian history, and with the Cossacks of yesteryear, that, despite all his misgivings, in 1867, when a Polish friend, Mme Przedziecka, to whom he seems to have been much attracted, sent him a book on eastern European history, urging him to be more sympathetic to the Poles, he playfully commented: "I have just received the book. It is well thought out and well-written, but has one mistake: It is a bit too Polish, and, as you know, I myself am a Cossack."[42] This statement, frequently quoted in Ukrainian appreciations of Mérimée, aptly summed up his stance on Ukrainian, Polish, and Russian history.

# FOUR

Contested Canvases:
Rembrandt's *Polish Rider*
and Repin's Satirical Cossacks

## CHAPTER EIGHT

# Deciphering Rembrandt's
# *Polish Rider*

REMBRANDT HARMENSZOON VAN RIJN (1606–1669) was the foremost artist of the Golden Age of Dutch painting and one of the most brilliant of all European artists. A "realist" who eschewed classical perfection and decorum to depict life as it really was, complete with its flaws and its mundane side, he was a master of the psychological portrait, with an extraordinary capacity to infuse his canvases with life, vitality, and movement, to express personality, to raise contradictory emotions, and even to shock. Yet there is always something solemn and mysterious about his pictures, especially his portraits, and the people depicted are usually thoughtful, and never without a certain depth. This immediacy, personalism, and depth are evident in almost all of his some 300–600 acknowledged paintings (critics have exposed many imitators and shrunk the canon over the years), and many hundreds of drawings, sketches, and prints, which are prized by collectors and museums all over the world.[1]

In eastern Europe too Rembrandt has always been highly esteemed, and for a long time the Hermitage Museum in St Petersburg had one of the largest collections of his paintings in the world. During the twentieth century, however, parts of this trove were sold off or dispersed in other ways, while the Dutch, anxious to preserve their artistic heritage, conscientiously reassembled as much of it as they could. Today in Amsterdam the Rijksmuseum holds the most Rembrandt paintings in the world and the Rembrandt House Museum the biggest assemblage of his prints.[2]

In Poland, patrons have been collecting Rembrandts for many years. In addition to many of his prints and drawings, at least three of his paintings grace Polish museums: *Landscape with the Good Samaritan* (Czartoryski Museum in Cracow) and *Scholar at a Lectern* and *Girl in a Hat* (both in the Royal Castle Museum, Warsaw). The last two belonged to the last king of Poland, Stanisław Augustus Poniatowski (reigned 1764–95), an avid collector and patron of the arts. Poland entered Rembrandt's *œuvre* during his lifetime, as we see in *The Polish Nobleman* (1637) (National Gallery, Washington, DC), believed perhaps a portrait of the Protestant diplomat Andrzej Rej, and *The Polish Rider* (c. 1655) (Frick Collection, New York City), long considered a portrait of an unknown person. The much-discussed *Polish Rider*, exceptional in every way, yet immediately recognizable as the master's, is the subject of the present chapter.[3]

## Who Is the "Polish Rider"?

*The Polish Rider* (c. 1655), oil on canvas, 46 in x 53½ in/116.8 cm x 134.9 cm, is of moderate size, about half life, and depicts a young man, perhaps eighteen to twenty-five years old, mounted on a slender white horse that is trotting across a dark and barely discernible landscape dominated by browns and deep orange (Plate 12). It appears to be at either early dawn or late dusk. The subject's face is serious but calm and self-assured, bright and handsome, with regular, square features. He is gazing off into the distance, as if to search out his future destiny. His hair is fairly long and partly covered by a fur cap with flaps on either side that look like they can fold down to protect his ears from the cold when necessary. The equestrian is armed for war, with a saber on one side and a saber or short sword on the other. He carries a mace or war-hammer in his right hand and the horse's reins with the other. A full quiver of arrows hangs at his waist, and the end of his bow protrudes behind him. Both rider and mount sport apparently "Oriental" costume: the man, a long coat extending to his ankles and tied at his waist, and tight red breeches, and his horse, an ornamental horsetail banner hanging from his bridle and blown backward by his movement. From beneath the high saddle to just above the short stirrup spreads a seeming leopard-skin saddlecloth.

Man and mount stand out clearly from the dark background, across which they are moving quickly. Rising in the distance behind them is a domed building – perhaps a fortress, church, or some other antique building – and barely visible to the right are a stream and a small campfire. The whole picture unites exotic arms, costume, and scenery with the attractive confidence and innocence of a youth with whom we immediately identify. But who is this young man? What is he thinking? And to what battle does he ride with such confidence? This mysterious picture has haunted viewers, art critics, and historians for the century since it left eastern Europe for Henry Clay Frick's gallery in New York.[4]

## Out of the Shadows (1870s–1910)

When in the 1890s the painting first came to the attention of the Western art community, it hung in the private collection of Count Zdzisław Tarnowski (1862–1937), in the ladies drawing room in his family home, Dzików Castle, in Austrian Galicia, in what is today part of Tarnobrzeg district in Poland. The castle, a venerable building, had recently been renovated in the neo-gothic style. The Tarnowskis were a great landowning family, with estates in both Poland and Ukraine and including entire towns and cities like Tarnobrzeg, Tarnów, and Ternopil associated with their name.

The picture itself seems to have been esteemed by the Poles – who call it *Lisowczyk* (after an irregular light-cavalry unit) – and was noted in print as early as 1842 (by the poet Kajetan Koźmian); in 1843 the historian Maurycy Dzieduszycki printed a somewhat fanciful engraving of it in a Galician scholarly journal and noted that in 1833 it had been sent to Vienna for "restoration" (*do odchędożenia*), where, in his words, it "delighted the experts who without any doubts recognized in it Rembrandt's brushwork."[5]

In the 1870s the painting was studied in greater detail by various Polish scholars, but Count Tarnowski – who did not believe it a family portrait, and perhaps also for taxation purposes – wished to sell it and sent it again to Vienna for restoration. Wilhelm Bode, a Rembrandt expert from Germany, citing its use of colour, dated it to "probably" 1654, in Rembrandt's late period (he died in 1669). "The picture depicted," Bode wrote in 1883, "a young Polish magnate who casually trots past the viewer in his national costume on an Arabian white horse." In a footnote, Bode added, "Even when Polish and other great men from half-civilized eastern Europe visited Holland, they showed a partiality for having themselves painted by Rembrandt." He wrote during the so-called *Kulturkampf* conflict (1872–78) between the new German government and the Catholic church, when German–Polish relations were quite tense.[6]

The first Western Rembrandt scholar to examine the original in detail was the Dutch scholar Abraham Bredius, who seems to have been encouraged by Bode and was invited to Dzików by the Polish art historian Jerzy Mycielski, a cousin of the Tarnowskis. In 1897, the two scholars visited Dzików, and Bredius described his experiences there in *De nederlandische Spectator*, no. 25 (1897), 197–9: "Just one look at it," he wrote, "a few seconds' study of the technique, were enough to convince me instantly that here, in this remote fastness, one of Rembrandt's greatest masterpieces had been hanging for nigh on a century." The two experts arranged to have the painting exhibited in Amsterdam the following year, and notices, reproductions, and reviews of the exhibition were widely printed. The picture instantly became a true sensation for the art world. Remnants of Rembrandt's signature – "Rem . . . " – were still visible at the bottom of the painting. Bredius, despite Bode's research, always considered the canvas his greatest discovery.[7]

Only one dissenter questioned its authenticity. Alfred von Wurzbach, in the first volume of his 1906 encyclopaedia of Dutch painting, assigned the work rather to Aert de Gelder (1645–1727), one of the master's last students, who copied his later style but, as the dissident put it, could not compete with his use of colour. He called the picture *A Tatar Rider* and noted that de Gelder was enamoured of Oriental costume, but gave no further explanation, and was generally disregarded.[8]

Meanwhile, Tarnowski still hoped to sell the work. Knowing that sending such a great national treasure abroad would cause an uproar in Poland, the count hid the matter. In 1910, he decided to sell it through the Carfax Gallery in London and Knoedler and Co. in New York. The prospective buyer was Henry Clay Frick (1849–1919), a steel, coke, and railway magnate, reviled for his merciless business practices and ruthless breaking of labour strikes. During the infamous Homestead Strike of 1892, which he pretty much provoked, ten men were killed and some sixty wounded, most of them poor immigrants – "foreigners" – many of them Poles, Slovaks, and other Slavs from central and eastern Europe.

Frick lived in Pittsburgh and from 1905 on in New York, where he built a home at East 70th Street and Fifth Avenue to house his exquisite collection of European Old Masters. He purchased *The Polish Rider* through the mediation of Roger Fry, an English writer, painter, and art critic, who, at Tarnowski's insistence, went to Dzików to finalize arrangements. Fry thought the castle and its furnishings "second rate," but was stunned by the painting. He later told a colleague that a cord was pulled, a curtain was rolled back, and there before his eyes "was revealed one of the world's masterpieces of painting." The agreed price for the work was £60,000, or $293,162.50, an enormous sum. Meanwhile, news of the sale was leaked to the press and became common knowledge in Poland, where the public was greatly aroused. Articles appeared in the press, and the Polish art historian Zygmunt/Sigismund Batowski, claiming great art as the property of the nation and lamenting the decline of appreciation for such art, objected to the sale in the Polish journal *Lamus*. The painting was exhibited in London on its way to New York, and a copy was made for the count. But in 1927 a fire broke out in Dzików Castle, and part of the collection, including the copy, was destroyed. Had *The Polish Rider* remained in Galicia, it too might not have survived.[9]

The assembling of the Frick collection and the arrival of this gem in New York stirred a new wave of publicity, including articles in the press and commemorative poems. In 1917, shortly before Frick's death, an article in a leading art magazine described the gallery and discussed the exotic and somewhat mysterious *Polish Rider*:

> Who the young man is, no one knows, but his red cap with a thick border of fur, his long tunic of a pale yellow note secured by blue buttons, his close-fitting red breeches and yellow boots proclaim him a Pole or a Russian, a man of the Slavs to the eastward who furnished light cavalry to western armies, the forerunners of the Hussars . . . [The art historian] Bode thinks that he can specify the regiment to which he belonged – Prince Lisowski's: at any rate that is the name this picture bore when in Count Tarnowski's collection.

The author concluded: "Rembrandt rarely painted horses and among the immense number of his etchings there is scarcely one. Yet what a horse this is! . . . It is not the somewhat barbaric harness and garb of the horse rider, nor the stern landscape well in keeping with the light, that compels the attention and urges conjecture . . . it is the human being, the expression of the face which is pondering, if not exactly dreamy – but the look is decipherable."[10]

Similar sentiments were expressed in poetry. As early as 1910, the *Lotus Magazine* reprinted F. Warre-Cornish's poem on "the Polish Rider" that had first appeared in the British journal the *Spectator*. With a direct reference to the Ottoman siege of Vienna and its relief by Jan III Sobieski in 1683, and an indirect allusion to the later partition of the country, he asked:

Does he ride to a bridal, a triumph, a dance, or a fray,
That he goes so alert, yet so careless, so stern and so gay?
Loose in the saddle, short stirrup, one hand on the mane
Of the light-stepping pony he guides with so easy a rein.
What a grace in his armor barbaric! Sword, battle-axe bow,
Full sheaf of arrows, the leopard-skin flaunting below.
Heart-conqueror, surely – his own is not given a while,
Till she comes who shall win for herself that inscrutable smile.
What luck had his riding, I wonder, romantic and bold?
For he rides into darkness; the story shall never be told:
Did he charge at Vienna, and fall in a splendid campaign?
Did he fly from the Cossack, and perish, ingloriously slain?
Ah, chivalrous Poland, forgotten, dishonored, a slave
To thyself and the stranger, fair, hapless, beloved of the brave![11]

After Frick's death in 1919, in accordance with his will, his widow lived in their home till her death in 1931, after which it was converted into a museum, which finally opened in 1935, and *The Polish Rider* was there for all to see.

## Stately Polish Ride:
## From Stanisław Augustus to Dzików Castle (1793–1910)

In 1944, a Jewish refugee from German-occupied Europe, Julius S. Held (1905–2002), who could read a little Polish, had done research in Poland, and in 1933 had even visited Dzików Castle, penned the first extensive English-language study of the picture. Others followed.

Research by these scholars and their Polish predecessors traced the provenance of *The Polish Rider* back to the end of the eighteenth century, when the multinational Polish–Lithuanian Commonwealth, one of the great states of central and eastern Europe, was on its last legs. Its last king, Stanisław Augustus Poniatowski, was a great patron of learning and the arts. His collection of European Old Masters was renowned, and he wished to expand it further. In August 1791, he received a letter from Michał Kazimierz Ogiński (1728?–1800), grand hetman of Lithuania and a composer, writer, and poet of note:

Sire,
I am sending Your majesty a Cossack whom Reinbrand had set on his horse. [*Odsyłam Waszey Królewskey Mości kozaka którego Reinbrand*

*osadził na koniu . . .*] This horse has eaten during his stay with me 420
German gulden. Your majesty's justice and generosity allows me to
expect that orange trees will flower in the same proportion.
Bowing to your feet, Your Majesty's,
My Lord Master's
most humble servant.
Michał Ogiński,
G[rand] H[etman] of L[ithuania].[12]

The scholar who discovered this letter, Andrzej Ciechanowski, believed that
since Ogiński had spent much of the previous year in western Europe, including Holland, he had purchased the painting, which he called "Cossack
on Horseback," for the king's collection, in return for which he wanted
some orange trees for the palace that he was building at Helenów near Warsaw. (The king possessed an orangery in the gardens of his Łazieńki Palace
in Warsaw.) Ciechanowski thinks that, apart from the suggested barter
agreement, the letter is "whimsical," and the reference to the "Cossack on
Horseback" fanciful.

   At any rate, the painting entered the king's collection, where it was
labelled *Cosaque à cheval*.[13] Nevertheless, many Poles blamed Ukrainian
Cossacks and their insurrection of the 1640s and 1650s for the decline and
fall of their Commonwealth, and as early as 1797 the king was referring
to the painting as a portrait of a "Lisowczyk" – a soldier of the Lisowski
company, a freebooting regiment of light cavalry often referred to as
"Cossacks" in Polish service. Its ranks included Poles, Ukrainians, and even
some Tatars; it was disbanded in the 1630s.[14]

   By the end of the 1790s, the Third Partition of Poland had occurred, the
Commonwealth had disappeared, and the king was dead. Some ten years
later the monarch's niece and heir, Countess Thérèse Tyszkiewicz, ordered
the sale and dispersal of the royal art collection. In 1810, while viewing
its contents, Countess Valèrie Tarnowska, née Stroynowska, expressed a
wish to buy this *Lisowczyk*, seeing in this "shining youth" not any lowly
Cossack, but rather a noble *condottiere* from the Lisowski Regiment,
perhaps even her distant relative Colonel Stanisław Stroynowski, who
commanded the regiment during the Thirty Years War. Therefore, argued
Andrzej Ciechanowski, it was probably she who talked her uncle, the bishop
of Vilnius, Hieronim Stroynowski, into buying the portrait for five hundred
ducats – a huge sum.

Bishop Stroynowski purchased the painting from Prince Franciszek Ksawery Lubecki (1779–1846), who had saved it from falling into the hands of the firmly anti-Polish Russian plenipotentiary, Nikolai Novosiltsev (1761–1836), who wished to acquire as many Polish cultural treasures as possible. After the bishop's premature death in 1815, the so-called *Lisowczyk* was inherited by Valèrie's father, Senator Valerien Stroynowski, and went from Vilnius to his castle at Horokhiv/Horochów in Volhynia in right-bank Ukraine (then under Russian rule). After the senator's death in 1834, it went to Dzików in Austrian Galicia, the residence of Valèrie Stroynowska and her husband, Count Jan Amor Tarnowski, where it remained until 1910.[15]

Although *Lisowczyk* was largely unknown to the Western world and to Western Rembrandt scholars before 1910, inside partitioned Poland it stirred up animated discussion. In the 1830s historian Dzieduszycki noted that the Lisowczyk forces had crossed the Rhine River twice, once in the early 1620s, when Rembrandt was fourteen, and again in 1636, when they even reached the Netherlands and one of them may have been sent to Amsterdam as an envoy and perhaps attracted the painter's attention. Dzieduszycki speculated that Rembrandt painted his Lisowczyk about this time, although he thought it unlikely that the subject was Stroynowski himself.[16] The expert's speculations influenced opinion in Poland for at least forty years, until Bode dated the work to Rembrandt's late period.

On the artistic level, two of the most successful nineteenth–century Polish painters of horses and battle scenes, Juliusz Kossak (1824–1899), whose name means "Cossack," and Józef Brandt (1841–1915), seem to have come under *Lisowczyk*'s powerful spell. Brandt, who loved painting Cossacks and the Polish–Cossack and Polish–Tatar wars of the seventeenth century, which occurred while Rembrandt was flourishng, painted *The March of the Lisowczyks* (1863), *Stroynowski Presenting Archduke Leopold Horses Seized by the Lisowczyks in the Rhine Palatinate* (1869), and *Lisowczyk (Bunczuczny)* (1885), while Kossak rendered his own striking, though inferior *Lisowczyk* (1860–65), in direct imitation of Rembrandt. Other Polish artists inspired by the canvas include Michał Płoński, A. Orłowski, and L. Kapliński. Moreover, around mid-century the Piller lithographic firm in Galicia's capital, Lemberg/Lwów, printed Karol Auer's lithograph of Rembrandt's canvas. In the 1890s, an engraved interpretation of the painting appeared in Zygmunt Gloger's influential *Encyklopedia Staropolska Illustrowana*. "The portrait of the young 'Polish Rider,'" concludes the art historian Michał Walicki, "was the best-known Rembrandt picture in Poland."[17]

The transfer of the masterpiece across the Atlantic occasioned grumbling in Poland and celebration in the United States, where it was almost universally deemed not a Lisowczyk but a somewhat more understandable and pronounceable "Polish Rider," romantically linked in many people's minds, as Cornish's poem clearly shows, to the Polish struggle for independence. A generation later, however, this link was put into question by Julius Held's pioneering 1944 article in the prestigious *Art Bulletin*.[18]

## Julius Held's Allegorical Interpretation

Julius Held, in his 1944 article on *The Polish Rider*, adhered quite closely to the professional standards of art history and accepted the work as Rembrandt's, but he put the word "Polish" in its title in quotation marks, thus seeming to question its Polish connection. He pointed out that the Lisowski Regiment was disbanded by the 1630s and thus Rembrandt could not have painted one of its members as a youthful rider in the mid-1650s. Indeed, it was doubtful whether the artist even knew about the unit. Held also agreed that the rider could not have been a Ukrainian Cossack, since they customarily wore bright-coloured clothing. As a clincher, he maintained that the Cossacks commonly sported loose, baggy pants (*sharavary* in Ukrainian), not tight breeches. like the rider. Held maintained that Polish scholars who identified the handsome sitter as Rembrandt's son, Titus, were wrong, since Titus was far too young to be mounted on a horse in the early or mid-1650s.

Held examined the subject's costume, weapons, and horse and concluded that these were not specifically Polish, but rather general accoutrements of central and eastern European soldiers, including Hungarian ones. Thus cap, coat, and weapons, and the horse's decorative horsetail standard, which Held called by a Hungarian name, *kutas*, and other equipment as well, were all generic items. Indeed, even the rider's personal grooming was un-Polish, since his hair was long and his moustache shaved, unlike most martial Poles of the time, who wore their hair short and sported bushy moustaches.

Held pointed to three possible models for the painting: the medieval statue of a rider in Bamberg Cathedral in Germany, Rembrandt's own sketch of the skeleton of a Dutch horse, and, following the Polish scholar Jan Bołoz-Antoniewicz (c. 1905), the sketches of Polish cavalrymen visiting Rome by the Italian artist Stefano della Bella. He concluded that the picture was not necessarily a portrait but rather a generalized allegory of the *Miles Christianus*, the good Christian knight, riding off to defend Christendom

from the Turks and Tatars. Held questioned not its author but its traditional connection with Poland. Had the rider been discovered in a Hungarian
castle instead of a Polish one, he concluded, it would today universally be
known as *Hungarian Rider*.[19]

Held's influential essay opened up a new trend, suggesting an allegorical
representation of some more ethereal or literary hero. For example, Jacob
Rosenberg closely followed suit in his highly influential *Rembrandt: Life and
Work* (1948).[20] Meanwhile, the same year, the veteran Rembrandt scholar
W.R. Valentiner identified the rider as Gijsbrecht van Amstel, the traditional
Dutch hero of a famous, eponymous play of 1638 by the prominent poet Joost
van den Vondel, which Rembrandt surely knew; the play was performed in
Amsterdam every New Year's Day till 1968. J.Z. Kannegieter thought the
equestrian was Sigismundus van Poolen from a play performed in 1647 and
available in print in 1654, and Colin Campbell (1970) proposed the Prodigal
Son riding out into the world after having received his "portion" (Luke
15:11–13). Leonard Slatkes's *Rembrandt and Persia* (1983) saw in him a biblical
"young David"; Reiner Hausherr viewed him as a kind of Jewish Messiah,
painted especially for the Jews; and a Canadian scholar, D.W. Deyell, in
1980 declared that the rider was St Reinold of Pantaleon, one of the few
popular seventeenth-century literary figures who, "as a soldier and a saint
gives acceptable meaning to the Frick Collection Rider." Finally, in 1985, the
distinguished Rembrandt expert Gary Schwartz opted for an equestrian
soldier from the play *Tamerlane* by Joannes Serwouters, first performed in
Amsterdam in 1657. Of course, all of these allegorical interpretations are
pure speculation, and none of them contradicts the fact that a real person in
real costume probably served as a model for the painting. Moreover, some
of them are far-fetched indeed, since, for example, as Held pointed out in
his "Postscript" of 1991, Gijsbrecht van Amstel was already an old man when
he supposedly fled to Poland, the Prodigal Son is usually depicted with a
purse to carry his inheritance; there is no iconic precedent for a "David"
on horseback; and finally, Rembrandt's rider looks rather nonchalant for a
Tamerlane or one of his men in pursuit of the Ottoman Sultan Bayazet, as
Schwartz claimed.[21]

Only one Polish scholar came up with an allegorical theory. Jan
Białostocki, writing in 1969, discovered a pamphlet by a Polish Socinian
group in Holland pleading for religious tolerance. The author signed
himself only "*Eques Polonus*" (A Polish Knight), but was otherwise known
as Jonasz Szlichting, a man of about sixty. Białostocki proposed this Polish

PLATE 1. *Hetman Petro Doroshenko* (1900), by Serhii Vasylkivsky.
From Volodymyr Nediak, *Ukraina kozatska derzhava*
(Kyiv: Emma, 2007), 355.

PLATE 2. *Hetman Ivan Mazepa* (1900), by Serhii Vasylkivsky.
From Volodymyr Nediak, *Ukraina kozatska derzhava*
(Kyiv: Emma, 2007), 406.

In Ukraine the title "hetman" came to designate the ruler of an autonomous or semi-independent Cossack polity. Ukrainian historians stress the quasi-monarchical nature of the Cossack "states" after Hetman Bohdan Khmelnytsky led the Ukrainian Cossacks to de facto independence in 1648. But in 1667, the Polish–Lithuanian Commonwealth and the tsardom of Muscovy tried to partition those Cossack lands between themselves, and resistance was led by Hetman Petro Doroshenko (1627–1698), who accepted the sovereignty of the distant Ottoman sultan. Hetman Ivan Mazepa (1639–1709) began his political career under Doroshenko and later ruled the Cossack state, or Hetmanate, in left-bank (eastern) Ukraine under Muscovite overlordship. But he too strove for more independence and sided disastrously with Swedish king Charles XII against the Muscovites at the battle of Poltava (1709). Doroshenko's attire (Plate 1), particularly in his "kaftan" or long dress, shows some definite "oriental," especially Persian influences, and contrasts with that of Mazepa in full, western armour (Plate 2).

PLATE 3. *Seated Mazepa*, from Homann's *Map of Ukraine* (Nuremberg, c. 1720).
Cover illustration from *Forum: A Ukrainian Review*, no. 90 (1994),
courtesy of Andrew Gregorovich, Toronto.

A hand-painted cartouche (title illustration) from Johann Baptist Homann's undated *Map of Ukraine*, printed probably at Nuremberg c. 1720. The title reads, "Ukraine, which is the Land of the Cossacks, and the Neighbouring Provinces of Wallachia, Moldavia, and Lesser Tatary." Some scholars believe that the illustration depicts a seated Mazepa smoking, with Charles XII of Sweden and Peter the Great of Russia on the left, and two Turkish Janissaries and a Cossack on the right. Peter appears to be threatening Mazepa, while the Turks, who opposed Peter, may be there to defend him. The fact that this map appeared about a decade after Mazepa's revolt reflects Ukraine's high profile in western Europe at that time.

PLATE 4. *Emir Rzewuski*: Taj al-Fahr, or "Goldenbeard," nineteenth-century
illustration. Based on a painting by Kazimierz Żwan (1792–1848),
based on a lithograph by Piotr Le Brun (1802–1879).

From the Kresy to the Middle East: The "Emir," Taj al-Fahr (Crown of Glory), was
born Count Wacław Rzewuski / Viacheslav Revusky in 1784 in the Ukrainian–Polish
borderlands (*Kresy*). Feeling the ignominy from his family's help in bringing about the
partition of Poland in the 1790s, he fled to Arabia. There he collected thoroughbred
Arabic horses, studied customs, language, and penmanship, and became an expert
sketch artist and calligrapher (see self-portrait in Plate 4). After his return to Ukraine,
he collected its folklore and musical instruments and patronized its poets. After a
skirmish between his private Cossack regiment and the Imperial Russian army in 1831,
he disappeared, allegedly fleeing back to Arabia, to live a long life and die peacefully.

PLATE 5. *Sadyk Pasha*, nineteenth-century illustration.

Also hailing from the *Kresy* was Sadyk Pasha (Plate 5), born Mykhailo Chaikovsky /
Michał Czajkowski (1804–1886). He took part in the Polish insurrection of 1830–31,
went into exile in France, and then wrote novellas on Cossack themes. He later went
to Turkey and commanded the Ottoman Cossack Brigade against the Russians in
the Crimean War (1853–56). After the war he returned to Ukraine. But this romantic
"neo-Cossack" always dreamed of restoring a free Cossack Ukraine.

PLATE 6. *Fight for the Turkish Standard* (1905), by Józef Brandt.
National Museum, Cracow.

Józef Brandt's 1905 painting is one of the great canvases depicting the seventeenth-century wars between the multinational Polish–Lithuanian Commonwealth and the equally multinational Ottoman Empire. The most famous battle occurred at Vienna (1683), where Poland's King Jan III Sobieski and his army (two-thirds of it from lands now part of Ukraine) defeated the Ottoman army besieging Vienna and captured a flag allegedly once owned by the Prophet Mohammed. But most of the wars' battles took place in the Ukraina (the south-eastern borderlands of the Commonwealth) and involved the Crimean Tatars more than Turks, and Orthodox Cossacks as well as Roman and Eastern Catholic gentry.

PLATE 7. *Return from Tatar Captivity*, by Leopold Loeffler, nineteenth century.

Leopold Löffler (1827–1898) depicts a young man returned to his home in Poland or Ukraine after being ransomed with the help of the (Catholic) Trinitarian order (founded 1198 to ransom Christian slaves). The captive is probably a *szlachcic* (gentleman) of the south-eastern borderlands (*Kresy*) of the old Polish–Lithuanian Commonwealth, the region that suffered most severely from Tatar raids. Although the icon above the door may be either Catholic or Orthodox, the cross by its side with a container for holy water below it suggests a Roman, or perhaps Eastern Catholic household, less likely Orthodox. For Eastern Catholics and Orthodox Ukrainians, ransom intermediaries were more often Armenians (also Eastern Christians) or others who had Christian and Muslim contacts. The *szlachcic*'s costume, as well as his loving wife and child, are typical for the Ukrainian gentry of that period.

PLATE 8. *Roxelana* (wife of Suleiman the Magnificent), oil on canvas,
by an unknown painter of the late sixteenth or early seventeenth century,
Topkapi Palace Museum, Istanbul.

This portrait of Roxelana, the Ruthenian consort and wife of Suleiman the Magnificent
(reigned as sultan 1520–66), by an unknown painter of the late sixteenth or early
seventeenth century, hangs in the Topkapi Palace Museum, Istanbul. In the upper left
corner, a Latin inscription reads: "Rossa Solymanni Uxor" (Rose, wife of Suleiman).

PLATE 9. *Taras Shevchenko* (1860), by Taras Shevchenko, pen drawing.
From Taras Shevchenko, *Mystetska spadshchyna*, vol. IV
(Kyiv: Vyd. AN UkRSR, 1963), plate 62.

Taras Shevchenko, Ukraine's national poet, was also a talented artist, who produced
many fine self-portraits (such as Plate 9). He executed these two pen drawings in
1859–60 after his return from central Asian exile. Mykhailo Maksymovych (1804–
1873) (Plate 10) was a prominent Ukrainian biologist and literary figure, who was
greatly influenced by the western European culture of his day, and whose pioneering
1827 collection of Ukrainian folksongs stimulated the sudden and rapid growth of

PLATE 10. *Mykhailo Maksymovych* (1859), by Taras Shevchenko, pen
drawing. From Taras Shevchenko, *Mystetska spadshchyna*, vol. IV
(Kyiv: Vyd. AN UkRSR, 1963), plate 43.

national consciousness among his compatriots. Like so many others, Maksymovych
was overwhelmed by Shevchenko's innovative verses, which remained so true to
spoken Ukrainian, yet clearly raised it to the literary level of other, more developed
European languages. But how the modest, soft-spoken biologist and university
administrator, with rather conservative political beliefs, could admire the poet's
fiery, even revolutionary verses remains an unsolved puzzle.

PLATE 11. *Shevchenko*, by Ilya Repin, Shevchenko Museum, Kyiv. From *Shevchenkivskyi slovnyk*, vol. I (Kyiv: Instytut literatury, AN URSR, 1976), frontispiece.

Both the Ukrainian poet Taras Shevchenko (1814–1861) and the Caucasian resistance leader Imam Shamil (1797–1871) were fierce opponents of the Russian Empire, though in different ways. From 1840 to 1859 Shamil led a Sufi Muslim imamate in the North Caucasus that defended its mountain homeland against the Russians. The poet's fiery verses condemned Russian imperialism in that same Caucasus and called out for truth, freedom, and glory. The portrait sets Shevchenko (Plate 11) against a flaming red field; Ukraine-born Ilya Repin executed it several years after the poet's death, and it conveys the revolutionary spirit of his incendiary poem "The Caucasus."

PLATE 12. *The Polish Rider* (c. 1655), by Rembrandt, oil on canvas.
Copyright Frick Collection, New York. Used by permission.

Rembrandt van Rijn almost certainly, about 1655, painted this handsome and somewhat mysterious young eastern European–looking rider, armed for war. It was originally titled *Cosaque à cheval*. The canvas's aristocratic provenance is Polish; its documentation does not antedate the eighteenth century. The young rider's identity remains uncertain, as does whether Rembrandt painted the picture, or only parts of it, and whether others – possibly a student – did the rest. Regardless, the work remains a masterpiece of striking originality and beauty, which could hardly have been created by a lesser artistic genius.

PLATE 13. *Zaporozhian Cossacks Writing a Satirical Letter to the Turkish Sultan* (1891), by Ilya Repin ("St Petersburg version"), oil on canvas. Russian Museum, St Petersburg.

This most famous version of Ivan Repin's *Zaporozhian Cossacks Writing a Satirical Letter to the Turkish Sultan* was completed in 1891 and hangs in St Petersburg's Russian Museum. It is the largest, most balanced, and in some ways most aesthetically pleasing version of this picture. The faces are taken from real people, almost all of Ukrainian background, whom Repin knew in St Petersburg or sketched in Ukraine. Despite the work's theme, and even though some of the attire, weapons, and objects clearly reflect "eastern" influences, it is difficult to see it as an "orientalist" creation à la Edward Said, since Repin definitely thought of these Cossacks as "our own," and not "the other." Both the floppy hat of the Cossack standing behind the Taras Bulba figure in red, and the upright-standing pole on the furthest left, bear what became the blue and yellow national colours of Ukraine during the 1917 Revolution.

PLATE 14. *Zaporozhian Cossacks Writing a Satirical Letter to the Turkish Sultan* (1880s–1890s), by Ilya Repin ("Kharkiv version"). Kharkiv Art Museum.

The second great version of Ivan Repin's *Zaporozhian Cossacks Writing a Satirical Letter to the Turkish Sultan*, which hangs in the Kharkiv Museum of Art, was begun before the 1891 St Petersburg version (Plate 14) but completed after it. Repin liked the latter very much, but wanted to do something more historically accurate. Here few Cossack faces can be recognized. Repin included descendants of the Zaporozhians, both free peasants and former serfs, whom he had sketched during research trips to central Ukraine and the Kuban. The Taras Bulba figure in red and the bare-chested Cossack on the left, however, have been identified.

PLATE 15. *Fire on the Steppe* (1848), by Taras Shevchenko, watercolour.

By the nineteenth century, Middle East and Islamic culture had a long history in central Asia, where the Ukrainian poet Taras Shevchenko was exiled in 1848 and spent over a decade as a common soldier, forbidden to paint or to write, but sometimes managing to do one or the other. Plate 15, *Fire on the Steppe* (1848), one of his most memorable watercolours, depicts a wildfire engulfing the steppe in what is today Kazakhstan. Such prairie fires are notorious for their violence and speed, especially when whipped up by a strong wind. Native Kazakhs are shown in the foreground. At that time, the Kazakh and Kirghiz nomads to the north of central Asian cities like Samarkand and Bukhara were only slightly Islamicized, but they made a deep impression on Shevchenko, who sketched them as often as he could.

knight as the Polish Rider, though a "spiritual" rather than a real one, since Szlichting was too old to be the horseman. But the Socinians were a radical Protestant sect, unitarian and pacifist, so hardly reflected, as Held pointed out, by Rembrandt's well-armed rider.[22]

## A Lisowczyk? Degrees of Polish

The proposed allegorical origin disturbed some scholars. Art historian Zdzisław Żygulski refused to abandon the idea of a real model into whom allegorical meaning could later be read, if desired. He rejected Held's idea of a generalized *Miles Christianus* and questioned the rider's supposed Hungarian connections. In a detailed and well-documented study of 1965, Żygulski pointed out that Rembrandt produced two distinct types of paintings of people in costume: artificial compositions of models dressed up for the occasion in clothing and accoutrements from his own large collection, and real portraits, which were remarkably accurate. He thought that *The Polish Rider*, which he still called *Lisowczyk*, belonged to the latter category.

Żygulski began by admitting that the subject could not be an actual Lisowczyk but proposed he was a Polish light cavalryman – a "Cossack" in seventeenth-century Polish – perhaps a Pole, Ukrainian, Walachian, Tatar, or other nationality. Żygulski stressed the "Cossack" label and the fact that "here served also the people from the Ukraine for whom war constituted the proper element, the source of support and fulfillment." He noted that the rider's steed was specifically Polish, light, and not of the heavier western European or even Hungarian variety, and that it was ridden in a specifically Polish style, upright but leaning slightly forward, and bent at the knee.

Żygulski added, about the horseman: like him, Poles visiting western Europe often imitated men there and wore their hair long and shaved their moustaches; the equestrian sported a fur cap called a *kuchma/kuczma*, which was most common in Poland and Ukraine, less so in Hungary; his coat was a *joupane/żupan*, most probably of closely woven silk, a kind of soft armour specific to Poland and its eastern neighbours; and his arms and especially his bow were unique to Poland (the bow of a type, Żygulski maintained, made only by Armenian artisans in Lviv/Lwów). Żygulski concluded that the saddle, harness, and brass stirrups were all of the Polish and Cossack style. Moreover, the horsetail standard was a typical *bunchuk/bunczuk*, widely used in the Commonwealth and adopted under Ottoman influence; these also were supposedly more popular in Poland than in Hungary.

Thus, all in all, Rembrandt's horseman was an exact replica of a "Polish
light cavalryman," which the artist could never have made up or created
from his own collection of artefacts without a real model. Żygulski hinted
that the artist had a "well-known" interest in Polish matters through his
family connections (his sister-in-law's husband was Polish), which perhaps
inspired him. Thus the "Lisowczyk" was a real person and no generic *Miles
Christianus* and most certainly not Hungarian. All allegorical interpretations of the picture, he concluded, must be relegated to secondary place.[23]

Żygulski's research was generally well received by Western art historians, but at least one had concerns. Mieczysław Paszkiewicz, a Polish émigré
scholar living in London, acknowledged Żygulski's detailed knowledge of
Polish arms and costume but disagreed about the painting's uniqueness. He
maintained that Żygulski's "either/or" approach to Rembrandt's pictures
of people in costume was too rigid, and he pointed out that the painter
sometimes copied and developed other artists' work, and that artefacts in
the picture also occurred in some of his other, non-Polish creations; at the
same time depictions of Poles in long hair, even in western Europe, were
very rare, thus indicating a non-Polish model.

Paszkiewicz suggested that the picture was based on the drawings of
Stefano della Bella and a Polish embassy (that of Opaliński and Leszczyń-
ki) of 1645 passing through Holland on its way to Paris, which Rembrandt,
with his lively interest in things exotic, might have witnessed. (Della Bella
drew this same embassy.) Thus Rembrandt was painting probably not a
commissioned portrait of a particular Pole, but rather a kind of composite
genre scene, very Polish, but not an exact likeness of a "Polish light cavalryman," much less a "Lisowczyk" of the 1630s. Paszkiewicz concluded that
the painting would be better titled "A Rider in Polish Costume."[24]

Needless to say, Paszkiewicz's arguments did not in the least convince
Żygulski. The *éminence* responded immediately, arguing, for example, that
the war-hammer (*nadziak*) was a weapon specific to lieutenants of the Polish light cavalry, just as the mace or "bulava" (a term in several Slavonic
languages) was specific to the hetman, and that while certain elements from
the picture might be found elsewhere in Rembrandt's *œuvre*, or in images
that the painter may have seen, such as certain Persian miniatures, it was
the detailed combination that was unique to the rider and marked him as
definitely Polish. Moreover, the Polish embassy to Paris had passed through
Holland some ten years prior to the artist's work (c. 1655) on the rider, which
seemed a rather long time for the artist to remember such details. Thus the

work remained likely a portrait of a real person rather than a copy of another artist's work or some kind of genre composition. Moreover, Żygulski concluded, Polish costume and armament changed very little between the 1620s and the 1660s, and thus *Lisowczyk* was not as far-fetched a name as it might seem.[25]

## Back to the Archives: An Ogiński Sitter?

About 1970, Mykhailo Bryk-Deviatnytsky, a Ukrainian living in Holland, was examining the Dutch archives for information on Poles living in that country in the 1650s. Because of Rembrandt's Polish family connection, he wondered about any contacts with Ukrainians from the Commonwealth, specifically Cossacks, as possible models for the rider. Some Ukrainians speculated about Hetman Bohdan Khmelnytsky (d. 1657), who was leading the Cossack insurrection when the work was being painted, or even a young Ivan Mazepa (1639–1709), later hetman, who, between seventeen and twenty, while a courtier to the Polish king, was sent to Holland to study artillery (1656–59).

Bryk-Deviatnytsky went to the archives of the Frisian Academy at Frankener, where Professor Jan Makowski (called Maccovius in Latin), the Polish husband of Rembrandt's wife's sister, had then been teaching theology and philosophy. He found some Ukrainians enrolled there, along with some members of the influential Ogiński family of Lithuania. He hypothesized that Makowski, always short of money, arranged for Rembrandt to paint one of these Ogińskis – brothers Bohdan (Theodorus in Latin) or Aleksander – in his national costume and mounted on his horse. The painting's turning up some 150 years later in the hands of this same family would thus be no coincidence.

The Ogiński family was actually Ruthenian (the old, generic name for Ukrainians and Belarusans in the Commonwealth) and in the 1650s still Orthodox and subjects of the Grand Duchy of Lithuania, not the Polish crown, and thus hardly "Polish." Bryk-Deviatnytsky suggested relabelling the painting as "Rembrandt's Cossack," or something similar.[26]

Rembrandt specialist B.P.J. Broos soon followed this lead. Broos also thought Żygulski's work underestimated, and he cited writings in both Dutch and Ukrainian by Bryk-Deviatnytsky. He identified several of Rembrandt's overlooked Polish connections and noted the existence of a stone relief of a *Poolse Cavalyier* (Polish Horseman) dating from

Rembrandt's time on an Amsterdam street but labelled *Poolsche Kozak* by a nineteenth-century scholar, which seemed to be "an interpretation of the 'Polish Rider' by a simple mason."

Broos also stressed Rembrandt's close relationship with the art dealer Henrick van Uylenburgh, in whose workshop he painted for four years and who got him commissions and promoted his career. Rembrandt married Uylenburgh's niece Saskia in 1634 and subsequently bought the house next door to his studio in Breestraat. The art dealer had grown up in Cracow in Poland and by 1620 was acting as an agent of the Polish king and buying art for his collection. Thus he may have arranged the sitter for *The Polish Rider*. It was Rembrandt's marriage to Saskia that connected him to Professor Jan Makowski at Frankener. Broos added three more possible Ogiński sitters from the Commonwealth: brothers Marcjan Aleksander, Jan, and Szymon Karol, who registered at Leyden University as "Poles" (*Polonus*, sing.). Broos seems to have favoured Szymon Karol, who had settled in Holland, married a Dutch woman, and fathered three children there, but concluded that at least one of these five Ogińskis was probably the model.[27]

Broos's careful scholarship, which publicized the Bryk-Deviatnytsky thesis from one or more little-known Ukrainian émigré newspapers, stunned the tight circle of established Rembrandt scholars when it appeared in 1974. Held noted it in a postscript to the 1981 German version of his article, and it attracted attention in Poland as well. Held seemed to awaken to the possibility of a real, live model, but he dismissed Szymon Karol as too old, at thirty-four in 1655. Instead, he proposed Marcjan – eighteen or nineteen in 1650.[28]

Meanwhile, in Poland, Juliusz Chrościcki, who thought Broos's article "brilliant," agreed and began research on Marcjan. He eventually discovered that Marcjan was portrayed in a picture by Ferdinand Bol, one of Rembrandt's students, and that Rembrandt's equestrian bore a striking resemblance. "Ogiński's face," he wrote in 1981, "is easily recognizable in the 'Polish Rider.'" As a clincher, he pointed to the fire faintly observable in the background and added that "Ogiński" in Polish means "of the fire," from the root "*ogień*." He failed to notice, however, another supporting element: Rembrandt's rider was mounted on a white horse moving across a dark background – a symbol on the coats of arms of the old Grand Duchy of Lithuania, the Commonwealth, and the modern republic. This armorial rider, today called *Vytis* (the chaser) in Lithuanian, carries a raised sword and rides a white steed set on a field of red. Thus Ogiński's presence in Holland in 1650, his age, nationality, status, and personal appearance, the "of the fire" argument, and the "white steed" all seemed to identify Rembrandt's rider, which, of course, turned up some 150 years later in the possession of this same family.[29]

Marcjan Aleksander Ogiński (1632–1690) was a perfect candidate. Born into one of the great landowning families of Lithuania, he was son of the last Orthodox senator in the *Sejm* (parliament) of the Polish–Lithuanian Commonwealth. Although this Ruthenian family, with lands in the Smolensk region, dated back to Kyivan Rus', it gained prominence in the sixteenth century when the Lithuanian Grand Duke Aleksander gave it the estate of Ogintai, which was the true source of its name.[30]

Marcjan was born and raised Orthodox and studied in Vilnius and Cracow before going to Holland; he enrolled at Leyden in 1650 but soon returned to the Commonwealth and entered military service; by 1654 he was a standard bearer (*chorążny*), and by 1656 he fought in the ranks of Prince Sapieha's Lithuanian army; he took part in the 1663–64 Muscovite expedition and became deeply involved in Commonwealth politics. He married Marcebella Anna Hlebovich in 1663 and through this marriage became one of Lithuania's wealthiest magnates. In 1668, he founded the Orthodox church in Śmiłowiczy, but he shortly afterwards converted to Catholicism and founded a Catholic church at Rogov and a Jesuit college in Minsk. He became grand chancellor of Lithuania in 1684 and died in 1690.[31]

The discovery of Bol's portrait of Ogiński and the identification of the "Polish Rider" with Marcjan convinced many Rembrandt scholars. Held himself largely accepted the evidence accumulated by Żygulski, Bryk-Deviatnytsky, Broos, and especially Chrościcki, retreated somewhat from his allegorical interpretation, which he claimed was not all that rigid, and wrote: "While I believe that Rembrandt's martially handsome rider derives some of his appeal from the old concept of the *Miles Christianus*, I never claimed that Rembrandt intended him to personify such an allegorical character, and always admitted the possibility that 'he may have called him by a definite name.'"[32] The British cultural historian Sir Simon Schama also accepted the new evidence, as did some Polish scholars, like the military historian Richard Brzezinski, who welcomed it and concluded that Chrościcki "had finally identified it as a portrait of a Lithuanian nobleman, Martin Alexander Ogiński."[33]

Of course, even all this compelling evidence did not convince everyone. Gary Schwartz ignored all this evidence and in 1985 proposed his somewhat fanciful *Tamerlane* theory about the origin of the picture;[34] and in

1983 Leonard Slatkes, echoing Held's earlier position, denied that the rider's arms and costume were specifically Polish, pointed out their general "Oriental" (that is, central Asian and Middle Eastern) qualities, flatly rejected the significance of the Bol portrait purported to be of Ogiński, and proposed his "young David" thesis.[35] A few years later, the Frick Collection's comprehensive catalogue of its paintings treated the Ogiński evidence as a mere "proposal," on the same level as Białostocki's "Socinian hypothesis": "The rider's costume, his weapons, and the breed of his horse have also been claimed as Polish. But if *The Polish Rider* is a portrait, it certainly breaks with tradition." The writer explained: "Equestrian portraits are not common in seventeenth century Dutch art, and furthermore, in the traditional equestrian portrait the rider is fashionably dressed and his mount is spirited and well-bred." The author concluded by returning to Held's original *Miles Christianus* theory, but only as another unverified proposal.[36]

## A "Cossack Rider"?

As late as 2007, Andrew Gregorovich, a Ukrainian researcher in Canada specializing in printed images and antique maps, somewhat more firmly rejected the identification with Marcjan Ogiński and again proposed restoring the original name, *Cossack Rider*. He returned to the older theory that the eighteenth-century Lithuanian Grand Hetman Michał Kazimierz Ogiński had purchased the painting and not inherited it. He also challenged Held's rejection of a Ukrainian Cossack subject because seventeenth-century Cossacks wore loose-fitting *sharavary* and not tight breeches. He printed several seventeenth-century pictures and drawings of Cossacks wearing such breeches and noted the similarity of the rider's *kuchma* and *zhupan* to those of the Ukrainian Cossack Hetman Bohdan Khmelnytsky (d. 1657) and his followers. Indeed, the words *kuchma* and *zhupan* remained current in Ukrainian until recent times, the former becoming a common surname.[37]

Gregorovich also pointed out that the rider's plain clothing and unimpressive horse were more likely to belong to a simple Cossack than to a great Polish magnate, and that Rembrandt probably knew something of the Ukrainian Cossacks because they threw off Polish rule about the time he created his canvas, and the Dutch and French press reported the uprising. Indeed, Gregorovich continued, even the cartouches of various maps of that time displayed Cossack figures that Rembrandt might have seen.

Gregorovich did not address Żygulski's argument about the complete authenticity of the rider's outfit (which required a sitter), but Bryk-Deviatnytsky, as noted above, had identified some Ukrainian students at Frankener. Moreover, there were then still many Ukrainian Cossacks enrolled as light cavalrymen in Polish armies, and even Ivan Mazepa was in Holland at exactly this time. However, no closer Ukrainian connections with Rembrandt and his painting have been established. Thus, while Gregorovich's hypothesis about a "Cossack Rider" may not convince everyone, it does reveal the extent to which some modern Ukrainians identify with Rembrandt's rider.[38]

## Who Done It? The Rembrandt Research Project

In the 1980s a massive challenge arose to all the previous scholarship on *The Polish Rider*. The Rembrandt Research Project, an informal committee at the Rijksmuseum in Amsterdam, had started in 1968 to investigate the master's entire corpus, which they believed had been greatly inflated over the years by false attributions, to see what was actually produced by Rembrandt himself as opposed to his students and imitators. The team, which was headed by Josua Bruyn of Amsterdam University, and included such eminent Rembrandt scholars as Bob Haak and Ernst van de Wetering, analysed the paintings using iconographic and technical methods, including autoradiography (analysis of brush strokes). At least two members of the team viewed each considered work in person, and the aim was to divide the *œuvre* into three categories: authentic Rembrandts, disputable works, and rejections.

In the 1980s, after many years of effort, the team rejected a great many canvases, including the famous *Man in a Golden Helmet* (Gemäldegalerie, Berlin), almost universally thought genuine and one of Rembrandt's greatest works. The prestigious Wallace Collection in London saw its twelve Rembrandts reduced to only one, although it had questions. Then in 1984, in a brief review of a book by Werner Sumowski on Rembrandt's school, Josua Bruyn, for the first time since von Wurzbach in 1906, questioned the authorship of *The Polish Rider* and cautiously proposed the master's student, Willem Drost.[39]

Other members of the Project expressed doubts about who painted the work but did not necessarily gravitate towards Drost. For example, to Żygulski, Bruyn pointed out the soft outline of the rider's figure, which he thought unlike Rembrandt and indicating a female artistic temperament. Haak criticized disproportions in the rider's figure, the strangeness of the horse, the nondescript background, and the lack of brush strokes typical of Rembrandt. For van de Wetering, the horseman lacked the usual "corporeality" and "stability" of Rembrandt's human figures and seemed too insubstantial and vibrating in the unreal gleam; he noted too the loose association between background and rider, again untypical of the master. These volleys re-opened the entire question of who created the painting, letting the much-feared authorship genie out of the bottle.[40]

In general, however, Bruyn's tentative but unexplained attribution to Drost, to say nothing of the private concerns of other team members, discombobulated the art world. The Frick Collection refused to change its attribution to Rembrandt; Held was indignant and in an interview even referred to the Rembrandt Research Project as "the Amsterdam mafia," and Anthony Bailey wrote *Responses to Rembrandt* (1994) pointing out the weaknesses in the team's arguments and anaysing *its* qualifications and methods, finding its documentation inadequate, its reliance on modern technology too rigid, and its judgments overly severe. He even quoted a limerick from the 1920s:

When the Rembrandt came to the cleaner
It began to look meaner and meaner.
Said Rembrandt van Rijn,
I doubt it is mine,
Ask Bode or else Valentiner.[41]

New York artist Russell Connor painted a canvas purporting to show Rembrandt creating his controversial picture and called it *Hands off the 'Polish Rider!'*[42]

This growing chorus of protest to the Project revisionists coincided with the retirement of Bruyn and several other of the team's members in 1993 and its public declaration that its methods, especially its "over-rigorous classification of the paintings into categories," would be changed.[43] A younger scholar, Ernst van de Wetering, took over both Bruyn's chair at Amsterdam University and chairmanship of the Project and soon expressed an opinion on *The Polish Rider* quite at variance with that of Bruyn: the painting was indeed by Rembrandt, but with certain parts completed later, possibly by one of his students. The faces of rider and horse seem to have been by the master, but the shank of the man's boot, the folded-back tail of his coat, and possibly his hose by that other hand.[44] A few years later, Jonathan Bikker published the first scholarly synthesis on Willem Drost and stated categorically that no arguments had been made supporting Drost's authorship of the canvas and he saw no reason for attributing it to him.[45] Robert Hughes, in the *New York Review of Books*, summed up Anglo–American opinion on the matter:

> There can be few paintings of comparable quality of which less is known for sure than the "Polish Rider." But the doubts cast on it by the Rembrandt Research Project are also guesswork. The efforts to reattribute it to one of Rembrandt's pupils, Willem Drost, about whose life and work very little is known, are quite inconclusive. They are like attempts to "prove" that Hamlet was really written by someone other than William Shakespeare – but someone who was still as good a writer as Shakespeare, for whose existence there is no actual evidence. Until such a phantom turns up, to imagine Rembrandt without the "Polish Rider" is rather like trying to imagine Wagner without *Parsifal*.[46]

Could the entire question have been stated any more clearly?

## Abiding Mysteries

By way of conclusion, *The Polish Rider* remains one of Rembrandt's most mysterious and controversial paintings. Its origin, provenance, and meaning have aroused debate since it first came to the attention of the Western public at the end of the nineteenth century. Was the rider really a Cossack as he was first identified? Or, less likely, was he a Tatar, as von Wurzbach thought? Or, again, was he a Pole, or a Lithuanian? And what meaning did these national categories have in the mid-seventeenth century when Rembrandt painted his canvas? More basically, did the painting originate as a portrait or merely an allegorical representation of some historical or literary figure? And most basically of all, was it Rembrandt himself who painted it, or one of his students or imitators?

The evidence presented above tends to support the idea that the creator of the painting, or at least the most important parts of it, was indeed Rembrandt and that it was a portrait of a very real person into which allegorical meanings (only perhaps intended by Rembrandt) have been read by certain modern scholars. Moreover, this person is almost certainly the Lithuanian magnate Marcjan Aleksander Ogiński.

We may thus end by saying that Rembrandt's rider of about 1650 was, if not a Pole by political origin, ethnicity, or religion, at least an actual subject of the great multinational Polish–Lithuanian Commonwealth who registered as a "Pole" in the University of Leyden and who later in a sense became a "Pole" through his conversion to Catholicism. Moreover, his family – Ruthenian and Lithuanian by origin, and Polish and Lithuanian by destiny – was to play an important role in that Commonwealth to the end of its existence. Thus, although some may refer to it in other ways, the picture's current label, *The Polish Rider*, remains more or less accurate both because of its provenance, through the royal collection of Stanisław Augustus and the Dzików Castle in Galicia, and also because of the complex personal history of the Ogiński family in general, and of Marcjan Aleksander Ogiński in particular, who is currently the best candidate for being Rembrandt's marvellous and eternally intriguing "Polish Rider."

## CHAPTER NINE

# Message to Mehmed:
# Repin Creates His *Zaporozhian Cossacks*

DURING THE RUSSIAN–UKRAINIAN WAR, which began in early 2014 and was somewhat misrepresented in Western media as a kind of Ukrainian "civil war," rather than a Russian invasion, there emerged a number of supposedly new images of Ukrainian warriors. One showed a group of soldiers decked out in typical modern military fatigues and gathered around a table in rough and ready style. In the centre a seated soldier was writing a letter. The other soldiers were quite clearly laughing and having a very good time. Although new to Western reporters and news media, this image was a contemporary take on one of the most famous paintings of the Russian Empire, by the beloved artist Ilya Repin (1844–1930). Repin was of Ukrainian origin from the Kharkiv area, the western part of Slobidska Ukraina/Sloboda Ukraine.

Ilya Repin's *Zaporozhian Cossacks Writing a Satirical Letter to the Turkish Sultan* (1878–91), oil on canvas, 203 cm x 358 cm/80 in x 141 in, hung for well over a century in St Petersburg's prestigious Russian Museum (Plate 13); we met this image above, in chapter 2. Those fighters were the most famous of all Ukrainian Cossacks and lived south of Kyiv, "beyond the rapids" (*za porohamy*), halfway down the Dnieper River towards its mouth on the Black Sea. The sultan was Mehmed (Mohammed) IV, Turkish ruler of the Ottoman Empire, the greatest foreign power to threaten Christendom since the Middle Ages. In 1676 this sovereign had supposedly written the Cossacks and demanded their submission to him in no uncertain terms. His missive started with a long list of his high-flown titles and the names of some of the many countries that he and his predecessors had conquered over the centuries. The Cossacks, who had no intention of submitting to him, were making fun of him and his extravagant claims, replying to him in a very vulgar way and mocking his various titles and claims.

Ukrainians in the 2010s who saw this new photo did not miss the satirical parallel, as they faced a new, secular sultan with similar grandiose dreams at Ukrainians' expense.[1] Ilya Repin, whose canvases are known far better in both Russia and Ukraine than those of the Moscow-born Wassily Kandinsky or Belarus'-born Marc Chagall (so rightly admired by Western art critics), still stands at the centre of Ukrainian and Russian art history, claimed by both countries as their own. Indeed, he was the central figure in the Russian national school of painting, which scorned Western models and the spirit of "academism" that had ruled in Russian art since the time of Catherine the Great.

Of Repin's various major paintings, his *Volga Barge Haulers* (1870–73, Russian Museum, hereafter RM) launched this new realistic, or "naturalist" trend, his *Ivan the Terrible Killing His Own Son* (1885, Tretiakov Gallery, hereafter TG) shocked Muscovite society out of its complacent, traditionalist slavophilism, his magnificent *Leo Tolstoy Barefoot* (just after 1900, TG) was seared into the mind of every Russian subject who loved Russian literature, and, finally, his *Zaporozhian Cossacks* has been almost universally admired throughout Russia. Tsar Alexander III proudly acquired the last for his new Russian Museum in St Petersburg; Joseph Stalin, attracted to the lavatory and other vulgarities indicated in the painting, hung a copy of it in his dacha outside Moscow and quietly made it known that it was a work of art to be admired by all "progressives." And who could disagree with Stalin?[2]

Consequently, Ilya Repin was declared by Soviet art critics and historians to be a "progressive" and a "realist," *persona grata* in the USSR, even though he had refused to return to Russia after the Revolutions of 1917 and quietly defied both Lenin and Stalin from his home just across the border in neighbouring Finland. To this day in the West, he is still little known or regarded, and his paintings may seem foreign and exotic, though not without a certain Romantic attraction, so some Western art historians have finally begun to pay some attention to him.

## Painting People and Places

So exactly who was Ilya Repin, and where does his corpus stand in the history of Russian and most especially Ukrainian art and culture? And again, what should a Western art enthusiast know about his great picture of those Zaporozhian Cossacks, who wrote that scandalous letter to the Ottoman sultan?[3]

Repin, as we saw, was a native son of Sloboda Ukraine, which began west of Kharkiv and extended eastward across the contemporary borders of Ukraine and Russia into the Kursk and Voronezh provinces of the Russian Federation. This was a region settled by free Ukrainian Cossacks in the seventeenth century fleeing the disorders of the old Polish–Lithuanian Commonwealth, which in older times had extended across most of what is today Ukraine. The Russian tsars accepted these Cossacks and granted them certain privileges and freedoms, including exemption from taxation for some years; hence Sloboda [free, non-enserfed] Ukraine.[4]

Repin himself was born into the family of a military colonist and from his youth knew well the local "Little Russian" (as he called it) or Ukrainian population, the "Little Russian" language, and Ukrainian Cossack history. Many years later, while living in the Russian North, he did his best to teach that language to his "half-Russian" children (if we may use that term). And in his prime, he was to paint those local people and depict their faces and their customs with great accuracy. In locales ranging from his hometown of Chuhuiv in western Sloboda Ukraine to the province of Kursk in the east, he vividly painted people and places, from a fleshy church deacon to colourful, crowded, and confused religious processions.

In 1863 he went to study at the St Petersburg Academy of Art, where he came under the strong influence of his slightly older countryman from Kursk, Nikolai Kramskoi/Mykola Kramsky (1837–1887), who had attracted him to the capital, and a little before had led a revolt in the Academy against its classical forms and academic disciplines. At that time, Repin, Kramskoi, and the others turned to realism and native "Russian" (including Ukrainian) motifs in their work and began a true revolution in Russian art. Eventually, both Repin and Kramskoi were to paint stunning portraits of the Ukrainian national poet, Taras Shevchenko (1814–1860) – see chapter 5, above – whose *Kobzar* (The Blind Minstrel, or The Kobza Player, 1840) changed the course of literature in Ukraine and was beloved by almost all Ukrainians.[5]

From St Petersburg, Repin went west to study in Paris, played with the impressionism that he found there, but shortly returned to Russia and eventually settled in the artistic colony at Abramtsevo just outside Moscow. There he briefly came under the influence of the local slavophilism that was so strong in Moscow, that old capital of the Muscovite state. But he did not much like the place and could never quite forget his Ukrainian roots. Sadly, his paintings on Muscovite themes are filled with darkness, anger, violence, and even ugliness. These include his graphic depictions of *Tsarina Sophia* (1879, TG) confined to a nunnery while her supporters are being executed outside her window; *Ivan the Terrible* (1885, TG), who had just murdered his own son in a furious fit of rage and was appalled by what he had done; and even *Choosing the Grand Prince's Bride* (1884–87, State Picture Gallery, Perm), in which the candidates are anything but beautiful.

The contrast of these dark works with his Ukrainian paintings was absolutely striking; and of all these, his happy Zaporozhians writing their satirical letter was by far the most important. Most of those canvases are filled with light and laughter, happiness and exuberance, and clearly reveal his attitude towards all things Ukrainian. Not only is his *Zaporozhian Cossacks* a study in laughter and joy, but so too is his *Evening Party* (1881, TG). The latter depicts a jovial peasant gathering in a cottage, with a young couple dancing in the middle and folk musicians and common people around them smiling, laughing, and clapping to the music, clearly delighted by the young dancers. These two works, dignified, yet warm and familiar to Ukrainians, are Repin's outstanding representations of what he seemed to think of as the Ukrainian spirit. And so, it was not without reason that Dmytro Dontsov, the twentieth-century ideologist of Ukrainian integral (quasi-fascist) nationalism, solemnly declared that for Repin, Russia was all violence and ugliness, Ukraine beauty, happiness, and joy.[6]

However, Dontsov was an extremist and only half right. Repin was primarily a portrait artist, and his portraits as opposed to his historical pictures do not reveal such a dichotomy. His portraits of Russian women are on occasion just as attractive as those of Ukrainian ones, his vision of the great Russian writer Leo Tolstoy just as dignified as that of the writer from Ukraine Vladimir Korolenko, who was of mixed Polish and "Little Russian," or Ukrainian parentage, and his depiction of the statesman Petr Stolypin, who was assassinated in the Kyiv Opera House in the presence of the tsar, just as dignified as that of Dmytro Bahalii, the historian of Sloboda Ukraine and president of Kharkiv University.

Moreover, in contrast to his dark view of old Muscovy with its autocracy and violence, his view of the imperial capital at St Petersburg and its surroundings is much brighter, as for example in his painting *What Freedom!* (1903, RM), which depicts an enthusiastic young couple (probably very much in love) wading into the waves on a Finnish beach in Kuokkala (now, aptly, Repino) on the Baltic seashore just outside the then-Russian capital, where for many years Repin taught and worked, including on many of his Ukrainian canvases. His impressions of St Petersburg seem to lack the usual dreariness, dampness, and mists of that city. It seems that he absorbed not only certain semi-conscious "national" differences between Ukraine and "Russia" (for Ukraine was then still very much a part of Imperial Russia), but also the very clear civic differences between western-looking, newer St Petersburg and self-absorbed and restrictively slavophilic old Moscow, where the autocracy had its roots.[7]

## The Zaporozhians' Letter: A Controversial History

And so it was that even in Abramtsevo, outside Moscow, Repin again turned his attention to Ukraine. It was there in 1878 that Repin did his first sketch (Figure 12) for a great panorama of the Zaporozhian Cossacks, suggested by his friend from Kyiv M.V. Prakhov (1840–1879), who excitedly brought him a copy of an article on this subject by the Ukrainian historian Mykola Kostomarov (1814–1885). Like the artist himself, Kostomarov hailed from Sloboda Ukraine, more exactly, the province of Voronezh.

Of course, having read Nikolai Gogol/Mykola Hohol and other Ukrainian authors, and being familiar with the Ukrainian *dumas*, or reflective songs, Repin knew the basic outlines of Zaporozhian history. He already seemed to fully accept the image of the Cossacks as defenders of popular liberty, as propagated by Romantic authors such as Gogol and Kostomarov, and extending as far back as Voltaire, who famously wrote that Ukraine had always wanted to be free. Repin also may have been aware of the differences between the more cultivated "town Cossacks" of central Ukraine and the more plebeian Zaporozhians of the south, who lived "beyond the rapids" on the Dnieper River and so out of reach of any civil authority. Moreover, he had actually heard of this famous letter, a popular folk motif in many Ukrainian villages.

In 1676, the Ottoman Sultan Mehmed (Mohammed in Arabic) IV, whose mother was said to have been of Ukrainian origin, allegedly sent the Zaporozhians a formal letter – complete with his extravagant titles and territorial claims – demanding their immediate submission to him. The Cossacks, led by their otaman, or commander, Ivan Sirko, or, in another version a different commander, were rather amused by this and ostensibly drafted a reply mocking these titles and calling the sultan all sorts of rude, indeed, exceedingly vulgar names. And so, when Repin at Abramtsevo again read a version of this letter in Kostomarov's article, he was seemingly immediately struck by the contrast between dark, absolutist Muscovy, with its restricting, authoritarian traditions, and the bright Ukrainian south, with its irrepressible spirit of liberty. On 26 July 1878, he did his first pencil drawing of the merry Zaporozhians drafting their missive.[8]

Repin certainly believed in the document's authenticity, or wanted to, as had the Ukrainian country folk among whom it circulated. But more circumspect historians of both Repin's time and later question whether such an epistle was really sent to the great ruler in Constantinople (today's Istanbul) on the straits separating Europe from Asia. And some historians even question whether such a text was originally written in Ukraine or was perhaps a copy of something drawn up elsewhere.

In Repin's time, two of his closest advisers, the Ukrainian historian Kostomarov and then the Cossack specialist Dmytro Yavornytsky, questioned this letter's authenticity, but thought that the legend revealed something very real about the Ukrainian Cossacks, especially the Zaporozhians. In Soviet times, the Ukrainian historian Volodymyr Holobutsky (1903–1993) too questioned the document, but printed the Zaporozhians' reply (though not the sultan's letter to them) in full in his history of the Zaporozhian Cossacks, despite heavy censorship by the Soviet authorities.[9]

Holobutsky's contemporaries the literary scholars M.D. Kagan-Tarkovskaia in Leningrad and N.D. Nudha in Ukraine thought the epistle probably original and believed it the model for later letters to the sultan from the Polish–Lithuanian Commonwealth and Muscovy. But in the 1970s, Daniel Clarke Waugh at Harvard, having created a more accurate chronology of the surviving manuscripts and editions, as well as analysing their content, concluded that the Ukrainian versions of the Cossack letter were copies of an earlier such letter probably composed in the chancellery of the Muscovite state and itself based on an even earlier Polish version produced in the Commonwealth. Ultimately, all of these letters, concluded Waugh, could be traced back to some very real letters from the Ottoman sultans to various sixteenth-century European rulers (especially in the Habsburg

Empire) and official clerks' dismissive responses to unacceptable demands. The Cossack letter, he believed, revealed absolutely nothing about the Zaporozhian Cossacks, and Repin's painting was simply "a museum piece."[10]

Of course, this stingy remark is completely off-base. A Cossack letter did in fact exist from the 1620s on, though based on earlier models. It was copied and circulated throughout the period of the Polish– and Cossack–Ottoman wars and appeared thereafter in many versions, including those later published by Kostomarov, Yavornytsky, and others. Indeed, one of these letters was retranslated into Polish, and even German and English, and publicized all over Europe in the late seventeenth century, especially in the face of the Ottoman siege of Vienna in 1683, when European interest in the subject was very high. So the fame of the Ukrainian Cossacks, and their valour and defiance, became more than a mere legend; it became a firm belief both in Ukraine, where versions of the epistle appeared in the Cossack chronicle of Velychko and elsewhere, and also in western Europe, where it gave hope to those struggling against the still very real Ottoman threat.[11]

Ultimately, of course, the sultan's letter goes right back to the beginnings of Islam and the Prophet Mohammed, who ostensibly wrote to Heraclius, the emperor of Byzantium, Khusrow, the shah of Persia, and the negus of Abyssinia and invited them to submit to the divine law given to the Prophet of Islam. The story of these invitations (as told by the early-tenth-century historian of Islam al-Tabari) was accepted in Muslim tradition, and was augmented by the legendary "Pact of Umar," allegedly between the Caliph Omar and the besieged Christians of Palestine. Throughout the centuries, Muslim rulers attacking non-Muslim cities and states usually would write such a letter demanding submission and, in accord with the legendary Pact of Umar, offer the protection of the Islamic State and security of person and property to those who would freely submit; such persons could even maintain their traditional Christian or Jewish religions on condition that they respected Islam, accepted their second-class status, and paid a special tax called the *jizya*. So Mehmed (II) the Conqueror, in 1453 before besieging the great Christian city of Constantinople, wrote in this way to the last emperor of Byzantium, and in 1683 Grand Vizier Kara Mustafa, when besieging Vienna, wrote to the Holy Roman Emperor Leopold I in similar terms.[12]

The bold Cossack letter ostensibly replied to such a summons. In 1683, it was translated into German, and even English, and gave hope to the defenders of Vienna and all Europe that the Turks would be repulsed, as indeed they were. In this way, the correspondence between the sultan and the Cossacks, although it may have started out with some legendary characteristics, and was not entirely original, became a real factor in European history, in which later Ukrainian historians like Nudha could justly take some pride.

Quite aside from the seventeenth-century English translation, the Cossack letter more recently has been translated into English several times, including by Bernard G. Guerney in *The Portable Russian Reader*, which was widely read in the English-speaking world during the Cold War.[13] At this point, I will quote the correspondence in full, both the sultan's summons and the Cossack response, from the translation of Kostomarov's version by Victor A. Friedman, which, despite the translator's untoward commentary accusing the Cossacks of doing nothing but raping, pillaging, and slaughtering defenceless people in pogroms, seems to be the linguistically most professional rendering:

### SULTAN MOHAMMED IV TO THE ZAPOROZHIAN COSSACKS

I, the Sultan, son of Mohammed, Brother of the Sun and the Moon, Grandson and Vicegerent of God, Sovereign of all kingdoms: of Macedonia, Babylonia, and Jerusalem, of Upper and Lower Egypt; King of kings; Ruler of all that exists; extraordinary, invincible Knight; Constant Guardian of the grave of Jesus Christ; Trustee of God Himself; Hope and Comfort of the Moslems, [the] Confusion [but also] Great Protector of Christians, command you, the Zaporozhian Cossacks, to surrender to me voluntarily and without any kind of resistance, and do not permit yourselves to trouble me with your attacks!
Turkish Sultan Mohammed

### ZAPOROZHIANS TO THE TURKISH SULTAN

You Turkish Satan, brother and comrade of the damned devil and secretary to Lucifer himself! What the hell kind of knight are you? The devil sh-ts and you and your army swallow it. You are not fit to have the sons of Christians under you; we are not afraid of your army, and we will fight you on land and on sea. You Babylonian busboy,

Macedonian mechanic, Jerusalem beer brewer, Alexandrian goat skinner, swineherd of Upper and Lower Egypt, Armenian pig, Tatar goat, Kamianets hangman, Podolian thief, grandson of the Evil Serpent himself, and buffoon of all this world and the netherworld, fool of our God, swine's snout, mare's asshole, butcher's dog, unbaptized brow, may the devil steam your ass! That's how the Cossacks answer you, you nasty gob of spit! You're unfit to rule Christians. We don't know the date because we don't have a calendar. The moon of the month is in the sky, and the year is in a book, and the day is the same with us as with you. So go kiss our butt!

Chief Hetman Zakharchenko with all the Zaporozhian Host[14]

In his biography of Ivan Sirko, Yavornytsky quotes a very similar letter, perhaps only slightly more insulting, and has it signed by "Otaman Ivan Sirko and the whole Zaporozhian army."[15]

Repin was seemingly well acquainted with both versions. Friedman translated the Kostomarov version, thinking that its more archaic language made it older and more original. Like Waugh before him, he also noticed Russian linguistic influences on the Ukrainian text, although, unlike Waugh, he did not suggest that these were due to copying from a Muscovite original, changing the context, and putting it into Ukrainian. Certainly, for Ukrainians, the references in the text to the "hangman of Kamianets" and the "Podolian thief" would have been perfectly clear and would have dated the document fairly precisely, because the great Polish fortress at Kamianets-Podolsky (The Place of the Rock), which dominated the Ukrainian province of Podolia, was captured by the Ottomans and the whole of the province annexed to the Ottoman Empire in 1672. That marked the apex of Ottoman power, after which the empire went into a rapid and irreversible decline. The Commonwealth recovered Podolia as early as 1699.[16]

## Repin's Tour of Ukraine (1880)

Of course, in a very general way, Repin was acquainted with most of these facts. Still, he wished to make his painting as historically and ethnographically accurate as possible. The dress, weaponry, physique, and faces of the Cossacks were to reflect the realities of old Ukraine. So he personally interviewed Kostomarov on these matters. The historian, who had pioneered the use of ethnography, especially historical songs, in his many histories, was enthusiastic about the project and charmed the artist with his stories of old Zaporozhia and even mapped out a research trip along the Dnieper for Repin to follow.[17]

From May to September 1880, Repin, who had long dreamed of visiting Kyiv and the Cossack country south of it, took up Kostomarov's suggestion and toured Ukraine in the company of V.A. Serov, his pupil. As a young schoolboy Serov had studied for some time in Kyiv and had acquired a real appreciation for the beauties of the Ukrainian language. The two travelled down the Dnieper, visiting Kyiv and Zaporozhia, and going as far south as Odessa on the Black Sea, visiting local museums, sketching artefacts, especially weapons and costumes, drawing the locals, especially those whom Repin thought might be descended from Cossack ancestors, and painting the countryside. Repin even sought out and painted what he believed to be the grave of the legendary Zaporozhian "Otaman" Ivan Sirko (d. 1680), whom he later made one of the central figures in the best-known version of his painting. For a month and a half, he stayed at Kachanivka, at the estate of the famous Ukrainian landowner in Chernihiv province, V.V. Tarnovsky the Younger (1837–1899), whose family had earlier hosted Gogol, Shevchenko, Kostomarov, Gay (Ge), and many others, and whose collection of Ukrainian Cossack artefacts Repin studied and whose portrait he painted at least twice: *The Cossack* (1880, TG) and *The Hetman* (1880, Sumy Art Museum).

In the second picture, Tarnovsky is dressed in an early-eighteenth-century scarlet Cossack costume with gold and silver trim, a pistol stuck in his cummerbund and a saber at his side; he is leaning on an old Cossack cannon. Repin at this time also copied what was (probably incorrectly) believed to be an old portrait (Dnipropetrovsk History Museum) of Hetman Ivan Mazepa (d. 1709), who had rebelled against Peter the Great. Repin also painted Tarnovsky's wife, Sofiia, at a piano (Sumy Art Museum).[18] Every evening Repin would visit the Ukrainian villages surrounding Kachanivka, observe the local customs, and sketch the country folk. It was at Kachanivka as well that Repin did crucial work on his exuberant *Evening Party*.

His last stop in Ukraine was at the estate of his colleague the painter Mykola Gay/N.N. Ge, also in Chernihiv province, where he painted the lady of the house, before returning to Moscow loaded with albums filled with drawings and studies.[19] Over the years, Repin painted portraits of at least four of his fellow artists, whose names were closely linked to Ukraine: Mykola Murashko, Mykola Gay/Ge, Ivan Kramskoi/Ivan Kramsky, and Arkhip I. Kuindzi.

Repin was clearly following not only Kostomarov's advice but also his example. That historian famously did not restrict himself to dry chronicles and documents, but also closely examined the life of the common people through study of their historical songs and ballads, their folklore, and their present customs, values, manners, and morals. "It cannot be," Kostomarov wrote, "that past centuries are not reflected in the lives and memories of their heirs." Similarly, Repin had undertaken that trip to Ukraine, and he had approached its people directly with a view to capturing the psychology and physical character of their predecessors. It was often said that Repin could paint only what he actually saw, and in Ukraine he most definitely saw those Zaporozhians of old.[20]

## Putting It Together: Laughter and Tears (1880s)

Back in Abramtsevo in September 1880, Repin began integrating his new materials to create a fuller version of his painting. On 6 November he wrote to Stasov:

> Ah, forgive me for not writing to you earlier. I am a man without a conscience. I was not able to answer you, Vladimir Vasilevich, and the 'Zaporozhians' are responsible for it. What a people! When I try to write about them, my head spins with their rowdiness and noise . . . I took up the palette and here it is two and a half weeks that I have lived with them without a break. It is impossible to tear oneself away from them, this happy people . . . Gogol did not write about them in vain and everything that he wrote was true! A devilish folk! No one in the entire earth felt *liberty, equality, and fraternity* as deeply as they! Throughout its entire life, Zaporozhia remained free, never submitting to anyone. [When the Muscovites tried to put the Zaporozhians down,] they left for Turkey and there lived freely to the end of their days . . . It may be a mocking picture, but all the same, I will paint it.[21]

Over the course of the next years, Repin's enthusiasm for the Zaporozhians never failed. His daughter, Vera, later recalled how immersed he was in Ukrainian history during this period. "Almost every day, Papa read verses aloud [to us] in Ukrainian: 'On the Three Brothers' [and other epics] . . . At that time, he painted his picture . . . We had gradually come to know all the heroes, Otaman Sirko with his grey whiskers . . . , Cossack Holota 'who feared neither fire, nor sword, nor swamp' . . . There was Taras Bulba with [his sons] Ostap and Andrii, and Vakula the blacksmith. Papa modeled the figures of the Zaporozhians from yellow clay, Taras Bulba and the others. Some have been preserved to this day."[22]

However, Repin's conception of the final large canvas was of epic proportions, and it could not be completed in only a few years. He was to work on it intermittently in three different versions from 1878 to 1891. After a few years, he moved to St Petersburg, but still continued to labour at his masterpiece. In 1885, the year that Kostomarov died, the Ukrainian archaeologist Dmytro Yavornytsky (1855–1940), driven out of his homeland by charges of "ukrainophilism," arrived in the capital, and Repin made a point of meeting him.

After a memorial service in honour of the poet Shevchenko at the Kazan Cathedral in St Petersburg, Repin walked up to Yavornytsky and introduced himself. The two Zaporozhian enthusiasts became immediate friends, and the historian put his extensive collection of Zaporozhian artefacts at the artist's disposal. In turn, Repin drew some illustrations for one of Yavornytsky's books, *Zaporozhe v ostatkakh stariny i predaniiakh naroda* (Zaporozhia in the Relics of the Past and the Legends of the People, 1888). It may even be that the archaeologist's arrival stimulated Repin to begin work again on his masterpiece. In 1888, possibly at his new friend's suggestion, Repin undertook a new research trip to the Kuban in search of the descendants of the Zaporozhians among the Kuban Cossacks. (At one point Yavornytsky hoped to accompany Repin, together with Tarnovsky, on this trip, but his academic duties prevented it.) Moreover, in 1889, Yavornytsky published an outline history of the Zaporozhians with a special section on the apocryphal letter as a Ukrainian folk motif written especially for Repin's use.[23]

At this time, the Ukrainian artists and intellectuals in St Petersburg would often gather at evening parties for discussions and song. Repin frequently attended. Ukrainian history, including the raids of the Crimean Tatars, who carried off into Turkish captivity as many younger people as they could, and Cossack reprisal raids even into Istanbul, often came up (see chapter 3). At one such event, the painter Opanas Slastion (1855–1933; see Figures 7 and 8), who played the kobza well, and the artist Khoma Bondarenko, who sang well, performed the famous *duma* "The Lament of the Poor Slaves in Turkish Captivity." The company was deeply moved, and Repin himself, as Yavornytsky recalls in his memoirs, "cried more than a single tear."[24] It was this view of Ukrainian history, of the conflict of Christendom and the Islamic power on the Ukrainian Steppe, that forms the background to Repin's *Zaporozhians*. On 19 February 1889, at a time when he was most absorbed by his Zaporozhian brotherhood, Repin wrote to the Russian literary figure, N.S. Leskov:

> I have to say to you that even in the 'Zaporozhians' I had an idea. I have always been attracted to the communal life of citizens, in history, in the monuments of art, and especially in the architectural planning of cities – most often feasible only under a republican form of government. In each trifle remaining from these epochs, one may observe an unusual spirit and energy; everything is done with talent and energy, and bears wide common, civic meaning. Italy gives us so much material of this kind!!! Up to today, this tradition is alive and well there . . . And our Zaporozhia delights me with this same love for freedom and heroic spirit. There the brave elements of the Russian people renounced a life of comfort and founded a community of equal members to defend the principles of the Orthodox faith and human personality that they most cherished. Today these will seem like obsolete words, but then, in those times, when thousands of Slavs were carried off into slavery by the powerful Muslims, when religion, honor, and freedom were being desecrated, this was a powerfully stirring idea. And thus, this handful of daring men, of course the best of them . . . rose up, not only to defend Europe from the eastern plunderers, but even to threaten that civilization and laugh to their very souls at that eastern arrogance.[25]

Thus did Repin juxtapose the tears of the poor slaves in Turkish captivity to the laughter of his happy Zaporozhians.

Of course, Repin's reference in the letter to the *Russkii narod* (Russian people) did not imply that the Zaporozhians were "Russians" in the modern sense, or some kind of Muscovite immigrants to Ukraine; rather he used this term, as most people did in those days, in a general way, as we might say "Eastern Slavs" – Ukrainians, Russians, and Belarusans. The Zaporozhians were central to Ukrainian history, and Repin usually spoke of "Little Russians" when referring to the Ukrainians of his time. Repin seems to have envisioned a kind of hierarchy or symbiosis of simultaneously held identities, Russian, Ukrainian, and Zaporozhian, which is alien to modern notions of mutually exclusive national identity. This is an important point to which we shall return later in this chapter.

Throughout these many years, Repin's enthusiasm for the Zaporozhians never seriously flagged. This was true even though he sometimes feared that certain persons who could expect to enjoy favour at the imperial court would accuse him of spreading Ukrainian "separatist" ideas. In general, Repin was very uncomfortable with Russian nationalist elements, men like the fiery journalist Mikhail Katkov, who helped instigate the official ban on the printing of the Ukrainian language in the empire during the last quarter of the nineteenth century, and whom he detested as a hopeless reactionary.[26]

## Models for the Painting

When the most famous version of his magnum opus was finally finished in 1891, it was an epic canvas, vigorous and exuberant, and reflecting every kind of laugh or smile that one could imagine. A very large painting (203 cm x 358 cm/80 in x 141 in), it contained more than sixteen well-developed figures closely grouped around a table on which the scribe was penning the letter. Each Cossack is dressed in a period costume, and there are a great variety of facial types among them. Weapons and other artefacts, based on models from the collections of Tarnovsky, Yavornytsky, and the museums, are prominently displayed across the picture. The fictional Taras Bulba, dressed in red, holding his enormous sides, stands to the right. Otaman Sirko, pipe in mouth, leans forward over the scribe, and to the left, a Cossack in a black fur hat of the type once worn by Hetman Sahaidachny looks on intently.

All of the major figures are based on real models, many of them peasants originally drawn in Ukraine, but others were more famous Ukrainians or personal friends of Repin's from St Petersburg. Repin chose his models carefully, including only those who were good natured or revealed interesting smiles or laughter: Taras Bulba was O.I. Rubets, a professor of the St Petersburg Conservatory, a collector of Ukrainian folksongs, and from the same town as Repin in the Kharkiv area; Sirko was Repin's friend the wily but good-humoured General Mykhailo Drahomirov, commander of the Kyiv garrison and a protector of nationally conscious Ukrainian activists; the Cossack in the black Sahaidachny hat was the enormously rich Cossack enthusiast V.V. Tarnovsky; the Cossack putting his fist on the back of another Cossack was the painter Ya.F. Tsionhlynsky; another Cossack was the artist from Poltava P.D. Martynovych; and the scribe was Yavornytsky himself. Rubets, moreover, was the first composer to rework the famous Ukrainian folksong *Zasvystaly kozachenki* (The Cossacks Whistled) into an orchestral and choral piece. In some ways, perhaps, Repin's happy Zaporozhians mirror the spirit of that particular song.[27]

In his memoirs, Yavornytsky writes about what lengths he and Repin went to to obtain proper models for the painting. They decided that Georgii Alekseev, an official of the tsar's court, a coin collector, a man who held imperial decorations, and an honorary citizen of Ekaterinoslav in the old Cossack country (today Dniepropetrovsk in central Ukraine) was an excellent candidate. However, when Repin approached Alekseev, he was shocked and even a bit offended, exclaiming: "What is this? What kind of laughter are you leaving for future generations? No!" Yavornytsky therefore worked out a clever strategy. One day he invited Alekseev over to Repin's home to see his extensive collection of old coins that he had loaned him especially for the purpose. Unaware of the plan, Alekseev came over, and while he was poring intently over the coins, Repin quietly sketched him from behind. In the painting, he is that impressive Cossack with the shaved head and bare back turned towards the viewer.[28]

## Critical Reception

After its first showing in St Petersburg in November 1891 the painting was a great success, and on its initial tour of Europe it was applauded in Stockholm, Munich (where it won a gold medal), and elsewhere. In St Petersburg itself, it was generally appreciated for its native "Russian" character, and Tsar Alexander III, after seeing the generally positive reaction in Europe, immediately purchased it, for the enormous sum of 35,000 rubles, for his new Museum of Russian Art (Russian Museum, RM) in St Petersburg. Moreover, both the critics and Repin himself (often very critical of his own work) agreed that it was one of his finest productions. It was especially well received in Ukraine, where reproductions and copies soon turned up in many towns and cities, and it even came to be imitated in folk art.[29]

Of course, Repin's masterpiece was not to everyone's liking. Prestigious or powerful art critics like the reactionary nationalist publisher A.S. Suvorin and the cosmopolitan art connoisseur A. Benua (Alexandre Benois) stood back from the work; it was looked on with suspicion by certain elements in official court and government circles, who seemed to fear the bold statement of freedom and independence that it represented; and, of course, some of the painter's contemporaries were envious.[30]

A few years later, Benua, a scion of old French and Italian émigrés long
settled in Russia, and the young ideologist of the new Modernist trend in
Russian art and "art for art's sake," published a pioneering history of Russian painting, and, of course, devoted an entire section of it to Repin. But it
was scathing. Benua acknowledged that Repin had been "the greatest and
most remarkable" Russian artist of the 1870s and 1880s, but he attacked
him for what he believed to be his superficiality, lack of method, lack of
consequential thought, and "anecdotism." He particularly disliked what he
thought of as Repin's growing reverence for the early-nineteenth-century
classicist K.P. Briullov and that painter's style of "academic" art; he further
charged that Repin's works could now be seen as merely "drafts" – they
seemed unfinished and incompletely thought out, not expressing any kind
of whole. Of Repin's *Zaporozhians*, he could barely speak, and he did not
even mention it in his history, saying only that Repin was most of all "given
to satire, smiles, caricature, and spiteful anecdote." All in all, he bitterly
concluded, Repin "over-salts things and falls into painting cartoons."[31]

Of course, such scathing criticism of one of Russia's greatest painters,
and the person who, like Tolstoy in literature, or even Mussorgsky in music,
personified Russian art, did not pass without comment. So in a review of
Benua's opinion, the equally young Kornei Chukovsky defended Russian
art and Repin in particular. He charged Benua with a superficiality of his
own, with being more concerned with "decoration" than true art, and with
simply demeaning Russian culture. "I am glad to say that I live in a world
in which Repin is [still] alive," he concluded. Chukovsky was to remain an
admirer of Repin's through the Revolution and well into Soviet times, and
eventually published an officially approved, Soviet biography of the artist.[32]

However, neither Benua nor Chukovsky touched on the Ukrainian aspect of Repin's corpus, even in his picture of the Zaporozhians. Perhaps
they simply did not feel it important. Or perhaps restrictions on Ukrainian
culture, including the official ban on printing the language, were generally enforced during the reign of the reactionary Alexander III and
inhibited open discussion of the "local," or national Ukrainian rather than
pan-"Russian" character of Repin's epic canvas. For example, the principal
ukrainophile journal (purely cultural, of course) in the Russian Empire –
*Kievskaia starina* (Kyivan Antiquity) – which normally would have been
quite interested, printed nothing about it.

By contrast, the canvas was discussed in Ukrainian-populated Austrian
Galicia, where the censor was no problem. "Artist," for example, from the

Russian Empire, wrote about two exhibitions in St Petersburg, that of Polish painter Józef Brandt's *Victory Song of the Zaporozhians* (Figure 13), where the Cossacks are riding towards the viewer on their spirited horses, and that of Repin's Zaporozhians writing their letter. "Artist" remarked that Brandt's picture was vivid, filled with colour, and made a very good impression, but the faces of his riders looked more Hungarian than Ukrainian, and one could hardly make them out, whereas Repin's Zaporozhians were remarkable for their individual laughing faces that put Brandt's entirely out of mind. "Artist" seemed proud to conclude that Repin's canvas, that is, the picture of his "fellow countryman" (*zemliak*), was far more successful than Brandt's.[33]

Also of note was the second major version of the painting, which the artist had begun prior to the 1891 Russian Museum version but completed after it and which today hangs in the Museum of Art in Kharkiv. After Repin finished this version, the Ukrainian sugar magnate, I.N. Tereshchenko, wished to buy it, but seemingly he was outbid by the Trekiakov Gallery, and it went to Moscow. In 1933, when Kharkiv was still the capital of Soviet Ukraine, as the country swayed between the earlier purges of the national intelligentsia and the massive purges yet to come, and while the Great Ukrainian Famine was at its worst, this version of the painting was transferred to Kharkiv. It stayed there after Kyiv became the capital, and it survived the Second World War. The work remains an attraction to the present, although it is much less known outside of independent Ukraine.[34]

Art critics generally agree that the Kharkiv version (Plate 14) is somewhat less impressive than the St Petersburg version. It is slightly smaller and lacks the harmony and some of the power of the latter. Repin executed it in part because he wanted a version that was more historically accurate than its predecessor. Its general plan is similar, but Otaman Sirko, who appears in the centre of the original, is missing. And while the artefacts and dress may be slightly more accurate, and the Cossacks' faces just as varied, the identities of few of its models are known. Repin most probably here used unnamed Ukrainian country folk and also some Cossacks from the Kuban for its models. Ukrainian art historians, however, love it, and delight in its less formal character, its accuracy, its even greater variety of facial types, and generally what they call its more "democratic" character.[35]

There remains one full-scale oil "sketch" (1879) of the picture. Repin eventually gave it to Yavornytsky as a token of his esteem and in recognition of his considerable help. But the impoverished archaeologist had nowhere to hang it, and it remained in Repin's studio for several years. Eventually, it was sold off, and today it hangs in the Tretiakov Gallery in Moscow.[36] Although it is far less sophisticated than the two main versions, the faces being somewhat uniform and stereotypical, this canvas has many of the basic elements, including the structure of the picture, with the Cossacks around the table, the scribe writing, and also many of the vibrant colours, that remained in the painting to the end of the creative process. As such, it forms an important intermediate stage between that very first pencil sketch in 1878 and the finished versions of the late 1880s and early 1890s.

As has been intimated above, the appearance of Repin's *Zaporozhians* was greeted enthusiastically in Ukraine, where Repin was unequivocally accepted as a native son. Indeed, it was only a few short years after the first exhibition showing this painting that the Ukrainian publisher and patron of scholarship and the arts, Yevhen Chykalenko (1861–1929), invited Repin to take on the mantle of "Ukrainian national artist" in the same way that Jan Matejko had become "a Polish national artist," who inspired his compatriots to struggle on for the good of their native land. Repin courteously rejected his idea, saying that he did not consider himself "a Ukrainian" in the modern sense and that he believed that Ukraine had been so integrated into Russia that they were now indivisible.[37]

Of course, this was only one statement of this time by the artist, and he never seems to have repeated it in correspondence or conversations with others, including those Ukrainians who knew him quite well, such as Yavornytsky. He remained enthusiastic about things Ukrainian throughout his life. Also, his reply to Chykalenko came before the Revolution of 1905, when the Ukrainian national movement really took off. That movement reached full flight during the Revolution of 1917 and gathered strength after the declaration of an autonomous Ukrainian People's Republic later that same year and its declaration of full independence in 1918. Moreover, Ukrainian national consciousness garnered some very real depth in the mid- and later 1920s, when a period of very intense "ukrainianization" occurred under Soviet auspices.

Repin lived through all of this in faraway Finland, and his attitude towards Ukrainian independence is not clear. He was an old man (he was born in 1844), with a fully formed identity, and his attitude towards Russia and Ukraine and their inter-relations may not have much changed. But he remained in touch with Yavornytsky and, to the end, continued to paint on those Ukrainian subjects so dear to his heart, especially Cossacks. Perhaps his earlier identity, which, like most Ukrainian intellectuals, contained both Little Russian and "pan-Russian" elements, evolved towards a more clearly Ukrainian one, which accepted independence, and he passed from simultaneously held identities to a more mutually exclusive kind of modern national identity. We simply do not know.[38]

Abroad, however, except for the Ruthenians/Ukrainians of the Habsburg Empire, especially in the large and populous province of Galicia, the world outside of the Russian Empire still simply saw him as a "Russian" painter. So in 1892, about the time that Repin first exhibited his Zaporozhians, the American travel writer and student of all things Russian Elizabeth Hapgood characterized Repin simply as "A Russian National Artist," though one who came from "Little Russia" and had some very definite Little Russian characteristics. Extremely well-informed on Russia, Hapgood featured Repin's Zaporozhians in a lead article in the *Century Magazine* and throughout stressed his Ukrainian connections. She even argued that his famous depictions of oppositionists in *Arrest of a Propagandist* (1880–92, TG) and other canvases were all probably located in Ukraine, which, she reported, had consistently displayed a rebellious spirit to the tsars since the time of the Cossacks; and of course, she also highlighted Repin's family background among the Cossacks of the Kharkiv region, who, she believed, reflected that very old spirit of rebellion. Hapgood seems to have attended the first exhibition of *Zaporozhian Cossacks* in St Petersburg, or at least had heard news of it. Shortly later, she wrote the significant *Russian Rambles* (1895) about her travels and included a long section on Kyiv as a religious centre for all "Russians," Great, Little, and otherwise, but in this volume, unfortunately, she did not develop or repeat her earlier perceptive observations on the painter's rebellious heritage.[39]

Over the years, Repin continued to attract some attention in the United States. For example, in 1906, in a well-informed and detailed article in *Scribner's Magazine*, Christian Brinton hailed him as "Russia's Greatest Painter," and a number of years later, after war and revolution, when "Ukraine" was already beginning to appear on certain maps and in the daily news, Louis E. Lord wrote in the American *Art Bulletin* that Repin still "epitomizes the Russian painting" of the pre-Revolution period. The Kharkiv version of his defiant Zaporozhians was the first in a string of his works to illustrate

Brinton's article, and the St Petersburg version was printed in Lord's. Although neither author fully understood what was going on in Ukraine, both explicitly acknowledged the importance of the Zaporozhians in Repin's corpus and pointed to his roots in what they still called "Little Russia."[40]

Meanwhile, in Europe too, Repin's magnum opus continued to attract attention. The most notable western European writer to discuss the canvas was the idiosyncratic French poet and art critic Guillaume Apollinaire (1880–1918), a cosmopolitan first son of the iconoclastic European "Avant-Garde." A friend of the painter Picasso, he coined and defined "Cubism," "Surrealism," and "Orphism" and helped welcome these revolutionary artistic movements to pre-1914 Europe. In Repin's masterwork, he clearly saw defiance, rebellion, and an attack on propriety, decorum, and classical taste.

He was so impressed by Repin's painting and the rough, rude, and disrespectful Cossack letter that inspired it that he produced his own version of the letter in his poem *La chanson du mal-aimé* (The Song of the Unwanted), a series of verses that placed personal feelings of desire, anger, and pain on a landscape of vast historical and mythological proportions, where the sultan was again labelled *Le Bourreau de Podolie* (the executioner of Podolia). *La chanson* formed the centrepiece of Apollinaire's collection *Alcools* (Alcoholic Spirits) of 1913. Certainly, it was no coincidence that this revolutionary poet was the son of a Polish noblewoman named Angelika Kostrowecka. Tellingly, his Polish family coat of arms displayed a serpent with an apple in its mouth.[41]

A generation later, Repin again came to be discussed by Western art critics, but in a completely different context. By 1939, the Revolution in Russia was over, Benua had fled to France, and the Modernist and Avant-Garde movements that had broken loose in the USSR of the 1920s had come to an abrupt end. War, Revolution, Stalinism, the Great Depression in the Western countries, and, finally, the rise of fascism and Nazism changed the political prospects and cultural landscape of Europe. Concerned by these developments, and the general crisis of their times, certain New York art critics sought to explain the sudden suppression of the Avant-Garde in Germany by Hitler, and particularly in the Soviet Union by Stalin. Some simply thought the socialist state responsible for this change.

But one, a young Marxist by the name of Clement Greenberg, dug deeper and penned a revolutionary article titled "Avant-Garde and Kitsch," expanding the meaning of the German term *Kitsch* from simple commercial art to include all art that in some way imitated older times and, in his opinion, restricted the progress of culture and formed a kind of "rear-guard" that was inferior to its progressive counterpart. Greenberg, like Friedman many years later, seemed to have no love for either peasants or Cossacks, and chose Repin for his special target. For him, Repin was not high art and Avant-Garde like Picasso, but rather backward "kitsch":

> Let us see, for example, what happens when an ignorant Russian peas-ant . . . turns next to Repin's picture and sees a battle scene . . . That Repin can paint so realistically that identifications are self-evident immediately and without any effort on the part of the spectator – that is miraculous. The peasant is also pleased with the wealth of self-evident meanings that he finds in the picture: 'It tells a story.' Picasso and the [peasant] icons are so austere and barren in com-parison. What is more, Repin heightens reality and makes it more dramatic: sunset, exploding shells, running and falling men. There is no longer any question of Picasso or icons. Repin is what the peasant wants, and nothing else but Repin.

Greenberg then goes even further: this type of kitsch also exists in North America and western Europe and is sweeping everything before it. It serves country folk who have invaded not only Russian cities but so too American cities to form the working classes, "the masses," for whom there is no time or money to appreciate higher art forms, the Avant-Garde. It is they who reject Picasso, and it is they who turn to lower art forms, to "kitsch" in art, architecture, and literature. And it is they to whom the Nazis and the Communists were now appealing.[42]

Greenberg's analysis was extremely influential in its day and later. But it had its problems. It was suitable for its time, when movement from the coun-tryside to the cities was commonplace, indeed, massive, but less relevant afterwards. It was terribly elitist, and ipso facto restricted the apprecia-tion of art to a select few. And, finally, its example from Repin was completely erroneous: Repin never once painted warfare with running and falling men, and the exploding of shells, at least in battle! In fact, as a portraitist, he almost never painted movement, and hardly ever touched on war itself. The closest that he ever came to it was that picture of his Zaporozhians writing their defiant letter, with smiles, fun, and belly-shaking laughter in the foreground, some exotic weapons and even a musical instrument scattered around, and only the suggestion of the aftermath of some great battle in the distant background! (The fizzing grenade dimly depicted in that painting – most likely as a mischievous afterthought – may well have been launched by the Cossacks themselves in their victory celebration!) The composition points to a certain rough strength, reckless bravado, and the firm confidence of victory over enemies, but does not openly depict blood or violence, only suggesting sure triumph. Greenberg had certainly heard of Repin's popularity in the USSR and did not like it. But perhaps in some strange way he also mixed up that unfortunate Cossack enthusiast with the anti-war artist V.V. Vereshchagin (discussed further below), who indeed painted the horrors of war, but fell out of favour in Stalin's time, especially after June 1941.

## Repin and the "Orient"

There remains the question of "the Orient" and where Repin's picture stands in the artistic trend depicting that Orient in the late nineteenth century, which was the heyday of Western imperialism. In the later twentieth century, as Middle Eastern problems rose to become a matter of world politics and the daily news, this question took on new political implications. Thus on the very centenary of Repin's first pencil sketch of his Zaporozhians, that is in 1978, an important book by a Palestinian–American author named Edward Said savagely attacked what he called "Orientalism." Before that time, European "Orientalists" were known simply as expert scholars, writers, or artists who wrote about or depicted the Orient, especially the Middle East. The word was used in exactly the same way as "Classicists," who studied ancient Greece and Rome, or later on, "Slavists" who studied the Slavonic peoples of central and eastern Europe. It was a given that they loved and were really interested in the sometimes rather arcane subjects that they studied.

But Said injected a new, negative side into the word, associating it with a put-down or disparagement of the East, that is, what he thought those Europeans considered to have been "the other." Said charged that they did this in order to subjugate and rule that "Orient." Said's book was an attack on what he saw as "imperialism," and even "racism" in scholarship and the arts. But he concentrated most of his fire on Britain and France and ignored Germany and Russia, both of which in the late nineteenth century also held large empires of a sort, though "continental" ones, not primarily overseas. So how did Said's thesis apply to the Russian Empire, and to the work of Ilya Repin in particular, who seemed to have painted so many "Eastern" motifs, and also (we might venture to say) "anti-Eastern" motifs, into his Zaporozhians?[43]

Although in the nineteenth century both Germany and Russia had produced a fair number of "Orientalist" scholars and artists, and Germany was perhaps the scholarly heart of that movement, neither of them had any direct political control of or influence on Said's homeland and concern, which was Palestine. But by 1914 Russia had annexed large parts of Transcaucasia, central Asia, and the Far East, bordered on Turkey, Persia, Afghanistan, and China, and even faced Japan across a branch of the Pacific Ocean. Russia was very concerned with "the Orient" in the form of Greater Asia, and this was revealed in its culture and its art. Indeed, when in 1920 Louis E. Lord published his American article on Repin, he noted that the "War Artist" Vasili Vereshchagin, who epitomized the Orientalist trend in Russian painting, was in his opinion still the best-known Russian painter of the nineteenth century. Vereshchagin was critical of warfare and ruthlessly pilloried "Eastern" violence, as well as the remnants of slavery in central Asia. But even he did not exactly fit Said's stereotype of the Orientalist painter, for he also opposed violence in general, Russian imperialism spread by violence and war, and the violence of British rule in India (especially Britain's reprisals for what it called the "Indian Mutiny" of 1857–59).[44]

Even less so did Repin fit Said's stereotype. Throughout his career, he had admired Old Masters among the European painters, artists like Rembrandt and Velázquez, but had no particular affection for the pioneers of European Orientalism such as Ingres, Delacroix, or even Gérôme, all of whom ostensibly painted "the other" in the Middle East. Indeed, he was much more concerned with "our own" at home. On a different level, although his Zaporozhians wore clothing quite foreign to the West and carried weapons and other artefacts of obviously Eastern origin, they were quite definitely "our own," and not "the other" for Repin, who was clearly himself of Ukrainian origin.

His great painting in its St Petersburg version depicted both the baggy *sharovary*, or trousers, typical of Cossack attire, and also a *kobza*, the stringed instrument that was already the Ukrainian national musical instrument par excellence, immortalized in the poetry of Shevchenko (beloved by Repin), which over numerous, ever-larger editions was, and still is, collected in a volume usually called *Kobzar* (The Blind Minstrel, or The Kobza Player, 1840). However, both *sharovary* and the *kobza* are Ukrainian artefacts and words of "Eastern" origin, and both originated in the Muslim world, which those Cossacks were defying. In this way, Ukraine was most definitely linked to and influenced by "the Orient;" that is, the Orient to its Islamic south in Turkey and the Middle East, and not so much to its geographical east in Asia, which was more typical of Russia to its north.[45]

These complementary and complicated facts do not seem to support Said's thesis about a hypothesized and iron-clad divergence or conflict between East and West, and they have nothing at all to do with Russian imperialism, from which Ukraine itself, it often came to be said, also suffered. Rather, as Repin saw it, those Zaporozhians were defenders of their own homeland against both the imperial power to its south, Ottoman Turkey, and (perhaps also) Russian imperial circles in St Petersburg, who were suspicious of the rebellious tone of his painting and, despite the tsar's stamp of approval, did not much like it. So Ilya Repin cannot in this sense be considered an "Orientalist" painter. Indeed, Kristian Davies, the influential Western art historian, who thought him one, and produced a beautiful book on the subject, defined that Orientalism in a non-pejorative way that emphasized the good and the bridge-building character of the nineteenth-century phenomenon, and not its darker side.[46] And so, although Repin could depict "Oriental" influences on Ukrainian culture, at one point even going on a pilgrimage to the Holy Land, and being, as he wrote, "moved, very moved" by the experience, and although his close friend and advisor Yavornytsky too visited the Middle East and even penned a brief biography of the Prophet Mohammed, Repin cannot be considered an "Orientalist" painter in the sense so over-confidently postulated by Edward Said.[47]

Of course, within contemporary Ukraine and Russia this question of the perceived "Orientalism" of Repin's Zaporozhians has thus far not found the kind of echo that it had in the West, and one acute English observer of contemporary Ukraine has completely ignored it. Andrew Wilson of London's School of Slavonic Studies in 2015 compared Repin's great work to two other monumental paintings of Ukrainian Cossacks at the height of their power and influence: Mykola Ivasiuk's *Triumphal Entry of Hetman Bohdan Khmelnytsky into Kyiv* (1912) and Oleksandr A. Khmelnytsky's *Eternal Unity* (1954). The former, on a subject that Repin had long considered painting, and on which the artist actually consulted with Repin, depicted the Ukrainian Cossack leader being greeted by the people and Orthodox clergymen of Kyiv after defeating and chasing the Catholic Poles out of Ukraine in the insurrection of 1648, and the latter picture portrayed the ostensible Ukrainian reception of the Treaty of Pereiaslav in 1654, whereby the Ukrainian Cossacks "united" with Muscovy by accepting some kind of vassalage to the Russian tsar.

Both are "monumental" pictures, but neither has the immediacy and vivacity of Repin's. The former, in a rather solemn, indeed "sanctified" mood, seems to concentrate principally on the Cossack and clerical élite, with nothing of the egalitarian spirit and spontaneity of Repin's master-piece, and the latter is a purely political and equally posed canvas, in which the central figure, Khmelnytsky, reminds one of the innumerable images all over the Soviet Union of V.I. Lenin with outstreached arm; it commem-orated the treaty's 300th anniversary in 1954. This canvas lost much of its relevance after the collapse of Communism and the Ukrainian declara-tion of independence in 1991, and all of its meaning after the beginning of the Russian–Ukrainian War in 2014. Wilson assures us that while *Bohdan Khmelnytsky* still hangs more proudly than ever in the Kyiv Museum of Fine Art, *Eternal Unity* has already been removed from the Museum of National History to its storage places. Meanwhile, of course, Repin's laugh-ing Zaporozhians are still prominently displayed in important museums in both Ukraine and Russia.[48]

## Conclusion: Caricatures and Continuing Responses

There is no doubt that Repin's *Zaporozhian Cossacks Writing a Satirical Letter to the Turkish Sultan* was his masterpiece. In more than one way, it de-fined that artist for Ukraine, for Russia, and for the outside world. Although the letter had apocryphal aspects, it was well grounded in Ukrainian his-tory, and it eventually came to play a significant role in that history. Repin tried to make his painting as historically accurate as possible, and in sev-eral ways succeeded. However, the work itself took on a certain legendary character and came to be interpreted in different ways by different viewers.

So Repin saw the matter in terms of defiance of the foreigner, who had invaded his native land and carried off so many of its people into foreign slavery, that is, as a defence of native liberty and national independence; but he also lived to see official Russia interpret it simply in terms of interna-tional relations, which had nothing to do with personal or national liberty and did not threaten the autocracy in tsarist times or the dictatorship of the proletariat later on. Meanwhile, taking the opposite view, Ukrainians such as Chykalenko saw its national significance principally for Ukraine, and by about 1900 clearly viewed Repin as a Ukrainian national painter, though one with some interests in "Russian" or Imperial Russian culture as a whole.[49] Indeed, during the Revolution, in a satirical pamphlet titled *Pro'stari' chasy na Ukraini* (About the Olden Days in Ukraine), the graphic artist P. Kotsky produced a caricature of Repin's painting with a group of Ukrainian autonomists in Cossack garb circled around the table. It sported none other than a bearded Professor Hrushevsky playing the part of Taras Bulba, and the Orthodox leader Oleksander Lototsky as secretary, or perhaps as the other bespectacled Cossack pointing off in the distance at Kerensky and defying the authority of the Russian Provisional Government in Petrograd (Figure 14).[50]

A few years later, after the Bolsheviks had established their new regime, they returned to that earlier view of the Zaporozhians as the defenders of the homeland from a foreign power, but with a very Soviet twist. So in 1923, the Soviet humour magazine *Krasnyi perets* (Red Pepper) (no. 6, p. 7) printed a caricature of the masterwork, depicting Soviet leaders writing a satirical letter defying the British minister Lord Curzon.[51] But the Soviets also put a new stress on the picture's social aspect and interpreted it as a shrill protest against the old Russian autocracy and the ruling classes in general.

In the 1930s, some Ukrainian satirists offered a much more confused view in a caricature of the Ukrainian political class in interwar Poland, which had annexed the former Austrian Galicia after defeating the Western Ukrainian People's Republic, established after the collapse of the Habsburg Empire in 1918. The Galician Ukrainians could not accept their defeat, and they continued to struggle both politically and militarily against the new Polish regime. In 1934, their leadership was united in appealing to the League of Nations in Geneva to protest their situation. At that point, the political satirists of the popular Galician-Ukrainian magazine *Komar* (The Mosquito) published a caricature of these leaders decked out as Repin's Zaporozhians writing to the League. They included every major Ukrainian political figure in Poland, from the quasi-fascist publicist Dmytro Dontsov on the far right to the democratic socialist Radical Party activist Matvii Stakhiv on the left.

However, to anyone unacquainted with Ukrainian political life in interwar Poland, this caricature loses much of its intended meaning. While the scribe looks a lot like Vladimir Kaye-Kysilewskyj, the legendary 1930s anglophile Ukrainian-Canadian lobbyist who ran the Ukrainian information bureau in London, the two pseudo-Cossacks standing directly behind the scribe look like the British comics Laurel and Hardy, who in the

1930s seem to have been famous across all of Europe. The caricature itself is very poorly done and strikes the modern reader as plainly insulting, with strongly racist overtones.

Indeed, a modern reader can hardly believe that it actually was published by Ukrainians themselves, as another of the pseudo-Cossacks (perhaps a Nazi sympathizer) sports a small, Hitler-style moustache and resembles the *Führer*. To the viewer today, the rugged defiance and spirit of protest that so animated Repin's original painting are completely missing, and sympathy here gives way to derision. Moreover, even to the Ukrainian public of the 1930s, the parallels with Repin's original were shaky: Repin painted a protest "against" the presumptuous sultan, while the Galician Ukrainians were protesting "to" the League of Nations for assistance.[52]

Westerners, however, from Elizabeth Hapgood and Apollinaire to more recent writers sympathetic to Communism or to Russia, evaluated the original canvas somewhat differently, and long felt the dignity and spirit of protest in Repin's stunning painting of 1891; many of the latter to some extent even today share Stalin's crass but positive view of it, largely ignoring the Ukrainian national aspect. Edward Said was a 1970s New York City Marxist, who sparked a new debate in Western scholarship, so at least one attempt to view the painting in that context was inevitable. But Said knew nothing of the Russian language and almost nothing about Russian history and did not dare to venture an opinion on "Orientalism" in the Russian Empire, let alone on Repin. The American enthusiast of "Orientalist" painting Kristian Davies was braver, but he too knew little of Russia and nothing of Ukraine, and completely misinterpreted the matter. Those brash Ukrainian soldiers who, during the Russian–Ukrainian War that began in 2014, posed as Zaporozhians, and wrote their satirical letter to Putin, thought that they knew much better. All this, we may modestly conclude, says much about Repin's great painting, which continues to spark interest and debate. And that is as it should be with all great art.

# Dmitrii E. Mishin on the *"Saqaliba"* in the Medieval Muslim World

IN A RECENT BOOK on the Slavonic peoples in the Middle East, the Russian Orientalist and historian Dmitrii E. Mishin examined a major but little-studied aspect of the historical relations between eastern Europe and the Middle East in *Sakaliba (Slaviane) v islamskom mire v rannee srednevekov'e* (Saqaliba: The Slavs in the Islamic World of the Early Middle Ages) (Moscow: Institut vostokovedeniia RAN, 2002), 365 pp. Its five substantial chapters discuss how Arabs and other Muslim peoples used the word *Saqaliba* in their languages, and its evolving meaning.

Mishin states (8) that *Saqaliba* was probably borrowed from the Greek ethnonym *Sklavos*, which was first rendered *Saklaby* in Arabic, and then later *Saqaliba*. Arab travellers and geographers used it to denote the various countries and peoples of Europe during the early Islamic centuries. (See, for example, Ibn Fadlan, *Ibn Fadlan and the Land of Darkness: Arab Travellers in the Far North*, trans. Paul Lunde and Caroline Stone [London: Penguin, 2012], 3, and the discussion on 222. Ibn Fadlan was a tenth-century Arab traveller to the northern Volga region.) Mishin then divides use of this Arabic word into two kinds. First, during the first Islamic century, the period of the Umayyads (661–744), it covered Slavic soldiers in the Byzantine armies, which the Arabs faced in Asia Minor during the early Muslim–Christian wars. These soldiers fought together in their own regiments and were easily identified as being of European and Slavonic origin. They spoke their own language and kept to their own traditions and customs. In time, some of them deserted the Byzantines and went over to the Muslim side, where for a long time they clung to their language and customs. They lived primarily on the frontiers of the early Caliphate, and for a while newcomers kept arriving from eastern Europe. Mishin identifies these people as Slavonic "colonists." And he seems to imply that they formed an early, distinct military corps somewhat like the later Mamluks in Egypt, or like other military slaves elsewhere, but as free men. However, with the ascendancy of the Abbasids (750–1258), more and more settlers from the eastern Iranian province of Khorasan were transplanted into Asia Minor, the principal centre of these military settlers, so the *Saqaliba* began to assimilate more rapidly.

Mishin's second class of *Saqaliba* consisted of European bondsmen or slaves pure and simple; that is, people who were captured in war or by Muslim raiding parties in Christian lands and sold into slavery for service in the wider *Dar al-Islam* (Realm of Islan). There existed a constant demand for slaves in the Muslim world because the principle of early manumission was deemed virtuous in Muslim tradition, and was often followed; freed slaves thus had to be replaced, and since the enslavement of free Muslims was strictly forbidden, their replacements had to come from outside the *Dar al-Islam,* that is, in the Christian north or the "pagan" (*kafir*) south and east.

During Carolingian times, that is, in the eighth and ninth centuries, the wars in central Europe between the Germans and the Slavs resulted in the enslavement of large numbers of people of Slavonic origin and their sale to the Muslim states to the south, especially to Muslim Spain, which was then still ruled by the Umayyads. The Umayyad Caliphate was rich, and the court at Cordova was splendid, and required a large number of slaves to help run the machinery of state. So it imported slaves from Christian Europe, and most especially castrated slaves, to be used as eunuchs in the administration and to guard the harems of the numerous elite. That terrible operation was usually performed in the Carolingian Empire to the north, as Islamic law forbade the procedure. Eventually, the word *Saqaliba* was restricted to those eunuchs who staffed the Umayyad court. With time, this usage of the word spread across the Islamic world and lost some of its original ethnic meaning.

There thus seems a parallel here with the use of the Latin *Sclavus* (originally meaning a Slavonic person), which in the Middle Ages replaced the ancient Latin *servus* for "slave," as the Latin *Sclavus* also lost its original ethnic sense with time and, as in the English word "slave," the French *esclave,* and so on, became the common name all over western Europe for an unfree person. Mishin argues that only in Islamic Spain did the *Saqaliba* ever attain any political power as a group. They existed also in North Africa and in the eastern Islamic lands, but as slaves, except in Fatimid Egypt, where certain members of the *Saqaliba* held some power. But Fatimid Egypt was an Ismaili Shia Caliphate, not recognized as legitimate by the Sunni powers. At any rate, the *Saqaliba* eventually lost power to other interest groups in Egypt, and by the time of the early Crusades, the Sunnis, in particular the Kurdish Sultan Saladin, put an end to the Fatimid dynasty. With more centrally organized states emerging in eastern Europe, argues Mishin (and he mentions Kyivan Rus'), slave raiding from the east and the south became more difficult, the slave trade went into a slow decline, and eventually the word itself disappeared from the common Arabic vocabulary.

Mishin ends his book with a summary of the *Saqaliba* in culture. Gradually Islamized, they were able to always keep their identity. The colonists kept their Slavonic names; the slaves did not forget their maternal language, and they remembered their Slavic traditions, and so forth. Even more important, the *Saqaliba* were conscious of their identity as part of a unified and homogeneous force. "This spirit of the *Saqaliba*," Mishin proposes, "shows that within the Islamic community, they formed a solid group that is worthy of the attention of researchers" (362–4).

Finally, Mishin reports that during the early Mongol era, the twelfth-century, Jewish-born Persian historian and vizier Rashid al Din (1247–1318), who composed a great world history that used even some European sources, distinguished at first, as did his predecessors, between the *Saqaliba* and the Rus', but was also one of the very first to note that later the Rus' were *Saqaliba* or Slavs (98). In this way, Rashid al-Din provides some external evidence to support the "Varangian," or Scandinavian theory of the origins of the Rus', who by then had affected European history as a whole.

# "Orientalisms" in Ukrainian, Polish, and Russian

ONE OF THE CLEAREST MARKERS of Eastern influences on Ukrainian and neighbouring cultures is the frequency of use of words of Eastern or "Oriental" provenance in their modern languages. These range from very old words, which we usually associate with Ukrainian or Slavonic roots, and do not think of as borrowed from Eastern sources, to relatively recent acquisitions, which stand out quite clearly. Some of the oldest are the name "Borys" and the term *boyaryn* (warlord) taken from old Bulgarian, which is a slavonized Turkic language, and the extremely old word *knyha* (Ukrainian) or *kniga* (Russian) meaning "book," which probably was taken via Armenian or another language from the ancient Assyrian word for "book." (The name "Borys," some etymologists claim, can be traced back through Bulgarian even to a very old Mongolian word meaning "little.")

Much more recent acquisitions include Eastern words such as *karavan* and *bazaar*, which were popularized or borrowed from Persian or Arabic into the various languages of Europe in the eighteenth century. That followed the translation of the *One Thousand and One Nights* (sometimes called *The Arabian Nights*) into French and then the other major languages of Europe. Some time before this, however, these two particular words did appear in the Ukrainian language from other sources.

"Orientalisms" in Ukrainian can be divided into four major kinds, by source language: first, Iranianisms, some of which are by far the oldest Oriental borrowings into the Slavonic tongues. A few of these entered the Slavonic "mother tongue" before it broke up into the different Slavonic groups, and some are still common to them all. Second, there are Turkisms, a few of which are also quite old, but many of which entered Ukrainian or became very common during early modern, Cossack times. Third, Arabisms range in type and age from medieval times almost to the present. Fourth, other Oriental loans are fewer in number and come from a range of languages, including Hebrew, Georgian, and Armenian.

**Iranianisms** are of great antiquity and play a notable role in most Slavonic tongues. Some are in fact pre-historic, dating from shortly after the breakup of the great Indo-European family of languages, when the ancient Slavonic and Iranian tribes were still close neighbours on the eastern European, or Pontic Steppe, and neighbouring areas. We know the names of a few of these peoples, such as the Cimmerians (of dubious origins), the Scythians, and the Sarmatians, but a few of the loans from Iranian languages may antedate these. Two of the most notable might be *Boh* (Ukrainian), *Bóg* (Polish), and *Bog* (Russian), meaning "God," and *mir* (Ukrainian and Russian), with the basic meaning of "peace," but sounding a bit archaic in Polish, although in the modern Polish tongue it retains the related meanings of "esteem" or "respect."

*Bagha* – "God" or "Lord" – is mentioned in the Avesta, the sacred scriptures of the Zoroastrians, a very old Iranian religion, dualist in nature, stressing the difference between good and evil, light and darkness, which faith first arose in central Asia. *Bagha* is a Sanskrit or ancient Indian word for "prosperity" or "good fortune." (The old Iranian tongues and Sanskrit were closely related.) As with *Boh*, which some scholars believe to be merely a cognate (having similar origins) rather than a true loan-word, *mir* is so old that it may have come to Slavonic directly from an ancient Indo-European root meaning "fair" or "fine." Nevertheless, it is closely related to the Iranian word *mitra*, meaning "friend," which later became the name of an old Iranian god, *Mithras*, whose worship eventually spread into the Roman Empire. At any rate, the alternate meanings of the modern Russian word *mir* as "peasant commune" and ultimately "world" are later developments from the older meaning of "peace," which, of course, is also associated with "prosperity."

There are also a few more mundane Ukrainian words that are probably of ancient Iranian origin. For example, *sobaka* means "dog." Many Slavonic etymologists believe that it also might be based on an old Iranian root, such as *spaka* in Avestan, an old Iranian language. This root is also preserved in the modern Persian word for dog, which is *sag*. The great Polish philologist Aleksander Brückner tells us that from the East Slavic languages, but particularly Ukrainian, in the seventeenth century, it passed as well into Polish.

The French Ukrainian scholar Iaroslav Lebedynsky suggests that the names of the rivers Don, Dnieper, Dniester, and most likely even Danube are all of ancient Iranian origin, even though the modern Persian word for river is *rudkhaneh*. Linguists, he says, determined this origin in part from studying the Ossetian language of the Caucasus, which is an Iranian tongue descended from those Sarmatians and Alans of late antiquity, for even in modern Ossetian *don* means "flowing water" or "river." The four river names given above were formed probably from the root "*don*," or something very close to it.

Of these four river examples, let us take a closer look at the most central one, the Dnieper, or *Dnipro* in modern Ukrainian. The river was named *Dunepru* in older forms of Slavonic, *Danapris* in Greek, and *Danaper* in Latin; philologists and specialists in old Steppe Ukraine, such as Iaroslav Lebedynsky, hypothesize their grounding in the old Iranian root *Danu* and a second element, also Iranian, such as Old Iranian *apara* (behind), or *apri* (west) as in Sanskrit, or *apra* (modern Ossetian *arf*), meaning "profound" or "deep." Put them together, and we have "The Western River," or "The Deep River."

Of course, as is well-known, the Greek historian Herodotus called the river *Borysthenes*, but it too seems to be of indisputably Iranian origin. According to Lebedynsky, it is derived from the Iranian word *varu*, meaning "large" (as in Avestan *vouru* and Ossetian *urukh*) and *stana*, meaning "country." (This latter Iranian word is still very common in modern Persian and other Eastern languages and appears on maps as Afghanistan, Pakistan, and so on.) Lebedynsky hypothesizes that the ancient Greeks took one of the names of the Scythian country, "large country," or even "the country of the large ones," and applied it to the river itself. At any rate, both the names Borysthenes and Dnieper are of clearly Iranian origin.

There are, of course, many lesser-known Ukrainian toponyms (place names) of ancient Iranian origin – more than two thousand, according to the Ukrainian philologist K.M. Tyshchenko. He also notes that other very common words like *khata* (a peasant cottage or simple one-storey house) are probably of ancient Iranian lineage. *Khata* in particular, he claims, is a "Sarmatianism" known exclusively to Ukraine and Belarus', which, in the province of Podolia has two separate, though related local meanings: a small home or a grave mound in a cemetery. The latter usage, he also claims, comes directly from the Zoroastrian *Avesta*, which seems to indicate (so he again claims) that the ancestors of modern Ukrainians and Belarusans were probably at one time in close contact with Iranians of the Zoroastrian religion on the European Steppe. Zoroastrianism, though originating in pre-historic central Asia, became a principal religion of the Persian Empire, especially under the Sasanian dynasty of late antiquity. Most Ukrainian philologists agree that *khata* is probably borrowed from the ancient Iranian *kad*, meaning "house." That word is preserved in the modern Persian language in the title *kadkhoda*, originally the "lord of the house," or today the "headman of a village."

Other very common Iranian-origin Ukrainian words, says Lebedynsky, are of cultural/religious import, such as *vira* (faith) from *vara* (to believe), and *vina* (fault) from *vinah*, and, quite surprisingly, titular words such as *Pan* (Mister) and *Pani* (Mrs). These last supposedly descend from the Old Iranian form *pana*, meaning "protector," and are also used in Polish, which greatly influenced their use in Ukrainian. (*Gau-pana* in Pashtu, an Iranian tongue spoken in Afghanistan and Pakistan, was once the name of "the Protector of the Cattle").

A parallel case is the Ukrainian word *bovvan*, meaning today "dumbbell" or "blockhead," that is, a person who is not very bright, but originally the up-right statues, poles, columns, "wooden blocks" or "idols" once erected on the Ukrainian Steppe. But this word too, according to Jaroslav Rudnyckyj and many others, is ultimately of Iranian origin, being related to the Persian word *pahlavan*, a "great hero," in honour of whom a statue was raised. Ultimately, notes the Iranian etymologist Ali Nourai, all these words come from the very ancient Indo-European root *pa*, meaning "protection." This root also gave us our common words for "father," *pater* in Latin and *pedar* in modern Persian.

Another interesting old Slavonic root is *konop*, which yields *konoplia* (hemp) in modern Ukrainian. It is clearly related to *cannabis* in Greek and Latin, which is not strange, says Lebedynsky, because they are both derived from the ancient Scythian word for "hemp," or "marijuana," as is attested by Herodotus and demonstrated by recent archaeology. Herodotus says that it served the Scythians as a psychedelic drug and as a kind of incense; in modern times Ukrainian women would use it to help their babies sleep while they themselves worked in the fields. This useful custom was even carried over to the prairies of western Canada by some of the early Ukrainian "pioneers" before 1914, although it seems to have largely disappeared by the 1920s.

It is difficult to distinguish between actual loans from Iranian and simple cognates with it, derived from their common ancestor, the very ancient

Indo-European "mother tongue" (Proto-Indo-European). How close the
Slavonic and Iranian languages are is clear from linguists' grouping them
as *satem* languages (from their words for a "hundred") as opposed to the
*centem* languages of western Europe. Geographers also note that the geographical area of Slavonic languages falls between the languages of western
Europe and those of central Asia and, later on, Iran, which are the historical
homelands of the Iranian peoples.

**Turkisms** make up the second great class of Orientalisms in Ukraine, after
Iranianisms. I.V. Muromtsev's encyclopaedia of the Ukrainian language de-
fines a Turkism as any "word or phrase borrowed from the Turkic languages
or through their medium from several other languages (predominantly
from Arabic and Persian), or constructed on their model." Muromtsev continues: "Turkisms are both general . . . (*harbuz*/melon or pumpkin), *tyutyun*
(tobacco), *kylim* (carpet or tapestry) and are also personal names (*Borys*
and *Bakhmach*)." He further divides Turkisms into historical ones, such as
*osavul* (lieutenant), *sahaidak* (a quiver or case for a bow), *yasyr* (captive),
and *bunchuk* (horsetail standard), and exoticisms, used primarily to describe Turkish culture, such as *harem* (women's quarters), *basha* ("pasha,"
or governor of an Ottoman Turkish province), and *sultan* (master or ruler).

A great many of the oldest Turkisms in Ukrainian do not feel in the
least foreign to the Ukrainian ear, especially the historical Turkisms. In
his article in the *Encyclopedia of Ukraine* on "Turkisms," Victor Swoboda
divides these chronologically. The oldest, dating to about the sixth century,
are words like *kahan* (ruler) and *bohatyr* (great hero). Vladimir the Great,
grand prince of Kyiv, claimed the quasi-imperial title *kahan*, or *kagan*,
which had been handed down from the Turkic-speaking Khazar Empire
after it had been extinguished by the Varangian Rus', and *bohatyr* was eventually used as a common personal name all over central Asia. As "Bahador,"
it is common enough in today's Iran.

With the decline of Kyivan Rus' many Turkic tribes swept across the
land and left their traces in both the physical features of the Ukrainian people and in their language. Words dating from the eleventh to the thirteenth
century include *zhemchuh* (pearl), *yevshan* (wormwood), *tlumach* (inter-
preter), and *tovar* (merchandise or goods, from the Turkic for "cattle" and
especially "sheep"), from which many common Ukrainian and Russian words

derive: for example, the Russian *tovarishch* (comrade) and the Ukrainian *tovarysh* (comrade), which originally meant "camp" or "wagon-train." The English etymologist Terence Wade believes that *tovarishch* may come from *tovar*, plus the ending *-ishch*, meaning "place," thus "place of trade," where one naturally made social connections. (The same ending also occurs in *kladbishche* or "cemetery," a "place" where people are buried.) However, Wade adds that the Ukrainian *tovarysh* may be even closer to Turkic, where the ending *-ish* means "friend," thus initially rendering "a friend in trade" or "a trading partner." It is an irony of history that this word, which was once so closely associated with commerce and business, became ideologically associated with a militantly anti-business form of socialism, Soviet Communism. In the Slavonic languages, even today, the word does not always have the military connotation of the English "comrade." For example, the great Ukrainian historian Mykhailo Hrushevsky, who was anything but a military type, used it simply to mean "friend," even when addressing his students at the University of Lemberg/Lviv.

*Tovarysh* and *tovarishch* seem to have entered the Eastern Slavonic languages as early as the fourteenth century, but many more Turkic words entered Ukrainian later, during Cossack times, when Ukrainians interacted closely with Turks and Tatars, the latter of whom spoke a Turkic language of the so-called Kipchak branch. So the name "Cossack" itself (*kozak* in Ukrainian and Polish, *kazak* in Russian) was borrowed in this period; so also *vataha* (warband or herd), *chai* (tea), and *karyi* (dark brown or black, as in *kari ochi*, "black eyes"). The English form "Cossack" arrived in that language probably via the French *cosaque*, from the Polish *kozak*, from the Ukrainian *kozak* (not the Russian *kazak*).

Later Cossack times gave us *chaban* (shepherd), *tuman* (fog), *berkut* (golden eagle), *lyman* (estuary), *harbuz* (melon or pumpkin), *choboty* (boots), *chumak* (salt trader), *maidan* (town square), *kobza* (lute), *kaidany* (shackles or chains), and many, many others. Indeed, according to E.N. Shipova, some etymologists and historians, following the Orientalist Ahatanhel Krymsky, believe that even the archaic Ukrainian term of scorn for Russians, *Katsap*, may have been borrowed from one of the Turkic languages. Recent Ukrainian etymology favours the more obvious one that ridicules persons who wear long beards, as did the Muscovites of old. (*Tsap* is a billy-goat in Ukrainian.)

In all, according to the Ukrainian philologist O.M. Harkavets, about four thousand Turkisms populate modern Ukrainian – about as many as Arabisms in modern Spanish. (For the Spanish figure, see Michel Malherbe, *Les langages de l'humanité* [Paris: Bouquins, 1995], 160.) And like the Iranians, the Turks and Tatars have also shaped Ukrainian topography. So the names of the towns Kremenchuk and Karasu are both of Turkic origin, the former according to Metropolitan Ilarion from the Tatar *ke* or *kyr*, meaning "high place," as in the Turkish *kerman* "fortress," and the latter in particular meaning "black water."

**Arabisms** form the third general class of Orientalisms in Ukrainian. Many entered Ukrainian via Turkish or Tatar, both of which absorbed a great many Arabic words and phrases as Islam spread through their homelands. Virtually all Turks or Tatars were historically Muslim, and, in Europe generally, "turning Turk" was the phrase for conversion. "Muslim" in Ukrainian (*Musulman*) comes to Ukrainian not from Arabic but rather indirectly through Persian and then Turkic. Ukrainians and Russians often corrupted it into the sometimes-pejorative *Busurman*.

A second class of Arabisms reached Ukraine via Latin (or sometimes Greek) and western European tongues. Most of these were scientific, medical, geographical, or mathematical terms such as *algebra*, *admiral*, *alcohol*, *arsenal*, *zenith*, and *talisman*. Others were less scientific but very common, such as *kava* for coffee, *khabar* meaning bribe, and *zhasmyn* for the jasmine flower, this last, possibly a Persian word reaching Ukrainian through Arabic, Turkish, or Tatar. Still others arrived more directly from Arabic and are used in Ukrainian and some other Slavonic languages, but not in western Europe. A good example is *torba* (bag). *Zhupan* (trousers) is one word that did come from Arabic through western Europe, Italian in fact. Surprisingly, *mini-jup* (for a very short skirt) comes ultimately from an old Arabic word combined with a Latin prefix. Modern Ukrainian has a parallel word sporting an appropriate suffix: *mini-zhupka*.

A few Arabic words reached Ukraine through Tatar slave raiding of Ukrainian lands in early modern times and to this day evoke that era. These words include *yasir* (captive) and, as mentioned above, *kaidany* (shackles or chains). A Greek word loaned into Arabic and Turkish also arrived in Ukraine this way: *katorga* originally meant "slave rowing on a Mediterranean galley," from Byzantine Greek *katá* (down or below) and *érgon* (work). But in modern Ukrainian and Russian it means "punitive exile." Such exile, especially to Siberia, was common in Imperial Russia and massive under the Soviets.

**Other languages**, such as Armenian, Georgian, and Hebrew, provide the fourth general class of Orientalisms in Ukrainian, Polish, and Russian. As we saw above, the word for "book" – *knyha* (Ukrainian), *kniga* (Russian), and *książka* (Polish) – reached Slavonic possibly from ancient Assyrian via the Armenian *knik*. Terence Wade informs us that a *kunukku* in ancient Assyrian was originally a "sealed clay tablet, or seal impression." To this, from Georgian should be added *zubr* (bison) in Ukrainian and *żubr* (meaning the same) in Polish. (Even today, the eastern European bison survives in the forest region joining Poland to Belarus'.)

From Hebrew, of course, came a great many biblical terms, often via the Old Church Slavonic of the southern Balkans. As in English, *seraphim* and *cherubim* are good examples. In the 1920s, Aleksander Brückner, who compiled one of the first etymological dictionaries in a Slavonic language, estimated that about one third of all modern Polish words are of foreign origin. For Polish, he reports, German provided more new or non-Slavonic words than any other language. He does not say what proportion came from the East, but the figure must be high, especially for Ukrainian and Russian, which were usually in much closer and more direct contact with "Oriental" cultures than was Polish.

## Bibliographical Note

Most of the material in this brief essay comes from various specialist encyclopaedias treating the Ukrainian language. See, in particular, O.M. Harkavets, "Tiurkizm," in *Ukrainska mova: Entsyklopediia*, ed. V.M. Rusanivsky (Kyiv: Vyd. Ukrainska entsyklopediia, 2004), 694–5, and also his "Ukrainsko–Tiurkski movni kontakty," 747–8, in the same volume. Also see the articles on Iranianisms, Arabisms, and Turkisms in I.V. Muromtsev, ed., *Ukrainska mova Entsyklopediia* (Kyiv: Vyd. Maister-klas, 2011), which is a valuable revision and abridgment of Rusanivsky's volume, and the article on "Turkisms," by Victor Swoboda, in *Encyclopedia of Ukraine*, vol. V (Toronto: University of Toronto Press, 1993), 321–2.

For a survey of older, pre-Islamic "Orientalisms" preserved in modern Ukrainian, see K.M. Tyshchenko, "Davnii skhid u slovnyku i toponimii Ukrainy," in I.P. Bondarenko, ed., *Movni ta literaturni zv'iazky Ukrainy z krainamy Skhodu* (Kyiv: Vyd. Dmytro Buraho, 2010), 7–57. Tyshchenko is a specialist in Iranian influences on Ukrainian. Also see Iaroslav Lebedynsky, *Scythes, Sarmates, et Slaves: L'influences anciens nomades iranophones sur les Slaves* (Paris: L'Harmattan, 2009), especially 117–47, on languages. I also consulted an unusual volume featuring a new arrangement of materials made possible by recent technology: Ali Nourai, *An Etymological Dictionary of Persian, English and Other Indo-European Languages*, 2 vols. (N.p.: Xlibris, 2013), and available online at https://archive.org/details/ AnEtymologicalDictionaryOfPersianEnglishAndOtherIndo-european-Languages/page/n377, 14 February 2011. For a detailed study of a very old Iranianism in Ukrainian, see my "The Word *Maidan*: Where It Comes from and What It Means," https://www.slideshare.net/ThomasMPrymak/ the-word-maidan-illustrated, 15 October 2016.

Etymological dictionaries for the various Slavonic languages are also of considerable use. In this regard, see the great four-volume work of Metropolitan Ilarion (Ivan Ohienko), which was edited and completed by Yurii Mulyk-Lutsyk, *Etymolohichno-semantychnyi slovnyk ukrainskoi movy* (Winnipeg: Tovarystvo 'Volyn,' 1979–94), Aleksander Brückner, *Słownik etymologiczny języka polskiego* (Warsaw: Krakowska spółka wydawnicza, 1927), and Terence Wade, *Russian Etymological Dictionary* (London: Bristol Classics, 1996). Also see Wacław Przemysław Turek, *Słownik zapożyczen pochodzenia arabskiego w polszczyźnie* (Cracow: Universitas, 2001), Stanisław Stachowski, *Słownik historyczny turcyzmów w języku polskim* (Cracow: Księgarnia akademicka, 2007), and E.N. Shipova, *Slovar tiurkizmov v russkom iazyke* (Alma-Ata: Nauka Kazakskoi SSR, 1976). More generally, see Jurij Kočubej/Yury Kochubei, "Les éléments orientaux dans la culture et dans la vie quotidienne des Cosaques ukrainiens," in Michel Cadot and Émile Kruba, eds., *Les Cosaques de l'Ukraine* (Paris: Presses de la Sorbonne nouvelle, 1995), 117–24.

I would also sometimes check the materials found in these dictionaries and sources against the widely respected *Etymolohichnyi slovnyk ukrainskoi movy*, 6 vols (Kyiv: Naukova dumka, 1982–2012), and, where possible, Jaroslav B. Rudnyckyj's incomplete *Etymological Dictionary of the Ukrainian Language*, in 15 fasciculae (Winnipeg: UVAN, 1962–76). Always opinionated, Rudnyckyj's dictionary gives meanings in English, and often offers quite learned and balanced disquisitions on the entries, but covers only the first letters of the Ukrainian alphabet.

# Shevchenko and the Muslims

ALTHOUGH THE COMMON Ukrainian/Russian terms for a Muslim, *Musulman,* or in literary Ukrainian *Musulmanyn,* do not occur in Shevchenko's poetry, the (today) disparaging term *Busurman* and the related *Busurmanskyi* ("Muslim" in its noun and adjectival forms) do, but very rarely indeed. See the *Slovnyk movy Shevchenka*, 2 vols. (Kyiv: Naukova dumka, 1964), especially I, 50. This lacuna suggests that the poet took little notice of Muslim religious developments. With particular regard to the word "*Busurman,*" Metropolitan Ilarion [Ohienko], *Etymolohichno-semantychnyi slovnyk ukrainskoi movy*, 4 vols. (Winnipeg: Tovarystvo 'Volyn,' 1979–94), I, 190, states that this term was loaned into Ukrainian and the other Slavonic languages from the Turkic languages, which often replaced an "m" with a "b" and an "l" with an "r," and that among the Eastern Slavonic peoples it is found as early as the fifteenth century in the travel writings of Afanasy Nikitin, who visited Eastern lands as far away as India. Consequently, by origin at least, the word was definitely not a pejorative. Yet C.H. Andrusyshen, *Ukrainian–English Dictionary* (Toronto: University of Toronto Press, 1957), 48, explains that the adjectival form *busurmanskyi* is associated with the meanings "to debauch" or "to lead a disorderly life," implications probably current during Shevchenko's lifetime in the nineteenth century.

*Tataryn* (Tatar) and *Turchyn* (Turk) appear more frequently in our poet's works, reflecting his interests in Ukrainian history, in which both Turks and Tatars, especially Tatars, played major roles. See, for example, his two great poems on the Cossack naval expeditions to free the slaves from Ottoman captivity: "Ivan Pidkova" (1840) and "Hamaliia" (1844). These poems were inspired in part by some of the *Cossack Tales* (1837) of Mykhailo

Chaikovsky/Michał Chajkowski/Sadyk Pasha, published in Paris, and *Campaign of Zbaraz* (1839), a poem by Józef Bohdan Zaleski, the ukrainophile Polish bard from central Ukraine, as well as by Ukrainian folk and other sources, such as the *duma* or reflective song "Lament of the Poor Slaves in Turkish Captivity." (On this, see Valeriia Smilianska, "Hamaliia," in *Shevchenkivska entsyklopediia*, vol. II [Kyiv, 2012], 46–7.)

But this "Turkish slavery" theme does not say much about the poet's views of Islam in general, which seem to have evolved and were never really hostile, unlike some of his contemporaries. As a young student of the famous Russian painter Karl Briullov, for example, Shevchenko was influenced by his master's interest in the "Orient." Briullov had toured Greece and Turkey and painted several "Orientalist" canvases, and it was probably under his influence that Shevchenko painted *In the Harem* (1843). The Ukrainian writer Petro Kraliuk ("Taras Shevchenko i musulmanskyi svit," in his *Taras Shevchenko: Nezauvazhene* [Kyiv: KNT, 2015], 218–28) wrote that the poet's "Kavkaz" (The Caucasus) even compared Russia's Orthodox Christianity unfavourably to Islam, and that this attitude showed later during his central Asian exile. For example, in *Son* (The Dream, 1847–48), written during his exile, in the land today called Kazakhstan, he compares the free life of the "Kirghiz" nomads, only superficially Muslim, with the oppression of the Orthodox Russian Empire:

> Blukav ia po svitu chymalo,
> Nosyv i svytu i zhupan . . .
> Nasho vzhe lykho za Uralom
> Otym Kyrhyzam, otzhe i tam,
> Ei zhe Bohu, luchshe zhyty,
> Nizh nam na Ukraini.
> A mozhe tym, shcho Kyrhyzy
> Shche ne Khrystiiany!

> (Around this world I have wandered about,
> Wearing my cloak and zhupan out.
> But why is it for the Kirghiz
> Across the Urals, so very bad?
> God, they've got more
> Than we in Ukraine ever had!

Maybe, that's the very reason
Why the Kirghiz aren't yet Christian?)
(Lines 80–8, in my rather loose translation from
– *Tvory u 6 tomakh* [Kyiv: Vyd. AN UkSSR, 1963], II, 43)

So for Shevchenko here, perhaps a bit obliquely, a free and relatively happy life on the Kazakh Steppe, which he associates with Islam, preserves liberty, while the political and social slavery associated with the empire promotes Christianity!

Shevchenko took a lively interest in the varied peoples of that central Asian region, both Muslim and non-Muslim, and he painted them often. One of his very best watercolours is the striking image of *Fire on the Steppe* (1848) (Plate 15), inspired by a local incident. He recorded examples of Kazakh folklore and superstition in his notes. On 9 June 1856, he recalled to his good friend and fellow exile Zigmund Sierakowski: "We have lived together in the East; we understand the deep meaning of the words: God is Great! *Allahu Akbar!*" On this, see Leonid Ushakov in an article on "Asia" in his compendium of reflections on the poet, *Moia Shevchenkivska entsyklopediia: Iz dosvidu samopiznannia* (Edmonton, Toronto, and Kharkiv: CIUS, 2014), 13–16, which also remarks that Shevchenko liked those central Asian peoples so much that he was even ready to join a Russian expedition to far-off Tibet to discover more about them.

Moreover, certain sharp cultural differences with the "East" did not shock the poet. For example, continues Ushakov ("Asia," 118–19), Shevchenko, like Briullov and many other artists in his time (as mentioned above), attempted to paint harem women, and in his poem *Saul*, on the biblical king, he did not outright condemn the custom of keeping harems: "*Saul, ne buduchyi durak, / Nabrav harem sobi chymalyi / Ta i zakhodyvsia tsariuvat*" (Saul, not being a dumbell, collected a substantial harem, and prepared himself to rule as a king). Kraliuk too points out ("Taras Shevchenko," 226–7) that the poet actually began work on a literary piece called *Satrap i dervish* (The Satrap and the Dervish), to be set somewhere in the East. In approaching this piece, he tried to avoid romanticizing Oriental women, but still wished to acknowledge their role in private life: "I do not know quite how to handle the matter of women. In the East, women are silent slaves. But in my poem they must be as they really are: silent, a soulless but key factor of the visible action [*bezdushnymy rygachamy pozornogo deistviia*]." Most probably, although he sketched a few, and could see their great beauty, he never got to know well a real "Oriental" woman, Kazakh, Kirghiz, Tatar, or other.

While acknowledging such problems, Shevchenko was far less patronizing of "Orientals," the various "conquered peoples," than were many of his contemporaries. And, of course, he was never an apologist for the Russian Empire, as was Pushkin or Lermontov. Kraliuk ("Taras Shevchenko," 226) remarks that he admired the Muslim view of paradise so often criticized by Westerners, though based only on one suggestion, perhaps in jest, about how pleasurable that highly sensual paradise must be! Moreover, he never became a Muslim, always retained a certain Christian identity, and always felt himself a member of the community of Ukrainian artists and intellectuals, who firmly acknowledged their Christian heritage, problematic though at times it was. Ushakov ("Asia," 13–16) states that the poet shared many of the "Eurocentric" ideas of his time, and sometimes contrasted European civilization to the ostensible "barbarism" of "the East." Within the general context of his time, however, Taras Shevchenko, the foremost poet of his country in the nineteenth century, was, in his sympathetic view of the Muslims with whom he came into contact or about whom he had heard or read, or painted or sketched, more open-minded than most.

# Notes

## EPIGRAPH

1 Victor Hugo, "Mazeppa" (no. XXXIV), in *Les Orientales* (1829), reprinted Ollendorf, 1912, 733–7, at https://fr.wikisource.org/wiki/Les_Orientales/Mazeppa, last modified 18 August 2018.

## INTRODUCTION

1 On the "great surprise in the chancelleries, universities and boardrooms of the West – a surprise that many are still adjusting to," see Andrew Wilson, *The Ukrainians: Unexpected Nation* (New Haven, Conn., and London: Yale University Press, 2000), especially xi. One of the most surprised of them all was the widely read British Communist E.J. Hobsbawm, *Nations and Nationalism since 1780: Program, Myth, Reality* (Cambridge: Cambridge University Press, 1990). For a previously published, but wide-ranging partial corrective, see Anthony D. Smith, *The Ethnic Revival in the Modern World* (Cambridge: Cambridge University Press, 1981).

2 On Hrushevsky, see my *Mykhailo Hrushevsky: The Politics of National Culture* (Toronto: University of Toronto Press, 1987), and Serhii Plokhy, *Unmaking Imperial Russia: Mykhailo Hrushevsky and the Writing of Ukrainian History* (Toronto: University of Toronto Press, 2005). Also see Ihor Hyrych, *Mykhailo Hrushevsky: Konstruktor ukrainskoi modernoi natsii* (Kyiv: Smoloskyp, 2016), and R.Ya. Pyryh and V.V. Telvak, *Mykhailo Hrushevsky: Biohrafichnyi narys* (Kyiv: Lybid, 2017).

3 On Lypynsky, see Ivan Lysiak Rudnytsky, "Viacheslav Lypynsky: Statesman, Historian, and Political Thinker," in his *Essays in Modern Ukrainian History* (Edmonton: CIUS Press, 1987), 437–46, and "Lypynsky, Viacheslav," in Volodymyr Kubijovyč and Danylo Husar Struk, eds., *Encyclopedia of Ukraine*, vol. III (Toronto: University of Toronto Press, 1993), 246–7.

4 See, for example, Lubomyr Wynar, *Mykhailo Hrushevsky: Ukrainian–Russian Confrontation in Historiography* (Kent, Ohio: Ukrainian Historical Association, 1988). In addition to Wynar's remarks, this little volume contains Hrushevsky's

programmatic essay: "The Traditional Scheme of 'Russian' History and the Problem of a Rational Organization of the History of the Eastern Slavs."

5  On Pritsak, see O.V. Yas, "Pritsak, Omelian Yosypovych," in *Entsyklopediia istoriii Ukrainy*, vol. IX (Kyiv: Naukova dumka, 2012), 15–16, which gives further references. Also see Pritsak's "L. Lypyns'kyj's Place in Ukrainian Intellectual History," *Harvard Ukrainian Studies* 9, nos. 3–4 (1985), 245–62, and his "Shcho take istoriia Ukrainy?," *Slovo i chas*, no. 1 (1991), 53–60. A version of this last title was first published during the Cold War in New Jersey / New York's venerable Ukrainian newspaper *Svoboda* (Liberty). Also see the chapter on Pritsak in Andrii Portnov, *Istorii istorykiv: Oblychchia i obrazy ukrainskoi istoriohrafii* (Kyiv: Krytyka, 2011), 185–200. For a brief sketch of Pritsak during his all-important American period, see my survey of "The Generation of 1919: Pritsak, Luckyj, and Rudnytsky," at https://www.slideshare.net/ThomasMPrymak/the-generation-of-1919, 10 April 2020, and my "Orest Subtelny as Historian: Personal Impressions and Professional Profile," at http://www.ucrdc.org/Publications_files/OREST%20SUBTELNY%20AS%20HISTORIAN%20with%20pics.pdf, 30 April 2020.

6  See Mykhailo Hrushevsky, *A History of Ukraine* (New Haven, Conn.: Yale University Press, 1940), and Dmytro Doroshenko, *History of the Ukraine*, trans. Hanna Chikalenko-Keller, ed. George Simpson (Edmonton: Institute Press, 1939). An updated version of Doroshenko's volume edited by Oleh Gerus was published in Winnipeg in 1975 as *A Survey of Ukrainian History*. Also see my two articles: "Dmytro Doroshenko: A Ukrainian Émigré Historian of the Interwar Period," *Harvard Ukrainian Studies* 25, nos. 1–2 (2001), 31–56, and "Dmytro Doroshenko and Canada," *Journal of Ukrainian Studies* 30, no. 2 (2005), 1–25.

7  See Orest Subtelny, *Ukraine: A History* (Toronto: University of Toronto Press, 1988). Also see my "Orest Subtelny as Historian."

8  Paul Robert Magocsi, *A History of Ukraine* (Toronto: University of Toronto Press, 1996). A revised and expanded edition appeared in 2010: *A History of Ukraine: The Land and Its Peoples*, where Magocsi added the history of the Crimean Khanate and relabelled that time as "the Lithuanian–Polish–Crimean period," c. 1450–c. 1750. Hrushevsky had never envisioned a "Crimean" period, focusing on the "Lithuanian and Polish" periods. My readings of both Magocsi and Subtelny are coloured by personal acquaintance with them both and by many interesting conversations, primarily with the former. Magocsi's survey was not the first territorial study. In 1994, the Austrian scholar Andreas Kappeler presented a highly articulate short history using the same approach. See his *Kleine Geschichte der Ukraine* (Munich: Verlag C.H. Beck, 1994) and my English-language summary in the *Journal of Ukrainian Studies* 20, nos. 1–2 (1996), 252–6.

9  See Volodymyr Kravchenko, "Fighting Soviet Myths: The Ukrainian Experience," in Serhii Plokhy, ed., *The Future of the Past: New Perspectives on Ukrainian History* (Cambridge, Mass.: Harvard Ukrainian Research Institute, 2016), 437–82, especially 441.

10  On Kukharenko and Shevchenko, see chapter 5 of this book, and on Kostomarov and Kramskoi, chapter 9. On Kostomarov, in particular, whose origins outside the borders of present-day Ukraine are sometimes overlooked, see my brief biographical sketch, "Nicholas Kostomarov," in *Forum: A Ukrainian Review*, no. 70 (Scranton, Penn., 1987), 20–3; and my more-detailed *Mykola Kostomarov: A Biography* (Toronto: University of Toronto Press, 1996). I treat Kostomarov's historical ideas in extenso in my "Mykola Kostomarov as a Historian," in Thomas Sanders, ed., *Historiography of Imperial Russia: The Profession and Writing of History in a Multinational State* (Armonk and London: M.E. Sharpe, 1999), 332–43, and I compare and contrast him with Hrushevsky in my "Kostomarov and Hrushevsky in Ukrainian History and Culture," *Ukrainskyi istoryk* 43–44, nos. 1–2 (2006–07), 307–19.

11  I address this point in chapter 6 of this volume. Balzac fell in love with and married Ewelina Hańska, née Rzewuska, an enormously rich Polish aristocrat from Kyiv province in right-bank Ukraine.

12  The geographically westward drift of Ukraine's notional borders over the centuries is seldom noted in the country's histories. It is also largely obscured by Paul Robert Magocsi's focus on Ukraine's present political borders and estimated ethnographic territory in his histories and historical atlases. See for example his *Ukraine: An Illustrated History* (Toronto: University of Toronto Press, 2007). But during the Cold War, when Ukraine was to be found on very few maps, this approach helped convince a sceptical scholarly world of the very existence of the country and its history, and its anachronistic character was a necessary price to pay. Magocsi uses the same technique in his various books on Subcarpatian Rus' and Carpatho-Rusyns, currently as controversial a subject as were Ukrainians in previous times.

13  Serhii Plokhy, *The Gates of Europe: A History of Ukraine* (New York: Basic Books, 2015); William H. McNeill, *Europe's Steppe Frontier 1500–1800: A Study of the Eastward Movement in Europe* (Chicago and London: Chicago University Press, 1964). Also see Liliya Berezhnaya, "A View from the Edge: Borderland Studies and Ukraine," in Serhii Plokhy, ed., *The Future of the Past: New Perspectives on Ukrainian History* (Cambridge, Mass.: Harvard Ukrainian Research Institute, 2016), 43–68, and the beautifully produced volume by Ihor Chornovol, *Komparatyvni frontyry: Svitovyi i vitchyznianyi vymir* (Kyiv: Krytyka, 2015). For a particularly stunning American example of this "frontier view" that saw Ukrainians as "the Texans" of Russia, that is, as "Texans in fur hats," see John Fischer, *Why They Behave like Russians* (New York and London: Harper and Brothers, 1947), 22–34.

14  Yury Bielichko / Belichko, "Tvorchist Illi Riepina v konteksti ukrainskoi khudozhnoi kultury druhoi polovyny XIX–pochatku XX stolit," *Narodna tvorchist ta etnohrafii*, no. 4 (1994), 3–12, especially 3.

15  In literature, Dmitri Likhachev offers an especially good example of a russifier and this russifying process. See especially his contributions to Dmitry Likhachev

et al., *A History of Russian Literature from the 11th to the 17th Centuries* (Moscow: Raduga Publishers, 1989), and the discussion of this book in chapter 1 below.

16  Myroslav Shkandrij, *Russia and Ukraine: Literature and the Discourse of Empire from Napoleonic to Postcolonial Times* (Montreal and Kingston: McGill-Queen's University Press, 2001), xv.

17  In the early 1980s, Valentine Moroz, a celebrated Soviet Ukrainian political dissident, newly arrived in the West, spoke at the University of Toronto and distinguished, as I recall, two different types of colonialism and imperialism. The first was the Greek type, wherein ancient Greece founded overseas colonies for economic purposes and did not attempt to absorb their inhabitants, or, at least, the surrounding "natives," into Greek civilization and culture. The second was the ancient Roman type, which Moroz claimed was a continental empire that did try to do this, and largely succeeded in both Gaul and Iberia. He claimed that the British Empire followed the Greek model, and the Russian Empire and its successor, the Soviet Union, the Roman model.

18  The "Introduction" to Shkandrij, *Russia and Ukraine, passim,* gives further references.

19  See the classic discussion by J.B. Rudnyckyj, "The Name of the Territory and Its People," in *Ukraine: A Concise Encyclopedia,* vol. I (Toronto: University of Toronto Press, 1963), 3–12. Of course, there are some complications to this general truth. See, for example, Andrii Danylenko, "On the Names of Ruthenia in Early Modern Poland–Lithuania," in M. Németh et al., eds., *Essays in the History of Languages and Linguistics Dedicated to Marek Stachowski on the Occasion of His 60th Birthday* (Cracow, 2017), 161–73.

20  Neither Sabbatai Zevi nor Mohammed Asad seems to have merited entries in Volodymyr Kubijovyč and Danylo Husar Struk, eds., *Encyclopedia of Ukraine,* 5 vols. (Toronto: University of Toronto Press, 1984–93), although Zevi was apparently very influential because of the distress caused to Ukrainian Jews during the Khmelnytsky revolt of 1648, and Asad's unusual biography deserves attention. However, Jewish literature treats of Zevi extensively, as does Islamic of Asad. In fact, the Islamic Cultural Centre in contemporary Lviv is named after Muhammad Asad, born Leopold Weiss.

21  For a comparison with the other major European source of slaves, see Robert C. Davis, *Christian Slaves, Muslim Masters: White Slavery in the Mediterranean, the Barbary Coast, and Italy, 1500–1800* (London: Macmillan Palgrave, 2003), based almost entirely on European narratives, and Jonathan A.C. Brown, *Slavery and Islam* (London: One World, 2019), by an American convert to Islam, who has examined the Muslim sources and addresses moral and ethical questions raised by slavery and its long acceptance, or at least tolerance, by major world religions. This book was published too late for its use in this chapter.

22  See chapter 7, on Mérimée, below. On Beauplan, Chevalier, Scherer, and other early French authors, see the classic work of Élie Borschak / Ilia Borshchak,

*L'Ukraine dans la littérature de l'Europe occidentale* (Paris: N.p., 1935), especially the first sections. This work was first serialized 1933–35 in the pioneering Paris journal *Le monde slave*. For a relevant anthology in Ukrainian translation, see Ievhen Luniak, *Kozatska Ukraina XVI–XVIII st. ochyma frantsuzkykh suchasnykiv* (Nizhyn: NDU, 2013), 508 pp.

23  See my "Voltaire on Mazepa and Early Eighteenth Century Ukraine," *Canadian Journal of History / Annales canadiennes d'histoire* 47 (2012), 259–83; illustrated and slightly revised version online at: https://www.slideshare.net/ThomasM-Prymak/voltaire-on-mazepa-and-early-eighteenth-century-ukraine, 10 October 2015; my "The Cossack Hetman: Ivan Mazepa in History and Legend from Peter to Pushkin," *Historian* 76, no. 2 (2014), 237–77; and my "The Polish Legend of Byron's *Mazeppa*," unpublished paper, 12 pp.

24  Yaroslav Dashkevych, "Ivan Mazepa: 300 rokiv protostoiannia v istorii ta polityt-si," in Ihor Skochylias, ed., *Ivan Mazepa i Mazepyntsi* (Lviv: NANU and NTSh, 2011), 15–28. I have also treated this question in my "Who Betrayed Whom? Or, Who Remained Loyal to What? Tsar Peter vs. Hetman Mazepa," unpublished paper, 13 pp.

25  The quote from Ilya Repin comes from his letter of 19 February 1889 to N.S. Leskov, in Repin, *Izbrannye pisma v dvukh tomakh*, 2 vols. (Moscow: Iskusstvo, 1969), I, 358–9. More generally, see Petro Kraliuk, *Kozatska mifolohiia Ukrainy: Tvortsi ta epihony* (Kharkiv: Folio, 2017). The first argument in English about Cossacks' contrasting roles in Ukrainian and in Russian history was Ivan Lysiak-Rudnytsky's review of Philip Longworth's *The Cossacks* (New York: Holt, Rhinehart and Winston, 1970): namely, "A Study of Cossack History," *Slavic Review* 31, no. 4 (1972), 870–5. Also see the respected survey of Cossack history by Andreas Kappeler, *Die Kosaken: Geschichte und Legenden* (Munich: C.H. Beck, 2013), especially 101, where Kappeler partly credits the poet Taras Shevchenko (on the Ukrainian side) for creating this "national myth." These points are less clearly stated in Iaroslav Lebedynsky, *Histoire des Cosaques* (Paris: Terre noire, 1995).

26  For some context, see Olga Andriewsky, "The Russian–Ukrainian Discourse and the Failure of the 'Little Russian' Solution, 1782–1917," in *Culture, Nation, and Identity: The Ukrainian–Russian Encounter (1600–1945)* (Edmonton and Toronto: CIUS, 2003), 182–214.

27  For a very brief English-language portrait of Shevchenko as a "social revolutionary," see Yevhen Kirilyuk's "Introduction" to *Taras Shevchenko: Selected Poetry*, trans. John Weir et al. (Kyiv: Dnipro, 1977), 5–12. For a more lengthy portrait, which pushed the limits for Soviet Ukrainian writers, see Yevhen Shabliovsky, *The Humanism of Shevchenko and Our Time*, trans. Mary Skrypnyk and Petro Krawchuk (Kyiv: N.p., n.d., but probably during the "Shelest Renaissance" of the 1960s). For the "national" interpretation, see Clarence A. Manning, *Taras Shevchenko: The Poet of Ukraine* (New York: Ukrainian National Association, 1945), and especially Luka Lutsiv, *Taras Shevchenko: Spivets ukrainskoi slavy i voli* (New York: NTSh and Svoboda, 1964), and R. Zadesniansky (pseud.), *Apostol ukrainskoi natsionalnoi*

*revoliutsii* (Munich: Ukrainska krytychna dumka, 1969). For a more moderate view, see Pavlo Zaitsev, *Taras Shevchenko: A Life*, trans. George Luckyj (Toronto: University of Toronto Press, 1988).

28  However, Mérimée, and possibly Balzac too, knew something of Gogol. Two generations later, a francophile Ukrainian émigré in Paris would write: *"Ces deux grandes écrivains, Gogol et Chevtchenko, se complètent parfaitment. Si l'on peut parler de l'âme ou du charactère d'un people, deux traits sont surtout typiques chez les Ukrainiens: le sens du comique [et] d'ironie, mais d'une ironie qui se transforme bientôt en pur lyrisme. Nos chansons nationales sont remplies de cette double tendence de l'âme ukrainienne."* See Alexandre Choulguine / Oleksander Shulhyn, *L'Ukraine contre Moscou (1917)* (Paris: Félix Alcan, 1935), 9. For an extensive but far from complete listing of French-language works on Ukraine, see Jacques Chevchenko, *Ukraine: Bibliographie des ouvrages en français XVIIᵉ–XXᵉ siècles* (Paris: L'est Européen, 2000). For recent general histories, see Iaroslav Lebedynsky, *Ukraine: Une histoire en questions* (Paris: L'Harmattan, 2008), and, with more detail, Pierre Lorrain, *L'Ukraine: Une histoire entre deux destins* (Paris: Bartillat, 2019), 670 pp.

29  For a Ukrainian take on the Orientalism controversy, see Yury Kochubei, "Edward Said (1937–2003), Humanizm proty 'Orientalizmu,'" *Skhidnyi svit*, no. 2 (Kyiv, 2004), 39–44, and for a brief survey of "Oriental" influences on Ukrainian art, including on the paintings of Taras Shevchenko, see Kochubei, "Orientalni motyvy v ukrainskomu obrazotvorchomu mystetstvi," *Skhidnyi svit*, no. 4 (2004), 132–7.

30  Many Slavonic philologists believe both *Boh* and *khata* very early borrowings from Iranian, and *kobza* a later borrowing from Turkish or Turkic, although some scholars think *Boh* derived directly from pre-historic Indo-European, so only a close cognate and not a loan-word from Iranian. For a reasoned introduction to the dispute, see Jaroslav B. Rudnyckyj, *An Etymological Dictionary of the Ukrainian Language*, Part 1 (Winnipeg: UVAN, 1962–69), 158–9.

31  The classic Cold War–era response to such Soviet positions, today much respected in independent Ukraine, was Borys Krupnytsky, *Ukrainska istorychna nauka pid Sovetamy* (Munich: Institute for the Study of the USSR, 1957), especially its last two chapters. An intellectual and political biography of the great western Ukrainian historian Ivan Krypiakevych (1886–1967), a student of Hrushevsky's who wrote successively under Austrian, Polish, Soviet, Nazi German, and then again Soviet authorities, would illuminate these processes. For some brief and scattered but titillating remarks, see Serhy Yekelchyk, *Stalin's Empire of Memory: Russian–Ukrainian Relations in the Soviet Historical Imagination* (Toronto: University of Toronto Press, 2004).

32  Again, see Krupnytsky, *Ukrainska istorychna nauka*.

33  See Mykhailo Hrushevsky, "Novi perspektyvy" (first pub. 1917), in O.T. Honchar et al., eds., *Velykyi ukrainets* (Kyiv: Veselka, 1992), 154.

34  Aside from his work on Ibn Fadlan, Kovalivsky's most important publication
    was his anthology of translations into Ukrainian from various "Oriental" litera-
    tures: *Antolohiia literatur skhodu* (Kharkiv: KhDU, 1961), 451 pp. On Ukrainian-
    Middle East studies generally, see L.V. Matvieieva, "Skhodoznavstvo (Oriental-
    istyka)," *Entsyklopediia istorii Ukrainy*, vol. IX (Kyiv: NANU, Institut istorii, 2012),
    925–6, which gives further references. Also see the collection of articles: Yaroslav
    Dashkevych, *Ukraina i skhid* (Lviv: NANU, 2016), 957 pp., which explores a num-
    ber of topics in Ukrainian Oriental studies, refers to many little-known works,
    and notes frequently the harmful effects of the Soviet censors, to this day not en-
    tirely resolved. Finally, Petro Kraliuk, *Pivtory tysiachi rokiv razom: Spilna istoriia
    ukraintsiv i tiurkskykh narodiv* (Kharkiv: Folio, 2018), is very useful but appeared
    too late for consideration in this book.

35  On Paul of Aleppo, compare for example the brief and laconic treatment of him
    in V.M. Beilis, "Pavlo Khalebsky," *Radianska entsyklopediia istorii Ukrainy*,
    vol. III (Kyiv: URE, 1971), 308, with the much more detailed and politically pointed
    one in "Alepsky, Pavlo," in Yevhen Onatsky, ed., *Ukrainska mala entsyklopediia*,
    vol. I (Buenos Aires: UAPTs v Argentini, 1957), 19–20, from which the quotations
    above are taken. Also see M. Kowalska, *Ukraina w połowie XVII wieku w relaji ar-
    abskiego podróznika Pawla, syna Makarego z Aleppo: Wstęp, przekład, komentarz*
    (Warsaw: PWN, 1986); and Paul of Aleppo, *Ukraina: Zemlia Kozakiv: Podorozhnyi
    shchodennyk*, ed. M.O. Riabii (Kyiv: Yaroslaviv val, 2008). The Soviet scholar Bei-
    lis did manage to mention, however, that Kovalivsky was able to publish a brief
    article on Paul in 1954 for the "300th Anniversary of the Reunification of Ukraine
    with Russia," a year after Stalin's death. Not only in the passages quoted above, but
    throughout his work, Paul calls Ukrainians "Rus" or "Cossacks," and Russians
    "Muscovites." See the newly rediscovered ms. by A.P. Kovalivsky, "Zviazky zi
    skhodom ta skhodoznavstvo u Kyievi i Naddniprianshchyni v seredni viky," in
    I.P. Bondarenko, ed., *Movni ta literaturni zviazky Ukrainy z krainamy skhodu*
    (Kyiv: Dmytro Burago, 2010), 120, n 81.

36  Karl Marx, *Secret Diplomatic History of the Eighteenth Century*, ed. Eleanor Marx
    Aveling (London: Swan Sonnenschein and Co., 1899), 77.

37  In the 1960s, a Soviet historian, K.V. Solovev, translated into Russian Marx's sum-
    mary of Kostomarov's "Hetmanite of Vyhovsky," but it was never published, and
    Ukrainian historians V.H. Sarbei and E.S. Shabliovsky also worked on it, but were
    stymied by the Communist Party censors. They did publish a carefully worded ar-
    ticle that concentrated on Marx's view of Kostomarov's *Stenka Razin* (which said
    nothing about Ukrainian history or Ukrainian Cossacks), but not his detailed
    notes on Vyhovsky and Ukrainian Cossack history. For the former, see Sarbei and
    Shabliovsky's "N.I. Kostomarov v istoriograficheskom nasledii Karla Marksa,"
    *Voprosy istorii*, no. 8 (1967), 49–59.

38  As for Marx's *Secret Diplomatic History*, reprinted in London and New York
    during the Cold War (1969), it remained "secret" till the 1990s primarily for

Soviet citizens. See the official statement by the Institute of Marxism–Leninism of the Central Committee of the Communist Party of the USSR: "Karl Marks: Razoblacheniia diplomaticheskoi istorii XVIII veka," in *Voprosy istorii*, no. 1 (1989), 3–11 (and following issues). Also see Mykhailo Kirsenko, "Marks i Engels pro vytoky rosiiskoi polityky: Analiz i zasterezhennia," *Vsesvit*, nos. 9–10 (Kyiv, 2008), 147–9. The first item prints a Russian translation of Marx's *Secret Diplomatic History*, and the latter, excerpts from a Ukrainian translation. For a commentary on and the text of Marx's précis, "The Hetmanate of Vyhovsky" (still not available, I believe, in the German original), see Sarbei's "Pro Marksiv konspekt rozvidky Kostomarova 'Hetmanstvo Vyhovskoho,'" *Pratsi tsentru pamiatkoznavstva*, no. 2 (Kyiv, 1993), 226–44. Also see O.V. Yas, "Karl Marks i Ukraina," online at the Vpered website at https://vpered.wordpress.com/2012/09/03/yas-Karl-Marx-Ukrainian, 4 October 2018, and J.P. Himka, "Marxism," in Volodymyr Kubijovyč and Danylo Husar Struk, eds., *Encyclopedia of Ukraine*, vol. III (Toronto: University of Toronto Press, 1993), 326–7.

## CHAPTER ONE

1  The general term "Middle East" is quite new, especially in its present sense. Originally coined by the British to fill in that great cultural and geographical expanse between what was once called "the Far East" and "the Near East," it eventually came to be centred around Greater Syria and its neighbours; that is, today's Turkey, Syria, Palestine, Israel, Egypt, Arabia, Iraq, and Iran – more or less how I understand it. It is used in this sense, for example, by Bernard Lewis in his many books and articles. See especially his *The Middle East: 2000 Years of History from the Rise of Christianity to the Present Day* (London: Phoenix, 2000) and his *Islam in History* (Chicago: Open Court, 1993). But this definition excludes most of North Africa, that is, the "Maghreb," or the Arab West, and also Afghanistan and most of central Asia in the east (the fuller *Mashrik Zamin* or "Eastern Lands"). In contrast to this "narrow" approach, the pioneering American anthropologist Carleton Coon, in his classic *Caravan: The Story of the Middle East* (New York: Holt, Rinehart and Winston, 1966), included both the Maghreb and Afghanistan, as well as Pakistan. Both scholars emphasized climatic, cultural, and especially religious factors in their definitions, although most of Lewis's work dealt either with the central Arab lands or Turkey, and most of Coon's experience was either in the Iranian / Afghan east, or in the Maghreb, that is, in the extremities of the region. For an introduction to the problem, see Nikki Keddie, "Is There a Middle East?" *International Journal of Middle East Studies* 4 (1973), 255–71.

2  Also relatively new, like "Middle East," are "eastern Europe" and "Kresy." "Eastern Europe" dates back to only shortly after 1700 (learned works usually applied the French "*L'Europe septentrionale*," or "*Le nord*") and "Kresy" to after about 1850, originating in the word *kres*, meaning "end" in Polish, but used for the first

time in the plural, *Kresy*, by the geographer / poet Wincenty Pol in his epic poem *Mohort* (1855), in this new sense of "eastern borderlands." The Balkans are outside the ambit of this book, as is Coon's sweeping definition of the Middle East. On "eastern Europe," see Larry Wolff, *Inventing Eastern Europe: The Map of Civilization on the Mind of the Enlightenment* (Stanford, Calif.: Stanford University Press, 1996); on "Kresy," see Jacek Kolbuszewski, *Kresy* (Wrocław: Wydawnictwo Dolnosląskie, 1995), especially 5-22.

3  For McNeill's introduction to the history of the region (including the Balkans, but winding down about 1800), see his *Europe's Steppe Frontier: A Study of the Eastward Movement in Europe* (Chicago: University of Chicago Press, 1964; reprint 1975). For some general surveys of travel from the region to the Middle East, see the relevant bibliography by Yury Kochubei, *Ukraina i skhid: Kulturni vzaiemozv'iazky Ukrainy z narodamy Blyzkoho i Serednoho Skhodu 1917-1992: Pidruchnyi bibliohrafichnyi pokazhchyk* (Kyiv: NANU, 1998), 227 pp. Also see his "Zv'iazky ukrainskoi literatury z literaturamy Blyzkoho i Serednoho Skhodu," in T.N. Denysova et al., eds., *Ukrainska literatura v zahalno-slov'ianskomu i svitovomu konteksti*, vol. III (Kyiv: Naukova dumka, 1988), 404-54. Yaroslav Dashkevych includes only one very short notice specifically about Ukrainian travellers to the Middle East in his "Ukrainski mandrivnyky XIX st. na Blyzkomy Skhodi ta ikhni memuary," in his *Maisternia istoryka: Dzhereloznavstvo ta spetsiialni istorychni dytsypliny* (Lviv: Pidamida, 2011), 126-7. Dashkevych mentions figures such as the "neo-Cossack" Mykhailo Chaikovsky, the writer Danylo Mordovets, the Galician-American priest Amvrosii Voliansky, the Orientalist Ahatanhel Krymsky, and a few others. On the Poles, see Jan S. Bystroń, *Polacy w Ziemi Święty, Syrji, i Egypcie 1147-1914* (Cracow: Orbis, 1930); Jan Reychman, *Podróżnicy polscy na Bliskim Wschodzie w XIX w.* (Warsaw: Wiedza powszechna, 1972); and Wacław Przemysław Turek, "Polskie kontakty socjokulturowe i językowe z krajami Islamu," *Przegląd polonijny* 29, no. 2 (2003), 63-86. There is also some material on Ukrainians and Poles in the various works of B.M. Dantsig, which concentrate on Muscovites and Russians. See, for example, his *Russkie puteshestvenniki na Blizhnem Vostoke* (Moscow: Mysl, 1965) or his *Blizhnii Vostok v russkoi nauke i literature (Do-oktiabrskii period)* (Moscow: Nauka, 1973). As well, there is much relevant material in I.A. Zakharenko, *Izuchenie vostoka urozhentsami Belarusi* (Minsk: Ekoperspektiva, 2006).

4  See Steven Runciman, *The Eastern Schism: A Study of the Papacy and the Eastern Churches during the 11th and 12th Centuries* (Oxford: Oxford University Press, 1955; reprint London: Panther, 1970), 104. Also see his *History of the Crusades*, 3 vols. (New York: Harper, 1965), II, 321, 485; and A.A. Vasiliev, *History of the Byzantine Empire*, 2 vols. (Madison and Milwaukee: University of Wisconsin Press, 1964), II, 393. *The Pilgrimage of the Russian Abbot Daniel in the Holy Land 1106-1107* was translated into English (via a French translation) by Charles W. Wilson, which was published in London in 1888; it was reprinted by the Palestine

Pilgrims' Text Society in 1895, and the part concerning the Holy Fire is available online at http://www.holyfire.org/eng/doc_Daniil.htm, 20 July 2016. Wilson also discusses those pilgrims from the Land of Rus' who preceded Daniel. Also see Bernard Leib, *Rome, Kiev et Byzance à la fin du XI siècle* (Paris, 1924; reprint New York: Bert Franklin, 1968), 280–5, which, like Runciman's later book, stressed the relatively good relations between Latins and Greeks in Palestine as seen through Daniel's eyes. More generally, see Theofanis G. Stavrou and Peter R. Weisensel, *Russian Travelers into the Christian East from the Twelfth to the Twentieth Century* (Columbus, Ohio: Slavica, 1986), a bibliographical work, which contains a valuable introduction.

5  For two characteristic Russian views of Daniel's account, see Vladimir Kuskov, *A History of Old Russian Literature*, trans. Ronald Vroon (Moscow: Progress Publishers, 1980), 105–9, and Dmitry Likhachev et al., *A History of Russian Literature from the 11th to the 17th Centuries* (Moscow: Raduga, 1989), 130–4, which on 588–9 lists the work's many translations into Western languages. For Ukrainian views, see Dmytro Čyževskyj, *A History of Ukrainian Literature from the 11th to the End of the 19th Century*, trans. Dolly Ferguson et al. (Littleton, Col.: Ukrainian Academic Press, 1975), 110–13, which compares some of Daniel's diction to that of the nineteenth-century Ukrainian poet Taras Shevchenko, and see Mykhailo Vozniak, *Istoriia ukrainskoi literatury*, 2 vols. (Lviv: Svit, 1992), I, 181–5, 652–63, which lists Slavonic editions of Daniel's work.

6  See Mykhailo Hrushevsky, *History of Ukraine-Rus'*, vol. III, *To the Year 1340*, trans. Bohdan Struminski, ed. Frank E. Sysyn (Edmonton and Toronto: CIUS, 2017), especially 310 and 370, where it states that Daniel's book "was without a doubt the most popular work of Old Rus' literature." Also see Hrushevsky, *Istoriia ukrainskoi literatury*, vol. II (New York: Knyho-spilka, 1959), 97–100.

7  See the discussion of this point in Klaus-Dieter Seemann's introduction to his edition of *Igumen Daniil Khozhenie / Abt Daniil Wallfahrtsbericht* (Munich: Wilhelm Fink Verlag, 1970), xxvi.

8  V.S. Buriak et al., eds., *Istoriia ukrainskoi literatury u vosmy tomakh*, vol. I (Kyiv: Naukova dumka, 1967), 133; On Dobrynia / Anthony of Novgorod in general, see "Antonii, Arkhiepiskop Novgorodskii," *Entsiklopedicheskii slovar*, vol. II (St Petersburg: Brogaus i Efron, 1890; photo-reprint Yaroslav: Terra, 1990), 858, and the brief noting of him in George J. Majeska, *Russian Travelers to Constantinople in the Fourteenth and Fifteenth Centuries* (Washington, DC: Dumbarton Oaks, 1984), 3. Likhachev et al., *A History of Russian Literature*, 134, like Hrushevsky before him, indicates the continuing popularity of Daniel's work by noting that over a hundred manuscripts of it have survived from earlier times. Likhachev's "great genius" view of Russian literature, which largely ignored sociological factors, as well as non-Russian origins and themes, coloured his take on the history of Russian, as well as "Old Ukrainian" culture, which, of course, he claimed for Russia. On this, see Robert Romanchuk's editorial remarks in Hrushevsky, *History of*

*Ukraine-Rus'*, III, 511. Also see V.M. Guminsky, *Russkaia literatura puteshestvii v mirovom istoriko-kulturnom kontekste* (Moscow: RAN, 2017), whose chapter on Daniel's influence I saw too late to use in this book.

9   See N.A. Meshchersky, "Drevnaia russkaia povest o vziatii Tsargrada Fragiami [*sic*] v 1204 godu," *Trudy otdel drevnoi russkoi literatury*, vol. X (St Petersburg: Pushkinskii dom, 1954), 120–35. Certain earlier Russian scholars had assumed that Anthony of Novgorod wrote this account, but Meshchersky's linguistic analysis showed that it was of *Iuzhno-russkii*, namely "South Russian," or Ukrainian origin. Also see Stavrou and Weisensel, *Russian Travelers*, 8–9, and the brief remarks in Likhachev et al., *History of Russian Literature*, 108–9, and Vasiliev, *History of the Byzantine Empire*, II, 461.

10   Bystroń, *Polacy w Ziemi Święty, Syrji, i Egypcie*, 1–5; Darius von Güttner-Sporzyński, *Poland, Holy War, and the Piast Monarchy 1100–1230* (Turnout, Belgium: Brepols, 2014), 10, 12, 136–59.

11   Bystroń, *Polacy w Ziemi Święty, Syrji, i Egypcie*, 6.

12   On Łaski and Radziwiłł, see ibid., 10–40, and Tomasz Kempa, *Mikołai Krzysztof Radziwiłł Sierotka* (Warsaw: Semper, 2000), on Radziwiłł, from whose influential work, says Kempa (121), "a great many Turkish and Arabic words" entered Polish vocabulary. Stanisław Stachowski compiled a 514-page historical dictionary of turkisms in Polish, many of them uncommon today: *Słownik historyczny turcyzmów w języku polskim* (Cracow: Księgarnia akademicka, 2007). Some of these turkisms entered via Ukrainian, which today has about four thousand – about the number of arabisms in modern Spanish. On this, and also for a survey of pre-Islamic "Orientalisms" in modern Ukrainian, see Appendix B above. On the enormous political impact of Radziwiłł's conversion to Catholicism, see Ambroise Jobert, *De Luther à Mohila: La pologne dans la crise de la Chrétienté* (Paris: Institut d'études slaves, 1974), 146 *et passim*.

13   David Frick translated Smotrytsky's Apology into English in his *Rus' Restored: The Selected Writings of Meletij Smotrytskyj (1610–1630)* (Cambridge, Mass.: Harvard Ukrainian Research Institute, 2005), 369–566. Also see Frick's biography of this controversial figure: *Meletij Smotrytskyj* (Cambridge, Mass.: Harvard Ukrainian Research Institute, 1995).

14   These three pilgrims are listed in Yury Kochubei, "Zv'iazky ukrainskoi literatury z literaturamy Blyzkoho i Serednoho Skhodu," in T.N. Denysova et al., eds., *Ukrainska literatura v zahalno-slov'ianskomy i svitovomu konteksti*, vol. III (Kyiv: Naukova dumka, 1988), 404–54, especially 411. Bibliographical information is given in Klaus-Dieter Seemann, *Die Altrussische Wallfahrtsliteratur* (Munich: Wilhelm Fink Verlag, 1976), 437, 441, which volume also notes, on 443, the *Putnik o grade Ierusalime sostavlen neizvestnym Galitsko-Russkim palomnikom mezhdu 1597–1607* (Guide to the City of Jerusalem Composed by an Unknown Galician-Ruthenian Pilgrim between 1597 and 1607), first published by the pioneering Galician-Ruthenian historian Antin Petrushevich in Lviv in 1872.

15  All of these characters are discussed in Zakharenko, *Izuchenie*, 72–7.

16  Ibid., 87–9. Further on Simeon, see Kuskov, *Old Russian Literature*, 336–41, and Likhachev et al., *History of Russian Literature*, 528–35, which ignore his anti-Islamic polemics, mentioning only his opposition to the Russian Old Believers.

17  Zakharenko, *Izuchenie*, 90 and 403, identifies Michael the Lithuanian as Michael Tyshkevych, ambassador 1538–40 of the Grand Duchy of Lithuania to the Crimean Khanate. Despite possible Ruthenian (perhaps "Belarusan") origins, Michael believed that the Lithuanians were descended from the ancient Romans, and he defended the administrative use of Latin as against "Ruthenian" in Lithuania. See Pietro U. Dini, *Prelude to Baltic Linguistics: Earliest Theories about Baltic Languages* (Amsterdam: Rudori, 2014), 53–6. For editions of *De moribus* and further references, see chapter 3 below.

18  Charles Verlinden, "L'origin de sclavus-esclave," *Archivum Latinitatis Medii Aevi*, 17 (1942), 97–128. This striking fact impressed the great early-twentieth-century Ukrainian poet Lesya Ukrainka, who wrote an understandably indignant poem about it. See her "Slavus – Sclavus," in her *Zibrannia tvoriv u dvanadtsiaty tomakh*, vol. I (Kyiv: Naukova dumka, 1975), 239; also available in English in *Spirit of Flame: A Collection of the Works of Lesya Ukrainka*, trans. Percival Cundy (New York: Bookman Associates, 1950), 67–8.

19  For a fascinating first-hand account of Suleiman and Roxelana, see E.S. Forster, ed., *The Turkish Letters of Ogier Ghiselin de Busbecq* (Baton Rouge: Louisiana State University Press, 2005), especially 28, 118–19, *et passim*. Busbecq was the imperial ambassador to Constantinople from 1554 to 1562. More generally, see Leslie Peirce, *Empress of the East: How a European Slave Girl Became Queen of the Ottoman Empire* (New York: Basic Books, 2017), which is to be used with care, and see my "Roxolana: Wife of Suleiman the Magnificent," *Nashe zhyttia / Our Life* 52, no. 10 (New York, 1995), 15–21. Also see chapter 3 below.

20  For further details, see chapter 3 below and, more briefly, Paul Robert Magocsi, *This Blessed Land: Crimea and the Crimean Tatars* (Toronto: Chair of Ukrainian Studies, 2014), 47–9 *et passim*. Again, Lesya Ukrainka wrote many poems on these themes, especially on the fate of female Ukrainian captives in Ottoman Turkey. Most of these are collected in her *Zibrannia tvoriv*, vol. I. For a Turkish view of what he calls "forced recruitment into the Ottoman élite," particularly the *Devşirme*, or collection of older boys from among the Christian inhabitants of the Balkans, for service in the Ottoman military as Janissaries, or in the civil administration, see Ilber Ortayli, *Discovering the Ottomans*, trans. Jonathan Ross (Markfield, England: Kube, 2009), especially 20–7. Ortayli is good on the voluntary movement of Christian Slavs into Islamic society, where they were in most cases quickly assimilated, but he does not discuss the Black Sea slave trade, or its implications for Turkish or Ukrainian and eastern European history.

21  George Vernadsky, *Bohdan: Hetman of Ukraine* (New Haven, Conn.: Yale University Press, 1941), especially 17.

22  Zbigniew Wójcik, *Jan Sobieski 1629–1696* (Warsaw: PIW, 1983), especially 51.

23  See Francisci à Mesgnien Meninski, *Thesaurus linguarum Orientalium Turcicae Arabicae Persicae . . . nemirum . . . Lexicon Turco-Arabo-Persicum . . . et Grammaticum Turcicam . . . etc.* (Vienna: N.p. 1680); and Wacław and Tadeusz Słabczyński, *Słownik podróźników polskich* (Warsaw: Wiedza powszechna, 1992), 222, which gives further references.

24  See Kuchubei, "Zv'iazky ukrainskoi literatury," 414, which quotes, in particular, the 1621 polemic of Zakhariia Kopystensky to the effect that "an Eastern Christian entering a land under Turkish rule is not killed or bothered in any way, but rather his faith experiences not the slightest bit of oppression."

25  For an English translation of Nikitin's text, see "Afanasy Nikitin's Journey across Three Seas," in *Medieval Russia's Epics Chronicles and Tales*, rev. and enlarged edition, ed. Serge A. Zenkovsky (New York: Dutton, 1974), 333–53.

26  See Pietro's own account of his adventures in the east in *The Pilgrim: The Travels of Pietro della Valle*, ed. and trans. George Bull (London: Century Hutchinson Folio Society, 1989), especially 117–92. Also see Oleksander Baran, "Kozaky v opysakh Pietra della Valle z XVII stol.," *Ukrainskyi istoryk* 17, nos. 1–4 (1980), 95–103, and 18, nos. 1–4 (1981), 128–36.

27  Kuchubei, "Zv'iazky ukrainskoi literatury," 413.

28  John Stoye, *The Siege of Vienna: The Last Great Trial between the Cross and Crescent* (New York: Pegasus, 2000); Taras Chukhlib, *Viden 1683: Ukraina-Rus' u bytvi za 'Zolote Iabluko' Ievropy* (Kyiv: Klio, 2013).

29  Andrew Wheatcroft, *The Enemy at the Gate: Habsburgs, Ottomans and the Battle for Europe* (New York: Perseus, 2010); Leszek Podhorodecki, *Jan III Sobieski* (Warsaw: Bellona, 2010); Miltiades Varvounis, *Jan Sobieski: The King Who Saved Europe* (London: XLibris, 2012); Borys Jaminsky, *Viden' 1683: Kozaky i Kulchytsky* (Vienna: Soiuz ukrainskykh filatelistiv Avstrii, 1983); Adam Zamoyski, *The Polish Way: A Thousand Year History of the Poles and Their Culture* (New York: Franklin Watts, 1988), especially chap. 12: "The Oriental Baroque." Also see Haydn Williams, *Turquerie: An Eighteenth Century European Fantasy* (London: Thames and Hudson, 2014).

30  See Vasyl Hryhorovych-Barsky / Vasilii Gregorovich-Barsky, *Mandry po sviatykh mistsiakh skhodu z 1723 po 1747 rik*, ed. P.V. Bilous (Kyiv: Osnova, 2000); B.M. Dantsig, *Russkie puteshestvenniki na Blizhnem Vostoke* (Moscow: Mysl, 1965), 68–73, and *Blizhnii Vostok v russkoi nauke i literature (Do-oktiabrskii period)* (Moscow: Nauka, 1973), 233–7, 246–9; Vozniak, *Istoriia ukrainskoi literatury*, II, 38–41; and V.M. Matiakh, "Hryhorovych-Barsky, Vasyl," in *Entsyklopediia istorii Ukrainy*, vol. II (Kyiv: Naukova dumka, 2004), 201, which termed Barsky's journal "a notable event in east Slavonic literature, in fact, starting the autobiographical genre within it." The journal is frequently listed together with the works of Theofan Prokopovych and Hrabianka as an outstanding example of the eighteenth-century Ukrainian literary language (not yet under strong Muscovite influence), although

many lesser examples have also survived. See on this point Ivan Franko, reviewing an essay by Pavlo Zhytetsky on Kotliarevsky's *Eneyda*: Ivan Franko, *Zibrannia tvoriv u p'iatdesiaty tomakh*, vol. XXXIII (Kyiv: Naukova dumka, 1982), 34.

31   That scholar was M.S. Petrovsky. See Kuchubei, "Zv'iazky ukrainskoi literatury," 411.

32   For the quote on Isfahan, see Father Krusinski / Tadeusz Jan Krusiński, *History of the Late Revolutions in Persia*, 2nd ed., vol. II (London: J. Pemberton, 1733), 8.

33   See Słabczyńskis, *Słownik*, 188–9; M. Kieffer-Kostanecka, "Polak pierwszym autorem europejskim historii Persji," *Notatki płockie*, no. 4 (1977), 45–6; and Bronisław Natoński, "Krusiński, Tadeusz," in *Polski słownik biograficzny* (hereafter *PSB*), vol. XV (Wrocław, 1970), 426–8, which states that Krusiński, a Polish Jesuit, passed through Turkey on his way back to Europe and eventually learned of the report by Durri Efendi, Ottoman ambassador to Iran, who described some of the events he had witnessed and was to write on. Krusiński later translated this report into Latin and published it in Lwów / Lviv (1733). Also, while he was in Istanbul, a high Ottoman official, Ibrahim Pasha, offered him a post in a planned School of Translators to serve the Ottoman government, which he declined. The Hollis Catalogue at Harvard lists several Latin titles by Krusiński, two, it says, translated into Ottoman Turkish throught the efforts of Ibrahim Mutifferika (a Hungarian convert to Islam) in the eighteenth century, and *Tarikh-e Afghan* (An Afghan History, 1860). Mutifferika's efforts at printing books in Islamic languages was cut short by the Turkish *ulema*, or religious scribes and jurisprudents, who feared for their jobs copying manuscripts and objected to the new technology as a foreign, un-Islamic influence. Also see Anna Krasnowolska et al., *Historia Iranu* (Wrocław: Ossolineum, 2010), 648.

34   For Potocki's travel writings, see Jean Potocki, *Œuvres*, 6 vols. (Louvain and Paris: Peeters, 2004). Volume I is on Turkey, Egypt, Holland, and Morocco, volume II covers the Caucasus, the European and Central Asian Steppes, and China, and volume III contains some of Potocki's historical writings, including his detailed study on Sarmatia, his *Histoire primitive des peuples de la Russie,* and his brief essay, "Coup d'œil sur les relations politiques entre la Russie et la Porte Ottomane" during the Napoleonic Wars. On Potocki and Jefferson, see Bohdan Yasinsky, "The Ukrainian Collections at the Library of Congress," online at the Library of Congress website at https://www.loc.gov/rr/european/coll/ukra.html, 11 July 2016. Also see my essay "From Podillia to the Pyramids: The Strange Life and Uncommon Death of Count Jan Potocki," *Ukrainian Weekly* (Jersey City), nos. 27–8, 1–8 July 2012, 8, at http://ukrweekly.com/archive/pdf3/2012/The_Ukrainian_Weekly_2012-27-28.pdf; and Słabczyński, *Słownik*, 250–1.

## CHAPTER TWO

1 Stefan Kieniewicz, "Rzewuski, Wacław Seweryn," *PSB*, vol. XXXIX, zeszyt 1 / 140 (Wrocław, 1992), 180–3; "Rzewuski [family]," in Volodymyr Kubijovyč and Danylo Husar Struk, eds., *Encyclopedia of Ukraine*, vol. IV (Toronto: University of Toronto Press, 1993), 487.

2 The historian, who basically accuses Rzewuski of being a "spy," was Jan Reychman. See his "Od fascynacji wschoda do Secret Service," *Twórczość*, no. 9 (1969), 38–44. More generally, see Wacław Słabczyński and Tadeusz Słabczyński, *Słownik podróżników polskich* (Warsaw: Wiedza powszechna, 1992), 269–71, which provides a detailed map of Rzewuski's expedition to the Middle East, and J. Chelrod, "Le voyage en Orient du Comte Wenslaus Rzewuski," *Arabia* 42, no. 3 (1995), 404–18; and Sarga Moussa, "Orientalisme et Rousseauism: La représentation des Bédouins d'Arabie par un voyageur polonais, Le Comte W. Rzewuski," *Revue d'histoire modern et contemporaine* 40, no. 2 (1998), 346–56.

3 Kieniewicz, "Rzewuski," 182.

4 Wacław Seweryn Rzewuski, *Sur les chevaux provenant des races orientales*, 3 vols. (Warsaw: Biblioteka narodowa, 2014), was not available to me to look at. But for a nicely illustrated Polish edition, see Rzewuski, *Podróż do Arabii: O koniach kohejlanach beduinach i przygodach w Arabii*, ed. and trans. Tadeusz Majda (Warsaw: Biblioteka narodowa, 2004).

5 Kieniewicz, "Rzewuski," 270–1. For a classic Ukrainian view of Rzewuski / Revusky, and also of Padura, see N.P. Dashkevich / Mykola Dashkevych, *Otzyv o sochinenii g. Petrova 'Ocherki istorii ukrainskoi literatury XIX stolettia = Zapiski Imperatorskoi Akademii Nauk* (St Petersburg, 1889), vol. LIX, 37–301, especially 191–5, which corrects the literary historian Petrov's view that writers of the Ukrainian School of Polish Literature like Padura have little place in the history of Ukrainian culture. Numerous versions of "Hej sokoly," both Polish and Ukrainian, are available on Youtube.

6 See in particular Jan K. Ostrowski, "Wacław Rzewuski w literature i sztuce: Prawda i legenda," in Elżbieta Karowska, ed., *Orient i Orientalizm w sztuce* (Warsaw: PWN, 1986), 193–216. An expanded and more prolifically illustrated version of this essay, with much additional material on related subjects, especially the Cossack Hetman Ivan Mazepa, is printed in Ostrowski, *Barok – romantizm – kresy* (Warsaw: DIG, 2017), which I discovered too late to include here.

7 On Goethe and von Hammer-Purgstall more generally, see Ingeborg H. Solbrig, *Hammer-Purgstall und Goethe "Dem Zaubermeister das Werkzeug"* (Bern and Frankfurt / M.: Verlag Herbert Lang, 1973), especially 195–6, on Rzewuski and the *Mines de l'orient / Fundgruben des Orients* project. The title page of the journal stated that it was produced by a society of lovers of science *"sous les auspices de M. Le Comte Venceslaus Rzewusky."* Also see Ananiasz Zajączkowski, "Z dziejów orientalizmu polskiego, doby mickiewiczowskiej," in Stefan Strelcyn, ed., *Szkice z*

*dziejów polskiej orientalistyki* (Warsaw: PWN, 1957), 69–94, especially 7, n 3, which quotes from von Hammer's memoirs describing Rzewuski's ride with him in July 1808, and T.F. Malenka, "Hafez, Goethe, Franko: Do problemy retseptsii perskoi klasychnoi poezii," *Skhidnyi svit*, no. 1 (2007), 111–15, which points out some parallels to Goethe's *Divan* in Ivan Franko's collection of lyric poetry, *Ziv'iale lystia* (Withered Leaves, 1896).

8   See Sibylle Wentker, "Joseph Freiherr von Hammer-Purgstall: Ein Leben zwischen Orient und Okzident," in Hannes D. Galter and Siegfried Haas, eds., *Joseph von Hammer-Purgstall: Grenzganger zwischen Orient und Okzident* (Graz: Leykam, 2008), 1–12, especially 5.

9   Jan Kieniewicz, "Poles vis-à-vis the Orient and Orientalism," in Tadeusz Majda et al., eds., *Oryantalizm: Orientalism in Polish Art* (Istanbul: Pera Müzesi, 2014), 22.

10   For a discussion of some of these points, see Marian Ursel, *Romantizm* (Wrocław: Wydawnictwo dolnośląskie, 2000), 165–6. A three-volume translation of Chateaubriand was published in Russia in 1815–16. See note 12 below for Viktor Guminsky's article on Gogol. Anna Kozak, "Between Fashion and Tradition: Orientalism in 19th Century Polish Painting," in Tadeusz Majda et al., eds., *Oryantalizm: Orientalism in Polish Art* (Istanbul: Pera Müzesi, 2014), 72, even argues that Polish Orientalism concerned the *Kresy* and old Poland, not the real Middle East.

11   On Shevchenko's "Kavkaz" (The Caucasus), see chapter 5 below. Yury Kochubei, "Zv'iazky ukrainskoi literatury z literaturamy Blyzkoho i Serednoho Skhodu," in T.N. Denysova et al., eds., *Ukrainska literatura v zahalno-slov'ianskomy i svitovomu konteksti*, vol. III (Kyiv: Naukova dumka, 1988), 423, notes that Shevchenko was interested enough in Mickiewicz's *Farys* to write to his Polish friend Bronisław Zaleski, questioning him about it. For Shevchenko's paintings and sketches on central Asian themes, see his *Mystetska spadshchyna*, 4 vols. in 5 books (Kyiv: Vyd. AN URSR, 1961–63), especially vol. II.

12   Viktor Guminsky, "Puteshestvie Gogola po sviatoi zemle v kontekste razvitie palmicheskoi literatury," online at the 'Russkoe voskesenie' website at http://www.voskres.ru/literature/critics/guminskiy1.html, 26 October 2017. Also see David Magarshack, *Gogol: A Life* (London: Faber and Faber, n.d.), 270–9. According to Guminsky, in the eighteenth century, each year only a few dozen pilgrims from the Russian Empire (mostly peasants) made their way to Jerusalem, but by the time of Gogol, the yearly number had reached four hundred (many of them nobles). This essay is printed in Guminsky, *Russkaia literatura puteshestvii*, 441–85, although I used the online version.

13   For some brief summaries of Chaikovsky's career, see my article "The Strange Life of Sadyk Pasha," *Forum: A Ukrainian Review*, no. 50 (Scranton, Penn., 1982), 28–31; Ivan Lysiak-Rudnytsky, "Michał Czajkowski's Cossack Project during the Crimean War: An Analysis of Ideas," in his *Modern Ukrainian History* (Edmonton: CIUS, 1987), 173–86; Adam Lewak, "Czajkowski, Michał (Sadyk Pasza)," in *PSB*,

vol. IV (Cracow, 1938), 155–9; and Mykola Rybak, "Mykhailo Chaikovsky: Mehmet Sadyk Pasha," in the *Almanakh Ukrainskoho Narodnoho Soiuzu na rik 1971* (Jersey City and New York), 86–97. The most detailed biography is in Polish by Jadwiga Chudzikowska, *Dziwne życie Sadyka Paszy: O Michałe Czajkowskim* (Warsaw: PIW, 1971), but also quite extensive is Vasyl Lutsiv's Ukrainian-language essay, "Legendarnyi nashchadok rodu Briukovetskykh: Mykhailo Chaika-Chaikovsky – Sadyk Pasha," in his *I slava i hordist* (State College, Penn.: N.p., 1969), 72–110. As well, there is an entire section on Chaikovsky in the journal *Khronika 2000*, no. 1 (2013), 411–42, which is a special issue on Turkish–Ukrainian relations.

14  Lewak, "Czajkowski," 155–6; Chudzikowska, *Dziwne życie Sadyka Paszy*, 11–61.

15  Chudzikowska, *Dziwne życie Sadyka Paszy*, 62–70.

16  Ibid., 71–130; Lewak, "Czajkowski," 156; Dashkevych, *Otzyv o sochinenii g. Petrova 'Ocherki istorii ukrainskoi literatury XIX stolettia*, 195–9.

17  Lewak, "Czajkowski," 156–9. More generally, Andrew A. Urbanik and Joseph O. Baylen, "Polish Exiles and the Turkish Empire, 1830–1876," *Polish Review* 26, no. 3 (1981), 43–53, summarizes Lewak's more extensive work: *Dzieje emigracji polskiej w Turcji (1831–1878)* (Warsaw: Nakładem instytutu wschodniego w Warszawie, 1935).

18  In addition to the various titles by Lewak cited immediately above in notes 14, 16, and 17, see Reychman, *Podróżnicy polscy*, 52, 68, 153.

19  See in particular Rybak, "Mykhailo Chaikovsky," 91, and Józef Fijałak's Introduction to Chaikovsky's Crimean War memoirs: Michał Czajkowski, *Moje wspomnienia o wojnie 1854 roku* (Warsaw: Wydawnictwo Ministerstwa Obrony Narodowej, 1962), v–xxxviii.

20  On the Cyril-Methodians, see my *Mykola Kostomarov*, 37–58, especially 57, and George S.N. Luckyj, *Young Ukraine: The Brotherhood of Saints Cyril and Methodius, 1845–1847* (Ottawa: University of Ottawa Press, 1991), especially 47–51. Also see Johannes Remy, *Brothers or Enemies: The Ukrainian National Movement and Russia from the 1840s to the 1870s* (Toronto: University of Toronto Press, 2016), chap. 1. On the Cossacks in the Crimean War, see Chaikovsky's *Moje wspomnienia o wojnie 1854 roku*, which is quite detailed.

21  In his various works on the subject, even the modern historian Lewak is quite critical of Chaikovsky, calling him "a renegade." (This was a term long used by Europeans to designate European converts to Islam; it was even common in scholarly work right through to the 1990s.) By contrast, Chudzikowska, Rybak, and others are more positive. As to Chaikovsky's contemporaries, the poet Mickiewicz was one of his biggest supporters and rushed to Istanbul to join the Ottoman Cossacks. But he took sick there and died in Chaikovsky's arms before he could do any fighting. See Chudzikowska, *Dziwne życie Sadyka Paszy*, 427–52, Ursel, *Romantyzm*, 143, and Chaikovsky's *Moje wspomnienia o wojnie 1854 roku*, 233. M. Sokolnicki, "Le mort de Mickiewicz en Turquie . . . 1855," *Belleten* 24 (1960), 111–27, was not available to me for this writing.

22  Dashkevych, *Otzyv o sochinenii g. Petrova 'Ocherki istorii ukrainskoi literatury XIX stolettia*, 196.

23  Reychman, *Podróżnicy polscy*, 252–61; Słabczyński and Słabczyński, *Słownik*, 56; Leon Płoszewski, "Chodźko, Aleksander Borejko," *PSB*, vol. III (Cracow, 1937), 380–1; and Zakharenko, *Izuchenie*, 168–72, which, as an example of Chodźko's ethnographic interests, tells his story, set in Azerbaijan, of the Virgin's Tower near Baku, supposedly built by Alexander the Great, but named after a young girl who preferred to throw herself to her death off the top rather than surrender to the carnal desires of a local potentate. Also see Harold Segel, "From the History of Polish Romantic Orientalism: Aleksander Chodźko's 'Derar,'" in Dietrich Gerhardt, ed., *Orbis Scriptus: Dmitrij Tchiżewskij zum 70 Geburtstag* (Munich, 1966), 707–15.

24  Reychman, *Podróżnicy polscy*; and Jean Calmard, "Chodźko, Aleksander Borejko," in *Encyclopedia Iranica*, vol. V, fasc. 5 (New York, 1991), 502–4.

25  See Bo Utas, "Borovsky, Izydor," in *Encyclopedia Iranica* at http://www.iranica-online.org/articles/borowsky-isidore, 20 July 2002, which gives further references, and also J. Fedirko, "Tragiczny Bohater Wyprawy Herackiej: General Izydor Borowski" (pdf), *Alma Mater*, 94 (Cracow, 2007), 121–5. Jan Reychman, "Podróżnicy polscy w Iranie," *Przegląd orientalistyczny*, no. 3 (1975), 235–43, further informs us that prior to 1838 a great many Poles in Russian service along the Turkestan and Terek lines fled the Russian Empire, and many took service in Persia. Under Russian diplomatic pressure, the Kajar government of Iran was compelled to expel some five hundred from its army on the eve of the siege of Herat. In this article, Reychman also gives a brief account of Chodźko's career in Iran.

26  See Calmard, "Chodźko," *passim*.

27  Ibid. Calmard writes that Chodźko's most controversial work was his *Grammaire persane* (1852), which was reviewed favourably by the distinguished Orientalist scholar Étienne Quatremère in the *Journal des savants* (1852) but attacked by the Iranian Mirza Kasem Beg in the *Journal asiatique* (1853).

28  See Louis Léger, "Chodźko," *Revue encyclopédique* 32, no. 2 (Paris, 1892), 491–4, which reports that Chodźko managed to calm things down at the Slavonic chair in Paris after Mickiewicz had stirred up quite a storm with his wild political prophesies that, he says, had turned the chair into a kind of "Sibylline Tripod." Léger concludes that Chodźko was "modeste, un peu timide . . . un poète délicat . . . un professeur consciencieux . . . un homme excellent."

29  Ibid.

30  Ryszard W. Wołoszyński, "Sękowski, Józef," in *PSB*, vol. XXXVI (Wrocław, 1995–96), 422–5; Słabczyński and Słabczyński, *Słownik*, 278–9; Zakharenko, *Izuchenie*, 110–11, 195–203.

31  Wołoszyński, "Sękowski, Józef," 423.

32  The book was *Collectanea z dziejopisów tureckich rzeczy do historii polskiej służących*, 2 vols. (Warsaw, 1824–25). See Wołoszyński, "Sękowski, Józef," 421–2.

Malenka, "Hafez, Goethe, Franko," notes that Sękowski also translated Hafez into Polish under the title *Wiersze perskiego poety Hafiza* (1838).

33  In English, the only work to treat Sękowski in any detail is Louis Pedrotti, *Józef Julian Sękowski: The Genesis of a Literary Alien* (Berkeley and Los Angeles: University of California Press, 1965), which concentrates on his career in Russian literature; but see 51–6 on Middle Eastern themes and 60 and 88 on the examples of satire mentioned here. As well, compare Wołoszyński, "Sękowski, Józef," with the parallel account by D. Korsakov in the *Russkii biograficheskii slovar*, vol. XVIII (St Petersburg, 1904), 316–25. Kochubei, "Zv'iazky ukrainskoi literatury," 423, speculates that Shevchenko may have learned something about Arabic culture from reading Sękowski. He certainly did take an interest in the Crusades, for, as he noted in his diary, he read in Russian translation J.F. Michaud's pioneering multi-volume history of the Crusades – this would be a translation of Michaud's *Histoire des croisades*, 6 vols. (Paris, 1812–22) or the six-voume 1840 edition; Michaud also compiled his *Bibliothèque des croisades*, 4 vols. (Paris, 1829), containing Western sources and, in volume IV, Arabic sources in French translation, and *Correspondence d'Orient*, 7 vols. (Paris, 1833–35), with letters relating to his travels in the Middle East.

34  Wiesław Bieńkowski, "Jabłonowski, Aleksander Walerian," in *PSB*, vol. X (Wroclaw, 1962–64), 214–16. Pedrotti, *Józef Julian Sękowski*, 184, notes that Jabłonowski also wrote on Sękowski, and cites his *Pisma*, vol.VII.

35  For one of the very few accounts in English, see my "Acquainting Two Worlds: Krymsky as Orientalist," *Nasha zhyttia / Our Life* 49, nos. 7–8 (New York, 1992), 21–4. For a fuller biography in Ukrainian, see Solomiia Pavlychko, *Natsionalizm seksualnist orientalizm: Skladnyi svit Ahatanhela Krymskoho* (Kyiv: Osnova, 2000).

36  See Jaroslaw Stetkevych, "Encounter with the East: The Orientalist Poetry of Ahatanhel Krymsky," *Harvard Ukrainian Studies* 8, nos. 3–4 (1984), 321–50.

37  See the brief popular article by Yury Kochubei, "Oriental iz Ukrainy," *Ukrainskyi tyzhden*, no. 13 (Kyiv, 2010), 46–8.

38  See Omeljan Pritsak, "Slovo pro Ahatanhela Krymskoho," *Visnyk AN URSR*, no. 6 (1991), 3–24.

39  Ibid., 15–16.

40  Ahatanhel Krymsky, *Tvory v p'iaty tomakh*, 5 vols. in 6 books (Kyiv: Naukova dumka, 1972–73). Volume IV contains most of his major (scholarly) "Orientalist" works in the Ukrainian language, which were, however, severely abridged by the Soviet censors for this edition. After the collapse of the USSR, his *Istoriia Turechchyny* (Kyiv and Lviv: Olir, 1996) was republished in full in independent Ukraine. For a bibliography of Krymsky's works and some works about him, see *A.Iu. Krymsky: Bibliohrafichnyi pokazhchyk* (Kyiv: Naukova dumka, 1972), which lists some 1,484 titles.

41  For an extensive article on Krymsky, with an updated bibliography, see O.V. Ias, "Krymsky, Ahatanhel," in *Entsyklopediia istorii Ukrainy*, vol. V (Kyiv: Naukova dumka, 2008), 362–4. A new and much fuller edition of Krymsky's *Collected Works* is presently in preparation in Kyiv; four volumes have already appeared.

42  See Agata Wojcik, "Nadworny malarz sułtana," *Alma Mater*, no. 124 (Cracow, 2010), 42–4, and "Jean-Léon Gérôme and Stanisław Chlebowski," *RIHA Journal*, at https://doi.org/10.11588/riha.2010.0.68542, 27 December 2010. Also see Mieczysław Treter, "Chlebowski, Stanislaw," in *PSB*, vol. III (Cracow, 1957), 296, and D.Kh. Murat, "Iz Stambula vo Lvova," at http://gazavat.ru/history3.php?rub=188art=132, 5 November 2016 (link defunct), which details how Chlebowski's portraits of the nineteenth-century Chechen rebel Shamil and his son Mohammed Shefi came to be painted, and Semra Germaner and Zeynep Inankur, *Constantinople and the Orientalists* (Istanbul: Isbank, 2002), 62, 65. There is also a considerable amount of material on Chlebowski, including many illustrations, in Majda et al., eds., *Oryantalizm*, *passim*, especially 140–61.

43  Both Bosphorus pictures, with commentary, are reproduced online at the website of the Polonia Institute in Istanbul at http://poloniaistanbul.wordpress.com/2012/01/04utopiona-w-bosforze/, 5 November 2016. Also see Reychman, *Podróżnicy polscy*, 75–6. On Matejko and the Ukrainians, in whom the painter also saw much that was "Oriental," see Adam Świątek, *'Lach serdeczny': Jan Matejko a Rusini* (Cracow: WUJ, 2013). On his "monumental" canvas on 1683, see my "Painting and Politics in the Vatican Museum: Jan Matejko's 'Sobieski at Vienna (1683)'," *Logos: A Journal of Eastern Christian Studies* 60, nos. 1–4 (2019); illustrated edition published online at https://www.academia.edu/42739074/Painting_and_Politics_ April, 3 May 2019.

44  Some of these are reproduced in Anna Bernat, *Józef Brandt 1841–1915* (Warsaw: Edipress, 2007), unpaginated, which gives further references. Also see the substantial article on Brandt in Aleksandra Górska, ed., *Wielka ensyklopedia malarstwa polskiego* (Cracow: Kluszczyński, 2011), 180–5. Brandt was preceded in such interests by Aleksander Orłowski (1777–1832), who was born in Warsaw but is sometimes considered "a Russian painter." He was the creator of the mysterious *Eastern Rider* (1805), which was almost certainly modelled on Rembrandt's *Polish Rider* (c. 1655), and also of *The Kirghiz Detachment* (1811–13), *The Persian Notable* (1811), and other such works. See Górska, ed., *Wielka ensyklopedia malarstwa polskiego*, 471–4. Brandt was succeeded a generation later by Wacław Pawliszak (1866–1903), who painted *Emir Rzewuski among the Arabs* and other such pictures; see Górska, ed., *Wielka ensyklopedia malarstwa polskiego*, 486.

45  See in particular my article "A Painter from Ukraine: Ilya Repin," *Canadian Slavonic Papers* 55, nos. 1–2 (2013), 19–43; illustrated version available online at both Slideshare and Academia.com <1 Jan. 2020>. On Yavornytsky in Egypt, see I.M. Hapusenko, *Dmytro Ivanovych Iavornytsky* (Kyiv: Naukova dumka, 1969), 23. Yavornytsky had lively interests in the Islamic world and Asia, published a histor-

ical and archaeological guide to central Asia from Baku to Tashkent (1893), and wrote a brief biography of the Prophet Mohammed, which was published only in 1992. See Serhii Kirzhaiev and Vasyl Ulianovsky, "Skhidni zori Akademika D.I. Yavornytskoho," *Vsesvit*, nos. 3–4 (1992), 168–81. Further on Repin's Zaporozhians, see chapter 9 in this volume.

46  For the full text of Ukrainka's "Vesna v Yehypti," see her *Zibrannia tvoriv*, I, 363–7, partly translated in Jaroslav B. Rudnyyckyj, *Egypt in the Life and Work of Lesya Ukrainka* (Ottawa: Slavistica, no. 83, 1983). She also wrote the play *Aisha and Mohammed* using an Islamic context to stress the idea of eternal love. See the brief note in Constantine Bida, *Lesya Ukrainka: Life and Work* (Toronto: University of Toronto Press, 1968), 62. In this, she was in part following the writer Panteleimon Kulish (1819–1897), the first Ukrainian poet to give serious attention to Islam. Kulish never visited the Middle East, but under the influence of John W. Draper became an "Islamophile" in late life and penned three poems or pieces on the Islamic world: "Mohammed and Khadija" (a love story), "Marusia Bohuslavka," and "Baida," all based largely on folk legends, but critical of "Cossack Barbarism." See George S.N. Luckyj, *Panteleimon Kulish: A Sketch of His Life and Times* (Bolder, Col.: East European Monographs, 1983), 174–5.

47  Khrystyna Sanotska and Ariadna Trush, "Arabski motyvy Ivana Trusha," *Vsesvit*, no. 11 (1979), 150–4. Also see Yury Kochubei, "Orientalni motivy v ukrainskomu obrazotvorchomu mystetsvi," *Skhidnyi svit*, no. 4 (2004), 1327, which also briefly treats Trush.

48  See O.M. Dziuba, "Yaroshenko, Mykola Oleksandrovych," in *Entsyklopediia istorii Ukrainy*, vol. X (Kyiv: Naukova dumka, 2013), 762, and "Nikolai Yaroshenko: Russkii i Ukrainskii zhivopisets i portratist," on the website of the "Itinerants" Association of Artists at http://www.tphv-history.ru/persons/Nikolay-Yaroshenko .html, 14 December 2016.

49  Stavrou and Weisensel, *Russian Travelers*, 616–17; V.P. Kovalenko, "Mordovets, Danylo Lukich," in *Entsyklopediia istorii Ukrainy*, vol. VII (Kyiv: Naukova dumka, 2010), 68–70.

50  See the official journal describing the pilgrimage: Vasyl Matsiurak and Yuliian Dzerovych, *Iak to Rus' khodyla slidamy Danyla: Propamiatna knyha pershoho ruskoho palomnytstva v Sviatu Zemliu vid 5 do 28 veresnia 1906* (Zhovka: Pechatnia oo. Vasyliian, 1907, 368 pp.; reprint Ivano-Frankivsk, 2015), with an introductory poem by Vasyl Shchurat on "The Monk Daniel [of Chernihiv]," two hundred illustrations, and modern spelling and orthography. The complete original text, which is the version that I consulted, is available online at www.anthropos.Inu. edu.ua/jspui/handle/1234567/2189, 28 March 2016. For information on the reprint, see Natalia Paliy, "A Book by Metropolitan Andrey Sheptytsky on Travel to the Holy Land Republished in Ivano-Frankivsk," Religious Information Service of Ukraine, 2 November 2015, risu.org.ua/en/index/all.news/catholics/ugcc/61570/. For more on the metropolitan, see "Sheptytsky, Andrei," in Volodymyr Kubijovyč

and Danylo Husar Struk, eds., *Encyclopedia of Ukraine*, vol. IV (Toronto: University of Toronto Press, 1993), 638–41, and for a detailed biography, see Cyrille Korolevskij, *Métropolite André Szeptyckyj 1865–1944* (Rome: Ukrainske bohoslovske tovarystvo, 1964), especially 47–8, which describes the pilgrimage and its commemorative book "magnifiquement imprimé par les Basiliens à Zovka." Sheptytsky, a long-time student of Hebrew, has recently become a renewed focus of Jewish–Ukrainian reconciliation because of his sheltering of Jews during the Second World War. See, for example, Paul Robert Magocsi and Yohanan Petrovsky-Shtern, *Jews and Ukrainians: A Millennium of Co-existence* (University of Toronto Press for the Chair of Ukrainian Studies, 2016), 77–8 *et passim*.

## CHAPTER THREE

1   For some context, see William H. McNeill, *Europe's Steppe Frontier* (Chicago: University of Chicago Press, 1964), especially 26–31; Paul Coles, *The Ottoman Impact on Europe* (London: Harcourt, Brace, and World, 1968), 28, 53; and Paul Robert Magocsi, *A History of Ukraine: The Land and Its Peoples* (Toronto and Buffalo: University of Toronto Press, 2010), 184–7. For general histories of the Crimean Tatars, which treat the khanate quite briefly, see Alan Fisher, *The Crimean Tatars* (Stanford, Calif.: Stanford University Press, 1978), and Paul Robert Magocsi, *This Blessed Land: Crimea and the Crimean Tatars* (Toronto: Chair of Ukrainian Studies, 2014). For a more detailed treatment, see Gulnara Abdulaeva, *Zolotaia epokha Krymskogo Khanstva* (Simferopol: Krimuchpedgiz, 2012). On the rulers, see Oleksa Haivoronsky, *Poveliteli dvukh materikov*, several vols. (Kyiv and Bakhchesarai: Maisterniia knigi, 2007– ), which "rehabilitates" the khanate for the Ukrainian and Russian publics, but does not discuss slave raiding, for which see Dariusz Kolodiejczyk, "Slave Hunting and Slave Redemption as a Business Enterprise: The Northern Black Sea Region in the Sixteenth and Seventeenth Centuries," *Oriente moderno* 86, no. 1 (2006), 149–59. Also see Maria Ivanics, "The Crimean Tatars," in Gábor Ágoston and Bruce Masters, eds., *Encyclopedia of the Ottoman Empire* (London: Facts on File, 2009), 158–61.

2   See, for example, M.A. Alekberli, *Borba ukrainskogo naroda protiv Turetsko-tatarskoi agressii* (Saratov: Izdat. saratovskogo universiteta, 1961). For a general bibliography on Ukraine and the Middle East, see Iu.M. Kochubei, *Ukraina i skhid: Kulturni vzaiemozviazky Ukrainy i narodamy Blyzkoho i Serednoho Skhodu 1917–1992* (Kyiv: NANU, 1998).

3   A major problem for historians is the paucity of references to the terms "Ukraine" and "Ukrainians" in the sources. Throughout the period, the ancestors of the modern Ukrainians were generally known (in different western European languages) as "Cossacks," "Ruthenians," "Russes," "Russiotes," and "Russians," and the ancestors of today's Russians, usually as "Russians" or more frequently "Muscovites." For an introduction with full references, see Brian J. Boeck, "What's in a

Name? Semantic Separation and the Rise of the Ukrainian National Name," *Harvard Ukrainian Studies* 27, nos. 1–4 (2004–5), 3365, and for greater detail: Natalia Yakovenko, "Choice of Name versus Choice of Path: The Names of Ukrainian Territories from the Late Sixteenth to the Late Seventeenth Century," in Georgiy Kasianov and Philipp Ther, eds., *A Laboratory of Transnational History: Ukraine and Recent Ukrainian Historiography* (Budapest and New York: Central European University Press, 2009), 117–48.

4  See, in particular, Murray Gordon, *Slavery in the Arab World* (New York: New Amsterdam, 1989); Bernard Lewis, *Race and Slavery in the Middle East* (New York: Oxford University Press, 1990); Ehud R. Toledano, *The Ottoman Slave Trade and Its Suppression: 1840–1890* (Princeton: Princeton University Press, 1982): and Y. Hakan Erdem, *Slavery in the Ottoman Empire and Its Demise 1800–1909* (Oxford: St Martin's Press, 1996). The briefer treatments of Hans Müller, "Sklaven," in B. Spuler, ed., *Handbuch der Orientalistik* part 1, vol. VI (Leiden and Cologne: Brill, 1977), 54–83, and R. Brunschvig, "Abd," in *Encyclopedia of Islam*, 2nd ed. (Leiden and London: Brill, 1960), I, 24–40, both completely ignore the role of eastern Europe after medieval times. More directly relevant are several titles by Alan Fisher, "Muscovy and the Black Sea Slave Trade," *Canadian–American Slavic Studies* 6, no. 4 (1972), 575–94, "Les rapports entre l'Empire ottoman et la Crimée: L'aspect financier," *Cahiers du monde russe et soviétique* 13 (1972), 368-81, "Azov in the Sixteenth and Seventeenth Centuries," *Jahrbücher für Geschichte Osteuropas* 21, no. 2 (1973), 164-74, "The Sale of Slaves in the Ottoman Empire: Market and State Taxes on Slave Sales: Some Preliminary Considerations," *Bogaziçi Universitesi Dergisi, Beşeri Bilimler* 6 (1978), 149–73, "The Ottoman Crimea in the Mid-Seventeenth Century: Some Problems and Preliminary Considerations," *Harvard Ukrainian Studies* 3 / 4 (1979–80), 215–26, and "Chattel Slavery in the Ottoman Empire," *Slavery and Abolition*, no. 1 (1980), 25–45. See also the pioneering essay by the distinguished Ottomanist Halil Inalcik, "Servile Labor in the Ottoman Empire," in his *Studies in Ottoman Social and Economic History* (London: Variorum, 1985), part 7, 26–52, and the more recent syntheses by Madeline C. Zilfi, "Slavery," in Gábor Ágoston and Bruce Masters, eds., *Encyclopedia of the Ottoman Empire* (London: Facts on File, 2009), 530–3; Alan Fisher, "Ottoman Empire," in Paul Finkelman and Joseph C. Miller, eds., *Macmillan Encyclopedia of World Slavery*, vol. II (New York and London: Macmillan, 1998), 660–63; E. Ann McDougall, "Islam," in Paul Finkelman and Joseph C. Miller, eds., *Macmillan Encyclopedia of World Slavery*, vol. I (New York and London: Macmillan, 1998), 434–9; and Suraiya Faroqhi, *The Ottoman Empire and the World around It* (London and New York: I.B. Tauris, 2007), 98–136. There are also several articles relevant to our theme ("Coran et Charia," "Mohamet," "Monde musulman," and "Orientalisme") in O. Pétré-Grenouilleau, ed., *Dictionnaire des esclavages* (Paris: Larousse, 2010). Also see W.G. Clarence-Smith, *Islam and the Abolition of Slavery* (New York: Oxford University Press, 2006).

5  See, in particular, O.I. Halenko, "Pro tatarski nabihy na ukrainski zemli," *Ukrain-skyi istorychnyi zhurnal*, no. 6 (2003), 52–68, and Ya. Dashkevych, "Bol'shaia granitsa Ukrainy: Etnicheskii bar'er ili etnokontaktnaia zona," in his *Maisternia istoryka*, ed. Andrii Hrechylo et al. (Lviv: Literaturna ahentsiia Piramida, 2011), 448–61.

6  Charles Verlinden, *L'esclavage dans l'Europe médievale*, vol. I (Brugge: De Tempel, 1955), 211–13 and *passim*; David Ayalon, "On the Eunuchs in Islam," *Jerusalem Studies in Arabic and Islam* 1 (1979), 67–124; Hans Müller, *Die Kunst des Sklavenkaufs nach arabischen persischen und türkischen Ratgebern von 10. bis zum 18. Jahrhundert* (Freiburg: Swartz, 1980), 79, 86, 104, 125; and, more briefly, John Tolan et al., *Europe and the Islamic World: A History* (Princeton, NJ, and Oxford: Princeton University Press, 2013), 66–7. On the *Saqaliba*, also see Appendix A in the present work.

7  In Mykhailo Hrushevsky, *History of Ukraine-Rus'*, vol. I, trans. M. Skorupsky (Edmonton and Toronto: CIUS, 1997), 227, citing G. Jacob, *Welche Handelartikel bezogen die Araber des Mittelalters aus den nordisch–baltischen Ländern,* 2nd ed. (Berlin, 1891), 12. Also see Tolan et al., *Europe and the Islamic World*, 67.

8  Walter Skeat, *A Concise Etymological Dictionary of the English Language*, 11th impression (New York: Pedegree, 1980), 491; and, most important, Charles Verlinden, "L'origine de *sclavus* = esclave," *Archivum Latinitatis medii aevi* 17 (1942), 97–128. Also see my article online: "Say 'Goodbye,' but Pause a Sec before Saying 'Chow,'" 4 pp., posted to Slideshare and at the blog of the Toronto Galician Genealogy Group: https://www.slideshare.net/ThomasMPrymak/say-goodbye-but-pause-a-sec-before-saying-chow-56408079, 23 December 2015, or http://www.onyschuk.com/wordpresstugg/?p=630, 5 November 2016. The classical Latin word for slave was *servus*. Also see O. Pétré-Grenouilleau, "Slaves," in O. Pétré-Grenouilleau, ed., *Dictionnaire des esclavages* (Paris: Larousse, 2010), 510–13. More generally, see Charles Verlinden, "Medieval Slavers," in David Herlihy, ed., *Economy, Society, and Government in Medieval Italy* (Kent, Ohio: Kent State University Press, 1969), 1–14, and M. Balard, *La mer noire et la Romanie génoise (XIII$^e$–XV$^e$ siècles)* (London: Variorum, 1989), which give further references.

9  Jaroslav Pelenski, "The Sack of Kiev of 1482 in Contemporary Musovite Chronicle Writing," *Harvard Ukrainian Studies* 3 / 4 (1979–80), 638–49; Mykhailo Hrushevsky, *Istoriia Ukrainy–Rusy*, 10 vols. (Lviv and Kyiv, 1898–1937), IV, 325–6. (I have used the second, or 1907 edition, published by the author simultaneously in Lviv and Kyiv.) This was technically not the first Crimean attack on Ukrainian territory, but it had incomparably greater political and psychological impact than previous raids.

10  See, in particular, Natalie Kononenko, *Ukrainian Minstrels: And the Blind Shall Sing* (Armonk and London: M.E. Sharpe, 1998). Also see her *Ukrainian Epic and Historical Song: Folklore in Context* (Toronto: University of Toronto Press, 2019), which I saw too late to incorporate into this chapter.

11  For more detail on this theme, see chapter 9 below.

12  Dariusz Kołodziejczyk, "Slave Hunting and Slave Redemption as a Business Enterprise: The Northern Black Sea Region in the Sixteenth to Seventeenth Centuries," *Oriente Moderno* 25 (86), no. 1, *The Ottomans and Trade* (2006), 150.

13  Adam Naruszewicz, *Tauryka czyly wiadomości starożytne i poźnieysze o stanie mieszkańcach Krymu do naszych czasów*, 2nd ed. (Warsaw: Tadeusz Mostowski w drukarnia przy Nowolipiu, 1805), 85, as quoted by Olgierd Górka, "Liczebność Tatarów i ich wojsk," *Przegląd Historyczno-Wojskowy* 8, no. 2 (1936), 232 / 48. I was unable to confirm this quotation in the original text. Also see O.V. Rusyna, *Ukraina pid Tataramy i Lytvoiu* (Kyiv: Alturnatyvy, 1998), 43–4.

14  Górka, "Liczebność Tatarów," 185–295, résumé in French, 327–30; also printed separately (Warsaw, 1936), 111 pp.

15  Leszek Podhorodecki, *Chanat Krymski i jego stosunki z Polska w XV–XVIII w.* (Warsaw: Książka i wiedza, 1987), 40–2. Similar figures have been given by Władysław Serczyk, *Na dalekiej Ukrainie: Dzieje Kozaczyzny do 1648 roku* (Cracow: Wydawnictwo literackie, 1984), 66, and Fisher, *The Crimean Tatars*, 37.

16  Alexandre Bennigsen et al., *Le Khanate de Crimée dans les Archives du Musée du Palais de Topkapi* (Paris: Mouton, 1978), 7, 21. The figure of eighty thousand has also been accepted by L.J.D. Collins, "The Military Organization and Tactics of the Crimean Tatars during the Sixteenth and Seventeenth Centuries," in V.J. Parry and M.E. Yapp, eds., *War, Technology and Society in the Middle East* (London: Oxford University Press, 1975), 257–76, especially 260, which closely follows S.M. Kuczyński, "Tatarzy pod Zbarażem," in his *Studia z dziejów Europy wschodniej X–XVIII w.* (Warsaw: PWN, 1965), 227–46, a severe critic of Górka.

17  Hrushevsky, *Istoriia Ukrainy–Rusy*, IV, 330–5.

18  Maurycy Horn, *Skutki economiczne najazdów tatarskich z lat 1605–1633 na Ruś Czerwona* (Wrocław: Ossolineum, 1964). In comparison, Muscovy, a very large state, lost only about 150,000–200,000 people to the Tatars between about 1600 and 1650. Its centralized, authoritarian state had established a fortified defensive "line" and warning system along its entire southern border, whereas highly decentralized Poland–Lithuania relied heavily on diplomacy, local strong points, border lords' private armies, and independent Cossack detachments. See A.A. Novoselsky, *Borba moskovskogo gosudarstva s Tatarami v XVII veke* (Moscow and Leningrad: AN SSSR, 1948), 368–72, on the "lines," and 434–6, on Muscovite demographic losses; see Podhorodecki, *Chanat Krymski*, 96, for a brief discussion of Polish–Lithuanian defences.

19  Bohdan Baranowski, *Chłop polski w walce z Tatarami* (Warsaw: Ludowa spółdzielnia wydawicza, 1952), 49. This text adds (56) that "the Tatars sold a significant part of the *yasir* to Turkey, which was the main receiver of this type of 'goods.' In the seventeenth century [the apparent apogee of the Black Sea slave trade] about 20,000 captives were yearly transported there from the Crimea."

20  Ya.R. Dashkevych, "Iasyr z Ukrainy (XV–persha polovyna XVII st.) iak isto-ryko-demohrafichna problema," *Ukrainskyi arkheohrafichnyi shchorichnyk*, no. 2 (Kyiv, 1993), 40–7.

21  Inalcik, "Servile Labor in the Ottoman Empire," 39; and Fisher, "Chattel Slavery in the Ottoman Empire," 32. Also see Victor Taki, *Tsar and Sultan: Russian Encounters with the Ottoman Empire* (London: I.B. Tauris, 2016), 53.

22  Halil Inalcik, *The Ottoman Empire: The Classical Age 1300–1600* (London: Weidenfeld and Nicolson, 1973), 131.

23  As does, for example, Iurii Zinchenko, *Krymski Tatary: Istorychnyi narys* (Kyiv: Holovna spetsializovana redaktsii literatury movamy natsionalnykh menshchyn Ukrainy, 1998), 43–4, which cites three hundred and fifty thousand lost and killed during the entire sixteenth century and three hundred thousand "captured" in the first half of the seventeenth. Most recently, I. Tymkiv, "Tatarski nabihy na ukrainski zemli v 30–40 rr. XVI st.," *Severnyi litopys*, no. 3 (2017), 3–19, found that Ukraine lost some thirty thousand people during the 1530s and 1540s. Kołodziejczyk, "Slave Hunting and Slave Redemption," 152, notes that such figures are comparable to the transatlantic slave trade for the same period. More generally, William J. Bernstein, *A Splendid Exchange: How Trade Shaped World History* (New York: Grove Press, 2008), especially the table on 276, shows the latter considerably smaller than the Black Sea trade throughout the sixteenth and seventeenth centuries, surpassing it only some years later, and reaching its peak in the late eighteenth. Of the approximately twenty thousand scholarly publications on slavery published since 1966, only the handful cited in the present study cover the Black Sea; for the twenty-thousand figure, see in particular Joseph C. Miller, *The Problem of Slavery as History: A Global Approach* (New Haven, Conn.: Yale University Press, 2012), 12–13.

24  Specialized studies of raids in certain times and places sometimes give startlingly low numbers. Thus D.I. Bahalii, *Istoriia Slobodskoi Ukrainy*, 2nd ed. (Kharkiv: Osnova, 1990), 49–50, says hundreds, not thousands, for even the large raids on eastern Ukraine under Russian rule during the 1680s and 1690s; Halil Sahillioğlu, "Slaves in the Social and Economic Life of Bursa in the Late 15th and Early 16th Centuries," *Turcica* 17 (1985), 43–112, offers similarly low figures – though at a time when the number of Ukrainian and Russian slaves in the Ottoman Empire was rapidly increasing; and Halil Inalcik, *The Customs Register of Caffa 1487–1490*, ed. Victor Ostapchuk, in *Sources and Studies on the Ottoman Black Sea*, vol. I (Cambridge, Mass.: Harvard Ukrainian Research Institute, 1996), contains very little on the slave trade. Fisher, "The Ottoman Crimea in the Mid-Seventeenth Century," plays down the slave trade, which, the author admits, involved about one quarter of the commerce in the bustling port of Kaffa.

25  Podhorodecki, *Chanat Krymski*, 59–60.

26  Ibid.

27   Ibid. For a first-hand account of Tatar raiding organization from a Muslim point of view, see Evliya Chelebi, *Księga podróży Ewliji Czebeliego*, ed. and trans. by Z. Abrahamowicz (Warsaw: Książka i wiedza, 1969), 232-5, which remarks on the fear that the Tatar raiders inspired among the Christian population. Also see Baranowski, *Chłop polski w walce z Tatarami*, 8-9. For certain periods, we have detailed knowledge of even small raids. For example, diplomatic sources in the 1540s reveal seventeen especially active leaders of Tatar raiding parties operating regularly out of Ochakiv and other Black Sea ports. Their names – Belek Murza, Sinan Aga, Taksari, Bigocha, Kormanak, Haji Lisan, and others – were known both in Cracow and in Istanbul. See Andrzej Dziubiński, "Handel niewolnikami polskimi i ruskimi w Turcji w XVI wieku i jego organizacja," in *Zeszyty Naukowe Uniwersytetu Warszawskiego*, vol. III (1963), 39-40. I obtained this title on interlibrary loan from the University of Warsaw. It is also sometimes listed as *Zeszyty Historyczne Uniwersytetu Warszawskiego*.

28   The classic, contemporary description of Tatar raiding and military tactics is by the French engineer in Polish military service, Guillaume le Vasseur Sieur de Beauplan, *A Description of Ukraine*, 3rd ed. (London, 1744; photo-reprint New York: Organization for the Defence of [the] Four Freedoms of Ukraine, 1959), 459-64. Also see Serczyk, *Na dalekiej Ukrainie*, 64-71, and Podhorodecki, *Chanat Krymski*, 52-9.

29   Yaroslav Kis, "Tatarski shliakhy na Ukraini v XVI–XVIII st.," *Zhovten*, no. 4 (1986), 134-6; Podhorodecki, *Chanat Krymski*, 57-8.

30   Sigismund von Herberstein, *Notes upon Russia*, vol. II (London, 1852; reprint New York: B. Franklin, n.d.), 65. Similarly, the Tatar chronicler Haji Mehmed Senai, in his *Historia Chana Islam Gereja III*, Ottoman Turkish text and Polish translation, ed. and trans. Z. Abrahamowicz (Warsaw: PWN, 1971), 116, boasted that during the great campaign of 1648, when "plunder beyond measure was taken," every Tatar would keep only the most beautiful girls and the handsomest boys and daily kill ten or fifteen prisoners. Haji Mehmed may have been exaggerating; certainly 1648 was an exceptional year. For a contemporary description of more usual tactics, see Beauplan, *Description of Ukraine*, 460, and for modern discussions, see Collins, "Military Organization and Tactics," 267-8, and Novoselsky, *Borba moskovskogo gosudarstva*, 434-6, which notes that the Tatars usually killed very few people, seeking mainly live *yasir*. On the low value of small children, see Gilles Veinstein, "Missionaires jésuits et agents français en Crimée au début du XVIIIᵉ siècle," *Cahiers du monde russe et soviétique* 10, nos. 3-4 (1969), 414-58, especially 435.

31   Text in Mykhailo Drahomanov, *Pro ukrainskykh Kozakiv, Tatar ta Turkiv* (Kyiv: Dnipro, 1991), 10 (my translation). This booklet, from the 1870s, is a popular-style distillation of research on the Tatar / Turkish theme as reflected in Ukrainian folk poetry collected in Volodymyr Antonovych and Mykhailo Drahomanov, *Istoricheskie pesni malorusskogo naroda*, 2 vols. (Kyiv: M.P. Frits, 1874-75). This work contains extensive historical and comparative-literary analysis and has recently been reprinted as volume I of Mykhailo Drahomanov, *Folklorystychni studii*, 4 vols.,

ed. V. Biliavsky (Donetsk: Nord-press, 2006–08), although I have used the first edition.

32    Marcin Broniewski, ambassador of the Polish King Stefan Batory (reigned 1576–86) to the Crimean court, has left a first-hand account of the return of a raiding expedition. Originally published in Cologne in 1595 in Latin as *Tartariae descriptio*, it was quickly translated into English and is available as Martin Broniovius, "Collections out of Martin Broniovius . . . containing a Description of Tartaria," in *Hakluytus Postumus or Purchas His Pilgrimes*, vol. XIII (Glasgow: James MacLehose and Sons, 1906), 461–91, especially 487. Broniewski states that the khan received a tenth of the booty, and Fisher, "Muscovy and the Black Sea Slave Trade," 583, follows him, pointing out, however, that Muslim rulers usually demanded a fifth, since, according to Islamic law, one-fifth of all booty "belongs to Allah." By contrast, Podhorodecki, *Chanat Krymski*, 58, states that the khan took a full fifth, and the *kalga sultan* or the *nureddin* a tenth. In this he follows Abrahamowicz (Haji Mehmed Senai), *Historia Chana Islam Gereja III*, 157–8, n 125, citing Evliya Chelebi, *Seyahat-name*, 10 vols. (Istanbul, 1896–1938), VII, 545, who notes that the khan would on occasion urge his followers on by promising them half of his share of "camp followers" (*chura / chora*) and "young girls" (*dimka*, from the Ukrainian *divka*).

33    Beauplan, *Description of Ukraine*, 460.

34    "Busurman" in this passage is a Slavonic rendering of the Persian / Ottoman term "Mosalman" (Muslim). (See Appendices B and C to the present work.) In Antonovych and Drahomanov, *Istoricheskie pesni malorusskogo naroda*, I, 89, no. 39, variant A; quoted in full and analysed in K. Ierofeev, "Krym v malorusskoi narodnoi poezii XVI–XVII vv. preimushchestvenno v dumakh," *Izvestiia Tavricheskoi Uchenoi Arkhivnoi Kommissii*, no. 42 (Simferopol, 1908), 73–87, especially 80 (my translation).

35    Chelebi, *Księga podróży Ewliji Czelebiego*, 308 (section on the Crimea). This passage refers to Turkish, not Tatar, slave traders in the Crimean town of Karasu. In theory at least, Islamic law prohibited slave raiding outside the bounds of *jihad* (Holy War), to extend or defend the faith. See "Coran et Charia," 165.

36    Hrushevsky, *Istoriia Ukrainy-Rusy*, VII, 95. In this case, with Poles and Cossacks in hot pursuit right up to the gates of Ochakiv.

37    V. Khenzel / W. Hensel, "Problema iasyria v polsko–turetskikh otnosheniiakh XVI–XVII vv.," in B.A. Rybakov, ed., *Rossiia Polska i Prichernomore* (Moscow: Nauka, 1979), 147–58, especially 158; Kołodziejczyk, "Slave Hunting and Slave Redemption," 157.

38    Baranowski, *Chłop polski w walce z Tatarami*, 50–2 and *passim*. Such instances were, however, the exception rather than the rule. In general, it was in the Tatars' self-interest to keep wealthy prisoners healthy, for if they got sick or died, they would be of no value at all; 52–3 gives several examples of captured military and civic leaders who were well treated by the Tatars.

39  Martin Broniovius (Broniewski), "Description of Tartaria," 487. The account of Captain John Smith of Pocahontas fame (who prior to his adventures in what became the United States had been in eastern Europe, where for a while he was a captive of the Tatars) seems to be somewhat exaggerated and directly contradicts Broniewski. In his *True Travels, Adventures and Observations* (London: Thomas Slater, 1630; photo-reprint Amsterdam: Da Capo Press, 1968), 30, Smith claimed of the Tatars that "the better they finde you, the worse they will use you, til you doe agree to pay such a ransome as they will impose upon you; therefore many great persons have indured much misery to conceale themselves." Perhaps it was best to be neither too rich nor too poor, but rather a middle-level gentleman not attracting special attention but able to pay a modest ransom.

40  Drahomanov, *Pro ukrainskykh Kozakiv Tatar ta Turkiv*, 13–14, gives the full text in Ukrainian. For the somewhat abbreviated form quoted here, see Mykhailo Hrushevsky, *A History of Ukraine* (New Haven, Conn.: Yale University Press, 1941), 160–1.

41  On Kaffa generally, see "Teodosiia," in Volodymyr Kubijovyč and Danylo Husar Struk, eds., *Encyclopedia of Ukraine*, vol. V (Toronto: University of Toronto Press, 1993), 190–1. Fisher, "Muscovy and the Black Sea Slave Trade," 583, states that the slave merchants "were mainly non-Muslim." Fisher claims that "Greeks, Armenians, Jews, and a few Italians handled the bulk of the sales." However, none of the authorities that he cites go so far. Alekberli, *Borba ukrainskogo naroda protiv Turetsko–tatarskoi agressii*, 104, observes: "On the markets of Kaffa, Evpatoria, Karasubazar, and Bakhchesarai, Turks and Tatars, Greeks and Jews, were occupied with the trade in human beings." Similarly, Nikolaus Ernst, "Die ersten Einfälle der Krymtataren in Südrussland," *Zeitschrift für osteuropaische Geschichte*, III (1913), 51, also cited by Fisher, takes a similar position. To be exact, he writes: "Viele Sklaven kamen ja auch in die Hände der Griechen, Italiener, Armenier, und Juden in den Städten der Krym. Die Hauptmasse der Sklaven aber wurde nach auswärts verkauft." (Indeed, in the cities of the Crimea many slaves also came into the hands of the Greeks, Italians, Armenians, and Jews. But the greater part of the slaves were sold to be sent abroad.) But neither Alekberli nor Ernst cites any source for these statements. C. Orhonlu, "Kefe," in *Encyclopedia of Islam* (Leiden and London: Brill, 1960), 2nd ed., vol. IV, part 2, 868–70, stresses the many Armenians and Greeks in the city – it was called "Istanbul the Lesser" because of its ethnic diversity – and notes that it was "a traditional centre of the slave trade." However, the entry otherwise ignores the subject.

42  Michael the Lithuanian / Mykolas Lietuvis, *De moribus Tartarorum, Lituanorum et Moschorum* (Basil: Apud Conradum Waldkirchium, 1615); photo-reprint with a Lithuanian trans., ed. K. Korsakas (Vilnius: Vaga, 1966), 11. I have also used the most recent Russian translation: Mikhailon Litvin, *O nravakh Tatar Litovtsev i Moskvitian*, trans. V.I. Matuzova (Moscow: Izdatelstvo moskovskogo universiteta, 1994), 72–3. "Non urbs [est] sed vorago sanguinis nostri" (12). The travails

of the Kaffa slave market remained legendary in Ukrainian culture right into the twentieth century. For example, it was alluded to by Taras Shevchenko, and after 1945 the refugee Ukrainian Bandurist Chorus composed and performed a *duma* (reflective song) about it, which was well received by audiences throughout western Europe and North America. See the *Shevchenkivska entsyklopediia*, vol. I (Kyiv: NANU, Institut literatury, 2012), 323, which refers to the "Nevolnychyi rynok u Kafi," (the slave market in Kaffa).

43  See Fisher, "Sale of Slaves in the Ottoman Empire," 156–7, citing the article on slaves in the *Istanbul Ansiklopedisi,* vol. X (Istanbul, 1971), 5271–3. Fisher gives a list of the mid-seventeenth-century Istanbul slave merchants, all Muslim. Thus the well-attested story that Jews predominated in the Istanbul trade (accepted by Robert Mantran, *Istanbul dans la second moitié du XVII$^e$ siècle* [Paris: A. Maissoneuve, 1962], 449, 506–7, and at one time by Fisher, "Muscovy and the Black Sea Slave Trade," 584) may be nothing more than a widely spread fable. Kołodziejczyk, "Slave Hunting and Slave Redemption," 155, analysing the same sources, states: "While in the 16th century most of the slave dealers had been Jews, in the following period this profitable profession was apparently dominated by Muslims." Compare Toledano, *The Ottoman Slave Trade and Its Suppression,* 59.

44  Quoted in Ahatanhel Krymsky, *Istoriia Turechchyny,* in his *Tvory v piaty tomakh,* vol. IV (Kyiv: Naukova dumka, 1974), 419.

45  In M.A. Berezhkov, "Russkie plenniki i nevolniki v Krymu," *Trudy VI arkheologicheskogo s"ezda v Odesse,* 4 vols. (Odessa, 1885–90), II, 342–72, especially 345. In 1568, the papal nuncio Ruggieri wrote of Poles and Ukrainians that "there are more slaves in Constantinople of this people [*sic*] than of any other"; Dziubiński, "Handel niewolnikami polskimi i ruskimi," 45. The Englishman Joseph Pitts, who was captured by Muslim pirates and in the 1680s taken as a slave throughout much of the Middle East, testifies to the same effect about the slave market in Cairo. See Joseph Pitts, William Daniel, and Charles Jacques Poncet, *The Red Sea and Adjacent Countries at the Close of the Seventeenth Century,* ed. W. Foster (London: Hakluyt Society, 1949), 15–16.

46  Brunschvig, "Abd," 32; Lewis, *Race and Slavery in the Middle East.*

47  Dziubiński, "Handel niewolnikami polskimi i ruskimi," 42–3, gives the prices at Akkerman; Inalcik, "Servile Labor in the Ottoman Empire," 44, note 3, gives prices at Edirne from 1500 to the 1630s.

48  Demetrius Cantemir, *The History of the Growth and Decay of the Othman Empire,* trans. N. Tindal (London, 1734), reprinted and quoted here from the Romanian abridgement: Dimitrie Cantemir, *Extracts from "The History of the Ottoman Empire",* trans. N. Tindal, ed. W.A. Duțu and P. Cernovodeanu (Bucharest: Association internationale des études du sud-est européen, 1973), 52–3.

49  Murray Gordon, a specialist on the modern period, generalizes about females in his *Slavery in the Arab World,* 82: "As long as Circassian, Slavic, Greek, and other white women were available at affordable prices, Arabs preferred them to blacks.

Their scarcity value tended to drive up their market value so that by the middle of the sixteenth century white slave women became a luxury that only the ruling sultans, Mamlukes, beys, and the very affluent could afford. From the end of the seventeenth to the middle of the nineteenth century, the average price of a white female slave was four to six times greater than that of a comparable black woman slave. In Egypt, according to [Edward] Lane, a white slave girl was worth anywhere from three to ten times the price of an Abyssinian."

50 Pitts et al., *The Red Sea*, 15; Berezhkov, "Russkie plenniki i nevolniki v Krymu," 345 (on Križanić) and 356-7 (on Ibrahim). On the constant shortage of slaves for the Ottoman navy, see Inalcik, "Servile Labor in the Ottoman Empire," 50-1, n 45, which remarks that galley slaves also supplied labour for monumental building projects such as the great Suleimaniye Mosque (1550-57) in Istanbul.

51 M. Fontenay, "Chiourmes turques au XVII$^e$ siècle," in Rosalba Ragosta, ed., *Le genti del Mare Mediterraneo*, 2 vols. (Naples: L. Pironti, 1981), II, 877-904; see especially Table 1. The Knights of St John clearly distinguished between Ukrainians (Fr: *Russiotes*), Russians (Fr: *Moscovites*), and Poles (Fr: *Polonais*), probably because the order supplied the freed captives with appropriate funds and a diplomatic letter requesting safe passage so that they could travel without restriction across Christendom to their original homeland.

52 Krymsky, *Istoriia Turechchyny*, 421; and Terence Wade, *Russian Etymological Dictionary* (London: Bristol Classical Press, 1996), 85, which notes that the word comes from the Greek *katá* (down below) and *érgon* (work); it had been loaned into Russian, in particular, in the fourteenth century, when the Ottomans were expanding rapidly in the Balkans, but before their push into the Ukrainian and Russian steppes.

53 For the Ukrainian text of "Vtecha Samiila Kishky iz turetskoi nevoli," with a collection of materials evaluating the legend, see Valerii Shevchuk, ed., *Samiilo Kishka: Istorychni rozvidky, dumy opovidannia* (Kyiv: Veselka, 1993). I follow the theory of Iurii Mytsyk, Serhiy Plokhii, and Ivan Storozhenko, *Iak Kozaky voiuvaly* (Dnipropetrovsk: Promin, 1990), 112-15. For an English translation of the *duma*, see *Ukrainian Dumy*, trans. George Tarnowsky and Patricia Kilina (Toronto and Cambridge, Mass.: CIUS, 1979), 46-63. There is an account of Jakimowski's adventures in English in Jerzy Pertek, *Poles on the High Seas*, trans. A.T. Jordan (Wrocław: Ossolineum, 1978), 103-6. Compare Taki, *Tsar and Sultan*, 60-2, which describes in similar terms the adventures of a Muscovite subject, Ivan Semenovich Moshkin, which occurred at about the same time.

54 "Si non castrantur, auribus tamen et naribus mutilantur, genis et frontibus cauteriantur." Michael the Lithuanian, *De moribus Tartarorum*, Latin text, 11; Russian trans., 72.

55 The testimony of Michael the Lithuanian (in ibid.) seems to imply that castration was usually performed in the Crimea itself or in the neighbouring countries. According to C. Orhonlu, "Khasi, Part III. In Turkey," *Encyclopedia of Islam*, 2nd

ed. (Leiden and London: Brill, 1960), vol. IV, part 2, 1092–3, that procedure in particular was strictly forbidden by Islamic law, and within the Ottoman Empire a private person had no legal right to castrate his slave. Orhonlu gives an example of a person who was prosecuted for trying to. Thus it was at the periphery of the empire, or even outside of it, that the operation usually seems to have been performed. However, some authorities seem to imply that it was also performed close to the sultan's palace itself in Istanbul or at least by people interviewed in Istanbul. For example, see the first systematic treatise (1608) devoted solely to Topkapi, by Ottaviano Bon, *The Sultan's Seraglio: An Intimate Portrait of Life at the Ottoman Court*, trans. John Withers (London: Saqi Books, 1992), 84. On the palace more generally, see Gülru Necipoğlu, *Architecture, Ceremonial and Power: The Topkapi Palace in the Fifteenth and Sixteenth Centuries* (New York: Architectural History Foundation and MIT, 1991).

56  Michael the Lithuanian, *De moribus Tartarorum*, Latin text, 12; Russian trans., 72–3.

57  Antonovych and Drahomanov, *Istoricheskie pesni malorusskogo naroda*, I, 208–30 (and reprinted in *Samiilo Kishka*, 90–5, especially 92), mentions Hasan Pasha. On the others, see A. Dziubiński, "Poturczeńcy Polscy, Przyczynek do historii nawroceń na Islam v XVI–XVIII w.," *Kwartalnik Historyczny* 102, no. 1 (1995), 19–37, and Baranowski, *Chłop polski w walce z Tatarami*, 55–7. From the above sources, it is evident that there is a real difficulty in distinguishing Ukrainian from Pole in the Ottoman Empire of that time. The principal distinguishing feature in Europe – religion, that is, Orthodox Ukrainian or Catholic Pole – was simply lost among such converts to Islam.

58  Baranowski, *Chłop polski w walce z Tatarami*, 55.

59  Fisher, "Ottoman Empire," 662; "Coran et Charia," 164–6. The Koran itself (sura 90, Balad, The City, 12–16) clearly recommends the liberation of slaves, and equates it to the giving of food to the hungry, to the orphan and to the indigent, though that liberation comes first on its list. The text then concludes: "Then will he be of those who believe" (line 17), meaning, of course, the former master. Also see Jonathan A. C. Brown, *Slavery and Islam* (London: One World, 2019), 70–100. The Bible too contains admonitions to gentle treatment of slaves, and St Paul (Galatians 2:28), stated: "There is neither Jew nor Greek, slave nor free, male nor female, for you are all one in Christ Jesus." So, taking into account Deuteronomy, the Koran, and Paul, we may conclude that while all three religions accepted the fact of slavery, all three were in some respects inclined towards its amelioration.

60  Ukrainian text and English translation in *Ukrainian Dumy*, trans. George Tarnowsky and Patricia Kilina (Toronto and Cambridge, Mass.: CIUS, 1979), 50–1.

61  Suraiya Faroqhi, "Crisis and Change, 1590–1699," in Halil İnalcik, with Donald Quataert, ed., *An Economic and Social History of the Ottoman Empire, 1300–1914* (Cambridge: Cambridge University Press, 1994), 411–636.

62  Herberstein, *Notes upon Russia*, II, 65–6.

63  Samiilo Velychko, *Litopys*, 2 vols., ed. and trans. into modern Ukrainian by Valerii Shevchuk (Kyiv: Dnipro, 1991), II, 191; Dmytro Yavornytsky, *Ivan Dmytrovych Sirko: Slavnÿi Koshovyi Otaman Viiska Zaporozkykh Nyzovykh Kozakiv*, in *Ivan Sirko: Zbirnyk* (Kyiv: Veselka, 1992), 9–103, especially 73. Sirko's controversial career as a Cossack leader gave rise to several *dumas* and historical songs, some printed in this collection. On the condition of slaves in the Crimea more generally, see Podhorodecki, *Chanat krymski*, 62–4, and (more briefly) Magocsi, *History of Ukraine*, 186–7.

64  Dmytro Yavornytsky, *Istoriia Zaporizkykh Kozakiv*, 3 vols. (Lviv: Svit, 1990–92), I, 247; Władysław Serczyk, *Na dalekiej Ukrainie: Dzieje Kozaczyzny do 1648 roku* (Cracow: Wydawnictwo literackie, 1984), 72. In Turkey, it was the custom for young unmarried women to wear white head scarves and married women to wear black ones. See Klára Hegyi and Vera Zimányi, *Muslime und Christen: Das Osmanische Reich in Europa* (Budapest: Corvina, 1988), 148.

65  "*Nam interdum ibi pensitantur auro et ponderibus suis, emuntur formosiores, et illibatae sanguinis nostri puellae.*" Michael the Lithuanian, *De moribus Tatarorum*, Latin text, 12; Russian trans., 73.

66  Brunschvig, "Abd," especially 27; Gordon, *Slavery in the Arab World*, 43, 79–104.

67  On Roxelana, see J.W. Zinkeisen, *Geschichte des osmanischen Reiches in Europa*, 8 vols. (Gotha: F. Perthes, 1840–63), III, 24–43; Krymsky, *Istoriia Turechchyny*, 425–40; S.A. Skilliter, "Khurrem," in *Encyclopedia of Islam*, 2nd ed. (Leiden and London: Brill, 1960), vol. V, part 1, 66–7; Ievhen Kramar, "Slavitna Ukrainka v sultanskomu dvori," in his *Doslidzhennia z istorii Ukrainy* (Toronto and Baltimore: Smoloskyp, 1984), 137–64; Galina Yermolenko, "Roxolana: 'The Greatest Empress of the East'," *Muslim World* 90, no. 2 (2005), 231–48, and, most especially, Leslie Peirce, *Empress of the East: How a European Slave Girl Became Queen of the Ottoman Empire* (New York: Basic Books, 2017), which, however, is quite speculative on many topics and mangles nationalities in eastern Europe. For a popularization by a non-historian, but with a good bibliography, see Andrew Gregorovich, *Roxelana: Ukrainian Consort of Emperor Suleyman the Magnificent* (Toronto: Forum Gregorado, 2014). For Turkish-language literature on Roxelana, see Stanford J. Shaw, *History of the Ottoman Empire and Modern Turkey*, vol. I (Cambridge: Cambridge University Press, 1976), 313.

68  Yavornytsky, *Istoriia Zaporizkykh Kozakiv*, I, 248; also see Iu. Mytsyk, S.M. Plokhii, and I.S. Storozhenko, *Iak Kozaky voiuvaly*, 153, a careful popularization, which devotes an entire chapter to "Cossack women."

69  Ukrainian text and English translation in *Ukrainian Dumy*, trans. Tarnowsky and Kilina, 37–41. (The translation quoted here, however, is my own.) Slave girls from Ukraine or Rus' (transformed into "Russia" in Latin and English-language sources) were found as far away as the court of the Mughal Emperor Akbar the Great (reigned 1556–1605) in India. See Bamber Gascoigne, *The Great Moghuls*

(London: Jonathan Cape, 1971), 85, citing Abu Fasl, *Ain-i-Akbari*, trans. H. Bloch-mann and H.S. Jarett, 3 vols. (Calcutta, 1873–94), I, 44–5.

70    Despite its legendary place in Ukrainian Cossack history – it was commemorated in verse and in a famous 1662 engraving in Kyiv – very little is known of Sahai-dachny's attack on Kaffa; even the alleged date – 1616 – is uncertain. For a crit-ical analysis of the problem see Hrushevsky, *Istoriia Ukrainy–Rusy*, VII, 354–5. The engraving is reproduced in the same author's *Iliustrovana istoriia Ukrainy* (Winnipeg, n.d.), 257. For an outline of events in English see Dmytro Doroshenko, *History of the Ukraine*, trans. H. Chikalenko-Keller (Edmonton: Institute Press, 1939), 188–90. More generally, see the detailed study of Victor Ostapchuk, "The Human Landscape of the Ottoman Black Sea in the Face of the Cossack Naval Raids," *Oriente moderno*, N.S. 20, no. 1 (2001), 23–95, and the specialized study of Viktor Brekhunenko, "Pokhid Ukrainskykh Kozakiv pid Kafu u 1616 r.," in *Osiahnennia istorii: Zbirnyk naukovykh prats na poshanu prof. Mykoly Pavlovy-cha Kovalevskoho* (Ostroh and New York: Ostroh Academy and the Ukrainian Historical Association, 1999), 166–70.

## CHAPTER FOUR

1    M. Dragomanov [Mykhailo Drahomanov], "M.A. Maksimovich: Ego literaturnoe i obshchestvennoe znachenie," *Vestnik Evropy*, vol. II, kn. 3 (1874), 442–53, espe-cially 453.

2    Volodymyr Zamlynsky, "Patriarkh ukrainskoi nauky," in M.O. Maksymovych, *Kiev iavilsia gradom velikim: Vybrani ukrainoznavchi tvory* (Kyiv: Lybid, 1994), 10–22.

3    Maksymovych's collected works appeared shortly after his death. See in particular M.A. Maksimovich [Mykhailo Maksymovych], *Sobranie sochinenii*, 3 vols. (Kyiv: Tip. M.P. Fritsa, 1876–80). Volume I, edited by Volodymyr Antonovych, contains his historical writings; volume II, by the same editor, his historico-topographical, archaeological, and ethnographical studies; and volume III, edited by Oleksander Kotliarevsky, his works on linguistics and the history of literature. His studies in the natural sciences and his popularizations of scientific thought have never been collected and published in the same way.

During the Soviet period, only his rather innocuous writings on Ukrainian folklore were published, which did not threaten Soviet stereotypes about Ukrainian and Russian national identities, especially of Russians as the "elder brothers" of the "younger" Ukrainians. However, a few secondary works by Soviet Ukrainian authors did appear, mostly during the Khrushchev thaw. These tended to portray Maksymovych as a "progressive," a forerunner of Darwin in biology, and a "fighter for the friendship of the Ukrainian and Russian peoples." See espe-cially D.F. Ostrianyn, *Svitohliad M.O. Maksymovycha* (Kyiv: Derzhpolitdav USRS, 1960). Moreover, throughout the Cold War, none of the handful of Ukrainian émigré scholars published a monograph or even an article on our protagonist, perhaps partly because he did not fit well into "nationalist" stereotypes about Ukrainian national identity.

However, the events of 1991 changed things. In 1994 a first collection of Maksymovych's selected works appeared (see note 2 above), and in 2004, on the bicentennial of his birth, beautifully illustrated collections of his works. See, in particular, Mykhailo Maksymovych, *Vybrani Tvory,* ed. and intro. by Viktor Korotky (Kyiv: Lybid, 2004), and *Vybrani tvory z istorii Kyivskoi Rusi Kyieva i Ukrainy,* ed. and intro. by P.H. Markov (Kyiv: Lybid, 2004); and his surviving letters: *Lysty,* ed. Viktor Korotky (Kyiv: Lybid, 2004). For some general studies in English that mention him, see David Saunders, *The Ukrainian Impact on Russian Culture 1750–1850* (Edmonton: CIUS, 1985), which discusses his place in Ukrainian and Russian history, and Zenon E. Kohut, *Russian Centralism and Ukrainian Autonomy: Imperial Absorption of the Hetmanate 1760s–1830s* (Cambridge, Mass.: Harvard Ukrainian Research Institute, 1988), and Serhii Plokhy, *Ukraine and Russia: Representations of the Past* (Toronto: University of Toronto Press, 2008), where chapters provide background information. For some conceptual issues, see Mark von Hagen, "Does Ukraine Have a History?" *Slavic Review* 54, no. 3 (1995), 558–73.

4 Biographical studies of Maksymovych began during his lifetime. See S.I. Ponomarev, *Mikhail Aleksandrovich Maksimovich: Biograficheskii i istoriko-literaturnyi ocherk* (St Petersburg: V.I. Golovnin, 1872). They continued during the pre-Revolution period. See in particular I. Steshenko, *Mikh. Aleks. Maksimovich: K stoletiiu godovshchiny ego rozhdeniia* (Kyiv: N.T. Korchak-Novytsky, 1904). And 1927 marked the centennial of his first and most influential work on folklore; see especially Mykhailo Hrushevsky, "'Malorossiiskie pesni' Maksymovycha i stolittia ukrainskoi naukovoi pratsi," *Ukraina,* no. 6 (1927), 1–13, reprinted in *Ukrainskyi istoryk* 21, nos. 1–4 (1984), 132–47; and Ihnat Zhytetsky, "Zhyttia M.O. Maksymovycha," *Ukraina,* no. 6 (1927), 14–24. The Khrushchev thaw of the 1950s brought studies like that of Ostrianyn (note 3 above). The Gorbachev reforms of the late 1980s allowed P.G. Markov, *Obshchestvenno-politicheskie i istoricheskie vzgliady M.A. Maksimovicha* (Kyiv: N.p., 1986), which is still a very "Soviet" work.

However, independence for Ukraine in 1991 initiated a Maksymovych renaissance. An early highlight was M.V. Tomenko, "'Shchyryi Malorossiianyn': Vydatnyi vchenyi, Mykhailo Maksymovych," in I.F. Kuras et al., eds., *Ukrainska ideia: Pershi rechnyky* (Kyiv: Tovarytstvo 'Znannia' Ukrainy, 1994), 80–97. Thereafter the floodgates opened; for a survey, together with an analysis of previous work, see Nadiia Boiko, *M. Maksymovych 'Ne pokynu z hynu moiu Ukrainu': Istoriohrafichnyi narys zhyttia i tvorchosti M.O.Maksymovycha* (Smila: Tiasmyn, 2001).

5 Mykhailo Maksymovych, "Avtobiografiia," in his *Kiev iavilsia,* 392.

6 Ponomarev, *Mikhail Aleksandrovich Maksimovich,* 5–6. Also see Volodymyr Panchenko, "Test na patriotism: Mykhailo Maksymovych, zabutyi arystokrat dukhu," in Larysa Ivshynam, ed., *Ukraina incognita*(Kyiv: Fakt, 2003), 159–69,

and V. Feyerherd, "Der Bildungsweg M.A. Maksimovič (1804–1873), des ersten Rektors der Kiever Universität," *Zeischrift für Slawistik* 27, no. 5 (1982), 684–99, which is particularly good on Maksymovych as a naturalist.

7  Ponomarev, *Mikhail Aleksandrovich Maksimovich*, 6ff. Also see A.N. Pypin, *Istoriia russkoi etnografii*, 4 vols (St Petersburg: M.M. Stasiulevich, 1891; reprint Kubon u. Sagner: Leipzig, 1971), III, 18–19, which is rather good on Maksymovych's intellectual formation.

8  See Pypin, *Istoriia russkoi etnografii*, III, 19, 35, which summarizes Maksymovych's address on Russian education: "O russkom prosveshchenii." Maksymovych's "Pismo o filosofii" – *Teleskop*, no. 12 (1833) – has been reprinted in Ukrainian translation as "Lyst pro filosofiiu," in *Khronika 2000* 9, nos. 37–8 (Kyiv, 2000), 397–401, and is summarized by Dmytro Chyzhevsky, *Narysy z istorii filosofii na Ukraini*, 2nd ed. (Munich: Ukrainskyi vilnyi universytet, 1983), 76–7.

   The *Book of Naum* was unavailable to me, but the beautiful title page, showing a farmer ploughing his field with a palm tree and beehive in the background, is nicely reproduced in Maksymovych, *Lysty*, 22, and discussed in Feyerherd, "Der Bildungsweg M.A. Maksimovič," *passim*. Naum, of course, is the Slavonic form of the Hebrew "Noam," meaning "pleasant." Noam was one the twelve minor prophets of the Old Testament. His feast day is 1 December on the eastern (Julian) calendar, and in many parts of Ukraine it was a holiday. Children born on that day were thought to turn out unusually intelligent: "*Nauma, toi vse zhyttia bude umnyi, sebto rozumnyi.*" See Yevhen Ontatsky, *Ukrainska mala entsyklopediia*, part V (Buenos Aires: UAPTs, 1959), 1097–8.

9  See his own Introduction, "O Malorossiiskikh narodnykh pesniakh," to M. Maksimovich, *Malorossiiskie pesni* (Moscow, 1827; photo-reprint Kyiv, 1962). This Introduction is reprinted in modern type and orthography in Maksymovych, *Vybrani tvory*, ed. Korotky, 346–56. More generally, V.F. Horlenko, "M.O. Maksymovych iak etnohraf: Do 180 richchia z dnia narodzhennia," *Narodna tvorchist ta etnohrafiia*, no. 6 (1984), 31–6, is a fairly good pre-*Glasnost* overview of our scholar's views on ethnography. Also see the discussions in George S.N. Luckyj, *Between Gogol and Ševčenko: Polarity in the Literary Ukraine 1798–1847* (Munich: Wilhelm Fink Verlag, 1971), 31–3, and in L.G. Frizman and S.N. Lakhno, *M.A. Maksimovvch: literator* (Kharkiv: KhNADU, 2003), 73–105. Many of the songs collected by Maksymovych are still sung in central Ukraine. See Svitlana Kytova, *Rodovid pisni: 'Malorossiiskie pesni' Mykhaila Maksymovycha (1827r.) ta ikhni suchasni zapysy* (Cherkasy, 2004).

10  This last point is especially stressed in Hrushevsky, "'Malorossiiskie pesni' Maksymovycha," *passim*. Later Ukrainian scholars would call Maksymovych's orthography *maksymovychivka*.

11  See the discussion in P.M. Popov, "Pershyi zbirnyk ukrainskykh narodnykh pisen,'" which is an Afterword to the facsimile edition of Maksimovich, *Malorossiiskie pesni* (photo-reprint Kyiv, 1962), 285–338, especially 322–3.

12  Maksymovych, "Avtobiografiia," 398. Also see Frizman and Lakhno, *M.A. Maksimovvch: literator*, 16.

13  At least this was the opinion of Drahomanov, "M.A. Maksimovich," 447, N.I. Petrov, *Ocherki istorii ukrainskoi literatury XIX stoletiia* (Kyiv: I. and A. Davidenko, 1884), 182, and many others who followed. Influenced, it seems, by his Muscovite environment, the young Maksymovych reacted positively to Pushkin's 1828–29 poem *Poltava*, about Mazepa, and defended its negative portrait from critics who thought it unhistorical. Later in life, Maksymovych's attitude seems to have eased, and he even suggested in a letter of 10 July 1865 to the Kyivan priest P.H. Lebedintsev that the Russian Orthodox curse on Mazepa should be lifted. For the text of this letter, see Maksymovych, *Lysty*, ed. Korotky, 154–5. More generally, see Tomenko, "'Shchyryi Malorossianyn'," 83–4, 94–5, which notes that even in the relatively liberal 1860s this was an unthinkable proposal for most Russian subjects. On Pushkin and Maksymovych more generally, see Mykhailo Popov, "Oleksandr Pushkin ta Mykhailo Maksymovych," *Kyiv*, no. 12 (1984), 142–6, which notes that when *Poltava* appeared, Maksymovych gave Pushkin a copy of the anonymous *Istoriia Rusov* (History of the Ruthenians, 1827), which effused Ukrainian autonomism, and Pushkin, somewhat embarrassingly for later Russian nationalists, tried to publish it.

14  In Pypin, *Istoriia russkoi etnografii*, III, 28. Also see Tomenko, "'Shchyryi Malorossianyn'," 83, and Mykola Zerov, *Lektsii z istorii ukrainskoi literatury (1798–1870)* (Oakville, Ont.: CIUS and Mosaic Press, 1977), 75.

15  Popov, "Pershyi zbirnyk," 325–6, citing N.P. Dashkevich, *Otziv o sochenenii g. Petrova* (St Petersburg: N.p., 1888), 92–3; Tomenko, "'Shchyryi Malorossianyn'," 83.

16  N.I. Kostomarov, "Avtobiografiia," in his *Istoricheskie proizedeniia. Avtobiografiia*, ed. V.A. Zamlinsky (Kyiv: Lybid, 1989), 448, and quoted in full in my *Mykola Kostomarov*, 8. The effect on the Ukrainian writer Panteleimon Kulish was similar. He writes: "Nikolai [Kostomarov], like all of us, students of the Russian schools, at first scorned everything Ukrainian and did his thinking in the language of Pushkin. Yet to both of us, in two different points in Little Russia, this unusual event happened. In Kharkiv, he came across the 1827 collection of Ukrainian songs [*Malorossiiskie pesni*] by Maksymovych[,] and I in Novhorod-Siversk, also by accident came into possession of the Ukrainian Dumas and songs of the same Maksymovych published in 1834 [as *Ukrainskie narodnye pesni*]. In one day both of us changed from Russian into Little Russian populists"; in Luckyj, *Between Gogol and Ševčenko*, 32–3. Popov, "Pershyi zbirnyk," 335–6, and Frizman and Lakhno, *M.A. Maksimovvch: literator*, 92–3, both claim that Maksymovych's collection of 1827 was known also to the prominent Polish poets Adam Mickiewicz, Juliusz Słowacki, and Józef Bohdan Zaleski (the last a member of the Ukrainian School of Polish Literature), as well as to numerous Polish folklorists.

17  On this see, in particular, Brian J. Boeck, "What's in a Name? Semantic Separation and the Rise of the Ukrainian National Name," *Harvard Ukrainian Studies* 27, nos. 1–4 (2004–05), 33–65.

18  Maksymovych, "Avtobiografiia," 399; Ponomarev, *Mikhail Aleksandrovich Maksimovich*, 23.

19  See the text of the speech in Mykhailo Maksymovych, "Ob uchastii i znachenii Kieva v obshchei zhizni Rossii," in Maksymovych, *Vybrani tvory*, ed. Korotky, 28–47. Also see the speaker's recollections about the audience's enthusiastic reception in his "Avtobiografiia," 401–2, where he called it "my victory" (*moe torzhestvo*), and also see the discussion in Pypin, *Istoriia russkoi etnografii*, III, 20, which, written from a Russian viewpoint, said Maksymovych had fulfilled his official duty "magnificently" both "as a Russian man and as a Kyivan." By contrast, Vitalii Shevchenko, "Mykhailo Maksymovych: Vydatnyi ukrainskyi uchenyi-entsyklopedyst, literaturnyi krytyk ta poet," *Vyzvolnyi shliakh* 57, no. 10 (2004), 46, from a more recent Ukrainian viewpoint, opined that the speaker "understandably and in an exculpatorable way veiled some sharp historical and political problems with a certain amount of obsequiousness."

20  Zamlynsky, "Patriarkh ukrainskoi nauky," 17. Despite his role in the depolonization of Kyiv and the formerly Polish-dominated Ukrainian territories, Maksymovych apparently earned the respect of Polish students and scholars at the university. Indeed, even the Polish populist historian and revolutionary of 1830, Joachim Lelewel, seems to have admired him and his work. This may simply have been because the Ukrainian Maksymovych, unlike most Russians, defended the unique nature (*samobutnost*) of the various Ukrainian lands. See B.S. Popkov, *Polskii uchenyi revoliutsioner Ioakim Lelevel* (Moscow: Nauka, 1974), 198.

21  Tomenko, "'Shchyryi Malorossianyn'," 85; Zamlynsky, "Patriarkh ukrainskoi nauky," 19.

22  See P.M. Fedchenko, *Materiialy z istorii ukrainskoi zhurnalistyky*, part 1 (Kyiv: Vyd. Kyivskoho derzhavnoho universytetu, 1959), 116, which quotes Borisov in Ukrainian translation: "It is not strange that the pitiful fate of the villagers in Little Russia arouses tears and bile in you. I very well know both the situation of the villagers whom the landlords take for granted and how difficult is their lot, and also the passionate nature and sensitivity of your expansive and philanthropic character."

23  For his early work, see M.A. Maksimovich / Mykhailo Maksymovych, "Pesn o polku Igoreve: Iz lektsii o russkoi slovestnosti chitannykh 1835 goda v Universitete Sv. Vladimira," in M.A. Maksimovich [Mykhailo Maksymovych], *Sobranie sochinenii*, 3 vols. (Kyiv: Tip. M.P. Fritsa, 1876–80), III, 498–563. On his interpretation of *Slovo o polku Igoreve* (Lay of Igor's Campaign), see Stepan Kozak, "Mykhailo Maksymovych i formuvannia romantychnoi dumky v Ukraini," *Journal of Ukrainian Studies* 9, no. 1 (Toronto, 1984), 3–32, and Frizman and Lakhno, *M.A. Maksimovvch: literator*, 134–65. Also see Mykola Korpaniuk, *Slovo i*

*dukh Ukrainy kniazhoi ta Ukrainy kozatskoi: Mykhailo Maksymovych – doslidnyk davnoukrainskoi literatury* (Cherkasy: Brama, 2004).

24  Reprinted in M.A. Maksimovich [Mykhailo Maksymovych], *Sobranie sochinenii*, 3 vols. (Kyiv: Tip. M.P. Fritsa, 1876–80), III, 345–471. Also see L. Gonczarow, "Mikhail Maksimovič et l'histoire littéraire russe de son temps," *Études slaves et est européennes / Slavic and East European Studies* 20–21 (1975–76), 31–43, which stresses Maksymovych's break with classical models and proposes: "*L'histoire est le premier ouvrage original consacré à l'étude de la littérature russe ancienne; c'est aussi le premier ouvrage sur l'histoire de la littérature russe*" (41).

25  M.F. Vladimirsky-Budanov, quoted in Zamlynsky, "Patriarkh ukrainskoi nauky," 21. Also see Ponomarev, *Mikhail Aleksandrovich Maksimovich*, 71–2.

26  On this period, see, in particular, the classic accounts of Luckyj, *Between Gogol and Ševčenko*, 162ff, and Zerov, *Lektsii*, 140ff. Also see Tomenko, "'Shchyryi Malorossianyn,'" 86.

27  See the documentary collection *Kyrylo–Mefodiivske tovarystvo*, 3 vols. (Kyiv: Naukova dumka, 1990), III, 340, partly quoted in Tomenko, "'Shchyryi Malorossianyn','" 86. On the Brotherhood more generally, see George S.N. Luckyj, *Young Ukraine: The Brotherhood of Saints Cyril and Methodius in Kiev 1845–1847* (Ottawa: University of Ottawa Press, 1991).

28  Zamlynsky, "Patriarkh ukrainskoi nauky," 22–3. The *Ocherk Kyiva* is reprinted in Maksymovych, *Vybrani tvory*, ed. Korotky, 62–77. *Nachatki russkoi folologii* is in M.A. Maksimovich [Mykhailo Maksymovych], *Sobranie sochinenii*, 3 vols. (Kyiv: Tip. M.P. Fritsa, 1876–80), III, 25–155. Maksymovych's pioneering work in classifying the Slavonic languages was praised two generations later by the great Croatian Slavist Vatroslav Yagich [Jagić]; see his *Istoriia slavianskoi filologii* (St Petersburg: Imp. Akademiia nauk, 1910, reprint Leipzig: Zentral Antiquariat, 1967), 489–92. However, Jagić considered the classification "purely geographical" rather than linguistic. For a sympathetic treatment, which claims that Maksymovych pioneered the now-canonical three-fold division of the Slavonic languages – East, West, and South, see M.Zh., "Movoznavchi pohliady M.O. Maksymovycha," *Movoznavstvo*, no. 5 (1979), 46–50.

29  Zamlynsky, "Patriarkh ukrainskoi nauky," 23–4. Ponomarev, *Mikhail Aleksandrovich Maksimovich*, 60, stresses the impact that Gogol's sudden and unexpected death had on Maksymovych.

30  The full work was published only in Soviet times (1947). A recent, fuller, Ukrainian-language edition has useful annotation. See Mykhailo Maksymovych, *Dni ta mistiatsi ukrainskoho selianyna*, ed. and trans. Viacheslav Hnatiuk (Kyiv: Vyd. Oberehy, 2002), 189 pp.

31  The title *Ukrainets* (The Ukrainian) is significant. The anonymous author of *Istoriia Rusov* (History of the Ruthenians, 1827) rejected the term *Ukraina* (Ukraine) as a Polish innovation in favour of *Malaia Rossiia* (Little Russia). Maksymovych apparently still preferred "Little Russia" and "Little Russians" to any other terms,

and in the 1850s, despite its use in the Russian translation of Beauplan, the term *Ukrainets* was making only halting progress. Kostomarov used it once in his secret "Books of the Genesis of the Ukrainian People" (1847), but nowhere else, and Shevchenko, although he rejected the term "Little Russia" and regularly extolled *Ukraina*, generally contrasted "Cossacks" to "Muscovites" and never actually used the term *Ukrainets*. Thus its use as the title of Maksymovych's almanac was a milestone.

32 See Maksymovych, *Lysty*, 27–78. For example, on 30 December 1846, Maksymovych wrote to Bodiansky to praise the latter's efforts at publishing controversial Ukrainian materials: "Especially we Ukrainians [*Ukraintsi*] are thankful for the publication of Konysky['s *Istoriia Rusov*] and the *Eyewitness Chronicle* [on the times of Hetman Khmelnytsky] . . . Finally!" (32). A decade later he informed Bodiansky that "in Kyiv it [*Istoriia Rusov*] is selling for [the enormous sum of] ten and twelve silver rubles and across Little Russia there is a rumor that it is a forbidden book! . . . That is what I hear from people returning from the fair [in that city]" (45). On Bodiansky, Shevchenko, Maksymovych, Shchepkin, and Gogol in Moscow, see Volodomyr Melnychenko, *Ukrainska dusha Moskvy* (Moscow: OLMA, 2010), 672 pp.

33 Taras Shevchenko, *Tvory v trokh tomakh* (Kyiv: Derzh. vyd. Khudozh. lit. URSR, 1961), III, 253, and quoted in part in Zamlynsky, "Patriarkh ukrainskoi nauky," 25.

34 First printed in *Osnova*, no. 6 (1861), 9. If we can believe *Istoriia ukrainskoi literaturnoi krytyky: Dozhovtnevyi period*, ed. P.M. Fedchenko (Kyiv: Naukova dumka, 1988), 62, this was a rebuke to Kulish, who claimed that Shevchenko had returned from exile a broken man.

35 Zamlynsky, "Patriarkh ukrainskoi nauky," 25. On Shevchenko at Mykhailova Hora, see O.K. Doroshkevych, "Shevchenko v selianskykh perekazakh," in *Spodahy pro Tarasa Shevchenka*, ed. I.O. Dzeverin (Kyiv: Dnipro, 1982), 398–401. His portrait of Maksymovych is reproduced in Maksymovych, *Vybrani tvory*, 8, and his portrait of Mariia Vasylivna in Maksymovych, *Lysty*, 306. Also see Frizman and Lakhno, *M.A. Maksimovvch: literator*, 234–48, and P.H. Markov, "U koli velykykh: Pro druzhbu M. Maksymovycha z Pushkinym ta Shevchenkom," *Vitchyzna*, no. 9 (1984), 181–6, both of which stress the accord between poet and scholar on political and social questions. But the "conservative" Maksymovych's relations with the fiery "revolutionary" Shevchenko, a topic muted in Soviet times, deserves further investigation.

36 Earlier editions of *The Book of Naum about God's Great World* had appeared thus: Moscow. 1833 and 1834; Kyiv, 1845; St Petersburg, 1847, 1848, 1851, and 1853; Moscow, 1859; and Kyiv, 1865, 1867, 1868 and, finally, 1876. See Zamlynsky, "Patriarkh ukrainskoi nauky," 406. There is a detailed analysis of Maksymovych and Kulish's disagreement about Gogol in Frizman and Lakhno, *M.A. Maksimovvch: literator*, 218–34.

37 On Maksymovych as a historian, see Ivan Krypiakevych, "Mykhailo Maksymovych: Istoryk," *Zapysky naukovoho tovarystva im. Shevchenka* 142 (1927), 165–72; and Pavlo Klepatsky, "M.O. Maksymovych iak istoryk," *Ukraina*, no. 6 (1927), 80–4. The most detailed Soviet-era treatment is P.H. Markov, *M.O. Maksymovych: Vydatnyi istoryk XIX st.* (Kyiv: Vyd. Kyivskoho universytetu, 1973). For a later exploration, see Viktor Kotsur and Anatolii Kotsur, *Vidomyi istoryk Ukrainy: M.O. Maksymovych* (Pereiaslav, Khmelnytsky, and Chernivtsi: Zoloti litavry, 2000).

38 Maksymovych's writings on the origins of Rus' are collected in Maksimovich [Maksymovych], *Sobranie sochinenii*, vol. I. See especially "Otkuda idet Russkaia zemlia po skazaniu Nestorovoi povesti i po drugim starinym pisaniiam russkim," 5–92. Unfortunately this piece has not been reprinted in any of the more recent collections of his works.

39 See especially Mykhailo Maksymovych, "O mnimom zapustenii Ukrainy v nashestvie Batyyevo i naselenii ee novoprishlym narodom: Pismo M.P. Pogodinu," in Maksymovych, *Vybrani tvory*, ed. Korotky, 48–61. For more on this "dispute between the Southerners and the Northerners," see the classic account of Pypin, *Istoriia russkoi etnografii*, III, 313–24, and more recently, Ivan Ohienko [Metropolitan Ilarion], *Ukrainska kultura: Korotka istoriia kulturnoi zhyttia ukrainskoho narodu*, 3rd ed. (Winnipeg, 1970), 256–61, and Petro Holubenko, *Ukraina i Rosiia u svitli kulturnykh vzaiemyn* (New York, Toronto, and Paris, 1987), 93–101.

40 Mykhailo Maksymovych, "O prichinakh vzaimnogo ozhestocheniia poliakov i malorossiian byvshego v XVII veke: Pismo k M.A. Grabovskomu," in Maksymovych, *Vybrani tvory*, ed. Korotky, 166–87.

41 Mykhailo Maksymovych, "Skazanie o hetmane Petre Sagaidachnom," in Maksymovych, *Vybrani tvory*, ed. Korotky, 166–87, 150–64, and "Pisma o Bogdane Khmelnitskom," in ibid., 190–257. On Kostomarov more generally, see my *Mykola Kostomarov*, 53–5 *et passim*.

42 Mykhailo Maksymovych, "Skazanie o Koliivshchine," *Russkii arkhiv* 2, no. 5 (1875), 5–27, and reprinted in Maksymovych, *Vybrani tvory*, ed. Korotky, 150–65. I have used only the reprint.

43 See, in particular, V.U. Pavelko, "M.O. Maksymovych: Arkheohraf," *Ukrainskyi istorychnyi zhurnal*, no. 1 (1962), 97–102. Also see the brief characterizations of Maksymovych's work in Ivan Krypiakevych, "Mykhailo Maksymovych: Istoryk," 165–72, and Klepatsky, "M.O. Maksymovych iak istoryk," 80–4.

44 See Mykhailo Maksymovych, "O pravopysanii malorossiiskogo iazyka: Pismo k Osnovianenku," first published in *Kyivlianin* (1841) and reprinted in P.M. Fedchenko et al., *Istoriia ukrainskoi literaturnoi krytyky ta literaturoznavstva: Khrestomatiia*, vol. I (Kyiv: Lybid, 1996), 120–1.

45 In Vasyl Chaplenko, *Istoriia novoi ukrainskoi literaturnoi movy XVIIst.–1933r.* (New York: The author, 1970), 82.

46  Maksymovych's orthography enjoyed more success in Galicia, where it was used with some modifications until 1895, and in Transcarpathia, where it continued in use right up to 1939. By then it had been abandoned everywhere. See O. Horbach, "Maksymovychivka," in Volodymyr Kubijovyč and Danylo Husar Struk, eds., *Encyclopedia of Ukraine*, vol. III (Toronto: University of Toronto Press, 1993), 285–6.

47  For Maksymovych's advice to the Galicians, see his letter of 22 April 1840 to Denys Zubrytsky, in Maksymovych, *Lysty*, 119–21. If we can believe Ponomarev, *Mikhail Aleksandrovich Maksimovich*, 67, Maksymovych to the very end of his life retained his doubts about the full development of Ukrainian literature. The classic interpretation of his hesitant views is by Serhii Yefremov, *Istoriia ukrainskoho pysmenstva*, 2 vols. (Kyiv and Leipzig: Ukrainska nakladnia, 1924), I, 286–8. By contrast, P.M. Fedchenko, writing in the *Ukrainska literaturna entsyklopediia*, vol. III (Kyiv: Ukrainska radianska entsyklopediia, 1995), 269–70, declares that Maksymovych "in all ways laid the foundation for the independence (*samostiinist*) and originality (*samobutnist*) of the Ukrainian language and defended its natural literary rights and future as a powerful tool for the creation of a single culture for the Ukrainian people divided by the political borders of that time." Strangely, Frizman and Lakhno, *M.A. Maksimovich: Literator*, says nothing about its subject's views on the future of Ukrainian literature. We may conclude that the entire question deserves further research.

48  So Zhytetsky, "Zhyttia M.O. Maksymovycha," 23–4.

49  Quoted in full, of course, by the Russian scholar Pypin, *Istoriia russkoi etnografii*, III, 35. Alluding to the nineteenth-century evolution of Ukrainian identity as seen by the intelligentsia – first Little Russian, then Ukrainophile, and finally Ukrainian – Pypin considered that Maksymovych "was not a 'Ukrainophile' in the fuller and later sense of the word." In 1904, the Ukrainian Steshenko's *Mikh. Aleks. Maksimovich*, 30, pointed out that our scholar eventually broke with the Russian slavophiles, who, with the passage of time, turned more nationalistic and intolerant of Ukrainian separateness.

50  On simultaneous identities more generally, see Paul R. Magocsi, "The Ukrainian National Revival: A New Analytical Framework," *Canadian Review of Studies in Nationalism* 16, nos. 1–2 (1989), 45–62, and also George Luckyj, *The Anguish of Mykola Hohol a.k.a. Nikolai Gogol* (Toronto: Canadian Scholars' Press, 1998).

51  Serhii Yefremov, "Maksymovych v istorii ukrainskoi samosvidomosty," *Zapysky istorychno-filolohychnoho viddilu VUAN* 16 (1928), 1–5. This article, long suppressed by the Soviets from the 1930s on, is reprinted in S.O. Yefremov, *Literaturno-krytychni statti*, ed. E.S. Solovei (Kyiv: Dnipro, 1993), 318–21.

52  Hrushevsky, "'Malorossiiskie pesni' Maksymovycha."

## CHAPTER FIVE

1 Ivan Franko, "Temne tsarstvo," in his *Zibrannia tvoriv u p'iatdesiaty tomakh*, vol. XXVI (Kyiv: Naukova dumka, 1980), 131–52; and reprinted without censors' deletions in Ivan Franko, *Shevchenkoznavchi studii*, ed. Mykhailo Hnatiuk (Lviv: Svit, 2005), 56–76; Taras Shevchenko, *Kobzar*, ed. Leonid Biletsky, 4 vols. (Winnipeg: Tryzub, 1952), II, 232.

2 Bohdan Lepky, *Zhyttiepys Tarasa Shevchenka* (Ivanofrankivsk: Nova zoria, 2004), 82–3. This volume was published as early as 1919.

3 George Grabowicz, *The Poet as Mythmaker: A Study of Symbolic Meaning in Taras Shevchenko* (Cambridge, Mass.: Harvard Ukrainan Research Institute, 1982), 86–7, 121, 143, 151, 157. Also see Grabowicz, "A Consideration of Deep Structures in Shevchenko's Works," in George Luckyj, ed., *Shevchenko and the Critics* (Toronto: University of Toronto Press, 1980), 481–96, one of the more translucent essays of this difficult author. Rory Finnin, "Mountains, Masks, Metre, Meaning: Taras Shevchenko's *Kavkaz*," *Slavonic and East European Review* 83, no. 3 (2005), 396–439, echoes, but also qualifies Grabowicz's theory, in a "post-colonial" interpretation of the poem. For two older treatments of Shevchenko's "Kavkaz" (The Caucasus) in English, see Vera Rich, "*The Caucasus* of Taras Shevchenko," *Ukrainian Review* 6, no. 1 (London, 1959), 45–53, which contains a good translation of the poem, and Clarence Manning, "*The Caucasus* of Taras Shevchenko," *Ukrainian Quarterly* 16, no. 4 (1960), 321–9, which is rich in Cold War polemics.

4 Hlafira Palamarchuk, "Balmen, Yakiv Petrovych de," in *Shevchenkivska entsyklopediia*, vol. I (Kyiv: NANU, Instytut Literatury, 2012), 321–2.

5 Ibid. Finnin, "Mountains, Masks, Metre Meaning," 433–5, adds that one of de Balmen's forefathers had participated in an earlier expedition against the mountaineers and may also have helped destroy the old Ukrainian Cossack Sich, or headquarters, on the Dnieper River in 1775. Shevchenko may have been partly aware of this family tradition.

6 Shevchenko, *Kobzar*, ed. Biletsky, II, 141 (my translation).

7 Palamarchuk, "Balmen," I, 321; photo-reprinted as *Wirszy T. Szewczenka* (Dniproderzhynsk: Andrii, 2008), though rare and unavailable to me to study. Also see M.I. Matsapura, *Doslidnyk na nyvi Shevchenkoznavstva* (Kyiv: Pulsara, 2011), 116–23, which prints several more of de Balmen's drawings and adds biographical details.

8 See the classic work of John F. Baddeley, *The Russian Conquest of the Caucasus* (London and New York: Longmans, 1908), and Moshe Gammer, *Muslim Resistance to the Tsar: Shamil and the Conquest of Chechnia and Dagestan* (London: Frank Cass, 1994). More generally, see T. Halasi-Kun, "The Caucasus: An Ethno-Historical Survey," *Studia Caucasica*, vol. I (1963), 1–47, which contains several explanatory maps.

9 In Baddeley, *Russian Conquest*, 114–15.

10  Yury Kochubei, "Zv'iazky ukrainskoi literatury z literaturamy Blyzkoho i Serednoho Skhodu," in T.N. Denysova et al., eds., *Ukrainska literatura v zahalno-slov'ianskomy i svitovomu konteksti*, vol. III (Kyiv: Naukova dumka, 1988), 404–54, especially 413. The expedition is described by Yakiv Markovych (1696–1770), a well-educated Ukrainian Cossack officer, in his extensive diary (1717–67), parts of which have been published, and later in the influential, anonymous, fanciful *Istoriia Rusov* (History of the Ruthenians, 1827), which was popular reading, in manuscript form, among the gentry of left-bank Ukraine about the time that Shevchenko first visited the area. Reading the latter deeply affected the poet, and it informed his depictions of old Ukraine.

11  Gammer, *Muslim Resistance*, 9–26.

12  Baddeley, *Russian Conquest*, 102ff., summarizes the testimony of the writer Leo Tolstoy, who in his tale *The Cossacks* (1863) stressed Yermolov's importance. Baddeley's invaluable history was published in 1908, two years before Tolstoy's death and before the publication of his last, short novel, *Hadji Murat* (1912), which dealt directly with the Caucasian War, in which Tolstoy served in 1851 (and also in the Crimean War). Sixty years later, *Hadji Murat* treated the resistance leaders Imam Shamil and Hadji Murat, both of whom played complex, and ultimately equivocating, parts in it, which Tolstoy clearly recognized. Harold Bloom in his *Western Canon* (New York: Harcourt Brace and Co., 1994), 332–49, chose Tolstoy as one of the twenty-six authors to make up "the Western Canon," and the novella *Hadji Murat* as representing Tolstoy's finest contribution to the "canon": "heroism," undiluted by the author's ethical objections to war. For a new, annotated translation of *Hadji Murat*, with independent material on Shamil, see Thomas Sanders et al., eds., *Russian–Muslim Confrontation in the Causasus* (London: Routledge, 2010).

13  Baddeley, *Russian Conquest*, 97–102.

14  Ibid. Also see Michael Whittock, "Ermolov: Proconsul of the Caucasus," *Russian Review* 18 (1959), 53–60, which discusses Yermolov's ostensible liberalism, and James Forsyth, *The Caucasus: A History* (Cambridge: Cambridge University Press, 2015), 279, n 31, which remarks that Yermolov was actually of Tatar Muslim ancestry. His forefather Arslan Murza Yermol had defected to the Russians and converted to Orthodox Christianity in 1506. Forsyth adds that it was "typical" of officers of such descent to be particularly harsh towards the non-Christian native peoples of Russia's colonies.

15  Aleksii Veselovsky, "Griboedov, Aleksandr Sergeevich," in *Entsiklopedicheskii slovar*, vol. XVIII (St Petersburg, 1893; reprint 1990), 689–96.

16  Alexander Knysh, "Shamil," in *Encyclopaedia of Islam*, 2nd ed., vol. IX (Leiden and London: Brill, 1996), 283–8, calls these *murids*, of whom there were about four to five hundred, "the core of his army," "career fighters," and "warrior monks," who were "always ready for maryrdom 'in the path of God.'" Of course, his army expanded to several thousands if one adds part-time conscripts. Also see Forsyth, *The Caucasus*, 246ff.; Gammer, *Muslim Resistance*, 47–110.

17 Finnin, "Mountains, Masks, Metre, Meaning," 400–1. For the military context, see Baddeley, *Russian Conquest*, 67–110, which mentions neither Shevchenko nor de Balmen. Nor does Forsyth, *The Caucasus*, 280–1, in its very brief account of Shamil's war against the Russians – but it notes the genesis of "Shamil." Knysh, "Shamil," explains that Shamil was actually named "Ali" at birth, but being sickly was remamed "Shamuil" (Samuel) to "repel" sickness. It worked, and the name stuck in a slightly altered form.

18 In Taras Shevchenko, *Zibrannia tvoriv u 12 tomakh*, vol. I (Kyiv: Naukova dumka, 2003), 736, citing A. Nikolai, "Iz vospominanii o moei zhizni: Darginskii pokhod 1845," *Russkii arkhiv*, no. 6 (1890), 272.

19 On his favourable treatment by the Russians, see especially T.M. Barret, "The Remaking of the Lion of Dagastan: Shamil in Captivity," *Russian Review* 8, no. 3 (1994), 353–66, which argues that this treatment of a vanquished enemy was gauged to sooth Russian pride after the empire's humiliating defeat in the Crimea.

20 Viacheslav Prokopenko, "Shamil u Kyievi," online at https://web.archive.org/web/20070820070820012707/http://www.dt.ua/3000/3150/45302/, 8 August 2016, writes that Shamil, contrasting it to isolated and chilly Kaluga, liked lively Kyiv, with its mild climate and hilly geography, which, as he wrote in a letter quoted in Prokopenko, "Shamil u Kyievi," reminded him of his home in the Caucasus. Unfortunately, this popular-style article does not cite any authorities for these statements.

21 See A. Manchuk, "Shamil na Pecherskykh Kholmakh," at https://web.archive.org/web/20081013122313/http://mycityua.com/history/2007/09/06/090007.html, 9 August 2016. Also see Shapi Kaziev, *Imam Shamil* (Moscow: Molodaia gvardiia, 2001), 352. Shevchenko's "Kavkaz" was first printed in Leipzig, in 1859, well beyond the reach of the Russian censors, and gradually filtered back into the Russian Empire. See Nina Ch., "Kavkaz," in *Shevchenkivska entsyklopedia*, III, 218. J.B. Rudnyckyj claims that the poem was circulated in hand-written copies and widely known in Ukraine even prior to this; see his "Introduction" to the photo-reprint edition of the Leipzig text, which is collated with the Biletsky text: J.B. Rudnyckyj, ed., *New Poems of Pushkin and Shevchenko: A Revised Version of the Leipzig Edition of 1859* (Winnipeg: University of Manitoba Press, 1959), 4. He further suggests that the poet's friend and colleague Panteleimon Kulish was probably responsible for sending the manuscript abroad.

22 D.Kh. Murat, "Iz Stambula vo Lvova," at http://gazavat.ru/history3.php?rub=188art=132, 5 November 2016, reproduces this portrait of Shamil, and also one of his son, which he says are today preserved in Lviv in western Ukraine. Also see Kaziev, *Imam Shamil*, 354.

23 Manchuk, "Shamil." Also see Gammer, *Muslim Resistance*, 257–95, which proposes that Shamil, despite his firm commitment to the cause, was no "fanatic," but rather a practical man, who knew when he was beaten and recognized reality when he saw it. Knysh, "Shamil," concurs. Ali Askerov, "Shamil," in his *Historical*

*Dictionary of the Chechen Conflict* (Lanham: Rowman and Littlefield, 2015), 120–1, informs us that there is currently much controversy about Shamil's legacy among the Chechens, some seeing him as the finest model of a resistance fighter, but others condemning his surrender to the Russians and subsequent withdrawal from the war. Askerov writes: "Many of his local officials received high ranks in Russia's colonial administration."

24  Yu.O. Ivakin, *Komentar do 'Kobzaria' Shevchenka: Poezii do zaslannia* (Kyiv: Naukova dumka, 1964), 282–3.

25  See "Kukharenko, Yakiv Herasymovych," in *Shevchenkivskyi slovnyk*, 2 vols. (Kyiv: AN UkRSR, 1976), I, 338. On Kostomarov, see my two studies: "Mykola Kostomarov and East Slavic Ethnography in the Nineteenth Century," *Russian History* 18, no. 2 (1991), 163–86, and *Mykola Kostomarov: A Biography* (Toronto: University of Toronto Press, 1996), especially 7–36, on his Kharkiv period and early interests in the Cossacks and folksongs about them.

26  See Shevchenko's first preserved letter to Kukharenko, dated 30 March 1842, in T.H. Shevchenko, *Zibrannia Tvoriv u 12 tomakh*, vol. VI (Kyiv: Naukova dumka, 2003), 18–19, which ends with a friendly greeting to "*mii shcheryi ridnyi brate Otomane* (my sincere and dear brother and Otoman)," and his letter of 31 January 1843, 22–3, which discusses the publication project.

27  In V.S. Borodin, ed., *Lysty do Tarasa Shevchenka* (Kyiv: Naukova dumka, 1993), 84. In addition to the titles cited above, also see V.K. Chumachenko, "Kukharenko, Yakiv Herasymovych," in *Entsyklopediia Istorii Ukrainy*, vol. V (Kyiv: Naukova dumka, 2008), 541, and Volodymyr Movchaniuk and Viktor Chumachenko, "Kukharenko, Yakiv Herasymovych," in *Shevchenkivska entsyklopediia*, III, 668–70.

28  Movchaniuk and Chumachenko, "Kukharenko," 669, quotes L. Melnikov, an early authority on the relationship between Shevchenko and Kukharenko, as follows: "[The very centrepoint of] their primary interest in the view of Shevchenko was the Black Sea region as a part of Ukraine, which more than any other preserved the invincible spirit and structure of glorious Zaporozhia, and on the part of Kukharenko, the same interest with regard to Ukraine – the mother of the Black Sea [Cossacks and region]."

29  O.S. Afanasiev-Chuzhbynsky, "Spomyny pro T.H. Shevchenka," in I.O. Dzeverin, ed., *Spodady pro Tarasa Shevchenka* (Kyiv: Dnipro, 1982), 92.

30  Mykola Zerov, *Lektsii z istorii ukrainskoi literatury* (Oakville, Ont.: CIUS and Mosaic Press, 1977), 174. The importance of this Canadian edition of Zerov's book is stressed by Viacheslav Briukovetsky, "Zerov i Shevchenko," in V. Panchenko, ed., *Mykola Zerov: Vybrani tvory* (Kyiv: Smoloskyp, 2015), 772–82, which notes that, in the absence of Zerov's proscribed works in Soviet Ukraine after 1930, a legend arose that Zerov, being a "Neoclassic" author, who translated ancient Greek and Roman texts into modern Ukrainian, denigrated Shevchenko as merely a folk poet. This Canadian edition of his lectures, says Briukovetsky, showed this to have been completely untrue.

31  On this, see especially Myroslav Shkandrij, *Russia and Ukraine: Literature and the Discourse of Empire from Napoleonic to Postcolonial Times* (Toronto: University of Toronto Press, 2001), 131–41.

32  Indeed, the name "Shamil" and even the very words *Musulman* or *Musulmanyn* (Muslim) do not occur in any of Shevchenko's known works, either in Ukrainian or in Russian. See Appendix C, "Shevchenko and the Muslims," at the end of this volume.

33  My translation of "Kavkaz" derives partly from that by John Weir, the pen name of Ivan Vyviursky (1906–1983), the Ukrainian Canadian newspaper editor and Communist political activist. For both the Ukrainian text and his translation, see Taras Shevchenko, *Selected Poetry* (Kyiv: Dnipro, 1977), trans. John Weir et al., 187–95, especially 192. For a text with accents added, see Shevchenko, *Kobzar*, ed. Biletsky, II, 141–5. Weir's translation captures the poet's anger and fire in a way that others do not, such as those of Alexander Hunter, *The Kobzar of the Ukraine* (Teulon, Man.: The Author, 1922), 68–78, and C.H. Andrusyshen and Watson Kirkconnell, *The Poetical Works of Taras Shevchenko* (Toronto: University of Toronto Press, 1964), 243–8. Unlike Weir, they make free use of some off-putting archaic forms of the English language, hardly suitable for a fiery "revolutionary" like Shevchenko. For other translations, see Taras Shevchenko, *Song out of Darkness: Selected Poems*, trans. Vera Rich (London, 1961), 69–73, which is one of the best, and *The Complete Kobzar: The Poetry of Taras Shevchenko*, trans. Peter Fedynsky (London: Glagoslav, 2013), especially 171–3, which, however, dispenses completely with rhyme.

34  See my *Mykhailo Hrushevsky: The Politics of National Culture* (Toronto: University of Toronto Press, 1987), especially chap. 8, 180–207; and on Symonenko, see Derek Jones, ed., *Censorship: A World Encyclopedia*, 4 vols. (London: Routledge, 2001), 2361, and the article on him by Ivan Koshelivets in Volodymyr Kubijovyč and Danylo Husar Struk, eds., *Encyclopedia of Ukraine*, vol. V (Toronto: University of Toronto Press, 1993), 143. Also see "Perekladannia tvoriv T.H. Shevchenka," in *Shevchenkivskyi slovnyk*, II, 95 (on Honcharenko), and II, 93 (on the Chechen translation). Similarly, the Prometheus theme was later resurrected by non-Russian refugees from the USSR in inter-war Poland, where the Polish government, wishing to use them against its threatening neighbour to the east, sponsored a Prometheus Movement aiming at the liberation of all these peoples from Soviet Russian rule, including Ukrainians, Crimean Tatars, central Asians, and Caucasians. With regard to Poland itself, in December 1846, through a member of the Brotherhood of Saints Cyril and Methodius, M. Savych, who was on his way abroad, Shevchenko sent a copy of his poem to the famous insurgent Polish poet Adam Mickiewicz, whom he greatly respected and admired. See Nina Ch., "Kavkaz," 219.

35  According to Knysh, "Shamil," an especially vociferous anti-Shamil literature arose in the 1950s and clearly labelled him a counter-revolutionary religious

"fanatic." This move seemed to coincide with Khrushchev's anti-religious drive but, of course, did not affect the official "Great Friendship of Peoples" policies.

36  See the discussion, with quotations from Pushkin and Lermontov, in Zerov, *Lektsii*, 174–5. On Tolstoy, see Henri Troyat, *Tolstoy* (New York: Doubleday, 1967), 77–108, especially 101, which quotes Tolstoy's diary entry of 6 January 1853, when he was living with the Cossacks in the Caucasus: "War is so unjust and ugly that all who wage it must try to stifle the voice of conscience within themselves." There are also some good comparisons of those Russian *literati* and Shevchenko in Manning, "*The Caucasus*," 22–8, and Oleksandr Tkachuk, *Intertekst poemy 'Kavkaz' Tarasa Shevchenka: Prometeizm v oriientalnomu dyskusi* (Ternopil: Ministerstvo osvity, 2012), which as well explores the concept of "Orientalism" as applied to these writers. Also see Shkandrij, *Russia and Ukraine*, 134–8, and Susan Layton, "Nineteenth-Century Russian Mythologies of Caucasian Savagery," in Daniel Brower and Edward J. Lazzerini, eds., *Russia's Orient: Imperial Borderlands and Peoples, 1700–1917* (Bloomington and Indianapolis: Indiana University Press, 1997), 80–100, which give further references.

37  See, for example, Mykola Zhulynsky, ed., *Istoriia ukrainskoi literatury*, vol. IV (Kyiv: Naukova dumka, 2014), 360–1; Dziuba is the author of this entire volume. On Dziuba himself, with a list of his most important works stressing internationalism and human rights, see M.H. Zhelezniak, "Dziuba, Ivan Mykhailovych," in *Entsyklopediia Istorii Ukrainy*, vol. II (Kyiv: Naukova dumka, 2004), 378–9.

38  Tsereteli was from a princely Georgian family, whose custom it was to send its sons to live with a peasant family for a time during their youth. This familiarity with peasant life may have drawn the young Georgian to Shevchenko, who certainly impressed him as a kind of grandfather figure. Tsereteli later wrote: "I confess that I first understood from his words how to love my homeland and one's own people." See Akaki Tsereteli, "Moi spohady pro Shevchenka," in M. Pavliuk, ed., *Spohady pro Taras Shevchenka* (Kyiv, 1982), 343–5. Also see Valerian Imedadze, "Shevchenko i Tsereteli," *Khronika 2000*, no. 43 (2001), 209–18.

39  Shauket Mufti, *Heroes and Emperors in Circassian History* (Beirut: Librarie du Liban, 1972), 125. Also see Forsyth, *The Caucasus*, 283–4. Strangely, even the Ukrainian specialist Iaroslav Lebedynsky, in his *La conquête russe du Caucase 1774–1864* (Chamalières: Lemme édit, 2018), mentions neither Shevchenko nor his poem.

40  Shkandrij, *Russia and Ukraine*, 134, writes that Shevchenko's poem "remained an embarrassment to both Tsarist and Soviet authorities for thirteen decades" and notes that Dziuba recalled that throughout the Soviet period the poem was not recited at public celebrations of the poet's name and that it was avoided by commentators.

41  I refer here to that of Clarence A. Manning, *Taras Shevchenko: The Poet of Ukraine, Selected Poems* (New York: Philosophical Library, 1945), and those of Rich, in Shevchenko, *Song out of Darkness*, trans. Rich, 69–73; of John Weir, in *Taras Shevchenko: Selected Poetry*, trans. John Weir et al. (Kyiv: Dnipro, 1977), 187–95; and of Peter Fedynsky, *The Complete Kobzar: The Poetry of Taras Shevchenko*,

trans. Peter Fedynsky (London: Glagoslav, 2013), especially 171–3. Indeed, even during the Cold War some of the best non-Communist – that is, émigré – literary figures and historians acknowledged the superiority of Weir's translations, which were published either in Soviet Ukraine or by a pro-Communist institution in Canada. For example, in the early 1980s, at a public lecture that I attended at the University of Toronto given by the poet Bohdan Rubchak, the literary historian George Luckyj pointed out the excellence of Weir's Shevchenko as compared to Kirkconnell's, in Andrusyshen and Kirkconnell, *The Poetical Works of Taras Shevchenko*. Rubchak agreed with him. However, for obvious reasons, during the Cold War such an opinion was not widely discussed by émigré Ukrainians in the West. See, for example, the extremely brief article on Weir as compared to the more extensive one on Kirkconnell's collaborator, Constantine Andrusyshen, in Mykhailo Marunchak, *Biohrafichnyi dovidnyk do istorii ukraintsiv Kanady* (Winnipeg: UVAN, 1986). During the Cold War, several hardy Ukrainian-Canadian "pro-Communists," such as Weir and Petro Krawchuk, stuck officially to the party line but quietly defied the Russian chauvinism coming from Moscow (as well as from some of their less well-informed non-Ukrainian, Canadian comrades) and remained staunch Ukrainian patriots and ceasely propagated the Shevchenko cult in the Western world. For a post-Soviet opinion that does appreciate their contributions, see the substantial article by Roksolana Zorivchak, "Kanadska literatura i Shevchenko," in *Shevchenkivska entsyklopediia* (Kiev, 2012), III, 250–4, with a very full bibliography.

42 Ivakin, *Komentar*, 282. For a post-Soviet treatment that gives Shamil somewhat more play, including a colour picture of him, see O.I. Rudenko and N.B. Petrenko, *Vichnyi iak narod: Storinky do biohrafii T.H. Shevchenka* (Kyiv: Lybid, 1998), 123–34.

43 Another personal anecdote is relevant here. Sometime about 1989, that is, after the Gorbachev reforms took off in the USSR, but before Ukrainian independence, the distinguished "Soviet" Ukrainian intellectual Serhii Bilokin visited Toronto, where he and I discussed the current state of scholarship about Hrushevsky and Shevchenko. He opined that Biletsky's edition of Shevchenko was "the worst" – whether he meant outside the USSR or ever he did not specify. On the censorship of Shamil and Chechen history in Soviet works, see Forsyth, *The Caucasus*, 604–13.

44 Askerov, "Shamil," 185–6. Askerov gives only a few biographical details about Pushkin and ignores his problematic attitude towards the Russian–Caucasian conflict. Askerov's *Historical Dictionary* (2015), where the article appeared, did not fully appreciate the significance for Caucasia of the new Russian–Ukrainian war, which began in 2014. However, it clearly affected Georgia, which only a few years before had confronted the Russians.

45 See Mykhailo Drahomanov, "Shevchenko, ukrainofily, i sotsializm," in his *Vybrane* (Kyiv: Lybid, 1991), 327–429, especially 400ff. Much of this essay is available in

English. See Mykhailo Drahomanov, "Excerpts from 'Shevchenko, the Ukraino-philes, and Socialism'," in George Luckyj, ed., *Shevchenko and the Critics* (Toronto: University of Toronto Press, 1980), 65–90. In this essay, Drahomanov summarized the positions of his predecessors: Kulish, Kostomarov, and Partytsky.

46  See the commentary to the poem by V.S. Borodin and others in Taras Shevchenko, *Povne zibrannia tvoriv u 12 tomakh* (Kyiv: Naukova dumka, 1989– ), I, 500, which gives further references. Unfortunately, there is still no mention of Shamil. Only the 2003 edition was to do so, in the passage in English translation on de Balmen's death quoted above. Also on Marx and the Ukrainian question, see the concluding paragraphs in the "Introduction" to the present volume.

47  See Hnatiuk's Introduction to Franko's *Shevchenkoznavchi studii*, especially 9–10, and his notes on 409–11. Hnatiuk restores (64) a few lines struck out by Soviet censors, which compared Pushkin unfavourably to Shevchenko and noted that Kondratii Ryleev was about the only political poet that Russia ever produced who openly tackled what he called "Saint Petersburg centralism."

48  Grabowicz, *The Poet as Mythmaker*. One exception to this trend is Myroslav Shkandrij, *Russia and Ukraine*, which termed Grabowicz's attempt to entirely cordon off the mythic-poetic from the political "unconvincing" (138).

49  Shkandrij, *Russia and Ukraine*, 141, suggests that Shevchenko generally considered and was bothered by this type of contradiction and in his "Kavkaz" revealed it to be "a national shame" for Ukrainians.

## CHAPTER SIX

1  An earlier version of this chapter appeared online without scholarly annotation at Slideshare and Academia.com <1 Jan. 2020>. The life of Balzac has been recounted many times. The most extensive life available in English is Graham Robb, *Balzac: A Biography* (New York: Norton, 1994). For a shorter treatment, see David Carter, *Honoré de Balzac* (London: Hesperus, 2008). Valuable biographies by Stephan Zweig (1946) and André Maurois (1965), written in German and French respectively, were translated into both English and Russian. Maurois was also translated into Ukrainian (1969) during the "Shelest Renaissance." A number of famed "Balzaciens," as Balzac scholars are called, have written biographies of both Honoré and his wife, Ève, the most notable being Marcel Bouteron's in the 1920s and Roger Pierrot's in the 1990s.

2  See the first pages of Elbert Hubbard, *Balzac and Madame Hanska* (East Aurora, NY: N.p., 1906) – a brief but pioneering work on the subject in English, of which I made extensive use. According to "Balzac," in *Encyklopedia powszechna S. Orgelbranda* (General Encyclopaedia of S. Orgelbrand), vol. II (Warsaw, 1898), 87–8, the Frenchman remained little-known in Polish lands (which then included much of today's Ukraine) until after his death, at which time a younger generation acknowledged him as a writer of "universal" importance, who for the first time in

European literature properly threw new light on the internal side of things, and thus was awarded a kind of unofficial title as a "doctor of the social sciences."

3  See A.I. Puzikov, "Balzak, Onore de," in *Kratkaia literaturnaia entsiklopediia* (Short Literary Encyclopaedia), vol. I (Moscow, 1962), 427–35, especially 431 (my translation).

4  See "Eve Hanska," in Vincent Cronin, *The Romantic Way* (Boston, 1965), especially 162–3, in a book about four fascinating European women, two of whom were Slavs, Hańska, and Marie Bashkirtseff, also of Ukrainian origin. Again, I have made extensive use of this account.

5  Ibid.

6  Ibid., 160.

7  There are several studies in French about Balzac's relationship with Hańska; especially good on the cultural milieu is Sophie de Korwin-Piotrowska, *Balzac et le monde slave: Madame Hanska et l'œuvre balzacienne* (Paris: H. Champion, 1933), even though the author is somewhat of an apologist for her. Roger Pierrot edited Balzac's *Lettres à Madame Hanska* in 4 vols. (Paris: Éditions du Delta, 1967–71), with extensive annotation. These remarkable letters are also available in an older English translation: Honore [sic] de Balzac, *Letters to Madame Hanska born Countess Rzewuska afterward Mme Honore [sic] de Balzac[,] 1833–1846*, trans. Katherine Prescott Wormeley (Boston, 1900; reprint Kessinger, 2010), 786 pp., which, however, was unavailable to me.

8  For general introductions to Ukrainian history that discuss the role of the Polish gentry in right-bank Ukraine, and even mention the Rzewuski family, see Paul Robert Magocsi, *A History of Ukraine: The Land and Its Peoples* (Toronto: University of Toronto Press, 2010), especially 309, and Orest Subtelny, *Ukraine: A History* (Toronto: University of Toronto Press, 2009), especially 189. Also see Daniel Beauvois, "Le monde de Madame Hańska: État de la société polonaise d'Ukraine au milieu du XIX siècle," *L'année balzacienne*, no. 14 New Series (Paris, 1993), 21–40, which is very forthcoming about the rather severe Ukrainian–Polish, and Russian–Polish, national and social tensions of that time, and also the looming Russian–Ukrainian conflict. There are also a few relevant observations in Serhiy Bilenky, *Romantic Nationalism in Eastern Europe: Russian, Polish, and Ukrainian Political Imaginations* (Stanford, Calif.: Stanford University Press, 2012); see the sections on Poland.

9  Beauvois, "Le monde de Madame Hanska," 22–3.

10  Ibid. Also see the useful collection of essays on this theme: Stanisław Makowski et al., *Szkoła ukraińska w romantyzmie polskim: Szkice polsko–ukraińskie* (Warsaw: Wydział polonistyki Uniwersytetu Warszawskiego, 2012), and on Ève in particular Zygmunt Czerny, "Hańska, Ewelina z Rzewuskich, Madame de Balzac," in *Polski Słownik Biograficzny*, vol. IX (Wrocław, 1960–61), 286–7.

11  See the discussion in chapter 2 of this volume, which gives full references.

12  Beauvois, "Le monde de Madame Hanska," 40.

13 On Balabin, and on Balzac in Russia generally, see Leonid Grossman, "Balzak v Rossii," *Literaturnoe nasledstvo*, nos. 32–3 (1937), 151–71, which is really a small book. Also see F. Savchenko, "Balzak na Ukraini (1847–1850)," *Ukraina* no. 1 (Kyiv, 1924), 134–51, a pioneering study in the initial issue of an epoch-making scholarly journal of Ukrainian studies; Ilko Borshchak, "Honore Balzak (1799–1850)" and "Ukraina i ukraintsi v lystuvanni Balzaka," *Ukraina*, no. 3 (Paris, 1950), 186–91; D.S. Nalyvaiko, "Ukraina u Balzaka," *Inozemna filolohiia*, no. 2 (1965), 133–41; and, most recently, Yevhen Luniak, *Mynuvshchyna Ukrainy v romantychnykh istoriiakh* (Kyiv: Knyha, 2011), 288–93.

14 On the Polish insurrection in 1846 in Austrian Galicia, see Aleksander Giesztor et al., *History of Poland* (Warsaw: PWN, 1979), 409–13, and, more briefly, Patrice M. Dabrowski, *Poland: The First Thousand Years* (Dekalb, Ill.: Northern Illinois University Press, 2014), 322–3. In the nineteenth century, it was often said that the "Ruthenian," or Ukrainian peasants of eastern Galicia were primarily to blame for the ferocious attacks on the noble Polish rebels, who in many cases were simply massacred. But recent scholarship agrees that the *jacquerie* was limited to western, or Polish Galicia. Balzac, of course, could not tell the difference and believed that the massacres extended further east than was in fact the case.

15 Marcel Bouteron was the first to publish Balzac's *Lettre sur Kiew*, in 1927; reprint in *Cahiers balzaciens* 5–8 (Geneva, 1971), with unsigned annotation by the Ukrainian scholar Ilko Borshchak; see especially 72.

16 In Borshchak, "Honore de Balzak," 189.

17 On the Cyril-Methodians, see my *Mykola Kostomarov: A Biography* (Toronto: University of Toronto Press, 1996), 37–58, especially 57, and George S.N. Luckyj, *Young Ukraine: The Brotherhood of Saints Cyril and Methodius, 1845–1847* (Ottawa: University of Ottawa Press, 1991), especially 47–50. Also see Johannes Remy, *Brothers or Enemies: The Ukrainian National Movement and Russia from the 1840s to the 1870s* (Toronto: University of Toronto Press, 2016), 22–60, which points out that members and the investigating police used the term "Society." The "Brotherhood" label came probably from anti-Communist émigré Ukrainian historians who disliked the secular Soviet interpretation of the group – and even the Soviets long used the term "Brotherhood."

18 Grossman, "Balzak v Rossii."

19 Ibid., 151.

20 See ibid., and Borshchak, "Honore de Balzak." Czerny, "Hańska, Ewelina z Rzewuskich, Madame de Balzac," 286–7, argues that Ève wrote most of Balzac's novel *Les paysans* (The Peasants), which paints a very dark picture of these country folk and supposedly used materials from Verkhivnia.

21 Moreover, readers of Soviet-era Russian, Polish, and Ukrainian encyclopaedia articles on Balzac were informed respectively that he was translated into Russian by Dostoevsky, in Poland he influenced Kraszewski, Prus, and even Słowacki, and in Ukraine he "always enjoyed great love and popularity," was read by Ivan

Franko and Lesya Ukrainka, and had a novel about his life written by Natan Rybak (1940) that was reprinted many times, as well as translated into both Russian and Yiddish. See, for example, *Ukrainska radianska entsyklopediia*, vol. I (Kyiv: URE, 1959), 431–2.

After Balzac's death, his widow financed and edited parts of his voluminous *Œuvres completes*, and many other French editions appeared thereafter. A few English editions of his collected works were then published, although none has been revised since. By contrast, a Russian edition in twenty volumes appeared in 1896–99, replaced by new Stalin-era editions in twenty volumes 1933–47 and in fifteen 1951–55, a Khrushchev-era edition in twenty-four volumes in 1960, and the same in Moscow 1997–99. This cornucopia testifies to the official Communist stamp of approval on Balzac, and his enormous reputation in the USSR and in Russia right up to the present day.

In Poland, an eight-volume edition of Balzac's *Wybór dzieł* (Selected Works) appeared 1880–84, but never a full collection, while in eastern Ukraine, readers relied on Russian translations until the 1920s, when a period of intense ukrainian- ization brought Ukrainian-language translations of several of his works. From the 1930s to the 1953 death of Stalin, very little contact with the outside world was al- lowed to Ukrainian readers, but in 1971, during the "Shelest Renaissance," a nicely illustrated one-volume edition of Balzac's *Tvory* (Works) appeared in Kyiv. One of the stories was translated into Ukrainian by a certain Ye. Rzhevuska (Rzewuska), which seems to indicate that at least one member of the Rzewuski family survived the tumultuous first half of the twentieth century. Finally, in 1989, during the ini- tial period of *Glasnost* and *Perestroika* in Ukraine, the Dnipro publishing house in Kyiv initiated a thorough-going collection of Balzac's *Tvory v desiaty tomakh* (Works in Ten Volumes). At least two thick volumes (in closely packed Cyrillic type) were published before the economic crisis of that time intervened.

22  Borshchak, "Honore de Balzak," 191. On Mérimée, see below, chapter 7.

23  D.S. Nalyvaiko, *Onore Balzak: Zhyttia i tvorchist* (Kyiv: Dnipro, 1985).

## CHAPTER SEVEN

1  In an exceptionally perspicacious encyclopaedia article, Guy Dumur notes these contradictions. See his "Mérimée, Prosper," in *Encyclopedia universalis*, vol. XI (Paris, 1985), 1118–19, which concludes that "Mérimée appartient au romantisme et à ses ombres." The best general accounts of Mérimée in English are those of A.W. Raitt, *Prosper Mérimée* (New York: Charles Scriber's Sons, 1970), and Maxwell A. Smith, *Prosper Mérimée* (New York: Twayne, 1972). For a biography in French, which I found useful, see Elizabeth Morel, *Prosper Mérimée: L'amour des pierres* (Paris: Hachette, 1988). For further references, listed alphabetically by author, see Pierre H. Dubé, *Bibliographie de la critique sur Prosper Mérimée 1825–1993* (Gene- va: Droz, 1997), which lists 2,386 titles.

2 *"Pessimist genug, um die Komödie mitspielen zu können, ohne sich zu erbrechen"*; Nietzsche, quoted in Erwin Laaths, *Geschichte der Weltliteratur*, 2 vols. (Munich and Zürich: Knaur, 1953), II, 232–3.

3 See Paul Léon, *Mérimée et son temps* (Paris: Presses universitaires de France, 1962), 397, which quotes a certain Mme Adam to this effect. It also quotes Armand Baschet's characterization of Mérimée: "Style net, ésprit sobre, il écrit peu mais bien. / Poèt à la surface, au fond voltairien. / Près du mot qui nous touche une phrase equivoque / Fait quelquefois douter s'il pleure ou s'il se moque. / Tout son oeuvre tiendrait en deux toms in-huit, / Mais rien n'est oublié de ce qu'il a produit."

4 Dumur, "Mérimée, Prosper," 1119: *"Cet hyper-Français, qui accumule en lui les qualitiés et les défauts de la race a été l'introducteur en France de la littérature russe en ses commencements: Pouchkine et Tourginiev."*

5 Prosper Mérimée, *Bogdan Chmielnicki: Facsimilé de l'édition originale (1865)* (Paris: L'Harmattan, 2007). Also see Michel Cadot, "Mérimée s'est il interessé à l'Ukraine?" *Littératures* 51 (Toulouse, 2004), 117–28. For a detailed analysis of Mérimée's relationship with Russia, but with no references in the Slavonic languages, see Thierry Ozwald, *Mérimée et la Russie* (Paris: Euredit, 2014). Ozwald relies heavily on Henri Mongault, "Mérimée et l'histoire russe," *Le monde slave* (Paris, Aug., Sept., Oct. 1932), 192–216, 349–73, 59–75, respectively, and others of his works listed below.

6 On all these authors, and some others as well, see Fedir Savchenko, "Kozachchyna u frantsuzkomu pysmenstvi ta kozakofilstvo Merime," *Khronika 2000*, nos, 1–2 (1995), 128–46; this pioneering article was first published in *Ukraina*, no. 5 (Kyiv, 1925). Also see Vasyl Fedorovych, "Merime i Kozaky," *Visti kombatanty*, no. 3 (Toronto, 1988), 22–7. Fedorovych, however, writes with much less authority than did Savchenko, a prominent Soviet Ukrainian scholar, who perished during the Stalin purges of the Ukrainian intelligentsia. For a general bibliography of works in French on Ukraine, see Jacques Chevchenko, *Ukraine: Bibliographie des ouvrages en français XVIIᵉ–XXᵉ siècles* (Paris: L'est européen, 2000), which, however, lists only three titles by Mérimée.

7 Prosper Merime [Mérimée], *Sobrannie sochinenii v 3 tomakh* (Moscow, 1934), and *Sobrannie sochinenii v 6 tomakh* (Moscow: Pravda, 1963), were unavailable to me for this writing. They are rare in the West, where most large academic libraries do not collect Russian translations of major Western classics. On the Ukrainian translations, see the discussion towards the end of this chapter.

8 For a brief account of Mérimée's major works, and that portrait of him dressed up as Clara Gazul, see Gustave Lanson and Paul Tuffrau, *Manuel d'histoire de la littérature française* (Paris and Boston: Hachette and Heath, 1938), 625–31.

9 See, for example "Merime, Prosper," in *Ukrainska radianska entsyklopediia*, vol. IX (Kyiv, 1962), 65. This important encyclopaedia was published during the Khrushchev thaw, when Soviet censorship was considerably loosened and foreign subjects like Mérimée were given more attention in both Russia and Ukraine. As

observed above, in note 7, the six-volume Russian edition of Mérimée's *Collected Works* actually came out in Moscow during this period, in 1963.

10  See Prosper Mérimée, *Carmen and Other Stories*, trans. Nicholas Jotcham (Oxford and New York: Oxford University Press, 1985), which contains a useful biographical introduction. Morel, *Prosper Mérimée,* proposes that this period helped define Mérimée's character and goals.

11  In A.W. Raitt, "History and Fiction in the Works of Mérimée, 1803–1870," *History Today* 19, no. 4 (1969), 240–7, especially 244 and 246. Also see Raitt, *Prosper Mérimée,* 241–2, and more generally Morel, *Prosper Mérimée,* 269–77. However, Mongault remarks, in "Mérimée et l'histoire russe" (Aug. 1932), 191, that the writer's literary works on a subject always preceded his historical studies of it. So, he tells us, *Carmen* antedated his historical analysis of Castile, his translations of Pushkin his exploration of the false Demetrius, and his essay on Gogol his study of the Ukrainian Cossacks.

12  "Merime, Prosper," in *Literaturnaia entsiklopediia*, vol. VII (Moscow: Sovetskaia entsiklopediia, 1934), cols. 199–206, especially 202.

13  "Merime, Prosper," in *Kratkaia literaturnaia entsiklopediia*, 9 vols. (Moscow: Sovetskaia entsiklopediia, 1962–78), IV, cols. 177–9.

14  Pierre-Georges Caster and Paul Surer, *Manuel des études littéraires françaises: XIX siècle* (Paris: Hachette, 1950), 171–6. Mérimée was to return to eastern European folklore at the very end of his literary career with the Lithuanian folktale *Lokis*, a story about monster bears (a kind of werewolf) set in the dark forests of that country. The story, typical for Mérimée, goes on about the ancient Lithuanian language and its relationship to Sanskrit. In English, see Mérimée, *Carmen and Other Stories*, trans. Jotcham, 291–331.

15  On *La Guzla,* see Raitt, *Prosper Mérimée,* 42–4, 59–60; and Smith, *Prosper Mérimée,* 48–66. A Pushkin scholar writing in Russian has recently questioned whether Pushkin was really fooled by this "mystification"; see E.G. Etkind, "Iz knigi 'Bozhestvennyi Glagol.' Pushkin prochitannyi v Rossii i vo Frantsii: 'Pesni zapadnikh Slavian' 'Pushkin perevodchik Merime,'" in N.V. Lindstom, ed., *Prosper Merime v russkoi literature* (Moscow: Rospen, 2007), 354–76. As an epigram to his study, Etkind quotes Dostoevsky as writing that Pushkin's translations of these songs were Pushkin's "masterpiece among his masterpieces."

16  See Gaston Cahen, "Prosper Mérimée et la Russie," *Revue d'histoire littéraire de la France* 28, no. 3 (1921), 388–96. Henri's book, *Une année en Russie* (1847), appeared ten years before the travelogues of writers such as Alexandre Dumas and Théophile Gautier, who are sometimes credited with "discovering" Russia for the French, or at least inventing a new kind of literature about it. Moreover, Henri was much more familiar with Russian culture and knew the language far better than they, says Cahen.

17  See especially Prosper Mérimée, "Alexandre Pouchkine," in his *Portraits historiques et littéraires,* 2nd ed. (Paris: Michel Lévy frères, 1894), 297–302. In this

essay, Mérimée compares Pushkin to Byron, saying both lived hard, died young, and were the outstanding poets of their lands. In this unusually enthusiastic essay, he also praised the Russian language for its "richness, sonority, accentuation, onomatopoeia, flexibility, nuances, and delicacy." He as well remarked that Russia had no dialects and the peasants spoke better and purer Russian than their lords. Only in Ukraine, he concluded, did the people speak a different "dialect" (302).

18  Ozwald, *Mérimée et la Russie*, 253–4. Also see Ilko Borshchak, "Marko Vovchok i ii zviazky v Paryzhi," *Ukraina*, no. 1 (Paris, 1949), especially 5–10, on Mérimée.

19  In Léon, *Mérimée et son temps*, 404. More generally, see Prosper Mérimée, *Histoire du règne de Pierre le Grand suivie de l'histoire de la Fausse Elizabeth II*, ed. with introduction and notes by Henri Mongault and Maurice Parturier (Paris: Louis Conard, 1947). In this book, about the early part of Peter's reign, Mérimée also discusses the Ukrainian Cossack hetman Ivan Mazepa and his early career, his service under Hetman Samoilovych, and the legend of his ride tied naked to the back of his horse by an irate, cuckolded husband and sent off to die on the Ukrainian steppes. Mérimée accepts part of this legend (very well known throughout Europe), but sets it in Poland (37): *"En somme, l'aventure qui parait avoir eu lieu, non pas sur le steppe, mais aux environs de Varsovie, fut moins tragique que la légende adoptée par Byron, mais assez ridicule pour oblige Mazepa à quitter la cour et le pays."*

20  See especially his letter of 16 June 1860 to Turgenev, in Maurice Parturier, *Une amité littéraire: Prosper Mérimée et Ivan Tourgeniev* (Paris: Hachette, 1952), 60–3. Also see Raitt, *Prosper Mérimée*, 282, on the comparison with Balzac, and more generally Borshchak, "Marko Vovchok i ii zviazky v Paryzhi," 5–10. Mérimée believed his own translation of *Kozachka* to be inferior, and it was never published. Today it is lost.

21  Ozwald, *Mérimée et la Russie*, 56.

22  In Léon, *Mérimée et son temps*, 400.

23  See Henri Mongault, "Introduction," in Prosper Mérimée, *Études de littérature russe*, 2 vols. (Paris: Champion, 1931–32), especially lxiv–lxv; and Ozwald, *Mérimée et la Russie*, 52–4. Some scholars even as late as the 1950s repeated the legend. See Borshchak, "Marko Vovchok i ii zviazky v Paryzhi," 5, citing [Felix] Chambon, *Notes sur Prosper Mérimée* (Paris, 1902), 257, which in turn cites E. Halperine-Kaminsky, *Ivan Tourgueneff d'après sa corresponance avec ses amis-français* (Paris: Charpentier, 1901), 14, which offers no source. Also see George Luckyj, *The Anguish of Mykola Hohol a.k.a. Nikolai Gogol* (Toronto: Canadian Scholars Press, 1998), 77, which, in contrast to Mongault, says nothing about Aleksandra's daughter Olga and paints a very positive picture of Rosset-Smirnova, who had happy memories of growing up in Ukraine; Luckyj concludes: "No wonder Gogol thought she was a kindred soul."

24  On Gogol, Mickiewicz, and Zaleski, see George S.N. Luckyj, *Between Gogol and Ševčenko: Polarity in the Literary Ukraine 1798-1847* (Munich: Wilhelm Fink

Verlag for the Harvard Series in Ukrainian Studies, 1971), 118, and also Luckyj, *The Anguish of Mykola Hohol*, 75, which both contain a long quote on Gogol's opinions from a letter of Zaleski to Duchiński. Boris Sokolov, *Gogol: Entsiklopediia* (Moscow: Algoritm, 2003), 261, quotes a Polish priest, who knew Gogol later in Rome, to the effect that Gogol "even undertook his fortunate journey to Paris in order to meet with Mickiewicz and [Józef] Bohdan Zaleski." Zaleski usually spelled his own given, middle name (i.e., Bohdan) with an "h" (Ukrainian style) rather than a "g" (Polish) – a telling distinction lost in Russian (Cyrillic) transliteration. Also see W. Hryshko, "Nikolai Gogol and Mykola Hohol: Paris 1837," *Annals of the Ukrainian Academy of Arts and Sciences in the US* 12, nos. 1–2 (1969–72), 113–42, which mentions those Ukrainian friends of Gogol's in Paris.

25  Mongault, "Introduction," lxx–lxxi. However, A.K. Vinogradov, *Merime v pismakh k Sobolevskomu* (Moscow: Moskovskoe khudozhestvennoe izdatelstvo, 1928), 55, reported that Sobolevsky's personal archive indicated that Sobolevsky, at the time Mérimée's closest Russian friend, decided, after meeting with Gogol in Italy in 1847, to use Mérimée to spread knowledge about Gogol and his writings in France.

26  Mongault, "Introduction," lxvi–lxvii. Also see Louis Léger, *Nicolas Gogol* (Paris: H. Didier, 1913), 98–103. Again, prior to Mongault, Léger had also rejected the idea that Mérimée and Gogol had ever met (204).

27  Prosper Mérimée, "Nicolas Gogol," in his *Études de littérature russe*, II, 6–7. It is also in this essay (6) that Mérimée (who had just begun his studies of Russian) compared Gogol to Balzac and even suggested that Balzac may have influenced Gogol. Also see Yevhen Sverstiuk, *Hohol i ukrainska nich: esei* (Kyiv: Klio, 2013), which twice (167, 179) quotes the above passage from Mérimée in Ukrainian translation. Sverstiuk was a famous Ukrainian political dissident of the 1980s, who later seems to have been influenced by the work of George Luckyj, with whom he carried on an extensive literary correspondence.

28  See Halperine-Kaminsky, *Ivan Tourgueneff d'après sa corresponance avec ses amis-français*, 15, on Dostoevsky, and more generally Sigismond Markiewicz, "La Pologne dans l'œuvre et la vie de Mérimée," *Revue de littérature comparée* 27 (April–June 1953), 148–59.

29  Raitt, *Prosper Mérimée*, 285–8. Also see Smith, *Prosper Mérimée*, 153–4. Here Raitt and Smith seem to be simply following Mongault, who treated this question at length in his "Mérimée et l'histoire russe" (Sept. 1932). Mongault, of course, knew some Russian, and Raitt and Smith did not. Also see Borshchak, "Marko Vovchok i ii zviazky v Paryzhi," which considered Mongault the ultimate expert on Mérimée and Russia. The era of these pretenders (1598–1613), who were all called Dmitri, is known as "The Time of Troubles"; it fell between the end of the Rurik dynasty and the enthronement of the Romanov Michael I and included a vast famine and an invasion by the Polish–Lithuanian Commonwealth. For the narrative history, see Prosper Mérimée, *Demetrius the Impostor: An Episode in Russian History*, trans. Andrew R. Scoble (London: Richard Bentley, 1853), especially 200–8, on the origins of Dmitri.

30  I have used the second edition: Prosper Mérimée, "Les Cosaques de l'Ukraine et leurs derniers atamans," in his *Mélanges historiques et littéraires* (Paris: Michel Lévy frères, 1859), 50–90. Also see Arkady Joukovsky, "Prosper Mérimée et la question ukrainienne," in *L'Ukraine et la France au XIXᵉ siècle* (Paris: L'université de la Sorbonne nouvelle, 1987), 21–32. Mérimée was, in fact, quietly critical of Napoleon III's policies in eastern Europe and not enthusiastic about the Crimean War, which interfered with his Russian interests. On this, see Léon, *Mérimée et son temps*, 119–29. Mérimée wrote "Les Cosaques de l'Ukraine" perhaps in response to a request from the French court, just as Charles-Louis Lesur penned his *Histoire des Cosaques* (Paris, 1814) at Napoleon's behest during his Russian campaign of 1812. On the latter invasion, see my summary of Borshchak's research: "1812: Napoleon and Ukraine," *Ukrainian Weekly* (New York), no. 47 (8 Nov. 2012), 8–9, which may, however, contain some errors, as Borshchak's work (always interesting) often contains false citations indicating what he wished to find in the sources, not what he actually found. I discovered how systematic this problem was only after publishing this 2012 article.

31  In Ozwald, *Mérimée et la Russie*, 170.

32  In a letter of 24 February 1863, Mérimée wrote to Turgenev: "Monsieur Kostomarof imagines that the whole world wants to know about the Cossacks and fills his book with beautiful words that no one can find in the dictionaries" (Parturier, *Une amité littéraire*, 86). And on 9 January 1863, in his last letter to Sobolevsky, he wrote: "I am reviewing Monsieur Kostomarof's *Bohdan Khmelnytsky* in the *Journal des savants*. I am very much displeased with all of the Little Russianisms in his book. Without Turgenev, I would have been able to get nothing at all out of it" (Vinogradov, *Merime v pismakh k Sobolevskomu*, 212). On Kostomarov in this regard, see in particular my two studies: *Mykola Kostomarov: A Biography* (Toronto: University of Toronto Press, 1996) and "Mykola Kostomarov and East Slavic Ethnography in the Nineteenth Century," *Russian History* 18, no. 2 (1991), 163–86.

33  In Parturier, *Une amité littéraire*, 26.

34  Mérimée, *Bogdan Chmielnicki*, 20–2.

35  Ibid., 1–2, 291–2. I have used Raitt's translation for the first part of this quote; see his *Prosper Mérimée*, 290. Also see Joukovsky, "Prosper Mérimée et la question ukrainienne," *passim*.

36  These included *hetman* (Ukrainian Cossack ruler) and *sich* (fortified Cossack headquarters on the Dnieper River). See E.P. Martianova, *Ot otrazhenii russko-frantsuzkikh kulturnikh sviazei vo frantsuzkom iazyke i literature XIX veka . . . P. Merime* (Kharkiv: Kharkivskii universitet, 1980), 131.

37  See Ozwald, *Mérimée et la Russie*, 302–3, especially n 220 and n 222, which cite Joukovsky, "Mérimée et la question ukrainienne."

38  There is a heavily censored Russian-language article on the relationship between Marx and Kostomarov by the Soviet Ukrainian scholars Ye. Shabliovsky and V.G.

Sarbei, "N.I. Kostomarov v istoriograficheskom nasledii Karla Marksa," *Voprosy istorii*, no. 8 (1967), 49–59. Further on this subject, see the "Introduction" to the present volume.

39 Dmytro Nalyvaiko, "Prosper Merime i Ukraina," *Vsesvit*, no. 9 (1970), 145–9.

40 Oleh Kupchynsky, "Prosper Merime i ioho tvir 'Bohdan Khmelnytsky'," *Zhovten*, no. 7 (Lviv, 1987), 16–22. Also see the reprint (which, however, lacks an introduction): Prosper Mérimée [Merime], *Ukrainski kozaky ta ikhni ostanni hetmany. Bohdan Khmelnytsky* (Kyiv: Biblioteka ukraintsia, 1998).

41 The fact that Mérimée's work on Khmelnytsky was researched, written, and first published on the eve and in the midst of the 1863–64 Polish insurrection against the Russian Empire, of which Mérimée was extremely critical, may have had something to do with his pro-Ukrainian opinions (if they can be called that) of that time. Certainly, he stressed the violence of both sides in the conflict.

42 Prosper Mérimée, *Lettres à une autre inconnu* (Paris: Michel Lévy frères, 1875), 118. "*C'est d'être un peu trop polonais. Vous savez que pour moi je suis Cosaque.*" According to Ozwald, *Mérimée et la Russie*, 75, Mme Przedziecka was born Lise Lachman, and was the wife of Charles Przedziecki, an officer in the Russian army and the son of "an illustrious family in Podolia" – one of the most westerly provinces of Russian Ukraine, at that time part of "the South Western Region." Although most of the nobility there was Polish, most of the peasants were Ukrainian.

## CHAPTER EIGHT

1 This chapter appeared first in the *Polish Review* 56, no. 3 (2011), 159–86. See especially Kenneth Clark, *An Introduction to Rembrandt* (New York: Harper and Row, 1978). For a particularly well-put brief characterization of Rembrandt, which devotes some attention to *The Polish Rider*, see Robert Hughes, "The God of Realism," *New York Review of Books* (6 April 2006), 6, 8, 10, also available as "Connoisseur of the Ordinary," *Guardian*, 11 February 2006, www.guardian.co.uk/artanddesign/2006/feb/11/art/print. For authoritative syntheses informed by recent scholarly debates, see Simon Schama, *Rembrandt's Eyes* (New York: Alfred A. Knopf, 1999), and Gary Schwartz, *The Rembrandt Book* (New York: Abrams, 2006). Both volumes are well illustrated, although the latter is missing a reproduction of *The Polish Rider*. Somewhat older, but with a respectable commentary on the rider, is Michael Kitson, *Rembrandt*, 3rd ed. (Oxford: Phaidon, 1982), especially section 34. For a recent synthesis in Polish, see M. Monkiewicz, "Rembrandt," in *Sztuka świata 7* (Warsaw, 1994), 137–59. My maternal grandfather, Jan Międzybrodzki (Miedzybrocki in Canadian orthography), a Polish *szlachcic* and native of eastern Galicia under the Habsburgs, inspired in his Canadian children and us grandchildren affection for their Polish heritage, which helped lead me to this study of *The Polish Rider*.

2  For some rather full collections of Rembrandt's paintings that list *The Polish Rider*, see, for example, Abraham Bredius, *The Paintings of Rembrandt*, 2 vols. (Vienna and New York: Phaidon Press, 1937), especially vol. I, no. 279, and Kurt Bauch, *Rembrandt: Gemälde* (Berlin: W. de Gruyter, 1966), especially no. 211. The latter labels the picture *Gijsbrecht van Amstel*, an allegorical interpretation discussed in the text below.

3  For some general observations, see H. Gerson, "Rembrandt in Poland," *Burlington Magazine* 98, no. 641 (Aug. 1956), 280-3, and Michał Walicki, "Rembrandt w Polsce," *Biuletyn historii sztuki*, no. 3 (1956), 319-48, with a synopsis in French, 347-8. Walicki's valuable article is reprinted in his *Obrazy bliskie i dalekie* (Warsaw: Wydawnictwa Artystyczne i Filmowe, 1963), 171-97, but all references in the present chapter are to the journal edition. On the "Polish Nobleman," see Otakar Odlozilik, "Rembrandt's Polish Nobleman," *Polish Review* 8, no. 4 (1963), 3-33. At mid-century there were four generally acknowledged Rembrandts in Poland: *Landscape with the Good Samaritan* (1638), *Portrait of Martin Day* (1634), *Self-portrait* (c. 1628), and *Portrait of Saskia* (1633). Some half-century later, only the first remained unquestionably a Rembrandt. Meanwhile, in the 1990s, Karolina Lanckorońska of Vienna donated both *Girl in a Hat* (1641), formerly called *The Jewish Bride*, and *Scholar at a Lectern* (1641), formerly *Father of the Jewish Bride*, to the Royal Castle (Zamek) Museum in Warsaw. In 2006, Ernst van de Wetering, a representative of the notably rigorous Amsterdam-based Rembrandt Research Project (discussed below in this chapter), opined that both paintings were true Rembrandts. See Dorota Jurecka, "Mamy prawdziwe Rembrandty," *Gazeta Wyborcza* (Warsaw), 4 Feb. 2006. For a more detailed history of the attribution of these canvases, see the website of the Royal Castle in Warsaw, page devoted to "Autorstwo obrazów," at www.zamek-krolewski.com.pl/?page=1434, 1 January 2020.

4  *The Polish Rider*, in *The Frick Collection: An Illustrated Catalogue*, vol. I: *Paintings* (New York: Frick, 1968), 258-65, with a brief bibliography. There is a serviceable colour reproduction of the painting under an article of the same name in the English-language Wikipedia. Unfortunately, this article is not linked to its Polish-language counterpart – "Jeździec Polski," 5 August 2010 – which displays the same photograph and contains additional information and many links to related Polish subjects.

5  M[aurycy] D[zieduszycki], "Wizerunek Lisowczyka, obraz olejny Rembrandta," *Biblioteka Naukowego Zakladu imienia Ossolińskich*, vols. VII–IX (1843), 157-9.

6  Wilhelm Bode, *Studien zur Geschichte der holländischen Malerei* (Brunswick: Friedrich Viewege, 1883), 499-500.

7  See Anthony Bailey, *Responses to Rembrandt* (New York: Tinken, 1994), which quotes Bredius on 118, n 5. For more detail on Bredius's research trip to Galicia, Poland, and Russia, on which he claimed to have discovered a number of "new"

Rembrandts, see Catherine B. Scallen, *Rembrandt: Reputation and the Practice of Connoisseurship* (Amsterdam: University of Amsterdam Press, 2004), 132–3.

8   Alfred von Wurzbach, *Niederländisches Künstler-Lexikon auf Grund archivali-scher Forschungen bearbeitet*, 3 vols. (Vienna and Leipzig, 1906–11; reprint 1963), I, 573: "Dzikow. Graf Tarnowski. Ein tatarischer Reiter . . . " (Dzikow, Count Tarnowski: A Tatar Rider . . . ).

9   *The Polish Rider*, in *The Frick Collection*, 258–65; Julius A. Chrościcki, "Rembrandt's 'Polish Rider': Allegory or Portrait?" in Alicja Dyczek-Gwiździ et al., eds., *Ars Auro Prior: Studia Ioanni Białostocki Sexagenario dictata* (Warsaw: PWN, 1981), 441–8 *et passim*, and Zygmunt Batowski, "Z powodu sprzedaży Lisowczy-ka," *Lamus* 3, no. 6 (1910), 189–96. Also see Bailey, *Responses to Rembrandt*, 4–5, which emphasizes Fry's experience. On Frick as an industrialist and "robber bar-on" as well as a collector of art, see, for example, Samuel A. Schreiner, *Henry Clay Frick: The Gospel of Greed* (New York: St Martin's Press, 1995). For a more positive assessment, see Martha Frick Symington Sanger, *Henry Clay Frick: An Intimate Portrait* (New York: Abbeville, 1998), with some speculations concerning Frick's feelings about *The Polish Rider* on 72–4 and 452–4. The role of eastern European immigrants, especially Slavs, in the Homestead Strike of 1892 is stressed in Paul Krause, *The Battle for Homestead 1880–1892: Politics, Culture and Steel* (Pittsburgh and London: University of Pittsburgh Press, 1992), 221–6, 315–28, which notes that these Slavic workers' efforts on behalf of organized labour have been seriously un-derrated. On the Tarnowski family and its varying fortunes during the twentieth century, see Andrew Tarnowski, *The Last Mazurka: A Tale of War, Passion and Loss* (London: Aurum, 2006), which mentions *The Polish Rider* on 4.

10  "The Henry Clay Frick Collection," *Art World* 1, no. 6 (March 1917), 374–8.

11  "Mr Frick's Rembrandt," *Lotus Magazine* 1, no. 3 (1910), 7–8. Another poem in honour of *The Polish Rider* was published in *Art in America* (Oct. 1920); the first stanza is quoted in full in Bailey, *Responses to Rembrandt*, 119, n 7.

12  In Andrew Ciechanowski, "Notes on the Ownership of Rembrandt's 'Polish Rid-er'," *Art Bulletin* 42, no. 4 (1960), 294–6.

13  Ibid., citing Inventory of 1795. Also see Walicki, "Rembrandt w Polsce," 329.

14  See Chrościcki, "Rembrandt's 'Polish Rider'," 443, and 448, n 9, citing T. Mańkow-ski, "Obrazy Rembrandta w Galerii Stanisława Augusta," *Prace Komisji Historii Sztuki PAU*, V (1930), 17–19, which refers to the king's letter. Chrościcki, howev-er, was unable to find this letter in the surviving correspondence. On the Lisow-czyks, who were basically brigands in royal and then imperial service, see Henryk Wisner, *Lisowczycy* (Warsaw: Książka i Wiedza, 1976), which sports a full-colour reproduction of *The Polish Rider* on the cover. See M[aurycy] D[zieduszycki], "Wizerunek Lisowczyka, obraz olejny Rembrandta (Portrait of a Lisowczyk, an oil painting by Rembrandt)," *Bibliotéka Naukowego Zakladu imienia Ossolińskich* [*Ossolineum*], vol. VII–IX (1843), 157–9, and Dzieduszycki's history of the Lisow-czyks, 2 vols. (1843–44).

15  Ciechanowski, "Notes on the Ownership of Rembrandt's 'Polish Rider'," 296; Chrościcki, "Rembrandt's 'Polish Rider,'" 441.

16  Dzieduszycki, "Wizerunek Lisowczyka," 158.

17  For a brief survey of Polish artists influenced by Rembrandt's painting, see Walicki, "Rembrandt w Polsce," 330. (Auer's lithograph may be the same image as that printed by Dzieduszycki in 1843, although I have not been able to examine the Piller version.) Also see Zygmunt Gloger, "Lisowczyki," in *Encyklopedia Staropolska Illustrowana*, 4 vols. (Warsaw, 1972), III, 145–6. (This work was first published 1900–3.) On Brandt in particular, see, for example, Anna Bernat, *Józef Brandt (1841–1915)* (Warsaw: Edipresse, 2007), which gives further references; on Kossak, see Kazimierz Olszański, *Juliusz Kossak* (Wrocław: Ossolineum, 1988), especially nos. 126, 127, 130, which is the most detailed account, and Maciej Masłowski, *Juliusz Kossak* (Warsaw: WAiF, 1986), especially no. 71, which contains the best reproduction of Kossak's *Lisowczyk on a White Horse*. Unlike Rembrandt's rider, however, Kossak's has a slight moustache but no fire or high "fortress" in the background. Also, his hat is more natural than that of Rembrandt's rider, lacking the puzzling black arc of the latter, which appears to have been added by a later hand, perhaps a "restorer," although the Frick (*The Polish Rider*, in *The Frick Collection*, 264, n 4) maintains that technical examination shows that "the peculiar shape results from the dark fur trimming of the two upturned flaps merging with some dark hair on the Rider's forehead." Somewhat strangely, the most extensive pre-independence Polish encyclopaedia does not even mention the "Lisowczyk"; see "Rembrandt," in *Encyklopedia Powszechna S. Orgelbranda*, vol. XII (Warsaw, 1902), 563; nor does that era's most detailed Russian-language encyclopaedia, which was widely read in Poland: A.A. Somov, "Rembrandt van Rein," in *Entsiklopedicheskii slovar*, vol. XXVI (St Petersburg: Brokgauz i Efron, 1899), 552–4.

18  Unless otherwise noted, I use the extensively revised edition of Held's article, which contains a valuable "Postscript": see Julius S. Held, "The 'Polish' Rider," in his *Rembrandt Studies* (Princeton, NJ: Princeton University Press, 1991), 59–97 and 194–9. For reasons of comparison, I have also consulted the original: "Rembrandt's 'Polish' Rider," *Art Bulletin* 26, no. 4 (1944), 246–65. Held's ideas are not fully accepted by A.J. Barnouw, "Rembrandt's Tribute to Polish Valor," *Polish Review* 5, no. 18 (1945), 8–9, 16, which assesses the painter's attention to Poland as a visionary and prophetic "token of gratitude" for Polish help in liberating Holland from the Germans in 1945. Barnouw's highly charged and enthusiastic speculation reflects the exhilaration of victory, not the likely facts.

19  Held, "The 'Polish' Rider" (1991), 59–97. On Stefano della Bella, whose sketches of Polish cavalrymen Rembrandt's rider very much resembles, see Phyllis D. Masser, "Presenting Stefano della Bella," *Metropolitan Museum of Art Bulletin*, new series, 27, no. 3 (1968), 159–76. Bołoz-Antoniewicz's comparison of the two dated from about 1905; see Held, "The 'Polish' Rider" (1991), 81, n 95. Held went on to say (82) that the rider's background – "this landscape, with its powerful fortress on top of

a steep and massive mountain" – is "an element quite foreign to Stefano's etchings with their wide plains and low horizon." For an eastern European, this building, with its broad, almost flat dome, evokes Orthodox churches of the eastern Mediterranean; it resembles that of the church / mosque of Hagia Sophia in Istanbul, minus the minarets added by the Turks. Walicki, "Rembrandt w Polsce," 343–6, compares it to the ruins of the Temple of Minerva in Rome, which appeared on a print of the later sixteenth century and on Rembrandt's own *David Taking Leave of Jonathan* (1642) in the Hermitage in St Petersburg.

20 This interpretation remained unchanged in later editions of the work. See, for example, Jacob Rosenberg, *Rembrandt: Life and Work*, rev. ed. (Ithaca, NY: Cornell University Press, 1986), 251–4. Clark, *Introduction to Rembrandt*, 57–9, also follows Held quite closely, although he sees an anti-classical "rebel" element in the rider's almost emaciated horse and "an almost feminine beauty" in the rider himself. He calls the canvas a "magical work typical of Rembrandt" and "one of the great poems of painting."

21 See Held, "The 'Polish' Rider" (1991), especially the "Postscript," 194–9, which outlines most of these theories and counters them. For the most widely influential theory, see W.R. Valentiner, "Rembrandt's Conception of Historical Portraiture," *Art Quarterly* 11 (Detroit, 1948), 116–35; Colin Campbell, "Rembrandt's 'Polish Rider' and the Prodigal Son," *Journal of the Warburg and Courtauld Institutes* 33 (1970), 293–303, and revised as "The Identity of Rembrandt's 'Polish Rider'," in Otto von Simon and Jan Kelch, eds., *Neue Beiträge zur Rembrandt-Forschung* (Berlin: Gebr. Mann, 1973), 126–37; Leonard J. Slatkes, *Rembrandt and Persia* (New York: Abaris, 1983), 60–92; and Gary Schwartz, *Rembrandt: His Life, His Paintings* (London: Viking, 1985), 273, 277–8. The St Reinold of Pantaleon theory was proposed in Daniel Wayne Deyell, "The Frick Collection Rider by Rembrandt van Rijn," MA thesis, University of British Columbia, 1980, to which Held did not respond.

22 Jan Białostocki, "Rembrandt's *Eques Polonus*," *Oud Holland* 84 (1969), 163–76. This "Socinian theory" is partly accepted by Pierre Descargues, *Rembrandt: Biographie* (Paris: Jean-Claude Lattès, 1990), 205–6. For Held's objections, see his "Postscript," 195–6.

23 Zdzisław Żygulski, "Rembrandt's 'Lisowczyk': A Study of Costume and Weapons," *Bulletin du Musée nationale de Varsovie* 6, nos. 2 / 3 (1965), 43–67. Rembrandt's *Lisowczyk* is also treated as a real example of Polish military history in Bronisław Gembarzewski, *Polska jej dzieje i kultura*, 3 vols. (Warsaw: N.p., [1930s]), II, 53–4, a highly respected work.

24 Mieczysław Paszkiewicz, "'Jeździec polski' Rembrandta," *Biuletyn historii sztuki* 31, no. 2 (1969), 216–26.

25 Zdzisław Żygulski, "Odpowiedź w kwestii 'Lisowczyka,'" 31, no. 2 (1969), 227–8. Also see Żygulski, *Polska: Broń wodzów i żołnierzy* (Cracow: Kluszczyński, 2003?), 54–5.

26   Mykhailo Bryk-Deviatnytsky, "Pro Rembrandta i ioho 'Polskoho Vershnyka',"
     *Vilne slovo* (Toronto), 6 May 1972. Through the good graces of archivist James
     Kominowski, I obtained an electronic copy of this rather rare newspaper arti-
     cle from the Oleksander Baran Collection, vol. "Kozaky," University of Manitoba
     Archives, Winnipeg, Manitoba.

27   B.P.J. Broos, "Rembrandt's Portrait of a Pole on His Horse," *Simiolus: Netherlands
     Quarterly for the History of Art* 7, no. 4 (1974), 192–218, particularly 214, which cites
     an article in Dutch by Mychalj Bryk-Dewjatnyckyj / Mykhailo Bryk-Deviatnytsky,
     "Morozenko in Frankener," *Ut de smidte* 1, part 4 (1969), 10–14, and refers to his
     work in Ukrainian. Held, "Postscript," 198, interpreted Broos to have already
     decided for Szymon Karol.

28   Held, "Nachwort zum 'Polnischen' Reiter" (1981), as quoted in Held, "Postscript,"
     198, n 13. Broos, "Rembrandt's Portrait of a Pole on His Horse," 215, quotes the
     register of Leyden University for 14 July 1650: "Martianus [Marcyan] Oginski Po-
     lonus, 19, Pol[itices]."

29   See Chrościcki, "Rembrandt's 'Polish Rider,'" 445–7, with a photograph of Bol's
     picture. Also, Rembrandt's rider wears a very light-coloured – indeed, almost
     white – "joupane" (*zhupan*), or coat, and the *Vytis* on the Lithuanian coat of
     arms is also generally white, as is the mounted St George slaying the dragon, who
     appears on the Ogiński family coat of arms. Aleksander Brückner, *Słownik et-
     ymologiczny języka polskiego* (Cracow: M. Arct, 1927), in his brief article on the
     "*żupan*," 668, reports two kinds worn by the Polish gentry: a white linen summer
     version and a winter one, of darker or grey wool. On Lithuanian heraldry, see
     Edmundas Rimša, *Heraldry: Past to Present*, trans. Vijolè Arbas (Vilnius: Versus
     aureus, 2005), especially 58–71, with several antique illustrations of the *Vytis*.

30   "Ogiński (Lith. Oginskis)," in *Encyclopedia Lithuanica*, 6 vols. (Boston, 1970–78),
     IV, 109. Since the family was of old "Ruthenian," or East Slavic origin (even spon-
     soring publications in the Ruthenian and Slavonic languages), "of the fire" would
     derive from an East Slavic, not Polish, word for "fire" (cf. the modern Belarusan
     *vahon*'), although these two cognate words sound very similar to an outside ear.
     On the Ogińskis (*Ahinski* in modern Belarusan), see *Polska encyklopedia szla-
     checka*, vol. IX (Warsaw, 1937), 135–6, with vital statistics on prominent family
     members, including Marcjan Aleksander.

31   Andrzej Rachuba, "Ogiński, Marcjan Aleksander," in *Polski słownik biograficzny*,
     vol. XXIII (Wrocław, etc., 1978), 618–20, makes no mention of Rembrandt's *Polish
     Rider*, nor does "Rembrandt," in *Wielka Encyklopedia Powszechna PWN*, vol. IX
     (Warsaw, 1967), 769–70.

32   Held, "The 'Polish' Rider" (1991), 197, n 11. Also by 1991, Held had dropped a Hun-
     garian origin for the painting, although he reprinted his earlier observations.

33   Richard Brzezinski, *Polish Armies 1596–1696*, 2 vols. (London: Osprey, 1987), I, 5;
     Schama, *Rembrandt's Eyes*, 599–603.

34  Schwartz has, however, dropped it in his most recent publication, *The Rembrandt Book* (2006).

35  Slatkes, *Rembrandt and Persia*, 60–92.

36  Bernice Davidson et al., *Paintings from the Frick Collection* (New York: Abrams, 1990), 58–60 (no pagination thanks to a printing error), boasts a beautiful colour reproduction of *The Polish Rider* with close-up details of the rider and his handsome face. Some fourteen years later, the Frick reported that the canvas "is not a conventional equestrian portrait, nor does it appear to represent a historical or literary figure, though a number have been proposed. Rembrandt may have meant only to portray an exotic horseman, a popular contemporary theme, or perhaps, intended the painting as a glorification of the latter-day Christian knights who in his time were still defending eastern Europe from the advancing Turks." See *The Frick Collection: Handbook of Paintings* (New York: Frick and Scala Publishers, 2004), 126. Such a consensus obviously influenced Sanger, *Henry Clay Frick*, 72–4, to speculate that the American magnate identified with the rider as a Christian knight, since he himself was a Masonic knight of the three highest orders of the York Rite – but Held first enunciated his *Miles Christianus* theory in 1944 and Frick died in 1919. As mentioned above, in Frick's time the rider was associated much more with the struggle for Polish independence than with Christendom as a whole.

37  It was even carried by President Leonyd Kuchma, who served 1994–2005. The word *kuchma* now also means "a bushy head of hair." Max Vasmer / Maks Fasmer, in his *Etimologicheskii slovar russkogo iazyka*, 4 vols. (Moscow, 1964–73), II, 438, informs us that it also entered Russian from Ukrainian, which had received it through the Polish *kuczma* from the Hungarian *kucsma*. As for *zhupan*, Metropolitan Ilarion, *Etymolohichno-semantychnyi slovnyk ukrainskoi movy*, 4 vols. (Winnipeg, 1979–94), II, 51, reports that it entered Ukrainian from the Polish *żupan*, which came from the Italian *giubhone* or *giupone*, a certain kind of jacket. Brückner, *Słownik etymologiczny języka polskiego*, 279 and 668, gives the same etymologies. Brückner's etymologies, if accurate, challenge Żygulski's theory that such apparel came to Poland from the east and not from Italy, or, more significantly, Hungary. Yet Brückner (49) also proffers that the word for the horsetail standard, "*buńczuk*," of Turkish origin, reached Polish from Ukrainian "*od Małej Rusi do nas.*"

38  Andrew Gregorovich, "Rembrandt's Painting: 'Cossack Rider'," *Forum: A Ukrainian Review*, no. 114 (fall / winter, 2007), 5–10. The legend of Mazepa's "ride" across the steppes, tied naked to the back of a wild horse by a cuckolded husband, dates from somewhat later. On Mazepa generally, see Clarence A. Manning, *Hetman of Ukraine: Ivan Mazeppa* (New York: Bookman Associates, 1957), especially 39–43, and Hubert F. Babinski, *The Mazepa Legend in European Romanticism* (New York: Columbia University Press, 1974). On Mazepa's stay in Holland, Theodore Mackiw, "Mazepa's Love Affair and Its Veracity," *Ukrainian Quarterly* 44,

nos. 1–2 (1988), 100–7, states that he spent one year (1657–58) studying in Deventer. He quotes F.J.G. Ten Raa and F. De Bas, eds., *Het Staatsche Leger, 1568–1795* (Breda, 1913), VII, 238: "Johannes Koledynski, latere Hetman Mazeppa, was een jaar in Nederland bij Geschutfabriek Willem Wegewaad in Deventer." For an introduction to Mazepa's portrayals in art, but not in *The Polish Rider*, see John P. Pauls, "[A] Great Maecenas of the Arts Glorified by Painters," *Ukrainian Review* 13, no. 4 (London, 1966), 17–32.

39 J. Bruyn, review of W. Sumowski, *Gemälde der Rembrandt-Schüler*, 5 vols. (Landau, 1983–90), in *Oud Holland* 98 (1984), 146–62, especially 158. Bruyn phrased his suggestion very carefully: "In the field of Drost research much remains to be done. This applies to the portraits . . . as well as to the history pieces. A further examination of the field reveals that a number of paintings still accepted as Rembrandts cannot be forgotten: 'A Man Seated with a Stick' in London (National Gallery, no. 51) which has already been questioned by MacLaren, and the so-called 'Polish Rider' in the Frick Collection, which shows at least [some] affinities with Drost's early work which was strongly influenced by Rembrandt" (original Dutch: . . . *of de z. g. Poolse ruiter in de Frick Collection die op zijn minst treffende verwant schappen vertoont met Drosts vroege, Rembrandtieke werk*) (translated with the help of Alta Vista Babel Fish translation service online).

40 Zdzisław Żygulski, "Further Battles for the *Lisowczyk* (Polish Rider) by Rembrandt," *Artibus et Historiae* 21, no. 41 (2000), 197–205, especially 203. Żygulski seems never to have doubted Rembrandt's hand. By contrast, Viktor Vlasov, "Polskii vsadnik," in *Novii entsiklopedicheskii slovar izobrazitelnogo iskusstva*, VII (St Petersburg, 2007), 576–7, referred to *The Polish Rider* as "a conventionally named picture which had been earlier ascribed to Rembrandt" and reproduced it but with a question mark after Rembrandt's name.

41 See Bailey, *Responses to Rembrandt*, 123, n 3, for the limerick, and 94 for Held's remark about "the Amsterdam mafia." On these issues more generally, see Donald Sassoon, "The Neverending Project," *Muse* 9, no. 3 (1 March 2005), 8, at eLibrary. Web, 1 October 2010.

42 Connor reproduced the painting (68 in x 64 in) from his personal collection on his website at www.russellconnor.com/gallery_7.html, 19 August 2010.

43 For the declaration, see Bailey, *Responses to Rembrandt*, 115–16.

44 Ernst van de Wetering, *Rembrandt: The Painter at Work* (Amsterdam: Amsterdam University Press, 1997), 207–11, with a portrait of the rider. The New York newspapers noticed van de Wetering's opinion; see, for example, Carol Vogel, "Rembrandt at Frick Passes," *New York Times*, 14 October 1997.

45 Jonathan Bikker, *Willem Drost (1633–1659): A Rembrandt Pupil in Amsterdam and Venice* (New Haven, Conn.: Yale University Press, 2005), sec. R16, with a portrait of the rider.

46 Hughes, "The God of Realism," 10.

## CHAPTER NINE

1   There are a number of photographs of these very real Ukrainian soldiers on the internet, for example: "Writing a Reply," 14 August 2015, at http://imgur.com/gallery/CaojH. Unsurprisingly, given the enormous Russian disinformation campaigns since about 2008, Vassily Nesterenko (b. 1967), a Russian painter of Ukrainian origin, but patronized by the Kremlin, executed his own version of Repin's *Zaporozhian Cossacks* – much more useful for propaganda purposes – titled *A Letter to Russia's Enemies*. As early as 1993, Nesterenko had been associated with a "New Wave of Russian Realism" and had a one-man show in the House of the Government of the Russian Federation (August 1993), and he had another in the Kremlin the next year. For his Russian version of the painting, and its association with an extreme Russian nationalist organization, see Neil MacFarquhar, "Patriotic Youth Army Takes Russian Kids Back to the Future," *New York Times*, 22 March 2018, https://www.nytimes.com/2018/03/22/world/europe/russia-soviet-youth-army.html.

2   Stalin's attitude towards Repin's *Zaporozhian Cossacks* mixed amusement at the content of the Cossacks' letter (his daughter later testified that he knew much of it off by heart and loved to quote it to visitors) with awareness of the artist's historical importance; see my article "A Painter from Ukraine: Ilya Repin," *Canadian Slavonic Papers* 55, nos. 1–2 (2013), 19–43. Illustrated version online at https://www.academia.edu/23138602/A_Painter_from_Ukraine_Ilya_Repin, 1 January 2020.

3   For an introduction to Repin's life and work, with special attention to Ukrainian affairs, see ibid., which contains full bibliographical information. A more general treatment in English is F. Parker and S.J. Parker, *Russia on Canvas: Ilya Repin* (University Park and London: Pennsylvania University Press, 1980), which reflects an older, pro-Soviet approach. Also see Elizabeth Kridl Valkenier, *Ilya Repin and the World of Russian Art* (New York: Columbia University Press, 1990), which, although it missed many important Ukrainian points, was the first critical non-Soviet account, and David Jackson, *The Russian Vision: The Art of Ilya Repin* (Schoten, Belgium: BAI, 2006), which includes information (previously suppressed) on Repin's portraits of Tsar Nicholas II, but, seemingly under a lingering pro-Soviet influence, pretty much ignores Ukrainian themes. In Ukrainian, there are three relevant studies. Two appeared during Soviet ideological thaws: Khrushchev–Shelest and just before the end: Iu. Bielichko / Iu. Belichko, *Ukraina v tvorchosti I. Iu. Repina* (Kyiv: Mystetstvo, 1963), handsomely illustrated, but mostly in two-tone, and the brief essay in Dmytro Stepovyk, *Skarby Ukrainy* (Kyiv: Veselka, 1991), 121–6. The third emerged just after the fall of the Soviet Union: Belichko, "Tvorchist Illi Riepina v konteksti ukrainskoi khudozhnoi kultury druhoi polovyny XIX – pochatku XX stolit," *Narodna tvorchist ta etnohrafiia*, no. 4 (1994), 3–12.

4  An extensive article with a good map is V. Kubiiovych and O. Ohloblyn, "Slobidska Ukraina," in Volodymyr Kubijovyč and Danylo Husar Struk, eds., *Encyclopedia of Ukraine*, 5 vols. (Toronto: University of Toronto Press, 1984–93), IV, 753–6.

5  There is a very brief, unsigned article, "Kramskoi," in Volodymyr Kubijovyč and Danylo Husar Struk, eds., *Encyclopedia of Ukraine*, vol. II (Toronto: University of Toronto Press, 1988), 657. Following the official Soviet line, this article describes him simply as a "Russian realist painter." This subject requires further investigation.

6  D. Snowyd / Dmytro Dontsov, *Spirit of Ukraine* (New York: United Ukrainian Organization of the United States, 1935), 102–3. Compare Kevin M.F. Platt, "On Blood, Scandal, Renunciation, and Russian History: Il'ia Repin's *Ivan the Terrible and his Son, Ivan*," in Marcus C. Levitt and Tatyana Novikov, eds., *Times of Trouble: Violence in Russian Literature and Culture* (Madison: University of Wisconsin Press, 2007), 112–22.

7  Even in "What Freedom" the waves are not clear blue but rather a sickly yellow. This caused some controversy when the painting was first exhibited, many observers seeing Russia's difficult political and social situation in that yellow. The art critic Vladimir Stasov, however, thought that the painting did represent some hope for the country's youth. See the reproduction and commentary in Seppo Miettinen et al., *Ilya Repin: Painting and Graphic Art from the Collection of the State Russian Museum* (St Petersburg: Palace Editions, n.d., c. 2005), 80–1, plate 48, and commentary on 112. Also, Repin's historical canvases dealing with St Petersburg or its founder, Peter the Great, lack the finish of his Ukrainian pictures. One finished painting, however, was his *Tsar Ivan V and Tsar Peter Initiating Young Falconers into the Toy Guards* (1900, Russian Museum, St Petersburg, hereafter RM); see ibid., 94, plate 60. Repin's attempts at painting Peter were never reproduced in the USSR and even today are seldom printed or reproduced online. (For a rare exception, see *Peter the Great on the Hunt* at https://www.wikiart.org/en/ilya-repin/peter-the-great-on-the-hunt, last modified 16 June 2011.) Similarly, his sketches of Nicholas II were never reproduced in the USSR, and only today are they being recognized for their beauty and accuracy in portraying that modest but ineffectual prince; three sketches are at http://www.ilyarepin.org/sitemap-7.html, 4 April 2017, or see Miettinen et al., *Ilya Repin*, 76, 77, plates 44 and 45, which are excellent reproductions of Repin's *Wedding of Nicholas II and Alexandra Feodorovna* (1894, RM) and *Portrait of Emperor Nicholas II* (1895, RM).

8  There is a considerable scholarly literature on *Zaporozhian Cossacks* in Russian, much of it rather technical, on its "painterly" aspects. See, for example, A. Davydova, "K istorii sozdannia kartiny Repina 'Zaporozhtsy,'" *Iskusstvo* 5 (1955), 36–42; N. Zograf, "Kartina I.E. Repina 'Zaporozhtsy'," ibid., 11 (1959), 56–66; A.S. Davydova, *Zaporozhtsy: Kartina Repina* (Moscow, 1962); and I.A. Brodskii, "Zaporozhtsy pishut pismo turetskomu sultanu 1878–1891," in V.M. Lobanov, ed., *Zamechatelnye polotna* (Leningrad: Khudozhnuk RSFSR, 1966), 271–80. The

literature in Ukrainian is much thinner, but very valuable for our purposes. See Bielichko, *Ukraina v tvorchosti Riepina*, *passim*, and Stepovyk, *Skarby Ukrainy*, 121–6.

9  See the brief discussion of these historians in Victor A. Friedman, "The Zaporozhian Letter to the Turkish Sultan: Historical Commentary and Linguistic Analysis," *Slavica Hierosolymitana* 2 (Jerusalem, 1978), 25–37. Also see the uncensored, post-Soviet Ukrainian-language edition of Holybutsky's history: *Zaporozhke kozatstvo* (Kyiv: Vyshcha shkola, 1994), 442–3. (The earlier, Soviet version had been published in Russian.) As well, see Dmytro Yavornytsky, *Ivan Dmytrovych Sirko: Slavnyi koshovyi otaman viiska zaporozkykh nyzovykh kozakiv*, in Yavornytsky, *Ivan Sirko: Zbirnyk* (Kyiv: Veselka, 1992), 75–6.

A personal anecdote is relevant here. In the 1970s, Andrew Gregorovich, the editor of the Toronto-based non-political cultural magazine *Forum: A Ukrainian Review*, told me of his trip to Soviet Ukraine less than a decade earlier, during the "Shelest Renaissance." Wanting to establish contact with Ukrainian historians and obtain materials on Ukrainian history for his illustrated magazine, he visited the Ukrainian Academy of Sciences Institute of History in Kyiv and there met Holobutsky and some other historians, who greeted him warmly. But to speak freely about their mutual interests, Holobutsky and some of the others spirited him away to a private room deep in the building, where they were not watched, and where there were no microphones. Gregorovich spoke to me respectfully of Holobutsky, who in the West was generally seen as simply repeating the party line on Ukrainian historical questions.

10  Daniel Clarke Waugh, "On the Origins of the 'Correspondence' between the Sultan and the Cossacks," *Recenzija: A Review of Soviet Ukrainian Scholarly Publications* 1, no. 2 (1971), 3–46. Also see his *The Great Turkes Defiance: On the History of the Apocryphal Correspondence of the Ottoman Sultan in Its Muscovite and Russian Variants* (Columbus, Ohio: Slavica, 1978), and H.A. Nudha's long essay on the Cossack letter in his *Na literaturnykh shliakhakh* (Kyiv: Dnipro, 1990), 260–348. The latter two works are both profusely illustrated.

11  See the numerous title pages of the various European editions of the Cossack Letter printed as illustrations in both Waugh, *The Great Turkes Defiance*, and also Nudha, *Na literaturnykh shliakhakh*.

12  Gerhard Bowering, ed., *Princeton Encyclopedia of Islamic Thought* (Princeton, NJ, and Oxford: Princeton University Press, 2013), 274; Frederic Baumgartner, *Declaring War in Early Modern Europe* (London: Palgrave Macmillan, 2011), 18–19, and n 20. Baumgartner cites the Koranic injunction: "We do not punish until we have sent a messenger (XVII, 15)." On Mehmed the Conqueror, see Steven Runciman, *The Fall of Constantinople, 1453* (Cambridge: Cambridge University Press, 1969), 95–6. Many Western historians treat the Letters of Mohammed to Heraclius and his contemporaries with caution. For example, Hugh Kennedy, *The Great Arab Conquests: How the Spread of Islam Changed the World We Live In*

(London: Weidenfeld and Nicholson, 2007), 74, notes the great respect the first Muslims had for the Emperor Heraclius, "modest and pious," but says little on the authenticity of the Prophet's letters. Authentic or not, the legend was accepted as fact in Islamic tradition and taken as a serious precedent, right to 1683 and after. In fact, in 1998, Osama bin Laden sent a parallel "Declaration of the World Islamic Front against the Jews and Crusaders" to a major Arabic newspaper in London, which was generally ignored by Westerners, but picked up by the Middle East scholar Bernard Lewis, who immediately saw its significance. The letter was shortly followed by the 9 / 11 airplane attacks on New York and Washington. See Bernard Lewis, *Notes on a Century: Reflections of a Middle East Historian* (New York: Penguin, 2013), 258–62.

13  Bernard G. Guerney, *The Portable Russian Reader* (New York: Viking, 1947); reprinted in 1959 and again in 1961; see 615–16. On other Cold War editions and English translations, see Andrew Gregorovich, "The Cossack Letter: *The Most Defiant Letter!*," 1999, at http://www.infoukes.com/history/cossack_letter/.

14  Friedman, "The Zaporozhian Letter." I have slightly smoothed out the language and punctuation of Friedman's translation.

15  Yavornytsky, *Ivan Sirko*, 75–6.

16  In Ukrainian historiography, the classic telling of this story is that in Dmytro Doroshenko, *A Survey of Ukrainian History*, 2nd ed. (Winnipeg: Trident Publishers, 1975), 283–308, where that historian describes the attempt of his distant relative Hetman Petro Doroshenko (1627–1698) to use Ottoman power to create an autonomous but united Ukrainian Cossack "state," independent of both the Polish–Lithuanian Commonwealth and the Tsardom of Muscovy, especially in the face of the 1667 agreement between those two powers to divide the country between themselves.

17  On Repin and Kostomarov, see Repin's memoirs, *Dalekoe blizkoe* (Leningrad: Khudozhnik RSFSR, 1982), 364, which are filled with "ukrainianisms"; Bielichko, *Ukraina v tvorchosti Riepina*, 37, and my *Mykola Kostomarov: A Biography* (Toronto and Buffalo, 1996), especially 237 n 67.

18  Both *The Hetman* and *S.V. Tarnovska* are reproduced in colour in I. Zilbershtein, "Repin v Kachanovke," *Ogonek* 5 (1953), 16–17.

19  The most detailed description of Repin's 1880 tour of Ukraine is the Ukrainian-language article by Iu.V. Belichko, "Istoryko-etnohrafichne znachennia podorozhi I. Iu. Repina na Ukrainu 1880 roku," *Narodna tvorchist ta etnohrafiia* 4 (1988): 28–37, which, of course, appeared only under the Gorbachev reforms. Note that in his article Belichko has dropped the Russian transliterations into Ukrainian of his own and Repin's surnames, which had always appeared in his Soviet-era publications. Now free to do so, he used standard Ukrainian orthography for Ukrainian names. There is a brief summary of Repin's trip in O.A. Liaskovskaia, *Ilia Efimovich Repin*, 3rd ed. (Moscow: Iskusstvo, 1982), 291ff.

20  See the discussion in Bielichko, "Tvorchist Illi Riepina," 10, which quotes from Kostomarov's autobiography: Mykola I. *Kostomarov, "Avobiografiia N.I. Kosto-marova, zapisannaia N.A. Bilozerskoi," Russkaia mysl'* 5 (1885): 185–223; 6 (1885): 20–43. For more detail on the historian's method, see my "Mykola Kostomarov and East Slavic Ethnography in the Nineteenth Century," *Russian History* 18, no. 2 (Salt Lake City, 1991), 163–86.

21  Ilya Repin, *Izbrannye pisma*, I, 240.

22  Vera Repina, "Iz detskikh vospominanii . . . ," *Niva* 29 (1914). 572, quoted in O.A. Liaskovskaia, *Ilia Efimovich Repin*, 2nd ed. (Moscow: Iskusstvo, 1962), 214.

23  Yavornytsky's outline history of the Zaporozhians was titled *Ocherki po isto-rii zaporozhkikh kozakov i novorossiiskogo kraia* (1889) and is a bibliographical rarity that I have not seen. On Repin and Yavornytsky, see the latter's memoir: Yavornytsky, "Kak sozdavalas kartina 'Zaporozhtsy'," ed. I.S. Zilbershtein, in *Khudozhestvennoe nasledstvo: Repin*, 2 vols. (Moscow: AN SSSR 1949), II, 57–105; M.M. Shubravska, *D.I. Yavornytskyi: Zhyttia folklorystychno-etnohrafichna diial-nist* (Kyiv: Naukova dumka, 1972), 31–3; and also Shubravska, "Istoryk i mytets," *Vitchyzna*, no. 9 (1968), 195–202. The last contains a photograph of Repin with an inscription dedicated to Yavornytsky dated 1898. On Yavornytsky more general-ly, see my "Dmytro Yavornytsky and the Romance of Cossack History," *Forum: A Ukrainian Review* 82 (Scranton, Penn., 1990), 17–23.

24  Yavornytsky, "Kak sozdavalas," 83.

25  Repin, *Izbrannye pisma*, I, 359.

26  On "separatism," see I.E. Repin, letter of 10 January 1892 to Tatiana Tolstaia, in *Perepiska s L.N. Tolstoym i ego semei*, vol. I (Moscow: Iskusstvo, 1949), 46. On Katkov, see Kridl Valkenier, *Ilya Repin*, 85, and Jackson, *The Russian Vision*, 196–7.

27  Yavornytsky, "Kak sozdavalas," 74–6; Brodskii, "Zaporozhtsy pishut pismo turets-komu sultanu 1878–1891," 278. Zilbershtein, in his Introduction to Yavornytsky's memoir, "Kak sozdavalas," 58, remarks that Repin intended later to add a section on the composition of the Zaporozhians to his memoirs, *Dalekoe blizkoe*, but that the outbreak of the First World War prevented it. This conflict proved a great loss for art historians and for Ukrainian and Russian culture generally. On Rubets, see Ivan Lysenko, *Entsyklopediia ukrainskoi pisni* (Zhytomyr: Ruta, 2017), 98 and 276.

28  Dmitrii Gromov, "Korrespondent: Veselye Zaporozhtsy. Istoriia sozdaniia kartiny. Zaporozhtsy pishut pismo turetskomu sultanu" at http://korrespondent. net/showbiz/1422142-korrespondent-veselye-zaporozhcy-historiya, 13 December 2016. Gromov gives a clear summary of Yavornytsky's story. For the original, see Yavornytsky, "Kak sozdovalas," 77.

29  Bielichko, *Ukraina v tvorchosti Riepina*, 75–7. David Jackson, *The Wanderers and Critical Realism in Nineteenth-Century Russian Painting: Critical Perspectives in Art History* (Manchester: Manchester University Press, 2006), 114–15, calls the *Zaporozhian Cossacks* "a popular and critical triumph for Repin" and "his greatest success, critically and commercially," but (astoundingly) he ignores the

Ukrainian angle. Bielichko, "Tvorchist Illi Riepina," 7, suggests that Repin could have finished the painting much earlier, but he did not wish to compete with his mentor and friend, Kramskoi, who was working on a major painting of his own. In fact, Repin finished the canvas only after Kramskoi's death in 1887.

30 On the general reaction in Russia and Ukraine, see Bielichko, *Ukraina v tvorchosti Riepina*, 75–7. Also see Stepovyk, *Skarby Ukrainy*, 125–6.

31 A. Benua / Alexandre Benois, *Istoriia russkoi zhivopisi v XIX veke* (Moscow: Respublika, 1995), 264–78. This work was first published in 1902–3. In later life, Benua remembered Repin much more kindly and actually gave him credit for opening his eyes to modern art. See Alexander Benois, *Memoirs*, trans. M. Budberg (London: Chatto and Windus, 1960), 109–11.

32 Kornei Chukovsky, "Repin i Benua," *Rech* (St Petersburg), 2 (15) April 1910. Also available online at http://www.chukfamily.ru/Kornei/Prosa/benua.htm, 8 August 2017. Also see K. Chukovsky, *Ilya Repin* (Moscow: Iskusstvo, 1969), 150 pp., 63 plates.

33 The ukrainophile Lemberg / Lviv journal *Zoria* for 1892 included three notes on the painting, in no. 1, 18-19 and 59–60, and no. 4, 217 (this last by "Artist" discussed in the text). During this period, writers in the Russian Empire who wished to publish in the Ukrainian language often sent their works to Austrian Galicia, where they were published uncensored and were much appreciated. This was true of some of the most popular writers, such as Ivan Nechui-Levytsky, Mykhailo Starytsky, Ahatanhel Krymsky, and even the young Mykhailo Hrushevsky. See my *Mykhailo Hrushevsky: The Politics of National Culture* (Toronto: University of Toronto Press, 1987), chap. 3: "Galician Piedmont 1897–1905," 45–69.

34 Bielichko, *Ukraina v tvorchosti Riepina*, 77; Stepovyk, *Skarby Ukrainy*, 125–6. Also see Davydova, *Zaporozhtsy*, 27–9, which mentions Tereshchenko's interest in this version.

35 Stepovyk, *Skarby Ukrainy*, 125–6, summarizes Bielichko's opinion and also adds his own. Also see Gromov, "Korrespondent: Veselye Zaporozhtsy"; the author queried several Ukrainian museum curators as to their opinions on the matter.

36 Shubravska, "Istoryk i mytets."

37 Yevhen Chykalenko, *Spohady (1861–1907)* (New York: UVAN, 1955), 191–2. There is a long extract from Repin's response to Chykalenko in Bielichko, *Ukraina v tvostchosti Riepina*, 4, 81. Also see the discussion in my essay "A Painter from Ukraine: Ilya Repin."

38 I have discussed these points more fully in my "A Painter from Ukraine: Ilya Repin."

39 Isabel F. Hapgood, "A Russian National Artist: With Pictures by Ilya Repin," *Century Magazine* 45, no. 1 (1892), 3–12, and *Russian Rambles* (Boston and New York: Houghton, Mifflin, and Company, 1895).

40 Christian Brinton, "Russia's Greatest Painter: Ilia Repin," *Scribner's Magazine* 40, no. 5 (Nov. 1906), 513–23; Louis E. Lord, "A Russian Painter of the Nineteenth Century, Elyas Repin," *Art Bulletin* 2, no. 4 (1920), 213–18.

41 See Guillaume Apollinaire, *Alcools: Poems 1898–1913*, trans. William Meredith (Garden City, NY: Doubleday, 1964), 24–8 (for both text and translation). In his edition of *Alcools* (London: Athlone Press, 1975), 133, Garnet Rees writes that the jilted poet's "Rabelaisian" tone in this section reflects his anger at his former lover, Annie: "The plea for fidelity put into the mouth of the *Cosaques* represents the voice of the poet venting his rage on Annie by proxy." On Apollinaire more generally, see Scott Bates, *Guillaume Apollinaire*, rev. ed. (Boston: Twayne, 1989), which describes his character as a combination of "a Slavic with a Latin personality" (1). More briefly, see Jennifer Birkett and James Kearns, *A Guide to French Literature from Early Modern to Postmodern* (London: Macmillan, 1997), 239–42. There is an illustration of his family coat of arms in Wikipedia <13 Dec. 2016>.

42 Clement Greenberg, "Avant-Garde and Kitsch," in Sally Everett, ed., *Art Theory and Criticism: An Anthology of Formalist Avant-Garde, Contextualist and Post-Modernist Thought*, (Jefferson, NC, and London: McFarland, 1991), 26–49, especially 34–5. This article was first published in the *Partisan Review* (New York, 1939). In later years, Greenberg turned more to the right, eventually editing the much more conservative Jewish magazine *Commentary*.

43 Edward Said, *Orientalism* (New York: Pantheon Books,1978). For rebuttals defending the Orientalist traditions in Europe, see especially the remarks of Said's special target, Bernard Lewis, "The Question of Orientalism," *New York Review of Books* (24 June 1982), 49–52, and Lewis's observations in his brief essay "On Occidentalism and Orientalism," in his *From Babel to Dragomans: Interpreting the Middle East* (Oxford: Oxford University Press, 2004), 430–8. For a much more detailed critique of Said, see Ibn Warraq, *Defending the West* (New York: Prometheus, 2007), 556 pp.

44 On Vereshchagin, see Vahan D. Barooshian, *V.V. Vereshchagin: Artist at War* (Orlando: University Press of Florida, 1993), which notes (xv) that Repin admired Vereshchagin greatly and even called him "a real Hercules" and "a genius."

45 On the *kobza*, the Ukrainian philologist Metropolitan Ilarion / Ivan Ohienko writes: "[The Kobza] is an eight stringed musical instrument, smaller than a bandura [which became more popular in the twentieth century]; it is derived from the Turkish *korpuz* whence it was accepted into Ukrainian and Bulgarian" culture. It "was known as early as the time of the Polovtsi [twelfth century] and [also] was known to the Crimean Tatars, and, certainly, the Cossacks got it from them. At one time, it was a single stringed instrument, but the number of strings grew later on, that is, in the sixteenth century. Whosoever plays a *kobza* is called a *kobzar*." See Metropolitan Ilarion / Ivan Ohienko, *Etymolohichno-semantychnyi slovnyk ukrainskoi movy*, 4 vols. (Winnipeg: Tovarystvo 'Volyn,' 1988–94), II, 234. On *sharovary*, see IV, 504, which observes of *sharovary* that "they were wide pants reaching down to high boots. [The word] comes from Persian, through the Turkish *shalvar*. [It] was also used in ancient Hebrew (see Dan. 3: 21) *'sarbalin,'* Greek *'sarabara.'*"

46  Kristian Davies, *The Orientalists: Western Artists in Arabia, the Sahara, Persia & India* (New York: Laynfaroh, 2005). The book reproduced the St Petersburg version of *Zaporozhian Cossacks* in full colour.

47  See Repin, *Izbrannye pisma*, II, 141, on his 1898 trip to the Holy Land, especially Jerusalem, which he thought so interesting that he could barely write about or paint it. Also see Kridl Valkenier, *Ilya Repin*, 8, on Repin in Jerusalem; and on Yavornytsky in the Middle East, see the latter pages of chapter 2 in the present volume.

48  See the brief discussion in Andrew Wilson, *The Ukrainians: Unexpected Nation*, 4th ed. (New Haven, Conn., and London: Yale University Press, 2015), 143–4. Wilson, or perhaps one of his unmentioned editors, seems to have confused the painter O.A. Khmelnytsky (b. 1924) with the Soviet Ukrainian painter Mykhailo Khmelko (1919–1996), who also painted a large canvas on the Treaty of Pereiaslav – *Forever with Moscow, Forever with the Russian People!* (c. 1951) – less stylized and a bit more cheerful than Khmelnytsky's. But the dour picture printed in Wilson's book (plate 36) is O.A. Khmelnytsky's, reproduced in 1954 on a Soviet postage stamp. For a brief discussion of these pictures, see *Istoriia ukrainskoi mystetsva v 6 tomakh*, vol. VI (Kyiv: URE, 1968), 122–3, with a reproduction of Khmelko's true painting. It is also available online in "Mykhailo Khmelko" on Wikipedia, 9 April 2018, and, together with the masterpieces of Repin and Ivasiuk, in the impressively produced Polish translation of Paul Robert Magocsi's magnum opus, *Historia Ukrainy: Ziemia i ludzie*, trans. Marek Król and Alicja Waligóra-Zblewska (Cracow: Księgarnia akademicka, 2017), plates 4.4, 4.5, and 4.7.

Mykola Ivasiuk considered his painting, today much loved by Ukrainians, a continuation and fulfilment of Repin's. He had begun it shortly after Repin completed his, and, like Repin, he spent many years working on it, finishing it in 1932. Sadly, he was executed by the Soviet political police in the Great Purge of 1937. By contrast, the two-time Stalin Prize winner, Khmelko, who, like the less talented O.A. Khmelnytsky, was a paragon of official Socialist Realism, taught for many years at the Kyiv State Art Institute, and died peacefully in his bed in 1996.

49  For a moderate interpretation of Repin, acknowledging both the Ukrainian and the "pan-Russian" aspects of his work, see Myroslav Popovych, *Narys istorii kultury Ukrainy* (Kyiv: ArtEk, 1999), 462–7. Compare Valentine Marcadé, *L'art d'Ukraine* (Lausanne: L'age d'homme, 1990), 151–63.

50  "Pro stari chasy na Ukraini, iliustrovana istoriia Ukrainy ne Hrushevskoho i ne Arkasa," reproduced in Svitlana Pankova and Hanna Kondaura, eds., *Facie ad Faciem: Iliustrovanyi zhyttiepys Mykhaila Hrushevskoho* (Kyiv: Lybid, 2017), 60.

51  Cited in the Russian version of Wikipedia in "Zaporozhtsy (Kartina)," 13 December 2016.

52  See "Modern Zaporozhians Write a Letter to the League of Nations," *Komar* 2, no. 19 (1934); as cited and reprinted on the cover of Andrzej A. Zięba, *Lobbying dla Ukrainy w Europie międzywojennej: Ukraińskie Biuro Prasowe w Londynie*

*oraz jego konkurenci polityczni (do roku 1932)* (Cracow: Księgarnia akademicka, 2010). Also on Kysilewskyj and the Ukrainian Bureau, itself an interesting experiment in West–Ukrainian contacts, see Orest Martynowych, "A Ukrainian Canadian in London: Vladimir J. (Kaye) Kysilewsky and the Ukrainian Bureau, 1931–1940," *Canadian Ethnic Studies* 47, nos. 4–5 (2015), 263–88; alternately numbered 42, nos. 2–3 (2015), my illustrated biographical article "Vladimir Kaye-Kysilewskyj in Europe, Canada, and Britain," online at https://www.slideshare.net/ThomasMPrymak/vladimir-kayekysilewskyj-in-europe-canada-and-britain?qid=6c482451-a9a1-4ba2-ad8a-87b3a4d656d3, 20 June 2019, and more briefly my *Maple Leaf and Trident: The Ukrainian Canadians during the Second World War* (Toronto: MHSO, 1988), 23–4 *et passim*.

# Index